.NET Domain-Driven Design with C#

.NET Domain-Driven Design with C#

Problem – Design – Solution

Tim McCarthy

WILEY

Wiley Publishing, Inc.

.NET Domain-Driven Design with C#

Published by
Wiley Publishing, Inc.
10475 Crosspoint Boulevard
Indianapolis, IN 46256
www.wiley.com

Copyright © 2008 by Wiley Publishing, Inc., Indianapolis, Indiana

Published simultaneously in Canada

ISBN: 978–0–470–14756–6

Manufactured in the United States of America

10 9 8 7 6 5 4 3 2 1

For general information on our other products and services or to obtain technical support, please contact our Customer Care Department within the U.S. at (800) 762-2974, outside the U.S. at (317) 572-3993 or fax (317) 572-4002.

Library of Congress Cataloging-in-Publication Data is available from the publisher.

About the Author

Tim McCarthy is a freelance consultant who architects, designs and builds highly scalable layered web and smart client applications utilizing the latest Microsoft platforms and technologies. Tim is a Microsoft MVP in Solutions Architecture, and his expertise covers a wide range of Microsoft technologies, including, but not limited to, the following: .NET Framework (ASP.NET/Smart Clients/VSTO/ Workflow/Web Services, Windows Presentation Foundation), SQL Server, Active Directory, MS Exchange development, UDDI, SharePoint, and Service Oriented Architecture (SOA) applications. Tim has worked as both a project technical lead/member as well as being in a technical consulting role for several Fortune 500 companies. He has held the Microsoft Certified Solution Developer (MCSD) and Microsoft Certified Trainer (MCT) certifications for several years, and was one of the first wave of developers to earn the Microsoft Certified Application Developer (MCAD) for .NET and MCSD for .NET certifications. He also holds the Microsoft Certified Database Administrator certification for SQL Server 2000. Tim is also certified as an IEEE Certified Software Development Professional, and he is one of only 550 people to hold this certification in the world.

Tim has been an author and technical reviewer for several books from Wrox Press. His other books include being a lead author on *Professional VB 2005*, several editions of *Professional VB.NET*, *Professional Commerce Server 2000*, and *Professional ADO 2.5 Programming*. He also has written and presented a DVD titled *SharePoint Portal Services Programming 2003*. Tim has written numerous articles for the Developer .NET Update newsletter, developed packaged presentations for the Microsoft Developer Network (MSDN), and wrote a whitepaper for Microsoft on using COM+ services in .NET. He has also written articles for *SQL Server Magazine* and *Windows & .NET Magazine*.

Tim has spoken at technical conferences around the world and several San Diego area user groups (including both .NET and SQL Server groups, and several Code Camps), and he has been a regular speaker at the Microsoft Developer Days conference in San Diego for the last several years. Tim has also delivered various MSDN webcasts, many of which were repeat requests from Microsoft. He also teaches custom .NET classes to companies in need of expert .NET mentoring and training.

Tim holds a B.B.A. in Marketing from the Illinois Institute of Technology as well as an M.B.A. in Marketing from National University. Before becoming an application developer, Tim was an officer in the United States Marine Corps. Tim's passion for .NET is only surpassed by his passion for Notre Dame Athletics.

Tim can be reached via email at tmccart1@san.rr.com.

Credits

Acquisitions Editor
Katie Mohr

Development Editor
Christopher J. Rivera

Technical Editor
Doug Holland

Production Editor
Rachel McConlogue

Copy Editor
Foxxe Editorial Services

Editorial Manager
Mary Beth Wakefield

Production Manager
Tim Tate

Vice President and Executive Group Publisher
Richard Swadley

Vice President and Executive Publisher
Joseph B. Wikert

Project Coordinator, Cover
Lynsey Standford

Proofreader
Jen Larsen, Word One

Indexer
Jack Lewis

Cover Image
Leandra Hosier

.NET Domain-Driven Design with C#

Contents

Contents

Contents

Acknowledgments

First of all, I would like to thank my family. To my wife Miriam and my daughter Jasmine—thank you for putting up with me the past year or so while I worked on this book. Everything I do is always with you guys in mind! I love you both! Jasmine, I think you may be writing books someday, too! To my Mom and Dad, who taught me the value of hard work, never giving up, and always believing in myself—thank you and I love you!

I also would like to thank my development editor, Christopher Rivera, who did a brilliant job of shielding me from things that I did not need to be bothered with and always kept me on track and kept on encouraging me the whole way. Thank you Christopher! To my technical reviewer, Doug Holland—Doug you did awesome work and were a pleasure to work with. I hope to work with you on another project some day, thank you! To my acquisitions editor, Katie Mohr—Katie, thank you for never giving up on my idea for this book and pushing it through! Also, thank you for your always kind words of encouragement; it always made me feel like I was appreciated.

I also would like to thank some of my friends at InterKnowlogy. To Kevin Kennedy—Kevin, thank you for taking the time to come up with a decent design for the layout of the WPF forms; you did more in 15 minutes with WPF than I would have done in hours! A big thank you to Dale Bastow and Staci Lopez—thank you so much for being so patient with me, and for always taking your time to educate me about the Architecture industry. To Dan Hanan and John Bowen   Guys, thank you for always taking time out for me whenever I had a WPF question, I really appreciated it. P.S. Don't forget to override GetHashcode and Equals. To Tim Huckaby—Tim, thank you for always encouraging me to write about whatever I was passionate about, and also for always being a good friend to me.

—Tim

Introduction

After reading Eric Evans' book *Domain-Driven Design, Tackling Complexity in the Heart of Software*, my way of designing software systems completely changed. Before that, I used to design software object models in a very data-centric way, and I did not really focus on how to combine behavior and data in objects. I was so inspired with this new way of thinking that I started trying to find any code samples I could get my hands on that demonstrated the concepts from Eric's awesome book. I did the usual Googling for answers to my Domain-Driven Design (DDD) questions, and I usually did find something that would help me, but I still thirsted for more knowledge on the subject.

I had to search for DDD answers in .NET because Eric's book is technology-agnostic. The main point of the book was the architectural concepts. There were code samples here and there in Java and Smalltalk, but that was about it. Then along came Jimmy Nilsson's book *Applying Domain-Driven Design and Patterns*, and it was then that I started to see a lot more of the patterns that could be used in conjunction with the DDD concepts. Jimmy tied together some of the concepts from Martin Fowler's excellent book *Patterns of Enterprise Application Architecture* and showed how they could help with good DDD design principles. Jimmy also did a great job providing lots of good .NET code examples in his book, as well as leading the reader down several paths to accomplish things the DDD way. Right after I finished Jimmy's book, I started subscribing to the DDD RSS Group feed on Yahoo! Groups, and this also helped me a great deal. One of the things I discovered while on the DDD group was that people kept asking for a .NET reference application that would showcase the DDD principles. After reading these posts for a while, I decided that I should write this book and give the developer community my take on how to build .NET applications using DDD techniques. I guess I probably felt a little bit guilty because I read so many other people's posts on the group, and I never posted very often. So now, instead of posting, I have written a book! Maybe this will be my catalyst to get more involved with the group.

My main goal in writing this book was to take the ideas and patterns from Eric's, Martin's, and Jimmy's books and use the ideas and concepts from them to build an actual end-to-end .NET application. I really wanted to show some of my ideas of how to build a domain model in .NET using DDD principles, but, I did not want to build just any old .NET application; I also wanted to try out some of the latest technologies from Microsoft in building the application, such as Visual Studio 2008 and the .NET 3.5 Framework.

Who This Book Is For

This book is targeted at experienced .NET developers who are looking to hone their object-oriented design skills and learn about DDD. If you are not at that level, that is okay, but I recommend that you at least have some experience writing .NET code or even Java code. If you have not written any .NET code before, this book may be a little bit hard to follow.

I also recommend that you read the books that I mentioned earlier from Eric Evans, Jimmy Nilsson, and Martin Fowler. You do not have to do this, but I highly recommend it, as it will help you understand better many of the designs and patterns in this book.

Since each chapter in this book builds upon the previous chapter, I recommend that you read the book in chapter order.

What This Book Covers

Chapter 1, "Introducing the Project: The SmartCA Application" —This chapter introduces you to the application that I am building, the SmartCA application. I outline the problems of the legacy application and the requirements for the new application, as well as what technologies and designs I plan to use to satisfy all of the requirements.

Chapter 2, "Designing the Layered Architecture" — This chapter covers the architectural foundations that will be used in the rest of the book. Several patterns are introduced in the chapter, which include the Layered Supertype pattern, the Separated Interface pattern, and the Model-View-ViewModel pattern. I also identify and explain several important DDD concepts. This also is the first chapter where I start to write the application code, with a focus on the infrastructure layer.

Chapter 3, "Managing Projects" — In this chapter, I start implementing the functionality for managing Projects in the application. I also discuss the concept of Contractors and how they relate to Projects as well as introducing the first iteration of code for the Model-View-ViewModel pattern.

Chapter 4, "Companies and Contacts" — In this chapter, I define and model Companies, Contacts, and Project Contacts. I also show how I deal with saving Entities that are not their own Aggregate Root. This was demonstrated by the techniques I used to save Project Contacts within the Project Aggregate. Last, I show a technique I came up with for displaying and editing Value objects in the UI.

Chapter 5, "Submittal Transmittals" — In this chapter, I introduce the concept of a Submittal Transmittal as used in the construction industry, and then I use the concept to model the Submittal Aggregate. I add a new concept to both the domain layer and the infrastructure layer, illustrating how to deal with saving child collections from the Entity Root repository. I also cover building User Controls that use the Xceed Data Grid Control.

Chapter 6, "Requests for Information" — In this chapter, I introduce the construction industry concept of a Request for Information (RFI). I also introduce a new pattern to the domain called the Specification pattern. I also do some major refactoring in this chapter on the Repositories and View Models for dealing with Transmittals.

Chapter 7, "Proposal Requests" — In this chapter, I introduce the concept of a Proposal Request in the construction industry. In this chapter, I start adding more behavior to the domain model and demonstrating richer Domain Model classes. I also cover handling broken business rules inside of my Domain Model classes, and tie in the Specification functionality.

Chapter 8, "Change Orders" — In this chapter, I introduce the concept of a Change Order in the construction industry. I continue to add more behavior to my Domain Model classes in this chapter, and continue to develop richer Domain Model classes. Two important interfaces are introduced in this chapter, the `IEntity` interface and the `IAggregateRoot` interface. This causes quite a bit of good refactoring throughout the domain model. Last, I create some more advanced `Specification` classes.

Chapter 9, **"Construction Change Directives"** — In this chapter, I introduce the concept of a Construction Change Directive in the construction industry. I do a lot of refactoring in this chapter, mostly focused on the various `ViewModel` classes. In this chapter, I demonstrate the power of combining interfaces with Generics.

Chapter 10, **"Synchronizing with the Server"** — In this chapter, I design and implement how to synchronize the client's offline data with the server. I show how to store transaction messages on the client, and also show how to synchronize those messages on the client with the messages on the server. I also show how to make sure that all of the synchronization logic is implemented in the domain model.

Chapter 11, **"The Client Membership System"** — In this chapter, I show you how to allow users to be able to perform membership-related tasks in an offline scenario by creating what I call my Client Membership System. This involves a very rich domain model for representing the Users and their membership data, as well as a new concept of using a Provider instead of a Repository for interacting with the data store. I also show how to take advantage of the Synchronization code from Chapter 10.

How This Book Is Structured

This book is essentially a very large case study. Throughout the chapters, a complete application is built from start to finish. The structure for each chapter is the same; it is generally a self-contained module with a problem, design, and solution that adds some new aspect of functionality to the application that is being built, followed by a summary at the end of the chapter.

Most of the time, the Problem sections are fairly short, whereas the Design and Solution sections make up most of the bulk of the chapters. The Solution section will always contain the code that implements what was designed in the Design section.

What You Need to Use This Book

You will need Visual Studio 2008 (which includes the .NET 3.5 Framework in its installation) in order to run all of the code samples in the book. I highly recommend using Visual Studio 2008 Professional Edition so that you can run all of the unit tests I have written as part of the code base.

In addition, you will need to install the following applications and components:

❑ **SQL Server Compact 3.5 (SQL CE)** — This is freely downloadable from the Microsoft SQL Server web site (`www.microsoft.com/sql/editions/compact/downloads.mspx`).

❑ **Version 1.3 of the Xceed DataGrid Control for WPF** — This also freely downloadable from the Xceed web site (`http://xceed.com/Grid_WPF_New.html`).

❑ **One of the available versions of SQL Server 2008** — This is necessary if you want to be able to use the SQL Server Management Studio to make changes to the SQL CE database. The Express Edition is freely downloadable from `www.microsoft.com/sql/2008/prodinfo/download.mspx`.

Source Code

As you work through the examples in this book, you may choose either to type in all the code manually or to use the source code files that accompany the book. All of the source code used in this book is available for downloading at www.wrox.com. Once at the site, simply locate the book's title (either by using the Search box or by using one of the title lists) and click the Download Code link on the book's detail page to obtain all the source code for the book.

> Because many books have similar titles, you may find it easiest to search by ISBN; this book's ISBN is 978-0-470-14756-6.

Once you download the code, just decompress it with your favorite compression tool. Alternately, you can go to the main Wrox code download page at www.wrox.com/dynamic/books/download.aspx to see the code available for this book and all other Wrox books.

Also, if you are interested in seeing how the code continues to iterate and grow after you finish the book, please visit my CodePlex site for this book's code at www.codeplex.com/dddpds. Here you will find new code that was written after the book was published.

Errata

We make every effort to ensure that there are no errors in the text or in the code. Nevertheless, no one is perfect, and mistakes do occur. If you find an error in one of our books, such as a spelling mistake or faulty piece of code, we would be very grateful for your feedback. By sending in errata you may save another reader hours of frustration, and at the same time you will be helping us provide even higher-quality information.

To find the errata page for this book, go to www.wrox.com and locate the title using the Search box or one of the title lists. Then, on the book details page, click the Book Errata link. On this page you can view all errata that has been submitted for this book and posted by Wrox editors. A complete book list including links to each book's errata is also available at www.wrox.com/misc-pages/booklist.shtml.

If you don't spot "your" error on the Book Errata page, go to www.wrox.com/contact/techsupport.shtml and complete the form there to send us the error you have found. We'll check the information and, if appropriate, post a message to the book's errata page and fix the problem in subsequent editions of the book.

p2p.wrox.com

For author and peer discussion, join the P2P forums at p2p.wrox.com. The forums are a web-based system for you to post messages relating to Wrox books and related technologies and interact with other readers and technology users. The forums offer a subscription feature to email you topics of interest of your choosing when new posts are made to the forums. Wrox authors, editors, other industry experts, and your fellow readers are present on these forums.

At http://p2p.wrox.com you will find a number of different forums that will help you not only as you read this book but also as you develop your own applications. To join the forums, just follow these steps:

1. Go to p2p.wrox.com and click the Register link.

2. Read the terms of use and click Agree.

3. Complete the required information to join, as well as any optional information you wish to provide, and click Submit.

4. You will receive an email with information describing how to verify your account and complete the joining process.

You can read messages in the forums without joining P2P, but in order to post your own messages, you must join.

Once you join, you can post new messages and respond to messages that other users post. You can read messages at any time on the web. If you would like to have new messages from a particular forum emailed to you, click the Subscribe to this Forum icon by the forum name in the forum listing.

For more information about how to use the Wrox P2P, be sure to read the P2P FAQs for answers to questions about how the forum software works as well as many common questions specific to P2P and Wrox books. To read the FAQs, click the FAQ link on any P2P page.

1

Introducing the Project: The SmartCA Application

The project for this book is based on a real application for a real company. The names of the company and the application have been changed for privacy reasons. The fictional company name will be Smart Design, and the name of their new application will be called SmartCA. Smart Design is a growing architectural, engineering, and interior design firm. One of its many service offerings is construction administration, which in its case consists mostly of document management, cost control, and project portfolio management.

The Problem

To manage its construction administration (CA) data and processes, Smart Design has been getting by for 10 years on a home-grown Microsoft Access database application, called the Construction Administration Database, which lives on its corporate network. The company has grown accustomed to this application, both the good parts and the bad. When the application was originally written, there were only a few users, the requirements were very simple, they already had licenses for Microsoft Office, and they had a very small budget. All of this made using Microsoft Access a good technology choice. Figure 1.1 shows the main screen of the application.

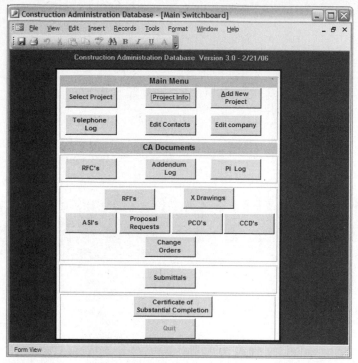

Figure 1.1: Legacy Construction Administration application
main screen.

As the years went by, the application became more and more important. It was modified many times, both with code and tweaks to the design of the user interface (UI). This led to UI forms with lots of logic embedded in them as well as some embedded logic in the database queries. The application is now, essentially, a poster child for the Smart Client anti-pattern.

> **The Smart Client anti-pattern is defined by Eric Evans as "Put all the business logic into the user interface. Chop the application into small functions and implement them as separate user interfaces, embedding the business rules into them. Use a relational database as a shared repository of the data. Use the most automated UI building and visual programming tools available" (Evans, *Domain-Driven Design: Tackling Complexity in the Heart of Software* [Addison-Wesley, 2004], 77).**

Figure 1.2 shows the architecture of the current application.

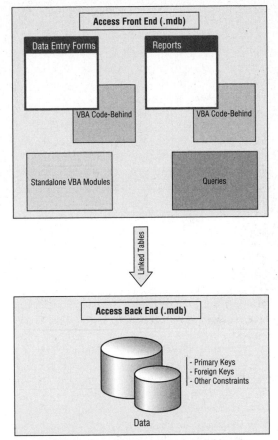

Figure 1.2: Legacy Construction Administration application architecture.

Recently, Smart Design merged with another architectural design company, and as a result the CA application became even more important. It is now being used more often than before by many more users from several remote offices. The increased use has caused scalability and performance problems with the application.

The problem with the Access application is that it has so much logic embedded into its forms, queries, and reports. This makes it very hard to maintain as well as very difficult to add new features to the application.

The Design

As far as a Microsoft Access application goes, the architecture is really not that bad. As shown in Figure 1.2, it is a two-tier application, with all of the UI, business logic, and queries in the first tier (which is a separate .mdb file), and all of the database tables in the second tier (also a separate .mdb file). Although the current solution for construction administration might have been a good fit 10 years ago, Smart Design has outgrown the application and needs a new solution that will support its new needs. Ten years ago, their needs were fairly simple—they just needed an organized way to capture information and be able to print reports on that information to send out to various people on various projects.

Originally, the main requirement was for a very simple information tracking and reporting tool. The first version of the application was made without any IT involvement, just a stakeholder and one Access programmer. Many changes were made to the program over the years, both by the stakeholder, and by the Access programmer. Several of the changes resulted in denormalized data structures, repetitious code, and various other code smells. Often, changes were made to the application that the Access programmer was not even aware of, and changing things to make them right would have taken a lot of time and effort, so the application just kept on moving along. As the data being tracked started to get larger, an archiving solution was put in place, which resulted in more Microsoft Access data files being created. In the end, almost every attempt to enhance the application has resulted in some type of "one-off" solution that has become very difficult to maintain over the years.

Now that the CA application has been deemed critical to Smart Design's business by their chief operating officer, it has become very apparent that it has greatly outgrown its original design. Smart Design has decided that they do not want to buy an off-the-shelf product; instead they want to rewrite the current application onto a different platform that will meet their growing needs.

Here are their most prevalent needs, in order of importance:

❑ Reliability and Availability

❑ Scalability

❑ Maintainability

❑ Rich client application functionality

❑ Offline capable

❑ Web access

❑ Intelligent installation and auto-update functionality

❑ Additional client device support

Reliability and Availability

One of the problems with the current application is that the database sometimes becomes corrupt and must be compacted or repaired regularly, which causes the application to be down for periods of time. The new system's database should be able to be backed up while the system is still in use, and should not be prone to data corruption issues.

Scalability

The system should be able to handle demands from a growing number of users and processes.

Maintainability

Because the code for the application is not correctly partitioned, updating the current application sometimes requires updating the same code and logic in several different places. The new application must be designed it such a way that the domain logic is centralized and is never duplicated.

Rich Client Application Functionality

Users are used to the current Microsoft Access application's rich controls and responsiveness, and they would like to continue to improve upon this type of user experience.

Offline Capable

The new application must be able to work even when the user is not connected to the network. For those users running the application with occasional or intermittent connectivity — such as those used by on-site construction managers, where connectivity cannot be guaranteed at all times — being able to work while disconnected is very important.

Web Access

The firm would like some parts of the application exposed to the web, such as reporting. Also, in the future, some parts of the application may need to be exposed to outside contractors. Another nice-to-have would be the ability to extend the application to support some type of an executive dashboard for showing key performance indicators (KPIs) or similar information to management.

Intelligent Installation and Auto-Update Functionality

Currently, the Smart Design IT department is challenged with making sure that users of the application have the right version on their desktops. IT has also had a tough time getting the application pushed out when new changes have been made to the application. IT would definitely prefer a deployment method similar to that of web applications, and would like SmartCA to be easily installed by clicking on a URL from their intranet. The application must be able to be updated while it is still running, and the updates should guarantee the integrity of the application and its related files.

Additional Client Device Support

The new application should be designed in such a way as to be able to reuse a good part of its core logic modules for different UI devices, such as personal digital assistants (PDAs), smart phones, and the like.

The current application and platform will not easily support these requirements. Therefore, Smart Design has decided to start from scratch and completely reengineer the new application to be able to meet the new requirements. The old Access application has served the company well for more than 10 years. Actually, it can still serve the company well by being the basis for the new design. There are lots of business rules captured in the old application that are not documented anywhere else, so the old application will be used as a guide in fleshing out some of the requirements for the new system.

The Solution

The new application, SmartCA, will be written using Microsoft Visual Studio 2008 (which includes the Microsoft .NET Framework 3.5) technologies for both the client-side and server-side partitions.

Fulfilling the Reliability, Availability, Scalability, Offline Capable, and Additional Client Device Support Requirements

Most of the current problems in the areas of reliability, availability, and scalability lie in the fact that the legacy application was implemented in Microsoft Access and used Access for its data store. The new solution going forward will be using both a database on the server as well as a database on the client.

On the Server

In order to support the Reliability and Availability requirements, the database server will be a SQL Server instance. All of the data from the legacy application will need to be migrated to the new SQL Server database. A SQL migration script or .NET program will be written that will facilitate this data transfer. This will allow the old application to continue working while the new application is still being built, since the script or migration tool will make it easier to refresh data on a regular basis from the production Access database into the development, testing, and staging database environments. Moving to a server-based relational database (SQL Server) will also lend itself well to the Scalability requirement, although the application design has just as much to do with that as the idea of using a database server instead an Access .mdb file for a data store.

On the Client

Yes, that's right, you see it correctly, a database on the client. You are probably saying to yourself, "That is worse than the original Access application's two-tier architecture, where at least the database lived on a network share!" Not so fast, my friend. One of the requirements of the application is to be able to support users who are not always connected to the network, such as those construction managers who may be inside of a construction trailer with no available connectivity, a.k.a. the Offline Capable requirement. The database used on the client will be a SQL Server Compact Edition 3.5 (SQL CE) database. Although SQL CE was originally only targeted for mobile platforms, such as PDAs and Tablet PCs, it now runs on all client platforms. According to Microsoft, SQL CE is a "low maintenance, compact embedded database for single-user client applications for all Windows platforms including tablet PCs, pocket PCs, smart phones and desktops. Just as with SQL Server Mobile, SQL Server Compact is a free, easy-to-use, lightweight, and embeddable version of SQL Server 2005 for developing desktop and mobile applications."

Another benefit of having a database on the client is the fact that it can help take some of the load off the database server, thus helping with the Scalability requirement.

At this point, you may be asking yourself, "Why not use SQL Server Express? At least with SQL Server Express I can use stored procedures!" While it is true that SQL Server Express supports stored procedures, while SQL CE does not, the real reason for using SQL CE is that I want to support multiple devices, not just Windows machines. With SQL CE I can reuse the same database on both a PC and a mobile device, and this functionality maps directly to the Additional Client Device Support requirement. I can live without stored procedures on the client.

Instead of using traditional replication to keep the schema and data between the database on the client and the database server in sync, the application will use Microsoft Synchronization Services for ADO .NET. The Synchronization Services application programming interface (API) provides a set of components to synchronize data between data services and a local store. Equally important is the need to synchronize the local copy of the data with a central server when a network connection is available. The Synchronization Services API, which is modeled after ADO.NET data access APIs, is a much more intelligent, service-based way of synchronizing the data. It makes building applications for occasionally connected environments a logical extension of building applications for which you can count on a consistent network connection. Think about how Microsoft Outlook works, and you will get the picture of the online/offline functionality that the Synchronization Services API will enable.

It should be noted that I will not be talking much about databases in this book, since the focus of this book is on Domain-Driven Design. One of the main tenants of Domain-Driven Design is persistence ignorance, and therefore, while the application is being designed, as far as you and I are concerned, the data could be coming from a text file. Therefore, from this point on, I will only talk about the 10,000 foot view when it comes to the database.

Fulfilling the Maintainability Requirement

In order to avoid embedding business logic in the behavior of the UI elements, such as the various forms, controls, and reports, or even embedded inside of database queries, a layered architecture (ibid., 69) will be used. Because the legacy application was implemented with such a Smart UI anti-pattern, the domain-related code became very difficult to decipher and track down. Unit testing was impossible, and sometimes trying to change one business rule meant tracing of UI code, Visual Basic for Applications (VBA) module code, and embedded SQL code. The layered architecture's main principle is that any element of a layer depends only on other elements in the same layer, or on elements of the layers beneath it. Using a layered architecture will make the code for this application much more maintainable, which maps directly to the Maintainability requirement. The layers that will be used in the SmartCA application will be:

❑ **UI (presentation layer)** — Probably the easiest to understand, this layer is responsible for showing information to the user and interpreting the user's commands. Sometimes, instead of a human, the user could be another system.

❑ **Application layer** — This layer is meant to be very thin and is used for coordinating the actions of the domain model objects. It is not supposed to contain business rules or domain knowledge, or even maintain state — that is what the domain model is for. The application layer is very useful for coordinating tasks and delegating actions to the domain model. Although it is not to be used to maintain state of a business entity, it can maintain the state that tracks the current task being performed by the user or system. It is very important that the application layer does not interfere or get in the way of the domain model representing the important parts of the business model (http://weblogs.asp.net)

❏ **Domain layer** — This is where the business logic and rules of an application live, and it is the heart of the software. The domain layer controls and uses the state of a particular business concept or situation, but how it is stored is actually delegated to the infrastructure layer. It is absolutely critical in Domain-Driven Design that the domain layer contains the business model, and that the domain logic is not scattered across any other layers.

❏ **Infrastructure layer** — This is where general technical, plumbing-related code happens, such as persisting objects to a database, sending messages, logging, and other general cross-cutting concerns. It can also serve as a place for an architectural framework for the pattern of interactions between the four layers. In the next chapter, you will see an example of a framework for the SmartCA domain model that is contained in the infrastructure layer.

Generically, Figure 1.3 shows what the SmartCA layered application architecture looks like.

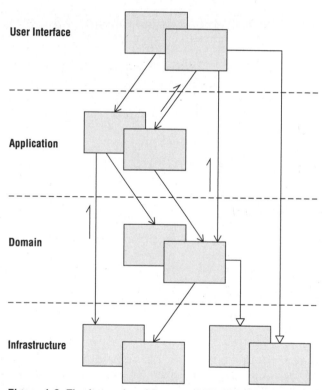

Figure 1.3: The layered architecture (adapted from Evans, 68).

Figure 1.4 shows what the application architecture looks like with all of the technologies and patterns layered on top of the layered architecture model.

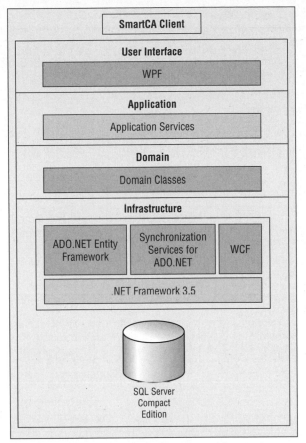

Figure 1.4: The SmartCA application architecture.

Fulfilling the Rich Client Application Functionality Requirement

Since the users of the current application have become used to a Windows application, the new application will also be Windows-based, but it will be much more than just a traditional Windows application. The SmartCA application will be a smart client application implemented using the Windows Presentation Foundation (WPF). You might be asking yourself, OK, what exactly do you mean by smart client?

A smart client is a type of application that combines the best of both Windows applications and web applications.

Windows Application Benefits

The advantages of Windows applications are that they are able to provide a rich user experience, they are not too complex to develop, and they can use local resources. Using local resources allows Windows applications to be responsive, interact with connected devices, and do other things that web applications cannot do (at least not very easily).

Web Application Benefits

The positive aspects of a web application are that it is easy to deploy and manage, since you deploy it to a server not to the client computer, and it has a very broad reach — even PDAs and cell phones can access a web application!

Smart Client Definition

The term "smart client" means different things to different people. For the purposes of this book, I will classify a smart client application (note this is adapted from the MSDN Smart Client FAQ) as follows:

❑ It uses local resources and provides a rich user experience. This satisfies the rich client application functionality requirement.

❑ It is a connected application that can exchange data on the Internet or on an enterprise network.

❑ Even though it is a connected application, it is offline capable so that it can be used even if it is not currently connected. This satisfies the Offline Capable requirement.

❑ It has an intelligent deployment and update story, maintaining relatively the same ease of deployment and management as web applications, thus satisfying the Intelligent Installation and Auto-Update Functionality requirement.

Intelligent deployment means that the smart client application is deployed to an application server, and from there it is deployed onto the local client system. Intelligent update means that the application on the client system is able to receive updates that are deployed to the server.

Windows Presentation Foundation (WPF)

WPF is intended to be the next-generation graphics API for Windows applications on the desktop. Applications written in WPF are visually of a higher quality than Windows Forms applications. Some of the relevant highlights of WPF for the SmartCA application are:

❑ **Resolution independence** — Because of WPF's use of vector graphics, unlike most Windows-based applications of today, graphics and text that are viewed in a higher resolution do not get smaller; they actually get better! This means that a user can literally shrink or enlarge elements on the screen independently of the screen's resolution.

❑ **Declarative programming** — Windows Forms do not have built-in support for declarative UI definitions. The .NET Framework as a whole has allowed developers to use declarative custom attributes classes, methods, and assemblies, as well as XML-based resource and configuration files. WPF takes this declarative-based model to a new level with Extensible Application Markup Language (XAML). Using XAML in WPF is very similar to using HTML to define a UI for a web page, yet it is much better than that analogy. Not only does XAML give a great range of expressiveness for the look and feel of a UI, but it also allows for parts of the behavior of the UI to be declarative.

❑ **Rich composition and customization** — It is very easy to customize controls in WPF with little or no code. Almost any type of control can be composed with another control. There literally are no boundaries here; for example, you could bind a media clip to a text box if you wanted to, or make it spin around, and so on. It is also very easy to "skin" applications with very different looks, without requiring any code. These advantages help satisfy the Rich Client Application Functionality requirement.

❑ **Easy deployment** — Using the .NET Framework's ClickOnce technology will provide a way to install and run SmartCA on the client machines simply by clicking on a URL. ClickOnce ensures that installation will not affect other applications because all files required for the application are placed in an isolated area and it also prevents any custom registration.

Fulfilling the Web Access Requirement

Although I have not talked much about the server-side partition of this application, the mere fact that there will be a server-side implementation means that it is possible for the application's data and behavior to be exposed to the web via a web application or even via web services. In fact, I will show later in the book how each SmartCA client application instance will be using web services to synchronize its transactions with the server.

Fulfilling the Intelligent Installation and Auto-Update Functionality Requirement

The SmartCA application will take advantage of the Visual Studio 2008's ClickOnce deployment tools and .NET Framework technology to satisfy the Intelligent Installation requirement. Since the .NET Framework also has built-in support for automatic updates and for rolling back to previous versions, the Auto-Update requirement will also be satisfied.

Since SQL CE is so lightweight (it only eats up about 1.5 MB worth of hard disk space), it will be very easy to deploy, which will also help support the Intelligent Installation requirement.

Summary

In this chapter, I introduced you to the fictitious company Smart Design, and more importantly, the new application that I am building for them, the SmartCA application. I also outlined the problems of the legacy application, the requirements for the new application, as well as what technologies and designs I plan to use to satisfy all of the requirements. In the next chapter, I will delve into the details of the layered architecture model and implementation for the SmartCA application.

2

Designing the Layered Architecture

Since I have decided that the application architecture will use a layered approach, it is time to create the Visual Studio solution to host these layers.

The Problem

In order to implement the layered approach correctly, there are some steps that I will need to follow:

1. The Visual Studio solution must be organized make it very obvious where the layers have been implemented in the code modules.

2. Each individual layer needs to be designed as well, and needs to include the design patterns and technologies for each layer.

3. I need to decide what functionality belongs in each of the layers.

4. An application framework needs to be built that will simplify coding the application.

The Design

In this chapter, there are two main items that need to be designed, and those items are the Visual Studio solution and the actual architectural layers of the SmartCA application.

Designing the Visual Studio Solution

As stated earlier, the first step in implementing the layered architecture is to create a Visual Studio solution that will support the approach.

The initial skeleton for the solution will hold four projects, one for each layer of the application. Figure 2.1 below shows this initial design.

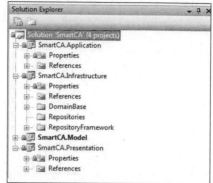

Figure 2.1: Initial code skeleton design.

The first three projects in the solution are basic C# Class Library projects, and the last project, SmartCA. Presentation, is actually a WPF project.

As can be seen from the names of the projects in the solution, the namespace pattern that will be used is always SmartCA.<Layer Name>. There will be cases where an extra project may be required even though it still belongs in one of the four layers. Usually, this happens in the infrastructure layer, where you may be implementing some functionality that needs to be separated from the rest of the Infrastructure project. In that particular case, the naming standard that I will follow is SmartCA.<Layer Name>.<Some other functionality name>. An example is a project with a name and namespace combination of SmartCA.Infrastructure.Caching. These types of projects can be added later if and when they are needed.

Designing the Architectural Layers

Now that the namespace naming pattern has been established for the layers, it is time to start the layers. Just to refresh your memory from Chapter 1, the layers I will be building are the application, domain, infrastructure, and presentation (a.k.a. UI) layers.

Designing the Application Layer

I would like to approach the application layer as an application programming interface (API), or almost a façade, to the domain model. The reason I say *almost* a façade is because the application will be doing a little bit more than just making it simple to use the domain model; it will also be coordinating actions between different domain objects as well as maintaining the state of a particular task. The classes in this layer will be composed of mostly static methods, thus making it easy for a class in the presentation layer to do some work. An example is having a ProjectService class in the application layer that has very simple methods to load and save a Project, such as Project.GetProject(1) and Project .Save(project). This could also be the layer that web service methods would call to get or save their data. Another example is using the application layer to coordinate actions between domain objects and infrastructure objects, such as saving a project and then sending an email to all of the interested parties in management.

Designing the Domain Layer

The domain layer will be designed using the POCO approach (POCO stands for Plain-Old CLR Objects). It is my intent to make the domain model as free from any distractions as possible, including having to implement several persistence-related interfaces or inherit from classes that have nothing to do with the business model. The idea is for the classes in the domain layer to be as persistent-ignorant as possible.

Important Domain-Driven Design Concepts

Before getting too deep into the design of the SmartCA application, there are some common Domain-Driven Design terms and concepts that must be discussed. Although I am not going to go into great detail about them here, they still need to be talked about before moving forward. In order to get a deeper understanding of these concepts I highly recommend reading *Domain-Driven Design: Tackling Complexity in the Heart of Software* (Addison-Wesley, 2004) by Eric Evans; *Applying Domain-Driven Design and Patterns, With Examples in C# and .NET* (Addison-Wesley, 2006) by Jimmy Nilsson; and *Patterns of Enterprise Application Architecture* (Addison-Wesley, 2003) by Martin Fowler. The main point of this book is to adhere to these concepts as much as possible while building the SmartCA application.

Entities

One of the most important fundamental concepts to understand is the definition of Entity in Domain-Driven Design. According to Evans "An object primarily defined by its identity is called an Entity." Entities are very important in the domain model, and need to be designed carefully. Sometimes what people think of as an entity in one system is not an entity in another system; for example, an address. In some systems, an address may not have an identity at all; it may only represent attributes of a person or company. In other systems, such as a cable television company or a utility company, the address could be very important. In those systems, the address is important as an identity because the billing may be tied directly to the address. In that case, the address would definitely be classified as an entity. In other systems, such as an e-commerce web site, the address may only be used for determining where to send an order, and the identity of the address may not really matter much, just the attributes of the address so that the order can be fulfilled. In those types of cases, the address becomes what is called in Domain-Driven Design a Value object.

Value Objects

Unlike Entity objects, Value objects have no identity. There is no need to track the object's identity, and it is very easy to create and discard. Most of the time, Value objects usually contain either just data or just behavior. The ones that contain only data are also known as Data Transfer Objects (DTOs) (Fowler, *Patterns of Enterprise Application Architecture*, 401). A very common scenario is for an Entity to contain other Value objects. There are also times where Value objects can contain other Value objects, even other Entity objects. Most of the time, as in the case of the address example used earlier, they are a group of attributes that make up a conceptual whole but without an identity.

It is recommended that Value objects be immutable, that is, they are created with a constructor, with all properties being read-only. To get a different value for the object, a new one must be created. A perfect example of this is the `System.String` class. Value objects do not always have to be immutable, but the main rule to follow is that if the object is going to be shared, then it needs to be immutable.

In distinguishing between Entity objects and Value objects, if the object does not have an identity that I care about, then I classify it as a Value object.

Services

Sometimes, when designing a domain model, you will have certain types of behavior that do not fit into any one class. Trying to tack on the behavior to a class to which it really does not belong will only cloud the domain model, but .NET, and all other object-oriented languages, requires the behavior to live in some type of object, so it cannot be a separate function on its own (as you might find in JavaScript or other scripting languages). The type of class that becomes the home for this behavior is known in Domain-Driven Design as a Service.

A `Service` class has no internal state and can simply act as an interface implementation that provides operations. This concept is very similar to web services. Services typically coordinate the work of one or more domain objects, and present the coordination as a well-known operation. It is also important to note that some services may live in the application layer, some may live in the domain layer, and others may live in the infrastructure layer.

Application Layer Services

The services that live in the application layer typically coordinate the work of other services in other layers. Consider an order fulfillment service. This service probably takes in an order message in the format of XML data, calls a factory to transform the XML into an object, and then sends the object to the domain layer for processing. After processing has been completed, the service may need to send out a notification to a user, and it may delegate that to an infrastructure layer service.

Domain Layer Services

In keeping with the order fulfillment example, the domain layer service would be responsible for interacting with the right Entity objects, Value objects, and other domain layer objects necessary to process the order in the domain. Ultimately, the service would return some type of result from the operation so that the calling service could take the necessary actions.

Infrastructure Layer Services

In the same order fulfillment scenario, the infrastructure layer service may need to do things like sending the user an order confirmation email letting them know that their order is being processed. These types of activities belong in the infrastructure layer.

Aggregates

In Domain-Driven Design speak, an Aggregate is a term used to define object ownership and the boundaries between objects and their relationships. It is used to define a group of associated objects that are to be treated as one unit in regard to data changes. For example, an `Order` class and its associated line items can be considered to be part of the same Order Aggregate, with the `Order` class being the root of the Aggregate. That brings me to a very important rule, and that is each Aggregate can only have one root object, and that object is an Entity object. The root of an Aggregate can hold references to the roots of other Aggregates, and objects inside of an Aggregate can hold references to one another, but nothing outside of the Aggregate boundary can access the objects inside of the Aggregate without going through that Aggregate's root object.

It is easier to understand this concept with an example. The example I always use is the canonical Order Aggregate. An Order object is the root of its own Aggregate, and it contains objects such as Line Items (which can contain Products) and Customers. To get to a Line Item object, I would have to go through the Order Aggregate root object, the Order object. If I only wanted get some data about a Customer, and not the Order, I might choose to start from the Customer Aggregate. I could move from the Order Aggregate to the Customer Aggregate, since the Order Aggregate contains an instance of a Customer object. On the other hand, I could get to a Customer's Order by going through the Customer Aggregate first, and then traversing the relationship between a Customer and his Orders. In this case, the relationship is bidirectional, and I could choose to start from the Customer Aggregate or from the Order Aggregate, depending on the use case. The key to remember is that both the Customer and the Order are the roots of their own Aggregate, and can also hold references to other Aggregate roots. I could not go directly from a Customer to a Line Item; I would first need to go to the Customer's Order, and then travel from there to the Line Item.

Defining the Aggregates in a domain model is one of the hardest activities to get right in Domain-Driven Design, and this is where you really need the help of an expert in the business domain that you are dealing with to determine the right boundaries and associations. It is also an area that I end up refactoring a lot as I begin to understand more about the business model of an application.

Repositories

According to Eric Evans, a repository "represents all objects of a certain type as a conceptual set (usually emulated)" (Evans, *Domain-Driven Design: Tackling Complexity in the Heart of Software*, 151). He also goes on to say that for every object that is an Aggregate, create a repository for the object and give it the look and feel of an in-memory collection of objects of that particular type. The access to the repository must be through a well-known interface. The main point of repositories is to keep the developer focused on the domain model logic, and hide the plumbing of data access behind well-known repository interfaces. This concept is also known as *persistence ignorance*, meaning that the domain model is ignorant of how its data is saved or retrieved from its underlying data store or stores.

Factories

As the Entities and their associated Aggregates start to grow in the domain layer, it becomes increasingly more difficult to build up objects consistently just using constructors. Lots of times there is intimate knowledge needed to construct an Aggregate and all of its relationships, constraints, rules, and the like. Instead of making the Entity objects themselves responsible for this creation, it is better to have a Factory that knows how to build these types of objects, and thus avoid clouding up the code of an Entity object.

In Domain-Driven Design, there are two types of Factories, those for building the root Entity of an Aggregate (usually from some type of resultset data) and those for building Value objects (usually from some type of configuration data).

Using Repositories in the Domain Layer

If I can get away with it, I will try not to let any of my domain model classes know about any of the repositories. This goes a long way towards persistence ignorance, but it is not always an easy thing to accomplish. I would like to restrict repositories so that only their interfaces will live in the domain layer. If I am successful, a domain model class can talk to a repository interface if it really needs to, yet the implementation of the actual repositories will be in the infrastructure layer. This is better known as the Separated Interface pattern (Fowler, *Patterns of Enterprise Application Architecture*, 476–479), where the interface is defined in a separate assembly from its implementation. My goal can also be aided by having a factory provide the implementation of the interface requested, and therefore the domain model classes may need to have an extra dependency on the Repository Factory if they need to create and use the repository implementation classes.

Using the Layered Supertype Pattern

Since Evans defines an Entity as "an object that is distinguished by identity, rather than its attributes" (Evans, *Domain-Driven Design: Tackling Complexity in the Heart of Software*, 92), we know that all of our entity classes are going to need some type of data type to distinguish their identities. This would be a good opportunity to use Fowler's Layered Supertype pattern, which is defined as "a type that acts as the supertype for all types in its layer" (Fowler, *Patterns of Enterprise Application Architecture*, 475). Having all entities inherit from an entity base class type will help eliminate some duplicate properties and behavior in the domain entity classes. The use of this base class is purely for convenience, and I feel that it will not distract our model at all; in fact, it will be easier to distinguish between which classes are entities and which ones are value objects.

Designing the Infrastructure Layer

The infrastructure layer is where all of the SmartCA application's *plumbing* lives. Any type of framework, data access code, calls to web service calls, and so forth will live in this layer. A perfect example of this is the SmartCA application's Repository Framework implementation, which I will dive into in the Solution section of this chapter, that lives inside of the infrastructure layer. Not only can the infrastructure layer hold infrastructure for the domain layer, but it can also hold infrastructure code and logic for any of the other layers, including those that meet its own needs.

Designing the Presentation Layer

The goal in designing the presentation layer is to keep it as thin as possible, very similarly to the application layer. One of the main pitfalls to avoid is embedding any business logic in the presentation layer. The presentation layer has two main responsibilities:

1. Interpret the user's commands and send the user's requests down to the application layer or domain layer.

2. Show information to the user.

In order to help the presentation layer carry out its responsibilities, I will be using a new pattern developed by John Gossman of the Microsoft WPF team, called the Model-View-ViewModel pattern. The implementation of this pattern will be discussed in the Solution section.

The Solution

Now that I have detailed how the Visual Studio solution and all of the architectural layers should be designed, it is time to start implementing these designs. That means I finally get to do my favorite thing, which is writing code!

Implementing the Visual Studio Solution

In keeping with the layered architecture diagram in Figure 1.2, the dependencies of the layers can only go down from higher levels to lower levels, that is, the presentation layer can depend on the application layer, but the application layer cannot have a dependency on the presentation layer. Figure 2.2 illustrates the dependencies by showing the references between the projects.

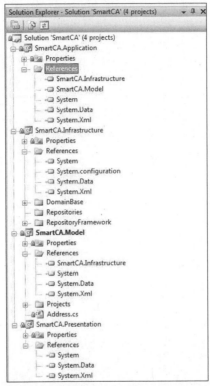

Figure 2.2: Initial code skeleton design with dependencies.

The project that is really the root of dependencies is the SmartCA.Infrastructure project, as it is referred to by all of the other assemblies and it does not refer to any of the other assemblies.

Implementing the Architectural Layers

This section may sound a little bit misleading, because if I were to implement all of the architectural layers here, then the application would be finished and the book would be over! What I am going to show you in this section is a lot of Infrastructure code that the other layers of the application will be using. I will first start with the Layered Supertype implementation, followed by the Repository Framework, and lastly I will conclude with the Model-View-ViewModel pattern implementation that will be used in the presentation layer.

19

Layered Supertype

The layered supertype I will use is an abstract class named `EntityBase`, with the intention that all Entity classes in the domain model will need to inherit from this class to gain their identity. This class will live in the `SmartCA.Infrastructure` project, as it is not really part of the domain logic, but it is providing necessary functionality to the domain model. Here is the code for this class:

```
using System;

namespace SmartCA.Infrastructure.DomainBase
{
    public abstract class EntityBase
    {
        private object key;

        /// <summary>
        /// Default Constructor.
        /// </summary>
        protected EntityBase()
            : this(null)
        {
        }

        /// <summary>
        /// Overloaded constructor.
        /// </summary>
        /// <param name="key">An <see cref="System.Object"/> that
        /// represents the primary identifier value for the
        /// class.</param>
        protected EntityBase(object key)
        {
            this.key = key;
        }

        /// <summary>
        /// An <see cref="System.Object"/> that represents the
        /// primary identifier value for the class.
        /// </summary>
        public object Key
        {
            get
            {
                return this.key;
            }
        }
    }
```

The first part of the class contains a default constructor and an overloaded constructor that allow a key value to be passed in. The key that was passed in is also exposed as a read-only property. Currently, I am leaving the `Key` property's type as a `System.Object`, because I am not really sure yet if the keys to the entities will be Guids, Integers, an so on. Also, some key data types on entity objects may be different from others, and so for right now this gives me the most flexibility.

The next part of the code implements all of the necessary equality tests to determine whether two entity objects are equal to each other. These come in very handy later when comparing entity values in collections, trying to find matches, and so forth.

```
#region Equality Tests

/// <summary>
/// Determines whether the specified entity is equal to the
/// current instance.
/// </summary>
/// <param name="entity">An <see cref="System.Object"/> that
/// will be compared to the current instance.</param>
/// <returns>True if the passed in entity is equal to the
/// current instance.</returns>
public override bool Equals(object entity)
{
    if (entity == null || !(entity is EntityBase))
    {
        return false;
    }
    return (this == (EntityBase)entity);
}


/// <summary>
/// Operator overload for determining equality.
/// </summary>
/// <param name="base1">The first instance of an
/// <see cref="EntityBase"/>.</param>
/// <param name="base2">The second instance of an
/// <see cref="EntityBase"/>.</param>
/// <returns>True if equal.</returns>
public static bool operator ==(EntityBase base1,
    EntityBase base2)
{
    // check for both null (cast to object or recursive loop)
    if ((object)base1 == null && (object)base2 == null)
    {
        return true;
    }

    // check for either of them == to null
    if ((object)base1 == null || (object)base2 == null)
    {
        return false;
    }

    if (base1.Key != base2.Key)
```

(continued)

(continued)

```
            {
                return false;
            }

            return true;
        }

        /// <summary>
        /// Operator overload for determining inequality.
        /// </summary>
        /// <param name="base1">The first instance of an
        /// <see cref="EntityBase"/>.</param>
        /// <param name="base2">The second instance of an
        /// <see cref="EntityBase"/>.</param>
        /// <returns>True if not equal.</returns>
        public static bool operator !=(EntityBase base1,
            EntityBase base2)
        {
            return (!(base1 == base2));
        }

        /// <summary>
        /// Serves as a hash function for this type.
        /// </summary>
        /// <returns>A hash code for the current Key
        /// property.</returns>
        public override int GetHashCode()
        {
            return this.key.GetHashCode();
        }

        #endregion
    }
}
```

This behavior is necessary for comparing, sorting, and matching entity objects. This is nice because this *plumbing* type of code is encapsulated in the infrastructure layer and keeps the domain layer's entity objects free from these distractions.

Repository Framework

For the SmartCA application, I have decided to implement a hybrid Repository Framework. By hybrid, I mean a cross between a pure Repository Framework, where all repositories have the same interface, and a custom repository implementation for each aggregate root.

The Interfaces

The hybrid framework will contain a generic IRepository<T> interface, which will live in the SmartCA.Infrastructure.RepositoryFramework namespace in the SmartCA.Infrastructure assembly, which has the following signature:

```
using System;
using SmartCA.Infrastructure.DomainBase;

namespace SmartCA.Infrastructure.RepositoryFramework
{
    public interface IRepository<T> where T : EntityBase
    {
        T FindBy(object key);
        void Add(T item);
        T this[object key] { get; set; }
        void Remove(T item);
    }
}
```

Using .NET Generics helps a great deal here, as it allows for the IRepository<T> interface to be reused in many places of the application, and because of the where clause on T, it restricts the data type to being a class that derives from EntityBase, the domain model's layered supertype. An interesting note about this interface is that there is actually an indexer (T this[*object key*] { get; set; }). I added this to emphasize the concept that a repository should emulate a collection of objects in memory.

You may have noticed that I did not put a Find or FindBy method on this interface that takes some type of generic predicate or expression. I did this intentionally. Based on my previous experience, this can get pretty complicated, and so I have decided to put all of the Find type of methods in Aggregate-specific types of repositories, an example of which would look like the IProjectRepository interface shown below:

```
using System;
using System.Collections.Generic;
using SmartCA.Infrastructure.RepositoryFramework;

namespace SmartCA.Model.Projects
{
    public interface IProjectRepository : IRepository<Project>
    {
        IList<Project> FindBy(object sector, object segment,
            bool completed);
    }
}
```

This way, if you want to program against the general interface (IRepository<T>) you can, but you can also program against a more specific interface if you need to add more specialized methods to your repository, such as more granular Find methods. It essentially gives you the option to refactor things later without too much pain.

The Repository Factory

Earlier in the Design section of this chapter I talked about the importance of the domain model classes being able to use a particular Repository interface without needing a reference to the associated repository implementation in the infrastructure layer. This concept was defined as the Separated Interface pattern, and I mentioned that I would need a Factory to provide the implementation of the Repository interface that was requested. That Factory is called the Repository Factory and is exactly what I going to implement in this section.

Configuration Section

In order to eliminate any hard-coding of repository class names in the Repository Factory, I have chosen to use configuration along with the Factory to make it very easy to change what repositories get created at runtime by changing a few configuration settings. Not only does this make use of the previously mentioned Separated Interface pattern, but it also very closely resembles the ASP.NET Provider pattern, in that the provider's Factory creates its objects based upon configuration settings.

Here is what the configuration section for the Repository Factory looks like:

```xml
<?xml version="1.0" encoding="utf-8" ?>
<configuration>
  <configSections>
    <section name="repositoryMappingsConfiguration"

type="SmartCA.Infrastructure.RepositoryFramework.Configuration.RepositorySettings,
SmartCA.Infrastructure, Version=1.0.0.0, Culture=neutral, PublicKeyToken=null"/>
  </configSections>
  <repositoryMappingsConfiguration>
    <repositoryMappings>
      <repositoryMapping interfaceShortTypeName="IProjectRepository"

repositoryFullTypeName="SmartCA.Infrastructure.Repositories.ProjectRepository,
SmartCA.Infrastructure.Repositories, Version=1.0.0.0, Culture=neutral,
PublicKeyToken=null" />
    </repositoryMappings>
  </repositoryMappingsConfiguration>
</configuration>
```

The configuration section is really just storing the mappings of interface types to their implementations, as can be seen in the `repositoryMapping` element in the configuration file. What this means is that a repository implementation could be changed in the application's configuration file without having to recompile the application.

Configuration Section Handling

In order to support this functionality, I have added a `Configuration` folder under the `RepositoryFramework` folder of the `SmartCA.Infrastructure` project (see Figure 2.3).

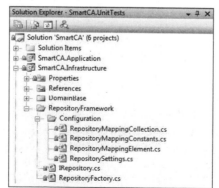

Figure 2.3: RepositoryFramework Configuration folder.

The job of the classes in the Configuration folder is to read and copy the settings from the `repositoryMappingsConfiguration` configuration section into a nice object model that the `RepositoryFactory` can consume in order to do its job. The root class for this configuration-section-handling functionality is the `RepositorySettings` class, which inherits from the .NET Framework `ConfigurationSection` class.

```
using System;
using System.Configuration;

namespace SmartCA.Infrastructure.RepositoryFramework.Configuration
{
    public class RepositorySettings : ConfigurationSection
    {

[ConfigurationProperty(RepositoryMappingConstants.ConfigurationPropertyName,
            IsDefaultCollection = true)]
        public RepositoryMappingCollection RepositoryMappings
        {
            get { return
(RepositoryMappingCollection)base[RepositoryMappingConstants.ConfigurationProperty
Name]; }
        }
    }
}
```

The class is very simple, since the .NET Framework's `ConfigurationSection` class does most of the work. Its main purpose is to return the collection of repositories defined in configuration into a `RepositoryMappingCollection` data type. I have defined the name of the configuration element that represents the collection of repositories in a separate class named `RepositoryMappingConstants`.

```
using System;

namespace SmartCA.Infrastructure.RepositoryFramework.Configuration
{
    internal static class RepositoryMappingConstants
    {
        public const string ConfigurationPropertyName = "repositoryMappings";
        public const string ConfigurationElementName = "repositoryMapping";
        public const string InterfaceShortTypeNameAttributeName =
 "interfaceShortTypeName";
        public const string RepositoryFullTypeNameAttributeName =
 "repositoryFullTypeName";
        public const string RepositoryMappingsConfigurationSectionName =
 "repository
MappingsConfiguration";
    }
}
```

Since I have to refer to these string values more than once in the Repository Framework configuration code, it's a lot easier to define them with a static constants class. Note that the `RepositoryMappingConstants` class is marked `internal`, as the only code needing to know about these constants is in the `SmartCA.Infrastructure` assembly.

The `RepositoryMappingCollection` is a little bit more complicated than the `RepositorySettings` class. Its job is to wrap the `repositoryMappings` element from the configuration section, and expose it as a strongly typed collection.

```
using System;
using System.Configuration;

namespace SmartCA.Infrastructure.RepositoryFramework.Configuration
{
    public sealed class RepositoryMappingCollection :
ConfigurationElementCollection
    {
        protected override ConfigurationElement CreateNewElement()
        {
            return new RepositoryMappingElement();
        }

        protected override object GetElementKey(ConfigurationElement element)
        {
            return ((RepositoryMappingElement)element).InterfaceShortTypeName;
        }

        public override ConfigurationElementCollectionType CollectionType
        {
            get { return ConfigurationElementCollectionType.BasicMap; }
        }

        protected override string ElementName
        {
            get { return RepositoryMappingConstants.ConfigurationElementName; }
        }

        public RepositoryMappingElement this[int index]
        {
            get { return (RepositoryMappingElement)this.BaseGet(index); }
            set
            {
                if (this.BaseGet(index) != null)
                {
                    this.BaseRemoveAt(index);
                }
                this.BaseAdd(index, value);
            }
        }

        public new RepositoryMappingElement this[string interfaceShortTypeName]
        {
            get { return
(RepositoryMappingElement)this.BaseGet(interfaceShortTypeName); }
        }

        public bool ContainsKey(string keyName)
```

```
            {
                bool result = false;
                object[] keys = this.BaseGetAllKeys();
                foreach (object key in keys)
                {
                    if ((string)key == keyName)
                    {
                        result = true;
                        break;

                    }
                }
                return result;
            }
        }
    }
```

Like the `RepositorySettings` class, it too inherits from one of the `Sytem.Configuration` classes, this time the `ConfigurationElementCollection` class. There is really nothing very special about this class; it is basically just overriding various methods and properties on its base class. One thing that might look a little bit odd is the indexer property for the class.

```
public new RepositoryMappingElement this[string interfaceShortTypeName]
        {
            get { return
(RepositoryMappingElement)this.BaseGet(interfaceShortTypeName); }
        }
```

It is actually hiding the base class indexer (by using the `new` keyword) in order to make it strongly typed instead of exposing the collection item as a `System.Object`.

The child members that the `RepositoryMappingCollection` contains are `RepositoryMappingElement` instances. The `RepositoryMappingElement` class is what actually holds the mapping between an interface type name and a concrete repository type name.

```
using System;
using System.Configuration;

namespace SmartCA.Infrastructure.RepositoryFramework.Configuration
{
    public sealed class RepositoryMappingElement : ConfigurationElement
    {
[ConfigurationProperty(RepositoryMappingConstants.InterfaceShortTypeName
AttributeName,
            IsKey = true, IsRequired = true)]
        public string InterfaceShortTypeName
        {
            get
            {
                return (string)this[RepositoryMappingConstants.Interface
ShortTypeNameAttributeName];
            }
            set
```

(continued)

```
                {

this[RepositoryMappingConstants.InterfaceShortTypeNameAttributeName] = value;
                }
            }


        [ConfigurationProperty(RepositoryMappingConstants.RepositoryFullTypeName
AttributeName,
                IsRequired = true)]
        public string RepositoryFullTypeName
            {
                get
                {
                    return
(string)this[RepositoryMappingConstants.RepositoryFullTypeNameAttributeName];
                }
                set
                {

this[RepositoryMappingConstants.RepositoryFullTypeNameAttributeName] = value;
                }
            }
        }
    }
```

Like the other repository mapping configuration classes, this class also inherits from one of the `System.Configuration` classes, the `ConfigurationElement` class. With the help of some `System.Configuration` attributes decorating it, the `RepositoryMappingElement` class exposes two properties, `InterfaceShortTypeName` and `RepositoryFullTypeName`.

The RepositoryFactory Class

Now that the configuration is finished, the `RepositoryFactory` can use it to create repositories. The `RepositoryFactory` uses Generic type parameters combined with the mappings from the configuration in order to determine what kind of repository to create. The `RepositoryFactory` is a static class with one static method, `GetRepository`.

```
using System;
using System.Collections.Generic;
using SmartCA.Infrastructure;
using SmartCA.Infrastructure.DomainBase;
using SmartCA.Infrastructure.RepositoryFramework.Configuration;
using System.Configuration;

namespace SmartCA.Infrastructure.RepositoryFramework
{
    public static class RepositoryFactory
    {
        // Dictionary to enforce the singleton pattern
        private static Dictionary<string, object> repositories = new
Dictionary<string, object>();
```

```csharp
/// <summary>
/// Gets or creates an instance of the requested interface. Once a
/// repository is created and initialized, it is cached, and all
/// future requests for the repository will come from the cache.
/// </summary>
/// <typeparam name="TRepository">The interface of the repository
/// to create.</typeparam>
/// <typeparam name="TEntity">The type of the EntityBase that the
/// repository is for.</typeparam>
/// <returns>An instance of the interface requested.</returns>
public static TRepository GetRepository<TRepository, TEntity>()
    where TRepository : class, IRepository<TEntity>
    where TEntity : EntityBase
{
    // Initialize the provider's default value
    TRepository repository = default(TRepository);

    string interfaceShortName = typeof(TRepository).Name;

    // See if the provider was already created and is in the cache
    if (!RepositoryFactory.repositories.ContainsKey(interfaceShortName))
    {
        // Not there, so create it

        // Get the repositoryMappingsConfiguration config section
        RepositorySettings settings =
(RepositorySettings)ConfigurationManager.GetSection(RepositoryMappingConstants
.RepositoryMappingsConfigurationSectionName);

        // Create the repository, and cast it to the interface specified
        repository =
Activator.CreateInstance(Type.GetType(settings.RepositoryMappings[interfaceShortName]
.RepositoryFullTypeName)) as TRepository;

        // Add the new provider instance to the cache
        RepositoryFactory.repositories.Add(interfaceShortName, repository);
    }
    else
    {
        // The provider was in the cache, so retrieve it
        repository =
(TRepository)RepositoryFactory.repositories[interfaceShortName];
    }
    return repository;
}
}
}
```

The signature of this method is interesting because it uses two Generic type parameters, `TRepository` and `TEntity`, with the restrictions that `TRepository` is a class and implements the `IRepository<TEntity>` interface, and that `TEntity` derives from the `EntityBase` class. Because the Repository Framework is supporting interfaces other than just `IRepository<T>`, the method cannot just return a type of `IRepository<T>` for the `Repository` instance. It must also support returning any interface that implements `IRepository<T>`, since the repository interface being used can also have additional methods defined in it; that is why `TRepository` has been declared as a Generic type, so that the factory can support the Repository Framework requirements of being able to pass in a valid `Repository` interface type and get an instance of the interface (as long as it has been properly defined in the application's configuration file).

The code for the method first uses reflection to get the short type name of the interface type passed in via the Generic `TRepository` parameter. It then does a lookup in its static dictionary of repositories that have already been created to see if it can pull it out of memory. If it cannot, it then begins the process of using the custom repository configuration objects to find the right repository type to create based on the values in the mappings configuration. When the type is found, the method then uses the reflection capabilities of the Activator object to create an instance of the correct repository based on the mapped type from configuration. Then, after the repository has been created, it is put into the static dictionary of repositories so that it will be available the next time it is requested. Once the repository has been retrieved from memory or created, the instance is returned to the caller.

I decided to use a static dictionary to hold the repositories in order to make them behave like singletons. This is very important for performance reasons, since it can be expensive to build a Repository Factory using reflection every time you need one, especially in Domain-Driven Design architectures, where repositories are used quite frequently. Also, because the repositories are guaranteed to have only one instance per type, I can now do other interesting things, such as enable domain model objects to be cached, refresh the cache when I choose to, and so on. This functionality can have a very positive impact on the performance of the application.

Unit of Work

Since I will be using several repositories to pull data in and out of the database (and possibly other resources), I need a way to keep track of what has been changed. I also need a way to define what sequences of events define a transaction and to be able to commit those sequences of events as a single transaction. One way of doing this is simply to avoid the problem altogether and every time an object changes, just write the change to the data store; however, this pattern usually does not work very well, especially when you need to group actions together into a single transaction.

The answer to this requirement that I am going to use is the Unit of Work pattern, as defined by Martin Fowler (Fowler, *Patterns of Enterprise Application Architecture*, 184). According to Martin, the Unit of Work "maintains a list of objects affected by a business transaction and coordinates the writing out of changes and the resolution of concurrency problems." The Unit of Work needs to know what objects it should keep track of, and Martin goes on to describe two basic ways this can be accomplished:

❑ **Caller registration** — The user of the object has to remember to register with the Unit of Work.

❑ **Object registration** — The objects register themselves with the Unit of Work.

Jimmy Nilsson describes a different approach to the Unit of Work, and that is to let the repositories delegate all of their work to a Unit of Work, and then the Unit of Work then makes all necessary database calls (or other types of resource calls) on behalf of the repositories (Nilsson, *Applying Domain-Driven Design and Patterns, With Examples in C# and .NET*, 200). One major benefit of this approach is that the messages sent to the Unit of Work are invisible to the consumer of the repositories, since the repositories are reporting what has been asked of them to the Unit of Work. This also helps promote persistence ignorance in the domain objects, which is what I am striving for.

In his solution, Jimmy implemented object persistence outside of the repository in his Unit of Work implementation. The reasoning for not letting the repositories completely hide the Unit of Work was that he wanted to synchronize changes across several Aggregates (and their respective repositories) in a single logical unit. In order for this to work, the repositories need to have a Unit of Work injected into them at creation time.

I really like Jimmy's idea of hiding the Unit of Work calls in the repositories because it eliminates lots of plumbing calls inside of domain objects or from application-level code. This way, the plumbing stays inside the repository, which itself represents plumbing, and shields the domain object from having to deal with the noise. With that being said, I also would like to have my cake and eat it too. What I mean by that is that I would like to keep the spirit of Jimmy's solution but also still have the repositories be responsible for the data persistence. In order to do that, I have created a few interfaces to help out. The first one being the obvious one, the IUnitOfWork interface:

```
using System;
using SmartCA.Infrastructure.DomainBase;
using SmartCA.Infrastructure.RepositoryFramework;

namespace SmartCA.Infrastructure
{
    public interface IUnitOfWork
    {
        void RegisterAdded(EntityBase entity, IUnitOfWorkRepository repository);
        void RegisterChanged(EntityBase entity, IUnitOfWorkRepository repository);
        void RegisterRemoved(EntityBase entity, IUnitOfWorkRepository repository);
        void Commit();
    }
}
```

The IUnitOfWork interface identifies for use the entities that have been added, changed, or removed from the repositories. An instance of this interface must be passed to all repositories that are to participate in a Unit of Work. Then, once all work is completed, I simply call Commit on the interface to commit all of my changes to the appropriate data stores. You may be asking yourself, how in the world can the Unit of Work implementation commit the changes if the repositories are supposed to do the work? The answer is to have the repositories implement a second interface to which the Unit of Work refers. That interface is the IUnitOfWorkRepository interface:

```
using System;
using SmartCA.Infrastructure.DomainBase;

namespace SmartCA.Infrastructure.RepositoryFramework
{
    public interface IUnitOfWorkRepository
    {
        void PersistNewItem(EntityBase item);
        void PersistUpdatedItem(EntityBase item);
        void PersistDeletedItem(EntityBase item);
    }
}
```

Because the repositories will implement the IUnitOfWorkRepository interface, the Unit of Work implementation will now be able to call back in to the repositories to make changes to the data store (or stores).

I have created a Unit of Work implementation class called UnitofWork (I know, very creative). It essentially keeps a list of the three types of changes, and then cycles through each of them during commit time and talks to the right repository to persist the changes.

```csharp
using System;
using System.Collections.Generic;
using SmartCA.Infrastructure.DomainBase;
using SmartCA.Infrastructure.RepositoryFramework;
using System.Transactions;

namespace SmartCA.Infrastructure
{
    public class UnitOfWork : IUnitOfWork
    {
        private Dictionary<EntityBase, IUnitOfWorkRepository> addedEntities;
        private Dictionary<EntityBase, IUnitOfWorkRepository> changedEntities;
        private Dictionary<EntityBase, IUnitOfWorkRepository> deletedEntities;

        public UnitOfWork()
        {
            this.addedEntities = new Dictionary<EntityBase,
                                    IUnitOfWorkRepository>();
            this.changedEntities = new Dictionary<EntityBase,
                                    IUnitOfWorkRepository>();
            this.deletedEntities = new Dictionary<EntityBase,
                                    IUnitOfWorkRepository>();
        }

        #region IUnitOfWork Members

        public void RegisterAdded(EntityBase entity,
            IUnitOfWorkRepository repository)
        {
            this.addedEntities.Add(entity, repository);
        }

        public void RegisterChanged(EntityBase entity,
            IUnitOfWorkRepository repository)
        {
            this.changedEntities.Add(entity, repository);
        }

        public void RegisterRemoved(EntityBase entity,
            IUnitOfWorkRepository repository)
        {
            this.deletedEntities.Add(entity, repository);
        }

        public void Commit()
        {
            using (TransactionScope scope = new TransactionScope())
            {
                foreach (EntityBase entity in this.deletedEntities.Keys)
                {
                    this.deletedEntities[entity].PersistDeletedItem(entity);
                }

                foreach (EntityBase entity in this.addedEntities.Keys)
                {
```

```
                    this.addedEntities[entity].PersistDeletedItem(entity);
                }

                foreach (EntityBase entity in this.changedEntities.Keys)
                {
                    this.changedEntities[entity].PersistDeletedItem(entity);
                }

                scope.Complete();
            }

            this.deletedEntities.Clear();
            this.addedEntities.Clear();
            this.changedEntities.Clear();
        }

        #endregion
    }
}
```

The methods in the IUnitOfWork Members region of the class will get called by the repositories, and the repositories actually pass in their own instances to the UnitOfWork class when they call these methods. When these methods are called, the entity and its associated IUnitOfWorkRepository instance are added to their respective dictionary object, depending whether the call was an add, change, or remove registration.

Then, in the Commit method, the UnitOfWork cycles through all of the deletions, additions, and updates, respectively, and calls back on the associated IUnitOfWorkRepository instance to persist the changes to the correct data store. The entire operation is wrapped up in a transaction using the .NET Framework's TransactionScope class, which knows how to enlist the right type of transaction properly, be it just a local transaction or a distributed transaction. Once everything has been committed, the entity-repository dictionaries are then reset to empty.

The Repository Base Classes

In order to eliminate a lot of duplicate code, I have decided to put in some abstract base classes from which the repositories will inherit common code. This should make it easier to code the concrete repository classes.

The RepositoryBase<T> Class

This is the first repository base class and its main job is to lend a helping hand to its derived repositories in regard to implementing the Unit of Work pattern. It also helps out with the indexer implementation of the IRepository<T> interface.

```
using System;
using SmartCA.Infrastructure.DomainBase;

namespace SmartCA.Infrastructure.RepositoryFramework
{
    public abstract class RepositoryBase<T>
        : IRepository<T>, IUnitOfWorkRepository where T : EntityBase
```

(continued)

33

(continued)

```
{
    private IUnitOfWork unitOfWork;

    protected RepositoryBase()
        : this(null)
    {
    }

    protected RepositoryBase(IUnitOfWork unitOfWork)
    {
        this.unitOfWork = unitOfWork;
    }

    #region IRepository<T> Members

    public abstract T FindBy(object key);

    public void Add(T item)
    {
        if (this.unitOfWork != null)
        {
            this.unitOfWork.RegisterAdded(item, this);
        }
    }

    public void Remove(T item)
    {
        if (this.unitOfWork != null)
        {
            this.unitOfWork.RegisterRemoved(item, this);
        }
    }

    public T this[object key]
    {
        get
        {
            return this.FindBy(key);
        }
        set
        {
            if (this.FindBy(key) == null)
            {
                this.Add(value);
            }
            else
            {
                this.unitOfWork.RegisterChanged(value, this);
            }
        }
    }
```

```
        #endregion

        #region IUnitOfWorkRepository Members

        public void PersistNewItem(EntityBase item)
        {
            this.PersistNewItem((T)item);
        }

        public void PersistUpdatedItem(EntityBase item)
        {
            this.PersistUpdatedItem((T)item);
        }

        public void PersistDeletedItem(EntityBase item)
        {
            this.PersistDeletedItem((T)item);
        }

        #endregion

        protected abstract void PersistNewItem(T item);
        protected abstract void PersistUpdatedItem(T item);
        protected abstract void PersistDeletedItem(T item);
    }
}
```

This class implements both the `IRepository<T>` interface and the `IUnitOfWorkRepository` interface, and it is optionally injected with the `IUnitOfWork` interface in its constructor. Its main job in implementing the `IRepository<T>` interface is mainly to call back into the `IUnitOfWork` interface instance to let it know when something has been added, removed, or changed. The other `IRepository<T>` method without an implementation in this class, `T FindBy(object key)`, is actually declared as an abstract method to be implemented by one of the derived repository classes.

All of the methods on the `IUnitOfWorkRepository` interface are implemented in this class, but really as a pass-through to some more abstract methods that the derived repositories have to implement. I did this to avoid having to cast from `EntityBase` to the types being used inside all of the repository implementations. Instead, the casting is performed in this class and then delegated to the more strongly typed, Generic-enabled abstract methods (`protected abstract void PersistNewItem(T item)`, `protected abstract void PersistUpdatedItem(T item)`, and `protected abstract void PersistDeletedItem(T item)`). This way, the code for the casting is centralized, and the concrete repositories can deal with the strongly typed entities that they know and represent.

The SqlCeRepositoryBase<T> Class

Since the architecture of this application dictates that we write and read all data to and from a local SQL Server CE database, a lot of duplicate SQL data access type of code can be eliminated in the `Repository` classes by building a base class to handle these types of operations. I decided to name this class

SqlCeRepositoryBase, in order to make its purpose obvious. This class makes it very easy for its derived Repository classes to talk to the local SQL CE database.

```
using System;
using System.Collections.Generic;
using SmartCA.Infrastructure.RepositoryFramework;
using SmartCA.Infrastructure.DomainBase;
using Microsoft.Practices.EnterpriseLibrary.Data.SqlCe;
using Microsoft.Practices.EnterpriseLibrary.Data;
using System.Data;
using System.Data.Common;
using SmartCA.Infrastructure.EntityFactoryFramework;

namespace SmartCA.Infrastructure.Repositories
{
    public abstract class SqlCeRepositoryBase<T> : RepositoryBase<T>
        where T : EntityBase
    {
        #region AppendChildData Delegate

        /// <summary>
        /// The delegate signature required for callback methods
        /// </summary>
        /// <param name="entityAggregate"></param>
        /// <param name="childEntityKey"></param>
        public delegate void AppendChildData(T entityAggregate,
            object childEntityKeyValue);

        #endregion

        #region Private Members

        private Database database;
        private IEntityFactory<T> entityFactory;
        private Dictionary<string, AppendChildData> childCallbacks;

        #endregion

        #region Constructors

        protected SqlCeRepositoryBase()
            : this(null)
        {
        }

        protected SqlCeRepositoryBase(IUnitOfWork unitOfWork)
            : base(unitOfWork)
        {
            this.database = DatabaseFactory.CreateDatabase();
            this.entityFactory = EntityFactoryBuilder.BuildFactory<T>();
            this.childCallbacks = new Dictionary<string, AppendChildData>();
            this.BuildChildCallbacks();
        }
```

```
#endregion

#region Abstract Methods

protected abstract void BuildChildCallbacks();
public abstract override T FindBy(object key);
protected abstract override void PersistNewItem(T item);
protected abstract override void PersistUpdatedItem(T item);
protected abstract override void PersistDeletedItem(T item);

#endregion

#region Properties

protected Database Database
{
    get { return this.database; }
}

protected Dictionary<string, AppendChildData> ChildCallbacks
{
    get { return this.childCallbacks; }
}

#endregion

#region Protected Methods

protected IDataReader ExecuteReader(string sql)
{
    DbCommand command = this.database.GetSqlStringCommand(sql);
    return this.database.ExecuteReader(command);
}

protected virtual T BuildEntityFromSql(string sql)
{
    T entity = default(T);
    using (IDataReader reader = this.ExecuteReader(sql))
    {
        if (reader.Read())
        {
            entity = this.BuildEntityFromReader(reader);
        }
    }
    return entity;
}

protected virtual T BuildEntityFromReader(IDataReader reader)
{
    T entity = this.entityFactory.BuildEntity(reader);
    if (this.childCallbacks != null && this.childCallbacks.Count > 0)
    {
        object childKeyValue = null;
        DataTable columnData = reader.GetSchemaTable();
        foreach (string childKeyName in this.childCallbacks.Keys)
```

(continued)

(continued)

```
                    {
                        if (DataHelper.ReaderContainsColumnName(columnData,
                            childKeyName))
                        {
                            childKeyValue = reader[childKeyName];
                        }
                        else
                        {
                            childKeyValue = null;
                        }
                        this.childCallbacks[childKeyName](entity, childKeyValue);
                    }
                }
                return entity;
            }

            protected virtual List<T> BuildEntitiesFromSql(string sql)
            {
                List<T> entities = new List<T>();
                using (IDataReader reader = this.ExecuteReader(sql))
                {
                    while (reader.Read())
                    {
                        entities.Add(this.BuildEntityFromReader(reader));
                    }
                }
                return entities;
            }

            #endregion
        }
    }
```

The class inherits from `RepositoryBase<T>` and does not implement any of its abstract methods; it simply overrides them and passes them on as abstract again. The real value it adds is in all of its protected methods to get data in and out of the local SQL CE database. One of the most interesting things about this class is that it is delegating out to a factory for building domain entity objects (`EntityBase`) from `IDataReader` instances.

When looking at the constructors, the first thing to notice is that I am using the Microsoft Enterprise Library 3.0 for data access, hence the use of the library's abstract `Database` class and its `DatabaseFactory` to create the `Database` class instance from configuration.

```
        #region Constructors

        protected SqlCeRepositoryBase()
            : this(null)
        {
        }

        protected SqlCeRepositoryBase(IUnitOfWork unitOfWork)
            : base(unitOfWork)
```

```
    {
        this.database = DatabaseFactory.CreateDatabase();
        this.entityFactory = EntityFactoryBuilder.BuildFactory<T>();
        this.childCallbacks = new Dictionary<string,
                            SqlCeRepositoryBase<T>.AppendChildData>();
        this.BuildChildCallbacks();
    }

    #endregion
```

When doing this I actually get a `SqlCeDatabase` instance, which is the Enterprise Library's nice encapsulation of common actions with a SQL Server CE database. The next item of interest is the instantiation of the `IEntityFactory<T>` interface instance; I will discuss the purpose of that interface in the next section of this chapter. The last thing the constructor does is delegate to its derived class and call its abstract method `BuildChildCallbacks`. This method initializes the private `Dictionary<string, AppendChildData> childCallbacks` member and represents a key-value pair of the name of a field in an `IDataReader` instance and a delegate of type `AppendChildData(T entityAggregate, object childEntityKeyValue)`. This will be talked about later, but it is used for allowing the `SqlCeRepository<T>` base class to call the method encapsulated in the delegate in order to help populate an aggregate object with data from another query in addition to the main query's results. It is very flexible in that it allows the derived class to use the base class's code for retrieving an entity, yet still leaves the door open for the derived class to append data on to the entity created by the base class.

The next section of code defines all of the abstract methods of the class:

```
    #region Abstract Methods

    protected abstract void BuildChildCallbacks();
    public abstract override T FindBy(object key);
    protected abstract override void PersistNewItem(T item);
    protected abstract override void PersistUpdatedItem(T item);
    protected abstract override void PersistDeletedItem(T item);

    #endregion
```

The `BuildChildCallbacks` method was just discussed, and it really is optional for the derived classes to put working code into it. What I mean by that is that the derived classes must implement the method signature, but they may decide to leave the body of the method blank if the derived class does not have a need for any methods to be called back when building its entities. The rest of the methods are just passing on the strongly typed Unit of Work methods defined on the `RepositoryBase<T>` class.

The two read-only protected properties on the class, `Database` and `ChildCallbacks`, are simply just encapsulating their respective private members. The next four protected methods are really the heart of the class. The first method, `ExecuteReader`, shown below, simply takes a SQL string and executes against the SQL CE database and returns an `IDataReader` instance.

```
    protected IDataReader ExecuteReader(string sql)
    {
        DbCommand command = this.database.GetSqlStringCommand(sql);
        return this.database.ExecuteReader(command);
    }
```

The next method, `BuildEntityFromSql`, uses the `ExecuteReader` method to help build an entity instance from a SQL statement.

```
protected virtual T BuildEntityFromSql(string sql)
{
    T entity = default(T);
    using (IDataReader reader = this.ExecuteReader(sql))
    {
        if (reader.Read())
        {
            entity = this.BuildEntityFromReader(reader);
        }
    }
    return entity;
}
```

It starts off by first getting an `IDataReader` from the `ExecuteReader` method, and then uses that `IDataReader` and passes it to the main method, `BuildEntityFromReader`, to build the entity. The Generic entity instance that is returned is a derivative of the `EntityBase` type.

The `BuildEntityFromReader` method is a little bit more complicated than the other methods in the class.

```
protected virtual T BuildEntityFromReader(IDataReader reader)
{
    T entity = this.entityFactory.BuildEntity(reader);
    if (this.childCallbacks != null && this.childCallbacks.Count > 0)
    {
        object childKeyValue = null;
        DataTable columnData = reader.GetSchemaTable();
        foreach (string childKeyName in this.childCallbacks.Keys)
        {
            if (DataHelper.ReaderContainsColumnName(columnData,
                childKeyName))
            {
                childKeyValue = reader[childKeyName];
            }
            else
            {
                childKeyValue = null;
            }
            this.childCallbacks[childKeyName](entity, childKeyValue);
        }
    }
    return entity;
}
```

It starts by delegating to the class's `IEntityFactory<T>` instance to build and map an entity from an `IDataReader`. I will discuss this *Entity Factory Framework* in the next section. It then checks the dictionary of child callback delegates (`Dictionary<string, AppendChildData> childCallbacks`) defined in the derived class to see whether any callback delegates have been defined. If there are some entries present in the dictionary, it iterates through the keys of the collection, which are really database foreign key field names from the derived class's main query. While iterating, it uses the `DataHelper` class to check to see whether the field name actually exists in the `IDataReader`'s set of fields (I will discuss the `DataHelper` class in the next paragraph). If it does exist, it then retrieves the value of the field name from the `IDataReader` instance. Once that foreign key value has been extracted, it then passes the value back to the callback method, along with the partially populated entity object, and executes the method, thus filling another part of the entity object. This is particularly useful for populating aggregate objects with many child objects attached to them.

The `DataHelper` class is used by the various Repositories and Factories to get data to and from ADO .NET objects, such as the `IDataReader`. In the code example above, I was using the `DataHelper`'s `ReaderContainsColumnName` method to determine whether a particular column name (or field name) existed in the `DataReader`'s set of data. Here is the method:

```
public static bool ReaderContainsColumnName(DataTable schemaTable,
    string columnName)
{
    bool containsColumnName = false;
    foreach (DataRow row in schemaTable.Rows)
    {
        if (row["ColumnName"].ToString() == columnName)
        {
            containsColumnName = true;
            break;
        }
    }
    return containsColumnName;
}
```

The next method, `BuildEntitiesFromSql`, is very similar to `BuildEntityFromSql`, except that instead of just returning a single entity instance, it returns a generic list (`IList<T>`) of them.

```
protected virtual List<T> BuildEntitiesFromSql(string sql)
{
    List<T> entities = new List<T>();
    using (IDataReader reader = this.ExecuteReader(sql))
    {
        while (reader.Read())
        {
            entities.Add(this.BuildEntityFromReader(reader));
        }
    }
    return entities;
}
```

The method starts by initializing the list of entities to be returned, and then similarly to `BuildEntityFromSql`, it calls the class's `ExecuteReader` method to get an `IDataReader` instance from the SQL statement passed in. It then iterates over the `IDataReader` instance and uses the `BuildEntityFromReader` method to build the entity and add it to its list.

The Entity Factory Framework

When I was originally building this application, I had hoped to be using the ADO.NET Entity Framework as my object-relational (OR) mapping solution. Since it was pulled from the Visual Studio 2008 release, I have decided to roll my own pseudo-mapping factory type of framework.

The IEntityFactory<T> Interface

The main concept of what I need the framework to do is extremely simple: to map field names contained in an instance of an `IDataReader` to fields of an object instance. Actually, it's really just mapping field names to class property names. To promote the simplicity of what I wanted, I created an interface, `IEntityFactory<T>`, to show my intent.

```
using System;
using SmartCA.Infrastructure.DomainBase;
using System.Data;

namespace SmartCA.Infrastructure.EntityFactoryFramework
{
    public interface IEntityFactory<T> where T : EntityBase
    {
        T BuildEntity(IDataReader reader);
    }
}
```

This interface is extremely simple, its one method, `BuildEntity`, takes an `IDataReader` and returns an object that derives from `EntityBase`. Now, since I have this interface in place, I need to have a way of figuring out how to get the right object instances of this interface. I will use a factory class to do this, named `EntityFactoryBuilder`.

Configuration Section

Just like the `RepositoryFactory`, I have chosen to use configuration along with my EntityFactoryBuilder. This keeps things very flexible.

Here is what the application configuration file with added support for the Entity Factory Framework looks like:

```
<?xml version="1.0" encoding="utf-8" ?>
<configuration>
  <configSections>
    <section name="dataConfiguration" type="Microsoft.Practices.EnterpriseLibrary
.Data.Configuration.DatabaseSettings, Microsoft.Practices.EnterpriseLibrary.Data,
Version=3.0.0.0, Culture=neutral, PublicKeyToken=null"/>
    <section name="repositoryMappingsConfiguration"

type="SmartCA.Infrastructure.RepositoryFramework.Configuration
.RepositorySettings, SmartCA.Infrastructure, Version=1.0.0.0, Culture=neutral,
PublicKeyToken=null"/>
    <section name="entityMappingsConfiguration"

type="SmartCA.Infrastructure.EntityFactoryFramework.Configuration
.EntitySettings,
SmartCA.Infrastructure, Version=1.0.0.0, Culture=neutral, PublicKeyToken=null"/>
  </configSections>
  <dataConfiguration defaultDatabase="SmartCA"/>

  <connectionStrings>
```

```xml
    <add name="SmartCA" connectionString="Data Source=|DataDirectory|\SmartCA.sdf"
        providerName="System.Data.SqlServerCe.3.5"/>
  </connectionStrings>

  <repositoryMappingsConfiguration>
    <repositoryMappings>
      <repositoryMapping interfaceShortTypeName="IProjectRepository"

repositoryFullTypeName="SmartCA.Infrastructure.Repositories.ProjectRepository,
SmartCA.Infrastructure.Repositories, Version=1.0.0.0, Culture=neutral,
PublicKeyToken=null" />
      <repositoryMapping interfaceShortTypeName="IEmployeeRepository"

repositoryFullTypeName="SmartCA.Infrastructure.Repositories.EmployeeRepository,
SmartCA.Infrastructure.Repositories, Version=1.0.0.0, Culture=neutral,
PublicKeyToken=null" />
      <repositoryMapping interfaceShortTypeName="ICompanyRepository"

repositoryFullTypeName="SmartCA.Infrastructure.Repositories.CompanyRepository,
SmartCA.Infrastructure.Repositories, Version=1.0.0.0, Culture=neutral,
PublicKeyToken=null" />
      <repositoryMapping interfaceShortTypeName="IContactRepository"

repositoryFullTypeName="SmartCA.Infrastructure.Repositories.ContactRepository,
SmartCA.Infrastructure.Repositories, Version=1.0.0.0, Culture=neutral,
PublicKeyToken=null" />
    </repositoryMappings>
  </repositoryMappingsConfiguration>

  <entityMappingsConfiguration>
    <entityMappings>
      <entityMapping entityShortTypeName="Project"

entityFactoryFullTypeName="SmartCA.Infrastructure.Repositories.ProjectFactory,
SmartCA.Infrastructure.Repositories, Version=1.0.0.0, Culture=neutral,
PublicKeyToken=null" />
      <entityMapping entityShortTypeName="Employee"

entityFactoryFullTypeName="SmartCA.Infrastructure.Repositories.EmployeeFactory,
SmartCA.Infrastructure.Repositories, Version=1.0.0.0, Culture=neutral,
PublicKeyToken=null" />
      <entityMapping entityShortTypeName="Company"

entityFactoryFullTypeName="SmartCA.Infrastructure.Repositories.CompanyFactory,
SmartCA.Infrastructure.Repositories, Version=1.0.0.0, Culture=neutral,
PublicKeyToken=null" />
    </entityMappings>
  </entityMappingsConfiguration>

</configuration>
```

Configuration Section Handling

Again, just as with the Repository Framework configuration, I have added a `Configuration` folder under the `EntityFactoryFramework` folder of the `SmartCA.Infrastructure` project (see Figure 2.4).

Figure 2.4: EntityFactoryFramework Configuration folder.

I am not going to show the configuration code for the Entity Factory Framework because it is almost exactly the same as the configuration code for the Repository Framework.

The EntityFactoryBuilder Class

Now that the configuration is finished, the `EntityFactoryBuilder` can use it to create repositories. The way the `EntityFactoryBuilder` works is that it uses a Generic type parameter representing the type of the entity that needs to be mapped, combined with the mappings from the configuration in order to determine what kind of `IEntityFactory<T>` to create. The `EntityFactoryBuilder` class is a static class with one static method, `BuildFactory`.

```csharp
using System;
using System.Collections.Generic;
using SmartCA.Infrastructure.DomainBase;
using SmartCA.Infrastructure.EntityFactoryFramework.Configuration;
using System.Configuration;

namespace SmartCA.Infrastructure.EntityFactoryFramework
{
    public static class EntityFactoryBuilder
    {
        // Dictionary used for caching purposes
        private static Dictionary<string, object> factories =
            new Dictionary<string, object>();

        public static IEntityFactory<T> BuildFactory<T>() where T : EntityBase
        {
            IEntityFactory<T> factory = null;

            // Get the key from the Generic parameter passed in
            string key = typeof(T).Name;
```

```
        // See if the factory is in the cache
        if (EntityFactoryBuilder.factories.ContainsKey(key))
        {
            // It was there, so retrieve it from the cache
            factory = EntityFactoryBuilder.factories[key] as IEntityFactory<T>;
        }
        else
        {
            // Create the factory

            // Get the entityMappingsConfiguration config section
EntitySettings settings = (EntitySettings)ConfigurationManager.GetSection
(EntityMappingConstants.EntityMappingsConfigurationSectionName);

            // Get the type to be created using reflection
            Type entityFactoryType =
Type.GetType(settings.EntityMappings[key].EntityFactoryFullTypeName);

            // Create the factory using reflection
            factory = Activator.CreateInstance(entityFactoryType) as
IEntityFactory<T>;

            // Put the newly created factory in the cache
            EntityFactoryBuilder.factories[key] = factory;
        }

        // Return the factory
        return factory;
    }
  }
}
```

The signature of this method is much simpler than the `RepositoryFactory` class's `GetRepository<TRepository, TEntity>` method. It has only one Generic type parameter, `T`, and that is the type of entity for which the factory was created. The `T` parameter has a restriction that it must be derived from the `EntityBase` class.

First, the code for the method uses .NET Reflection to find the short type name of the Generic parameter type being passed in via the `T` parameter. Then, the code looks in its static dictionary of entity factories to see whether it can pull the particular Factory out of memory. If it cannot, it then uses the custom Entity Factory Framework configuration objects to find the right entity factory type to create based on the values in the mappings configuration. When the type is found, the method then uses the reflection capabilities of the Activator object to create an instance of the correct Factory based on the mapped type from configuration. Then, after the Factory has been created, it is put into the static dictionary of repositories so it will be available the next time it has been requested. Once the Factory has been retrieved from memory or created, the instance is then returned to the caller.

The Model-View-ViewModel Pattern

Traditional Presentation Patterns

So far, I have covered the various patterns and principles being followed in the domain layer and the infrastructure layer. Since this book is about Domain-Driven Design, that is a good thing, but I still have an application to build; it cannot just be all domain objects and unit tests. I actually have to make the application present something fairly compelling to the user. If you remember, in Chapter 1 I stated that I was going to be using WPF for the presentation technology. That is all well and good, but there must be some type of strategy for hooking up domain objects to the user interface. Some very common presentation patterns are the Model-View-Controller (MVC) and the Model-View-Presenter (MVP). These patterns are very good, and I highly encourage you to study more about them; however, in my opinion, they have one major drawback when used with WPF: they do not take into account data-binding technology at all. What I mean by that, is that in those patterns, the Controller or the Presenter is responsible for acting upon the View, such as filling TextBoxes with text, loading ListBoxes, filling a grid, and so on. It just so happens that one of WPF's greatest strengths is its rich data-binding capabilities. By implementing either the MVC or the MVP pattern, I would be completely bypassing the data-binding facilities in WPF. There must be some way to make this concept of separating the View from the Model work in WPF without bypassing a whole slew of rich WPF features!

Model-View-ViewModel Definition

That way is the Model-View-ViewModel pattern. I first learned about this pattern by reading John Gossman's blog entries about it. He was a member of the Microsoft Expression Blend team and is currently on the WPF team at Microsoft. In his blog entries, he talks about how his team has created this new pattern, called Model-View-ViewModel, to separate the Model from the View but, at the same time, to take full advantage of WPF's features. According to John "The pattern was to take a pure Model, create an abstract view that contained state, and data bind a View created with a visual designer to that abstract view. That's a nice clean, formal pattern." In this case, the visual designer is the Microsoft Expression Blend tool, and the abstract view is the ViewModel. The key point is that there is a two-way connection between the View and the ViewModel via data binding. When properly set up, this means that every View will consist of almost nothing but pure XAML and very little procedural code, which is exactly what I want.

Because this pattern separates out the View and the Model so nicely, there are a lot of opportunities for graphic artist types to work in Blend all day, hand the XAML off to a developer working on the domain model, and have the developer wire everything up to the domain model. Shortly, I will show how I implemented this pattern for the SmartCA application.

What's a ViewModel?

You must be asking yourself this question by now. When I first read about it and looked at some sample code, it took me a while to grasp the full power of it. The purpose in life for a ViewModel is to adapt the Model to the View. This may mean that you have a method in the domain model that returns an `IList<Project>` type, but you would really like to convert that into a more WPF-friendly class for data binding purposes. Enter the ViewModel. In this case the ViewModel would transform the `IList<Project>` type from the domain model into something like a `CollectionView` class for a WPF UI Element to bind data to. The key is to expose public properties on the ViewModel for the things that the View needs to bind data to. Also, like a Controller, the ViewModel can be used to hold the View's state, as well as any commands that the View needs.

Since WPF natively implements the Command pattern, by which I mean certain UI elements such as Button controls, there is a property called `Command` that is of the WPF-defined `ICommand` type. I can place Commands into my ViewModel and expose them as public properties for my View to bind to. This is extremely powerful, as it allows me to bind executable code to a Button on a form without having to write any code to wire up the Button. WPF's Command pattern along with a public `Command` property on my ViewModel take care of this.

An Example

In order to understand this a little better, I will show you a part of the SmartCA application. The use case is extremely simple; it is to display a form to the user to show a list of projects, and have the user pick a project, and remember what project was selected. The selected project is what the user will be working on in his or her session until the user decides to change to another project. Since the point of this example is the Model-View-ViewModel presentation pattern, I will focus a little bit less on the domain and a little bit more on the presentation items.

To start off with, I first create a `Service` class in my domain model, called `ProjectService`. `ProjectService` has one method we care about right now, and that is `GetProjects`.

```csharp
using System;
using System.Collections.Generic;
using SmartCA.Model.Projects;
using SmartCA.Infrastructure.RepositoryFramework;

namespace SmartCA.Model.Projects
{
    public static class ProjectService
    {
        public static IList<Project> GetAllProjects()
        {
            IProjectRepository repository =
RepositoryFactory.GetRepository<IProjectRepository, Project>();
            return repository.FindAll();
        }
    }
}
```

The code is pretty straightforward; it is simply acting as a façade to the `IProjectRepository` instance and gets a list of all of the repository's Projects. So far so good; I now have a way of getting the data that I need.

The next step is to build a View for displaying the list of Projects to the user in the form of a dropdown list. Figure 2.5 shows what I want the form to look like.

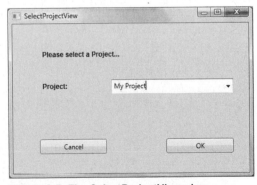

Figure 2.5: The SelectProjectView view

In order to get to this point, I need to build a ViewModel class that I can have the `SelectProjectView` class bind to. I only need to expose a list and two commands, one per button.

```csharp
using System;
using System.Collections.Generic;
using SmartCA.Model.Projects;
using System.Windows.Data;
using SmartCA.Infrastructure.UI;
using SmartCA.Presentation.Views;
using SmartCA.Application;

namespace SmartCA.Presentation.ViewModels
{
    public class SelectProjectViewModel
    {
        private CollectionView projects;
        private DelegateCommand selectCommand;
        private DelegateCommand cancelCommand;
        private IView view;

        public SelectProjectViewModel()
            : this(null)
        {
        }

        public SelectProjectViewModel(IView view)
        {
            this.view = view;
            this.projects = new CollectionView(ProjectService.GetAllProjects());
            this.selectCommand = new DelegateCommand(this.SelectCommandHandler);
            this.cancelCommand = new DelegateCommand(this.CancelCommandHandler);
        }

        public CollectionView Projects
        {
            get { return this.projects; }
        }

        public DelegateCommand SelectCommand
        {
            get { return this.selectCommand; }
        }

        public DelegateCommand CancelCommand
        {
            get { return this.cancelCommand; }
        }

        private void SelectCommandHandler(object sender, EventArgs e)
        {
            Project project = this.projects.CurrentItem as Project;
            UserSession.CurrentProject = project;
            this.view.Close();
        }
```

```
        private void CancelCommandHandler(object sender, EventArgs e)
        {
            this.view.Close();
        }
    }
}
```

The first thing to note about this class is its overloaded constructor. It first gives a reference to the View via the `IView` interface. This interface currently has two methods, `Show` and `Close`, and it just so happens that the WPF Window class happens to implement both of these methods.

```
using System;

namespace SmartCA.Presentation.Views
{
    public interface IView
    {
        void Show();
        void Close();
    }
}
```

This interface allows me to open and close the form from my ViewModel.

The next thing that the `SelectProjectViewModel` constructor does is to transform the `IList<Project>` list of projects into a WPF-friendly `CollectionView` class. This `CollectionView` is then exposed via the `Projects` public property.

```
        public SelectProjectViewModel(IView view)
        {
            this.view = view;
            this.projects = new CollectionView(ProjectService.GetAllProjects());
            this.selectCommand = new DelegateCommand(this.SelectCommandHandler);
            this.cancelCommand = new DelegateCommand(this.CancelCommandHandler);
        }
```

The next two lines are interesting not in that they are setting up the two `ICommand` properties for the two Buttons, but rather that they are using a class called `DelegateCommand` to represent the `ICommand` instances. The `DelegateCommand` class not only implements the `ICommand` interface but also allows a delegate to be called when the `ICommand`'s `Execute` method is called.

```
using System;
using System.Windows.Input;

namespace SmartCA.Infrastructure.UI
{
    public class DelegateCommand : ICommand
    {
        public delegate void SimpleEventHandler(object sender, EventArgs e);

        private SimpleEventHandler handler;
        private bool isEnabled = true;
```

(continued)

(continued)

```
                public DelegateCommand(SimpleEventHandler handler)
                {
                    this.handler = handler;
                }

                #region ICommand implementation

                /// <summary>
                /// Executing the command is as simple as calling that method
                /// we were handed on creation.
                /// </summary>
                /// <param name="parameter">Data used by the command. If the
                /// command does not require data to be passed,
                /// this object can be set to null.</param>
                public void Execute(object parameter)
                {
                    this.handler(this, EventArgs.Empty);
                }

                /// <summary>
                /// Determines whether the command can execute in its
                /// current state.
                /// </summary>
                /// <param name="parameter">Data used by the command. If the
                /// command does not require data to be passed,
                /// this object can be set to null.</param>
                /// <returns>True if the command can be executed.</returns>
                public bool CanExecute(object parameter)
                {
                    return this.IsEnabled;
                }

                /// <summary>
                /// This is the event that WPF's command architecture listens to so
                /// it knows when to update the UI on command enable/disable.
                /// </summary>
                public event EventHandler CanExecuteChanged;

                #endregion

                /// <summary>
                /// Public visibility of the isEnabled flag - note that when it is
                /// set, need to raise the event so that WPF knows to update
                /// any UI that uses this command.
                /// </summary>
                public bool IsEnabled
                {
                    get { return this.isEnabled; }
                    set
                    {
                        this.isEnabled = value;
                        this.OnCanExecuteChanged();
```

```
            }
        }

        /// <summary>
        /// Simple event propagation that makes sure someone is
        /// listening to the event before raising it.
        /// </summary>
        private void OnCanExecuteChanged()
        {
            if (this.CanExecuteChanged != null)
            {
                this.CanExecuteChanged(this, EventArgs.Empty);
            }
        }
    }
}
```

As advertised, the real power of this class is that, when its Execute method is called, it calls the delegate method that was passed in via the constructor. The reason why this is so powerful is that I can define the method handler for the delegate right inside of my ViewModel class, which keeps all of the presentation logic glue right where I want it.

So going back to the SelectProjectViewModel class, here are the handler methods for the two DelegateCommand properties.

```
        private void SelectCommandHandler(object sender, EventArgs e)
        {
            Project project = this.projects.CurrentItem as Project;
            UserSession.CurrentProject = project;
            this.view.Close();
        }

        private void CancelCommandHandler(object sender, EventArgs e)
        {
            this.view.Close();
        }
```

The handler for the SelectCommand property is a true example of why the ViewModel shines. Instead of having to talk to an element on the UI to know which project was selected, it simply asks the CollectionView for its CurrentItem property to get the selected project. This is made possible by the default two-way binding in the XAML, which I will show shortly. The handler method then sets the CurrentProject property of the application layer's UserSession class. Then, since its work is done, it tells the View to go away via the Close method of the IView interface.

The handler for the CancelCommand property is much simpler. It simply tells the View to close itself via the IView interface.

Now that the ViewModel class for the use case SelectProjectViewModel has been detailed, it's time to look at how the View actually uses it and communicates with it. The View class, SelectProjectView, has very little code behind in it. The only code that I wrote for it was in the constructor for wiring up the DataContext property of the form's Window element.

```
using System;
using System.Windows;
using System.Windows.Controls;
using SmartCA.Presentation.ViewModels;

namespace SmartCA.Presentation.Views
{
    public partial class SelectProjectView : Window, IView
    {
        public SelectProjectView()
        {
            this.InitializeComponent();
            this.DataContext = new SelectProjectViewModel(this);
        }
    }
}
```

The first thing to notice is that I added the implementation of the IView interface to the class. This was easy since the System.Windows.Window class already implemented the Close and Show methods. Then, in the constructor, after the auto-generated call to InitializeComponent, I set the Window's DataContext property to the SelectProjectViewModel class, passing in the Window instance (this) as the IView instance expected in SelectProjectViewModel's constructor. Finally, the form is wired up for data binding to the ViewModel.

The XAML markup for the View contains the ComboBox declaration, a few Label declarations, as well as a few Button declarations.

```
<Window x:Class="SmartCA.Presentation.Views.SelectProjectView"
    xmlns="http://schemas.microsoft.com/winfx/2006/xaml/presentation"
    xmlns:x="http://schemas.microsoft.com/winfx/2006/xaml"
    xmlns:vm="clr-namespace:SmartCA.Presentation.ViewModels"
    Title="SelectProjectView" Height="300" Width="437"
    Background="{DynamicResource FormBackgroundBrush}">
<Grid>
<ComboBox  Height="26" Margin="175.993333333333,98,28.006666666667,0"
        Name="projectsComboBox" VerticalAlignment="Top"
        IsSynchronizedWithCurrentItem="True"
        TextSearch.TextPath="Name"
        ItemsSource="{Binding Path=Projects}" IsTextSearchEnabled="True"
        IsEditable="True">
    <ComboBox.ItemTemplate>
            <DataTemplate>
                    <Grid ShowGridLines="True" >
                            <Grid.ColumnDefinitions>
                                    <ColumnDefinition Width="50" />
                                    <ColumnDefinition />
                            </Grid.ColumnDefinitions>
                            <TextBlock Grid.Column="0" Text="{Binding
Path=Number}"/>
                            <TextBlock Grid.Column="1" Text="{Binding Path=Name}" />
                    </Grid>
            </DataTemplate>
```

```
    <ComboBox.ItemTemplate>
    </ComboBox>
    <Label Margin="47,42,0,0" Name="selectProjectLabel"
        Style="{StaticResource boldLabelStyle}"
        VerticalAlignment="Top" HorizontalAlignment="Left"
        Width="153">Please select a Project...</Label>
    <Label Margin="47,98.04,0,0" Name="projectLabel"
        Style="{StaticResource boldLabelStyle}">Project:</Label>
    <Button Margin="47,0,0,35" Name="cancelButton"
        Command="{Binding Path=CancelCommand}" Style="{StaticResource baseButton}"
        HorizontalAlignment="Left" VerticalAlignment="Bottom">Cancel</Button>
    <Button Margin="0,0,28.006666666667,35" Name="okButton"
        Command="{Binding Path=SelectCommand}" Style="{StaticResource baseButton}"
        HorizontalAlignment="Right" VerticalAlignment="Bottom">OK</Button>
  </Grid>
</Window>
```

The first interesting thing to note about the ComboBox declaration is that it is bound to the `Projects` `CollectionView` property of the `SelectProjectViewModel`, and that its `IsSynchronizedWithCurrentItem` property is set to `True`. What this means is that whenever I change a selection in the ComboBox, I can always get the item selected from the `CollectionView` in the ViewModel to which it is bound, in this case the `Projects` property. The way I get that is by checking the `SelectedItem` property of that `CollectionView`. That is cool because I do not need to be tightly coupled to the UI elements in the ViewModel; data binding takes care of giving me the state that I need.

The next interesting thing about the ComboBox declaration is its use of a `DataTemplate` element to format how the dropdown will be displayed. In this case, the dropdown will show two columns instead of one, and each one of the columns is bound to properties of the child `Property` objects via the `Path` property of the `Binding` declaration. What's nice about using this pattern is that I can make the code for the UI View be more declarative, that is, keep most of it in XAML, and really get a good separation between the View and the Model, while at the same time take advantage of WPF's binding features to reduce the amount of code that I would have had to write to do this manually.

Summary

I covered quite a bit of ground in this chapter. I started out by designing the Visual Studio solution that will be used throughout the rest of the book, and then began the design for the four architectural layers, which were the application, domain, infrastructure, and presentation layers. In designing and implementing the layers, I introduced a few patterns that will be used throughout the book, such as the Layered Supertype pattern, the Separated Interface pattern, and the Model-View-ViewModel pattern. Also, when talking about the domain layer, I covered some very important Domain-Driven Design terms, which will be used throughout the remainder of the book.

I also wrote some code in this chapter! I started writing code for the infrastructure layer with the Layered Supertype implementation, followed by the Repository Framework and the Entity Factory Framework, and ending with the Model-View-ViewModel pattern implementation for the presentation layer. Overall, there is a good foundation on which to build for the rest of the application.

3

Managing Projects

Since I have just built the application architecture, it is time to start implementing the functionality of the application. Actually, the application architecture is not fully developed yet; in fact, I will probably refactor parts of it based on the needs of the application as I go along. In last chapter's example of a View and a ViewModel, I introduced what I will be talking about this chapter, the SmartCA's concept of Projects. I intentionally did not show you the `Project` class because that is the focus of this chapter. I will also be talking about the concept of Contractors and how they relate to Projects.

The Problem

Smart Design is an architectural, engineering, and interior design firm that is known for its expertise in the design and construction of complex facilities, such as hospitals and universities. Because they are involved from beginning to end in the construction projects, they are, by default, the "general contractor," meaning that they are the ones in charge of making sure that the facilities are built properly, according to both customer's and government's specifications. In order to carry out this large responsibility, they must manage several other parties involved in carrying out their architectural and engineering plans. This usually involves a lot of administration, mostly for keeping track of costs, project communications, documentation (such as requests for information, change orders, and proposal requests), and more. This construction administration is designed to ensure that the construction process is in general conformance with the architectural and engineering design documents as well as the applicable codes and standards. It is exactly these types of activities that the SmartCA application is intended to track and manage.

In the SmartCA domain, a Project is the center of all behavior: almost everything in the domain relates to a Project in one way or another. Construction Projects are, after all, what other companies hire Smart Design to do for them. A Project is a part of SmartCA's *core domain*.

The Design

In the SmartCA domain, the purpose of a Project is to bring together and manage all of the people involved in the construction process. In the next few sections I will be designing the domain model, determining the Project Aggregate and its boundaries, and designing the repository for Projects.

Designing the Domain Model

Listed below is a drawing showing the Entities that make up the Project Domain:

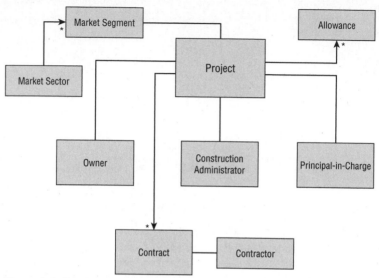

Figure 3.1: The Project Domain and its parts.

As you can see from Figure 3.1, every Project must have an Owner. An Owner is an outside party for whom the Project is being built. Other entities represented in every Project are the Construction Administrator and the Principal-in-Charge. These two roles will always be occupied by Smart Design employees. The Principal-in-Charge is the project director, the person who is ultimately responsible for the success or failure of the Project. The Construction Administrator will be using the SmartCA application the most. This person, and usually their assistant, is the domain expert of a Project.

One of the most important parts of the application is keeping track of the Contracts between Smart Design and the Contractors on the Project. Many of the aspects of the SmartCA application deal in communicating with the Contractors and documenting all of their costs in order to know what the current cost of the Project is and what the estimated cost of the Project will be.

One of the other items that must be tracked about a Project is what Market Segment the construction is for, that is, if it is for a university, a high school, a woman's hospital, and so on. Market Segments belong to Market Sectors, and are a bit more specific than Market Sectors. For example, a high school building would be classified in the education Market Sector, as would a university. A woman's hospital would be classified in the health care Market Sector. This information is later used by Smart Design management to analyze the company's portfolio of projects to identify trends within a particular Market Sector or Segment.

Defining the Project Aggregate

Now that the Project domain model has been designed, I need to design the Project Aggregate with the actual classes that will be used. Figure 3.2 shows a class diagram showing the classes that will be used in the Project Aggregate.

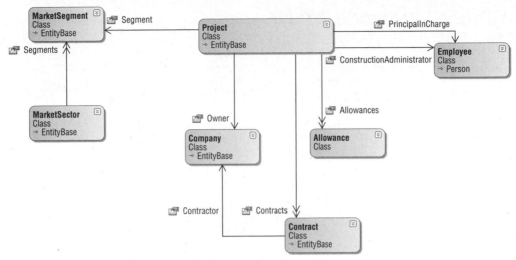

Figure 3.2: Classes constituting the Project Aggregate.

As you can tell from Figure 3.2, the class names are staying true to the model that I created in the previous section. There are some subtle differences though. For example, in the previous diagram, there was an association between the Project entity and the Principal-in-Charge entity. In the class diagram above, the association to Principal-in-Charge is a property on the Project class that is associated with an Employee class. The same pattern follows for the association to Construction Administrator. This is because the `PrincipalInCharge` and `ConstructionAdministrator` properties are both instances of an Employee class. The main idea here is to keep the code as consistent with the model as possible, and to strive to make the code become as easy to read as the model.

Defining the Aggregate Boundaries

Now that I have defined the Project Aggregate, it is time to determine where the boundaries are on this Aggregate. This is very important for when I start to design the Project repository in the next section.

Obviously, all of the classes in this diagram are part of the Project Aggregate, but the Project Aggregate also holds some references to the roots of other Aggregates. Figure 3.3 shows the Aggregate boundaries that I have determined so far in the domain model.

In Figure 3.3, I have identified two additional Aggregate Roots, `Company` and `Employee`. There is definitely a need to get `Company` and `Employee` information outside the context of a `Project`. In the context of a particular `Project`, if I wanted to get some detailed information about the `ConstructionAdministrator`, even though that represents an `Employee` instance, and `Employee` is an Aggregate Root, I would still need to navigate from the `Project` class to the `ConstructionAdministrator` property to get that information. If I just wanted to find some data about an `Employee` not in the context of a `Project`, I would go directly to the `Employee` aggregate itself, via the repository for the `Employee` aggregate. The same concept applies to accessing `Company` information; if you are in the context of a `Project`, for example wanting to find about the `Owner` of a `Project`, then you should go through the `Project` Aggregate's repository, but, if you just need information on a particular `Company` outside the concerns of a `Project`, then go directly to the repository for the `Company` Aggregate.

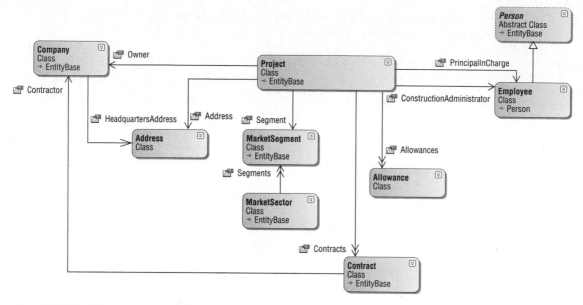

Figure 3.3: The Project Aggregate boundaries.

Designing the Repositories

Since I have just defined the boundaries for the Project Aggregate, identifying the classes that need Repositories is easy. The rule is that each Aggregate Root gets its own repository. Very simply, if a class has been identified as the Entity Root of an Aggregate, then a repository will be made for that class. This means that in the current domain model, we will have three repositories: one for the Project Aggregate, one for the Company Aggregate, and one for the Employee Aggregate (see Figure 3.4).

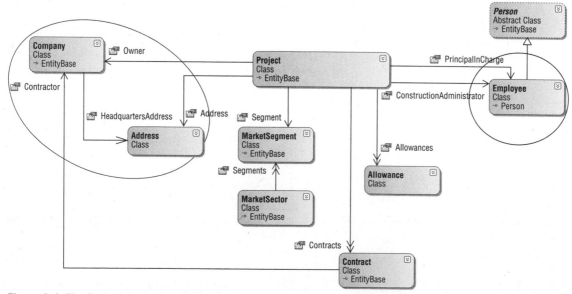

Figure 3.4: The Project Aggregate Repositories.

Because I will be covering Companies in the next chapter, I will not be showing the details of the Company Aggregate nor its respective repository in this chapter.

The IProjectRepository Interface

The `IProjectRepository` interface is the front to instances of Project Repositories. Currently, I have two implementations of this interface, one designed as a mock implementation, and the other one designed as real. As I was developing, I quickly decided that the mock implementations were not really necessary since I was writing to a local SQL CE database anyway, so my tests did not slow down at all. Here is the `IProjectRepository` interface:

```
using System;
using System.Collections.Generic;
using SmartCA.Infrastructure.RepositoryFramework;

namespace SmartCA.Model.Projects
{
    public interface IProjectRepository : IRepository<Project>
    {
        IList<Project> FindBy(IList<MarketSegment> segments, bool completed);
        Project FindBy(string projectNumber);
        IList<MarketSegment> FindAllMarketSegments();
    }
}
```

Notice how the `IProjectRepository` interface implements the `IRepository<T>` interface. This functionality is all handled by the `RepositoryBase<T>` class and the `SqlCeRepositoryBase<T>` class, which I showed in Chapter 2.

The IEmployeeRepository Interface

The `IEmployeeRepository` interface is the interface for instances of Employee Repositories. Here is the `IEmployeeRepository` interface:

```
using System;
using System.Collections.Generic;
using SmartCA.Infrastructure.RepositoryFramework;

namespace SmartCA.Model.Employees
{
    public interface IEmployeeRepository : IRepository<Employee>
    {
        IList<Employee> GetConstructionAdministrators();
        IList<Employee> GetPrincipals();
    }
}
```

Just like the `IProjectRepository` interface, the `IEmployeeRepository` interface also implements the `IRepository<T>` interface.

Writing the Unit Tests

Before implementing the solution for managing Projects, I am going to write some unit tests for what I expect of the Project and Employee repository implementations. I am not going to write any tests, yet, for the Project and Employee classes, just for their respective Repositories. You may be wondering how I can write these tests when the classes do not even exist yet. Since I have written the interfaces for these Repositories, and since I also have a Repository Factory implemented, I can write test code against the interfaces. The tests will fail, and that is what I expect. After the code is written for the repository implementations later on in the Solution section, then the tests should pass. The goal is to write code in the Solution section that will ultimately make the unit tests pass.

Setting Up the Unit Tests Project

For all of my unit tests, I have decided to use Visual Studio Team System (VSTS) to create my unit test projects. There is an excellent project template for doing this, and it is fairly straightforward. I simply add a new project to my Visual Studio solution, and choose "Test Project," as shown in Figure 3.5.

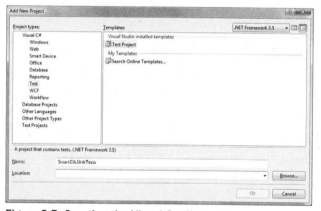

Figure 3.5: Creating the Visual Studio test project.

The next thing to do is to delete the default `UnitTest1.cs` file and create a real unit test file. In order to make things a little better organized, I have created folders in my test project for both Projects and Employees (see Figure 3.6).

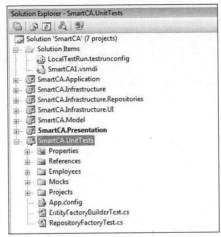

Figure 3.6: The SmartCA.UnitTests Project with folders.

The IProjectRepository Unit Tests

In order to get a jump start on writing the unit tests for the `IProjectRepository` interface, I use the VSTS New Unit Test Wizard to write test stubs automatically for each method in the `IProjectRepository` interface that I choose to test (see Figure 3.7).

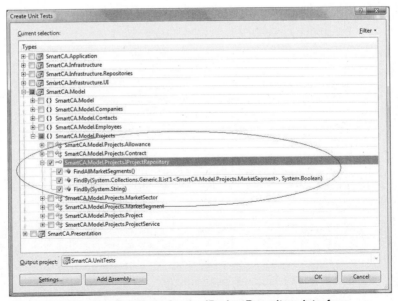

Figure 3.7: Creating Unit Tests for the IProjectRepository interface.

The next step is to modify the file created to use the `RepositoryFactory` class to build instances of the `IProjectRepository` interface. I have created a private class field for the unit test class to hold this reference, and I initialize it in the `MyTestInitialize` method of the unit test class. Here are the declarations for the private class fields:

```
using SmartCA.Infrastructure.Repositories;
using Microsoft.VisualStudio.TestTools.UnitTesting;
using SmartCA.Model.Projects;
using System.Collections.Generic;
using SmartCA.Infrastructure.RepositoryFramework;
using SmartCA.Infrastructure;

namespace SmartCA.UnitTests
{
    /// <summary>
    ///This is a test class for ProjectRepositoryTest and is intended
    ///to contain all ProjectRepositoryTest Unit Tests
    ///</summary>
    [TestClass()]
    public class ProjectRepositoryTest
    {
        private TestContext testContextInstance;
        private UnitOfWork unitOfWork;
        private IProjectRepository repository;
```

As you can see, I am also using a `UnitOfWork` private field (`unitOfWork`), and a `TestContext` private field (`testContextInstance`). The `testContextInstance` field was added automatically by the Visual Studio Wizard.

The next step is to initialize these fields in the `MyTestInitialize` method:

```
    /// <summary>
    /// Use TestInitialize to run code before running each test
    /// </summary>
    [TestInitialize()]
    public void MyTestInitialize()
    {
        this.unitOfWork = new UnitOfWork();
        this.repository = RepositoryFactory.GetRepository<IProjectRepository,
            Project>(this.unitOfWork);
    }
```

The code to create the `IProjectRepository` interface instance should look familiar to you, since I just covered that in the last chapter.

Now that the initialization is taken care of, it is time to fix the unit test methods that the Visual Studio Wizard generated.

The FindBySegmentsAndNotCompletedTest Method

The purpose of this test is to verify that I can query the `IProjectRepository` interface for all Projects that match the given Market Segments but have not been completed.

```
/// <summary>
///A test for FindBy(object sector, object segment, bool completed)
///</summary>
[DeploymentItem("SmartCA.sdf"), TestMethod()]
public void FindBySegmentsAndNotCompletedTest()
{
    // Create a list of Market Segments
    List<MarketSegment> segments = new List<MarketSegment>();
    segments.Add(new MarketSegment(1, null, "test", "test"));

    // Pass the Market Segments into the FindBy method, and
    // specify Projects that have NOT completed yet
    IList<Project> projects = this.repository.FindBy(segments, false);

    // Make sure there is one project that matches the criteria
    Assert.AreEqual(1, projects.Count);
}
```

The first thing to notice about this method is how it is decorated with the two different attributes, the `DeploymentItem` attribute and the `TestMethod` attribute. The `DeploymentItem` attribute lets the VSTS test host know to copy the `SmartCA.sdf` SQL CE project file to the output directory of the unit test project. This is important because otherwise I would not be able to connect to the database in the test. The `TestMethod` attribute lets VSTS know that this is a unit test, and it will be recognized as such by the VSTS unit testing UI.

This test code starts out by creating a dummy `MarketSegment` instance and adds it to a generic List of type `MarketSegment`. I then pass the list of Market Segments into the `IProjectRepository`'s overloaded `FindBy` method to have an `IList` of type `Project` returned. The test occurs on the last line, when I assert that there should be one Project returned from the `IProjectRepository` method. If the assertion is true, then the test will pass. As of this point in the chapter, this test (and all others in this class) should fail because I have not written the `IProjectRepository` implementation, yet.

The FindByProjectNumberTest Method

This method validates the ability to get a Project instance based on the Number of a Project:

```
/// <summary>
///A test for FindBy(string projectNumber)
///</summary>
[DeploymentItem("SmartCA.sdf"), TestMethod()]
public void FindByProjectNumberTest()
{
    // The Project Number
    string projectNumber = "12345.00";

    // Try to get the Project
    Project project = this.repository.FindBy(projectNumber);

    // Verify the Project is there and is the right one
    Assert.AreEqual("My Project", project.Name);
}
```

The method first starts out by initializing a Project Number string value. It then passes that value to the IProjectRepository in order to retrieve a Project with that particular Number value. Once the Project instance is returned from the repository, the Project's name is validated.

The FindAllMarketSegmentsTest Method

This method tests the last method on the IProjectRepository interface, the FindAllMarketSegments method:

```
/// <summary>
///A test for FindAllMarketSegments()
///</summary>
[DeploymentItem("SmartCA.sdf"), TestMethod()]
public void FindAllMarketSegmentsTest()
{
    // Get the list of all Market Segments
    IList<MarketSegment> segments =
        this.repository.FindAllMarketSegments();

    // Make sure there is at least one item in the list
    Assert.AreEqual(true, segments.Count > 0);
}
```

The code for this method is pretty straightforward; it simply calls the IProjectRepository interface to get the list of all Market Segments and then asserts that at least one has been returned.

The IEmployeeRepository Unit Tests

There are only two tests necessary for the IEmployeeRepository, and those are the tests for the GetConstructionAdministrators method and the GetPrincipals method. I am not going to go over the steps for creating the EmployeeRepositoryTest class; the steps are exactly the same as those I just outlined for the IProjectRepository unit tests.

The GetPrincipalsTest Method

This method tests the GetPrincipals method of the IEmployeeRepository interface:

```
/// <summary>
///A test for GetPrincipals
///</summary>
[TestMethod()]
public void GetPrincipalsTest()
{
    // Get the list of all Principals
    IList<Employee> principals = this.repository.GetPrincipals();

    // Make sure there is at least one item in the list
    Assert.AreEqual(true, principals.Count > 0);
}
```

This method is very similar to the FindAllMarketSegmentsTest method on the ProjectRepositoryTest class shown previously. It just validates that at least one Employee instance was returned from the GetPrincipals method of the IEmployeeRepository interface.

The GetConstructionAdministratorsTest Method

The code for this test is almost identical to the last test, only this time I am testing the GetConstructionAdministrators method of the IEmployeeRepository interface:

```
/// <summary>
///A test for GetConstructionAdministrators
///</summary>
[DeploymentItem("SmartCA.sdf"), TestMethod()]
public void GetConstructionAdministratorsTest()
{
    // Get the list of all Construction Administrators
    IList<Employee> administrators =
        this.repository.GetConstructionAdministrators();

    // Make sure there is at least one item in the list
    Assert.AreEqual(true, administrators.Count > 0);
}
```

This method validates that at least one Employee instance was returned from the GetConstructionAdministrators method.

The Solution

Now that the design is in place for the Project domain model, the Project Aggregate has been defined and its boundaries have been determined, and the Repositories have been designed with their associated tests, it is time to start the code implementation. In this section, I will be implementing these designs, as well as implementing the ViewModel and the View for Projects.

The Project Class

Currently, the Project class does not have any behavior. It only contains data at the moment, but this will change as I get further into the domain model. One of the things that should jump out at you about the Project class is that there is no persistence code in it, no code that calls any file operations, database operations, and the like. It is a Plain-Old CLR Object (POCO), and because of this it helps me to focus on the domain logic of a Project rather than worrying about persistence-related things. Those types of concerns will be left to the infrastructure layer.

The Private Fields and Constructors

Here are the private fields and constructors for the Project class:

```
using System;
using System.Collections.Generic;
using SmartCA.Infrastructure.DomainBase;
using SmartCA.Model.Companies;
using SmartCA.Model.Employees;

namespace SmartCA.Model.Projects
```

(continued)

(continued)

```
{
    public class Project : EntityBase
    {
        #region Private Fields

        private string number;
        private string name;
        private Address address;
        private Company owner;
        private Employee constructionAdministrator;
        private Employee principalInCharge;
        private DateTime? contractDate;
        private DateTime? estimatedStartDate;
        private DateTime? estimatedCompletionDate;
        private DateTime? adjustedCompletionDate;
        private DateTime? currentCompletionDate;
        private DateTime? actualCompletionDate;
        private decimal contingencyAllowanceAmount;
        private decimal testingAllowanceAmount;
        private decimal utilityAllowanceAmount;
        private decimal originalConstructionCost;
        private int totalChangeOrderDays;
        private decimal adjustedConstructionCost;
        private decimal totalChangeOrdersAmount;
        private int totalSquareFeet;
        private int percentComplete;
        private string remarks;
        private decimal aeChangeOrderAmount;
        private string contractReason;
        private string agencyApplicationNumber;
        private string agencyFileNumber;
        private MarketSegment segment;
        private List<Allowance> allowances;
        private List<Contract> contracts;

        #endregion

        #region Constructors

        public Project(string number, string name)
            : this(null, number, name)
        {
        }

        public Project(object key, string number, string name)
            : base(key)
        {
            this.number = number;
            this.name = name;
            this.address = null;
            this.owner = new Company();
            this.constructionAdministrator = null;
            this.principalInCharge = null;
```

```
        this.contractDate = null;
        this.estimatedStartDate = null;
        this.estimatedCompletionDate = null;
        this.currentCompletionDate = null;
        this.actualCompletionDate = null;
        this.contingencyAllowanceAmount = 0;
        this.testingAllowanceAmount = 0;
        this.utilityAllowanceAmount = 0;
        this.originalConstructionCost = 0;
        this.totalChangeOrderDays = 0;
        this.adjustedConstructionCost = 0;
        this.totalChangeOrdersAmount = 0;
        this.totalSquareFeet = 0;
        this.percentComplete = 0;
        this.remarks = string.Empty;
        this.aeChangeOrderAmount = 0;
        this.contractReason = string.Empty;
        this.agencyApplicationNumber = string.Empty;
        this.agencyFileNumber = string.Empty;
        this.segment = null;
        this.allowances = new List<Allowance>();
        this.contracts = new List<Contract>();
    }

#endregion
```

Since the `Project` class is an Entity, it inherits from the `EntityBase` type. Again, this is not to give the `Project` class any type of infrastructure functionality from its base class, it is merely to eliminate the duplicate code of having to decorate every `Entity` class with an `Id` property. This was mentioned before in Chapter 2, and it is my implementation of a Layer Supertype.

When analyzing the constructors for the Project class, you will notice that there are two overloads, one that requires a key value and one that does not. I used the two overloads because sometimes I may be loading an existing `Project` from a data store, and other times I may be creating a new `Project` that does not yet exist in the data store. When loading from the data store, I will use the key value to retrieve the `Project`.

The Properties

Currently, the `Project` class has several properties, which may make it a candidate to be split up into further classes later.

The Name and Number Properties

The first two properties, `Name` and `Number`, are actually read-only:

```
public string Number
{
    get { return this.number; }
}

public string Name
{
    get { return this.name; }
}
```

This means that once a number and name have been assigned to a `Project`, they cannot be changed. To change the name or number, you must delete the old `Project` instance and create a new one. The project number and project name are very important parts of a `Project`; many other parts of the application will refer to these properties later. Currently, the only way to set these values of the class is through the constructor.

Since C# 2.0, it is possible to add a private or protected set accessor to properties, but I have decided not to do that because right now I do not need it.

The Address Property

The next property, `Address`, actually represents a Value Object type.

```
public Address Address
{
    get { return this.address; }
    set { this.address = value; }
}
```

Since address information will be used on several other objects, it was put into its own class, so I only had to write the code for address information once. This class is a Value Object type because it has no conceptual identity that the SmartCA domain model cares about; it is simply holding the atomic value of an address.

Please do not confuse the term Value Object with a .NET Value type. .NET Value types are data types such as integers and DateTime structures. Strictly speaking in .NET terms, a Value Object is still a Reference type. In the Address example, the `Address` *class is a Value Object in DDD terms, but in .NET terms it is still a Reference type.*

A nice consequence of making the `Address` class a Value Object is that I do not have to write any code to track its identity. Here is the code for the `Address` class:

```
using System;

namespace SmartCA.Model
{
    /// <summary>
    /// This is an immutable Value class.
    /// </summary>
    public class Address
    {
        private string street;
        private string city;
        private string state;
        private string postalCode;

        public Address(string street, string city, string state, string postalCode)
        {
            this.street = street;
            this.city = city;
            this.state = state;
            this.postalCode = postalCode;
        }

        public string Street
```

```
        {
            get { return this.street; }
        }

        public string City
        {
            get { return this.city; }
        }

        public string State
        {
            get { return this.state; }
        }

        public string PostalCode
        {
            get { return this.postalCode; }
        }
    }
}
```

The interesting thing about this class is that it is immutable. What this means is that once it is created, it can never be changed. This is exactly how the .NET Framework's System.String class behaves, also. When I change the value of a String, or call a method on the String class to modify the String, I get an entirely new String returned to me. According to Eric Evans, if a class meets the requirements to be a Value Object, it should be conceptually whole (Evans, *Domain-Driven Design, Tackling Complexity in the Heart of Software*, 99). In the case of the class, it is conceptually whole and cannot be changed; it can only be copied or have new instances of it created.

In order to make sure that the address data from the constructor is valid, I have added some validation code to the Address class to make sure that only valid Address instances will be created:

```
using System;

namespace SmartCA.Model
{
    /// <summary>
    /// This is an immutable Value class.
    /// </summary>
    public class Address
    {
        private string street;
        private string city;
        private string state;
        private string postalCode;

        public Address(string street, string city, string state, string postalCode)
        {
            this.street = street;
            this.city = city;
```

(continued)

(continued)

```
            this.state = state;
            this.postalCode = postalCode;
            this.Validate();
        }

        public string Street
        {
            get { return this.street; }
        }

        public string City
        {
            get { return this.city; }
        }

        public string State
        {
            get { return this.state; }
        }

        public string PostalCode
        {
            get { return this.postalCode; }
        }

        private void Validate()
        {
            if (string.IsNullOrEmpty(this.street) ||
                string.IsNullOrEmpty(this.city) ||
                string.IsNullOrEmpty(this.state) ||
                string.IsNullOrEmpty(this.postalCode))
            {
                throw new InvalidOperationException("Invalid address.");
            }
        }
    }
}
```

Later, when I write the ViewModel for editing `Projects`, I will show a strategy for how to change the `Project`'s `Address` property value from the UI.

The Owner Property

The next property, `Owner`, represents a `Company` instance. A `Company` is an Entity that is also the root of its own Aggregate. This is not a problem, as we are only referring to the `Company` instance (`Owner`), and all information requested about the `Company` instance will need to go through its respective repository. I will show how I deal with this later in the chapter when looking at the repositories for the Aggregate Roots.

The code for `Company` is very simple right now, and following the principle of YAGNI (You Ain't Gonna Need It) (Wikipedia -`http://en.wikipedia.org/wiki/You_Ain't_Gonna_Need_It`), it only contains the code we need for the moment.

```csharp
using System;
using SmartCA.Infrastructure.DomainBase;

namespace SmartCA.Model.Companies
{
    public class Company : EntityBase
    {
        private string name;
        private string abbreviation;
        private Address address;

        public Company()
            : this(null)
        {
        }

        public Company(object key)
            : base(key)
        {
        }

        public string Name
        {
            get { return this.name; }
            set { this.name = value; }
        }

        public string Abbreviation
        {
            get { return this.abbreviation; }
            set { this.abbreviation = value; }
        }

        public Address HeadquartersAddress
        {
            get { return this.address; }
            set { this.address = value; }
        }
    }
}
```

The main note of interest in the Company class is that it is using the immutable Address class also being used by the Project class. This is great because we are getting immediate reuse of the Address class.

The ConstructionAdministrator and PrincipalInCharge Properties

The ConstructionAdministrator and PrincipalInCharge properties are both instances of the Employee class, which is also the root of its own Aggregate.

```csharp
using System;

namespace SmartCA.Model.Employees
{
    public class Employee : Person
```

(continued)

(continued)

```
        {
            private string jobTitle;

            public Employee(object key)
                : this(key, string.Empty, string.Empty)
            {
            }

            public Employee(object key, string firstName, string lastName)
                : base(key, firstName, lastName)
            {
                this.jobTitle = string.Empty;
            }

            public string JobTitle
            {
                get { return this.jobTitle; }
                set { this.jobTitle = value; }
            }
        }
    }
}
```

The interesting thing to notice about the Employee class is that it inherits from the Person class. The Person class is mainly to share common properties for some of the classes coming up in later chapters that are also people, such as Contacts.

```
using System;
using SmartCA.Infrastructure.DomainBase;

namespace SmartCA.Model
{
    public abstract class Person : EntityBase
    {
        private string firstName;
        private string lastName;
        private string initials;

        protected Person()
            : this(null)
        {
        }

        protected Person(object key)
            : this(key, string.Empty, string.Empty)
        {
        }

        protected Person(object key, string firstName, string lastName)
            : base(key)
        {
            this.firstName = firstName;
            this.lastName = lastName;
            this.initials = string.Empty;
        }
```

```
        public string FirstName
        {
            get { return this.firstName; }
            set { this.firstName = value; }
        }

        public string LastName
        {
            get { return this.lastName; }
            set { this.lastName = value; }
        }

        public string Initials
        {
            get { return this.initials; }
            set { this.initials = value; }
        }
    }
}
```

The main thing to note about the Person class is that it is abstract, that is, it cannot be created directly. I really just wanted this class to reuse some of the property code, but who knows, later on having it as an abstract class might turn out to be useful in other ways via polymorphism.

The Segment Property

The next property in the Project class, Segment, represents what market segment the Project is in:

```
using System;
using SmartCA.Infrastructure.DomainBase;

namespace SmartCA.Model.Projects
{
    public class MarketSegment : EntityBase
    {
        private MarketSector parentSector;
        private string name;
        private string code;

        public MarketSegment(MarketSector parentSector, string name, string code)
            : this(null, parentSector, name, code)
        {
        }

        public MarketSegment(object key, MarketSector parentSector, string name,
            string code) : base(key)
        {
            this.parentSector = parentSector;
            this.name = name;
            this.code = code;
        }

        public string Name
```

(continued)

(continued)

```
        {
            get { return this.name; }
            set { this.name = value; }
        }

        public string Code
        {
            get { return this.code; }
            set { this.code = value; }
        }

        public MarketSector ParentSector
        {
            get { return this.parentSector; }
        }
    }
}
```

The `MarketSegment` class holds a reference to the market sector in which it belongs, and this relationship is represented by the `ParentSector` property.

```
using System;
using System.Collections.Generic;
using SmartCA.Infrastructure.DomainBase;

namespace SmartCA.Model.Projects
{
    public class MarketSector : EntityBase
    {
        private string name;
        private List<MarketSegment> segments;

        public MarketSector(string name)
            : this(null, name)
        {
            this.name = name;
        }

        public MarketSector(object key, string name)
            : base(key)
        {
            this.name = name;
            this.segments = new List<MarketSegment>();
        }

        public string Name
        {
            get { return this.name; }
            set { this.name = value; }
        }
```

```
        public IList<MarketSegment> Segments
        {
            get { return this.segments; }
        }
    }
}
```

As you can see in the code for the MarketSector class, there is a bidirectional relationship between MarketSegment and MarketSector. MarketSector can contain zero or more MarketSegment instances, and MarketSegment refers to the appropriate market sector via its MarketSector property.

The ContingencyAllowanceAmount, TestingAllowanceAmount, and UtilityAllowanceAmount Properties

You may notice in the Project class that there are properties for ContingencyAllowanceAmount, TestingAllowanceAmount, and UtilityAllowanceAmount, and also one called Allowances. The first three are of type System.Decimal (for money), and the last one, Allowances, is an IList<Allowance>, which is just a list of name-value pairs of allowance names and allowance amounts. This gives the Construction Administrator the flexibility to have other allowance amounts without having to have them be hard-coded into the Project class.

```
using System;

namespace SmartCA.Model.Projects
{
    public class Allowance
    {
        private string title;
        private decimal amount;

        public Allowance(string title, decimal amount)
        {
            this.title = title;
            this.amount = amount;
        }

        public string Title
        {
            get { return this.title; }
        }

        public decimal Amount
        {
            get { return this.amount; }
        }
    }
}
```

Hopefully, from the code above you can ascertain that the Allowance class is a Value class. Because of its read-only properties and constructor, it has been made immutable. Just as with the other Value classes, the only way to change its value is to create another instance of the class.

The Contracts Property

The Contracts property represents a list of Contract types. The contract represents an agreement between the main or general contractor, in this case Smart Design, and another contractor:

```csharp
using System;
using SmartCA.Infrastructure.DomainBase;
using SmartCA.Model.Companies;

namespace SmartCA.Model.Projects
{
    public class Contract : EntityBase
    {
        private Company contractor;
        private string scopeOfWork;
        private string bidPackageNumber;
        private DateTime? contractDate;
        private DateTime? noticeToProceedDate;
        private decimal contractAmount;

        public Contract()
            : this(null)
        {
        }

        public Contract(object key)
            : base(key)
        {
            this.contractor = new Company();
            this.scopeOfWork = string.Empty;
            this.bidPackageNumber = string.Empty;
            this.contractAmount = 0;
        }

        public Company Contractor
        {
            get { return this.contractor; }
            set { this.contractor = value; }
        }

        public string ScopeOfWork
        {
            get { return this.scopeOfWork; }
            set { this.scopeOfWork = value; }
        }

        public string BidPackageNumber
```

```
        {
            get { return this.bidPackageNumber; }
            set { this.bidPackageNumber = value; }
        }

        public DateTime? ContractDate
        {
            get { return this.contractDate; }
            set { this.contractDate = value; }
        }

        public DateTime? NoticeToProceedDate
        {
            get { return this.noticeToProceedDate; }
            set { this.noticeToProceedDate = value; }
        }

        public decimal ContractAmount
        {
            get { return this.contractAmount; }
            set { this.contractAmount = value; }
        }
    }
}
```

As you can see, the `Contract` class contains the scope of work to be performed, how much the work will cost, when the contract is in effect, and when the contractor can start the work. The `BidPackageNumber` property allows the `Contract` to be tied back to the original bid for the work. Most important, the class contains a `Contractor` property, which represents the instance of the `Company` doing the work. More will be covered on the `Company` class in the next chapter.

The Repository Implementations

The next code to start writing is for the repositories. In this section I will be writing the code for the Project and Employee repositories.

The Project Repository

In order to implement the concrete `ProjectRepository` class, I just need to inherit from `SqlCeRepositoryBase<T>`, and also implement the `IProjectRepository` interface that I showed earlier in the Design section:

```
namespace SmartCA.Infrastructure.Repositories
{
    public class ProjectRepository : SqlCeRepositoryBase<Project>,
        IProjectRepository
    {
...
```

Refactoring the FindAll and FindBy Methods

During the process of writing the code for the `ProjectRepository` class and testing the Repository Framework, I noticed a nice refactoring I could do by putting the `FindAll` method inside of the `IRepository` interface:

```
using System;
using SmartCA.Infrastructure.DomainBase;
using System.Collections.Generic;

namespace SmartCA.Infrastructure.RepositoryFramework
{
    public interface IRepository<T> where T : EntityBase
    {
        T FindBy(object key);
        IList<T> FindAll();
        void Add(T item);
        T this[object key] { get; set; }
        void Remove(T item);
    }
}
```

To implement the `FindAll` method, I put in an abstract method in the `RepositoryBase<T>` class and then did an override of the method in the `SqlCeRepositoryBase<T>` class. Here is the signature in `RepositoryBase<T>`:

```
public abstract IList<T> FindAll();
```

Here is the implementation in the `SqlCeRepositoryBase<T>` class:

```
public override IList<T> FindAll()
{
    StringBuilder builder = this.GetBaseQueryBuilder();
    builder.Append(";");
    return this.BuildEntitiesFromSql(builder.ToString());
}
```

The `baseQuery` variable is a private string variable in the `SqlCeRepositoryBase<T>` class that I have added. It gets set by an abstract Template Method, `GetBaseQuery()`, which returns a string:

```
protected abstract string GetBaseQuery();
```

This allows all of the derived `SqlCeRepositoryBase<T>` classes to define their own base queries for their respective Aggregates. The `GetBaseQuery()` method is called from the constructor of `SqlCeRepositoryBase<T>`:

```
protected SqlCeRepositoryBase(IUnitOfWork unitOfWork)
    : base(unitOfWork)
{
    this.database = DatabaseFactory.CreateDatabase();
    this.entityFactory = EntityFactoryBuilder.BuildFactory<T>();
```

```
        this.childCallbacks = new Dictionary<string, AppendChildData>();
        this.BuildChildCallbacks();
        this.baseQuery = this.GetBaseQuery();
    }
```

I also noticed another refactoring opportunity, and that was to change the `FindBy` method in `SqlCeRepositoryBase<T>` from abstract to an implemented public method. Here was the old signature for the method in the `SqlCeRepositoryBase<T>` class:

```
public abstract T FindBy(object key);
```

Here is the new implementation of the method in the `SqlCeRepositoryBase<T>` class:

```
        public override T FindBy(object key)
        {
            StringBuilder builder = this.GetBaseQueryBuilder();
            builder.Append(this.BuildBaseWhereClause(key));
            return this.BuildEntityFromSql(builder.ToString());
        }
```

The `BuildBaseWhereClause` method is a private method in the `SqlCeRepositoryBase<T>` class:

```
        protected virtual string BuildBaseWhereClause(object key)
        {
            return string.Format(this.baseWhereClause, key);
        }
```

This method uses the private string variable, `baseWhereClause`, in the `SqlCeRepositoryBase<T>` class to substitute in a key value for the Aggregate's base query. It is set by another abstract Template Method, `GetBaseWhereClause()`, which returns a string, just like `GetBaseQuery()`:

```
protected abstract string GetBaseWhereClause();
```

This also allows all of the derived `SqlCeRepositoryBase<T>` classes to define their own `where` clauses for their respective Aggregate queries. The `GetBaseWhereClause()` method is also called from the constructor of `SqlCeRepositoryBase<T>`:

```
        protected SqlCeRepositoryBase(IUnitOfWork unitOfWork)
            : base(unitOfWork)
        {
            this.database = DatabaseFactory.CreateDatabase();
            this.entityFactory = EntityFactoryBuilder.BuildFactory<T>();
            this.childCallbacks = new Dictionary<string, AppendChildData>();
            this.BuildChildCallbacks();
            this.baseQuery = this.GetBaseQuery();
            this.baseWhereClause = this.GetBaseWhereClause();
        }
```

The end result of this refactoring is that now I do not have to implement the `FindAll` and `FindBy` methods in any of my concrete repositories, it is already done for me by the `SqlCeRepositoryBase<T>` class. This could save quite a bit of coding and testing in the long run.

The Organization of the ProjectRepository Class

Before going any further into the implementation of the ProjectRepository class, I wanted to take a moment to show you how I have it organized. I have divided the class into several collapsible regions (via the #region and #endregion keywords), as shown in Figure 3.8.

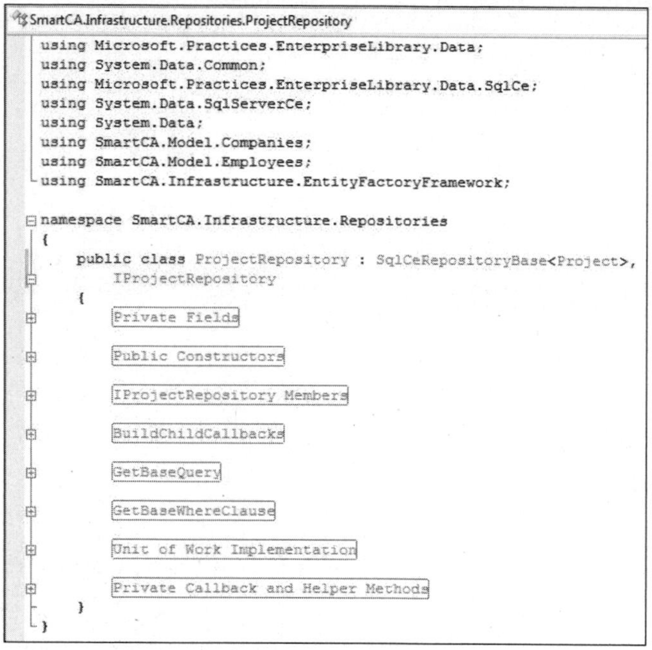

```
SmartCA.Infrastructure.Repositories.ProjectRepository
    using Microsoft.Practices.EnterpriseLibrary.Data;
    using System.Data.Common;
    using Microsoft.Practices.EnterpriseLibrary.Data.SqlCe;
    using System.Data.SqlServerCe;
    using System.Data;
    using SmartCA.Model.Companies;
    using SmartCA.Model.Employees;
    using SmartCA.Infrastructure.EntityFactoryFramework;

    namespace SmartCA.Infrastructure.Repositories
    {
        public class ProjectRepository : SqlCeRepositoryBase<Project>,
            IProjectRepository
        {
            Private Fields

            Public Constructors

            IProjectRepository Members

            BuildChildCallbacks

            GetBaseQuery

            GetBaseWhereClause

            Unit of Work Implementation

            Private Callback and Helper Methods
        }
    }
```

Figure 3.8: Repository code organization.

This type of code organization helps me quite a bit when I need to refactor code or just get to something quickly in the class.

The Constructors

There are two public constructors for the ProjectRepository class, a default constructor, and one that takes an IUnitOfWork instance (defined earlier in Chapter 2).

```
#region Public Constructors

    public ProjectRepository()
        : this(null)
    {
    }

    public ProjectRepository(IUnitOfWork unitOfWork)
        : base(unitOfWork)
    {
    }

    #endregion
```

These are very simple, and just pass on their data to the `SqlCeRepositoryBase<T>` constructor.

The IProjectRepository Implementation

Because of the infrastructure I have already built, the actual implementation of methods for almost all of the `Repository` interfaces are fairly simple. The usual pattern they follow is to build a SQL string, and then have the base class execute the SQL and return instances of Entity object(s) to the derived `Repository`. The `IProjectRepository` interface dictates that I need to implement three methods, `FindBy(IList<MarketSegment> segments, bool completed)`, `FindBy(string projectNumber)`, and `FindAllMarketSegments()`. The first one is the most complex of the three:

```
public IList<Project> FindBy(IList<MarketSegment> segments, bool completed)
{
    StringBuilder builder = this.GetBaseQueryBuilder();
    if (completed)
    {
        builder.Append(" WHERE p.ActualCompletionDate IS NOT NULL AND
p.PercentComplete > 99");
    }
    else
    {
        builder.Append(" WHERE p.ActualCompletionDate IS NULL AND
p.PercentComplete < 100");
    }
    if (segments ! = null || segments.Count > 0)
    {
        builder.Append(string.Format(" AND p.MarketSegmentID IN ({0})",
            DataHelper.EntityListToDelimited(segments).ToString()));
    }
    builder.Append(";");
    return this.BuildEntitiesFromSql(builder.ToString());
}
```

This method first filters the list of `Projects` based on whether the `Project` has been completed. It then builds another filter based on what `MarketSegment` instances were passed in to it. It uses the `DataHelper` class to help transform the `IList<MarketSegment>` object into a comma-delimited SQL IN clause via the `EntityListToDelimited` method. Finally, it passes the SQL it has built up to its base class, `SqlCeRepositoryBase<T>` for processing.

The next method, `FindBy(string projectNumber)`, is the simplest, thanks to the base class functionality in `SqlCeRepository<T>`:

```
public Project FindBy(string projectNumber)
{
    StringBuilder builder = this.GetBaseQueryBuilder();
    return this.BuildEntityFromSql(builder.Append(string.Format(" WHERE
p.ProjectNumber = N'{0}';",
            projectNumber)).ToString());
}
```

It does not have any logic in it except to build the SQL WHERE clause for the Project Number. It then follows the normal pattern of sending the SQL statement to the base class and getting an Entity back.

The last `IProjectRepository` method to look at is the `FindAllMarketSegments()` method. I was trying to decide whether `MarketSegment` objects belonged in their own repository, but right now they are not used outside of the Project Aggregate, so I have decided to leave them in the `ProjectRepository`.

```csharp
        public IList<MarketSegment> FindAllMarketSegments()
        {
            List<MarketSegment> segments = new List<MarketSegment>();
            string query = "SELECT * FROM MarketSegment mst INNER JOIN MarketSector
msr ON mst.MarketSectorID = msr.MarketSectorID;";
            IEntityFactory<MarketSegment> factory =
EntityFactoryBuilder.BuildFactory<MarketSegment>();
            using (IDataReader reader = this.ExecuteReader(query))
            {
                while (reader.Read())
                {
                    segments.Add(factory.BuildEntity(reader));
                }
            }
            return segments;
        }
```

This method is a little bit different in that it must build its own full SQL statement, use its own `IEntityFactory<T>` instance, `IEntityFactory<MarketSegment>`, and builds the list of `MarketSegment` instances "by hand." The `IEntityFactory<MarketSegment>` instance created by the `EntityFactoryBuilder` is actually a `MarketSegmentFactory` instance. In Chapter 2, I went over the Entity Factory Framework, and now you will see it actually put to use.

```csharp
using System;
using SmartCA.Model.Projects;
using SmartCA.Infrastructure.EntityFactoryFramework;
using System.Data;

namespace SmartCA.Infrastructure.Repositories
{
    internal class MarketSegmentFactory : IEntityFactory<MarketSegment>
    {
        #region Field Names

        internal static class FieldNames
        {
            public const string MarketSegmentId = "MarketSegmentID";
            public const string MarketSectorId = "MarketSectorID";
            public const string Code = "Code";
            public const string MarketSegmentName = "MarketSegmentName";
            public const string MarketSectorName = "MarketSectorName";
        }

        #endregion

        #region IEntityFactory<MarketSegment> Members

        public MarketSegment BuildEntity(IDataReader reader)
```

```
        {
            return new MarketSegment(reader[FieldNames.MarketSegmentId],
                            new
MarketSector(reader[FieldNames.MarketSectorId],
reader[FieldNames.MarketSectorName].ToString()),
reader[FieldNames.MarketSegmentName].ToString(),
                            reader[FieldNames.Code].ToString());
        }

        #endregion
    }
}
```

This class uses an internal static class, `FieldNames`, to hold the field names used in the mapping from database table field names to the class property names. The interface method `BuildEntity` uses the `IDataReader` instance passed to it along with the `FieldNames` static class to build an instance of a `MarketSegment` class. That is all there is to it, very nice and simple to maintain. The rest of the objects that get build by the repositories will all follow this same pattern.

The BuildChildCallbacks Method

Now that I have finished going over the `IProjectRepository` implementation, it is time to go back to how the `Project` class actually gets built. If you recall, this functionality was moved up into the base class, `SqlCeRepositoryBase<T>`, but it does make use of the Template Method pattern, and `BuildChildCallbacks` is one of those abstract template methods that the `ProjectRepository` must implement.

```
#region BuildChildCallbacks

protected override void BuildChildCallbacks()
{
    this.ChildCallbacks.Add(ProjectFactory.FieldNames.OwnerCompanyId,
        this.AppendOwner);

    this.ChildCallbacks.Add(
        ProjectFactory.FieldNames.ConstructionAdministratorEmployeeId,
        this.AppendConstructionAdministrator);

    this.ChildCallbacks.Add(ProjectFactory.FieldNames.PrincipalEmployeeId,
        this.AppendPrincipal);

    this.ChildCallbacks.Add("allowances",
        delegate(Project project, object childKeyName)
        {
            this.AppendProjectAllowances(project);
        });

}

#endregion
```

To refresh your memory from Chapter 2, the `ChildCallbacks` property of `SqlCeRepositoryBase<T>` is a dictionary of type `Dictionary<string, AppendChildData>`, with `AppendChildData` being a delegate type with the following signature:

```
#region AppendChildData Delegate

/// <summary>
/// The delegate signature required for callback methods
/// </summary>
/// <param name="entityAggregate"></param>
/// <param name="childEntityKey"></param>
public delegate void AppendChildData(T entityAggregate,
    object childEntityKeyValue);

#endregion
```

This takes in the entity Aggregate type, in this case a `Project` instance, and an entity key value, in this case the value of the primary key of the child entity's corresponding table. In the first example of `AppendOwner`, this would be the field name on the Project table representing the `Owner`.

The code in the `BuildChildCallbacks` method just adds entries to the `ChildCallbacks` dictionary, with the appropriate field names and delegate methods. The last entry is the most interesting, because the `AppendProjectAllowances` method has no parameters, so an anonymous delegate is used to make it fit:

```
this.ChildCallbacks.Add("allowances",
delegate(Project project, object childKeyName)
{
    this.AppendProjectAllowances(project);
});
```

Since it has no parameters, it does not need a field name on the Project table either; it will use the `Id` property of the Project class (I will show this method shortly). I added the `"allowances"` string value in order to give it a valid key value in the `ChildCallbacks` dictionary.

The AppendOwner Callback Method

The first entry made in the `ChildCallbacks` dictionary was for the `AppendOwner` method. This method uses the Company Repository to find the matching `Company` that represents the Owner of the Project:

```
private void AppendOwner(Project project, object ownerCompanyId)
{
    ICompanyRepository repository
        = RepositoryFactory.GetRepository<ICompanyRepository, Company>();
    project.Owner = repository.FindBy(ownerCompanyId);
}
```

As you can see, it follows the same pattern I have been using and is actually using the `IRepository<T>` interface's `FindBy(object key)` method implemented in `SqlCeRepositoryBase<T>`.

The AppendConstructionAdministrator and AppendPrincipal Callback Methods

These methods both need to get and set an `Employee` instance value on their respective properties in the `Project` class:

```
private void AppendConstructionAdministrator(Project project,
    object constructionAdministratorId)
{
    project.ConstructionAdministrator =
        this.GetEmployee(constructionAdministratorId);
}

private void AppendPrincipal(Project project, object principalId)
{
    project.PrincipalInCharge = this.GetEmployee(principalId);
}
```

Following the "Don't Repeat Yourself" (DRY) principle, I created a `GetEmployee(object employeeId)` method that the two methods could share:

```
private Employee GetEmployee(object employeeId)
{
    IEmployeeRepository repository
        = RepositoryFactory.GetRepository<IEmployeeRepository, Employee>();
    return repository.FindBy(employeeId);
}
```

This method is very similar to the `AppendOwner` method in that it also uses the `IRepository<T>` interface's `FindBy(object key)` method implemented in `SqlCeRepositoryBase<T>` in order to build the Employee instance.

The AppendProjectAllowances Callback Method

As mentioned earlier, the `AppendProjectAllowances` method is a little bit different from the previous three callback methods:

```
private void AppendProjectAllowances(Project project)
{
    string sql =
        string.Format("SELECT * FROM ProjectAllowance WHERE ProjectID =
'{0}'", project.Key);
    using (IDataReader reader = this.ExecuteReader(sql))
    {
        while (reader.Read())
        {
            project.Allowances.Add(ProjectFactory.BuildAllowance(reader));
        }
    }
}
```

The Project Allowance data does not belong to another repository; it is part of the `ProjectRepository`. Therefore, since it is not covered by the base query for the `ProjectRepository`, the `Allowance` instances must be built by hand, very similarly to the `FindAllMarketSegments` method seen earlier in this chapter. In fact, this method is almost identical except for the SQL statement and the `ProjectFactory` method used to build the Entity. In this case the method is using a static method on the `ProjectFactory` class to build the Entity.

```
public static Allowance BuildAllowance(IDataReader reader)
{
    return new Allowance(reader[FieldNames.AllowanceTitle].ToString(),
            DataHelper.GetDecimal(reader[FieldNames.AllowanceAmount]));
}
```

As you can see in the code for the method, it is a very simple mapping. I had to make it a static method in the `ProjectFactory` class because the `Allowance` class is not an Entity, it is a `Value` class; therefore, it cannot use the Entity Factory Framework.

The GetBaseQuery Method

The next abstract Template Method that the `SqlCeRepositoryBase<T>` calls is the `GetBaseQuery` method. Here is the `ProjectRepository` class's override of the abstract method:

```
#region GetBaseQuery

protected override string GetBaseQuery()
{
    return "SELECT * FROM Project p INNER JOIN MarketSegment ms ON
p.MarketSegmentID = ms.MarketSegmentID";
}

#endregion
```

This simply returns the SQL statement for the Project Aggregate. By abstracting the base query out, the `SqlCeRepositryBase<T>` class is able to pull in the two "FindBy" methods, thus eliminating repetitive code in all of the derived repositories.

The GetBaseWhereClause Method

The `GetBaseWhereClause` method is very similar to the `GetBaseQuery` method just shown, only this time the string returned is just a formatted SQL WHERE clause for the Project Aggregate with a placeholder for the `ProjectID` field.

```
#region GetBaseWhereClause

protected override string GetBaseWhereClause()
{
    return " WHERE ProjectID = '{0}';";
}

#endregion
```

The `SqlCeRepositoryBase<T>` class handles filling in the `ProjectID` placeholder at runtime.

The Unit of Work Implementation

In order to implement the Repository Framework's Unit of Work defined in Chapter 2, I only need to override three methods, PersistNewItem(Project item), PersistUpdatedItem(Project item), and PersistDeletedItem(Project item). I am not going to show all of the code for PersistNewItem, since it is rather lengthy, but here is an abbreviated version of it:

```
protected override void PersistNewItem(Project item)
{
    StringBuilder builder = new StringBuilder(100);
    builder.Append(string.Format("INSERT INTO Project
({0},{1},{2},{3},{4},{5},{6},{7},{8},{9},{10},{11},{12},{13},{14},{15},{16},{17},
{18},{19},{20},{21},{22},{23},{24},{25},{26}) ",
        ProjectFactory.FieldNames.ProjectId,
        ProjectFactory.FieldNames.ProjectNumber,
        ProjectFactory.FieldNames.ProjectName,
```

```
        DataHelper.GetSqlValue(item.AgencyFileNumber),
        item.Segment.Key));

    this.Database.ExecuteNonQuery(this.Database.GetSqlStringCommand(builder
.ToString())));
}
```

The code is building up an insert statement composed of the values from the Project instance and then executing the query using the Microsoft Enterprise Library's Database object.

PersistUpdatedItem is very similar, only it does an update to the table:

```
protected override void PersistUpdatedItem(Project item)
{
    StringBuilder builder = new StringBuilder(100);
    builder.Append("UPDATE Project SET ");

    builder.Append(string.Format("{0} = {1}",
        ProjectFactory.FieldNames.ConstructionAdministratorEmployeeId,
        item.ConstructionAdministrator.Key));

    builder.Append(string.Format(",{0} = {1}",
        ProjectFactory.FieldNames.PrincipalEmployeeId,
        item.PrincipalInCharge.Key));
    builder.Append(string.Format(",{0} = {1}",
        ProjectFactory.FieldNames.AgencyFileNumber,
        DataHelper.GetSqlValue(item.AgencyFileNumber)));

    builder.Append(string.Format(",{0} = {1}",
        ProjectFactory.FieldNames.MarketSegmentId,
        item.Segment.Key));
```

(continued)

(continued)

```
            builder.Append(" ");
            builder.Append(this.BuildBaseWhereClause(item.Key));

    this.Database.ExecuteNonQuery(this.Database.GetSqlStringCommand(builder
    .ToString()));
        }
```

The last method to implement, `PersistDeletedItem`, follows the same pattern:

```
        protected override void PersistDeletedItem(Project item)
    {
        string query = string.Format("DELETE FROM ProjectAllowance {0}",
            this.BuildBaseWhereClause(item.Key));
        this.Database.ExecuteNonQuery(this.Database.GetSqlStringCommand(query));
        query = string.Format("DELETE FROM Project {0}",
            this.BuildBaseWhereClause(item.Key));
        this.Database.ExecuteNonQuery(this.Database.GetSqlStringCommand(query));
    }
```

It is a little different from the other two persistence methods in that it actually has to execute two SQL statements, one to delete rows from the `ProjectAllowance` table and then one for deleting the single row from the `Project` table. Notice, also, how the last two methods make use of the `SqlCeRepositoryBase<T>` class's `BuildBaseWhereClause` method. The refactoring of code into `SqlCeRepositoryBase<T>` keeps paying off.

The Employee Repository

Similar to the `ProjectRepository` class, in order to implement the concrete `EmployeeRepository` class I just need to inherit from `SqlCeRepositoryBase<T>`, and also to implement the `IEmployeeRepository` interface shown earlier in the Design section of this chapter:

```
namespace SmartCA.Infrastructure.Repositories
{
    public class EmployeeRepository : SqlCeRepositoryBase<Employee>,
        IEmployeeRepository
    {
...
```

The Constructors

The public constructors for the `EmployeeRepository` class are exactly the same as those in the `ProjectRepository` class:

```
        #region Public Constructors

        public EmployeeRepository()
            : this(null)
        {
        }

        public EmployeeRepository(IUnitOfWork unitOfWork)
            : base(unitOfWork)
```

```
        {
        }

        #endregion
```

The IEmployeeRepository Implementation

The `IEmployeeRepository` interface dictates that I need to implement two methods, `GetConstructionAdministrators()` and `GetPrincipals()`. Both of these methods are fairly simple, and both return a type of `IList<Employee>`.

```
        #region IEmployeeRepository Members

        public IList<Employee> GetConstructionAdministrators()
        {
            //Construction Administrator
            StringBuilder builder = this.GetBaseQueryBuilder ();
            return this.BuildEntitiesFromSql(builder.Append
                (" WHERE JobTitle LIKE '%Construction Administrator%';")
    .ToString());
        }

        public IList<Employee> GetPrincipals()
        {
            //Principal-in-Charge
            StringBuilder builder = this.GetBaseQueryBuilder();
            return this.BuildEntitiesFromSql(builder.Append
                (" WHERE JobTitle LIKE '%Principal%';").ToString());
        }

        #endregion
```

I am not going to worry about the string matching going on in the SQL WHERE clauses of these two methods because that is not my concern right now. This can always be refactored later to get rid of the string references and made to use a more normalized table structure with foreign key relationships.

The GetBaseQuery Method

Here is the `EmployeeRepository` class's override of the `GetBaseQuery` abstract method:

```
        #region GetBaseQuery

        protected override string GetBaseQuery()
        {
            return "SELECT * FROM Employee";
        }

        #endregion
```

This just follows the same Template Method pattern I have shown all along.

The GetBaseWhereClause Method

Again, I am just following the Template Method pattern for implementing the `GetBaseWhereClause` method:

```
#region GetBaseWhereClause

protected override string GetBaseWhereClause()
{
    return " WHERE EmployeeID = {0};";
}

#endregion
```

The Service Class Implementations

The only `Service` classes I have implemented up to this point are all Service classes that live in the domain model layer and are acting as facades to their respective `Repository` interfaces. These `Service` classes are intended to be called directly from the `ViewModel` classes; the idea is that they will greatly simplify access to the domain model operations. In this section, I will cover the `ProjectService` and the `EmployeeService` classes.

The ProjectService Class

The `ProjectService` class is responsible for retrieving and saving `Project` instances, as well as retrieving `MarketSegment` instances:

```
using System;
using System.Collections.Generic;
using SmartCA.Model.Projects;
using SmartCA.Infrastructure.RepositoryFramework;
using SmartCA.Infrastructure;

namespace SmartCA.Model.Projects
{
    public static class ProjectService
    {
        private static IProjectRepository repository;
        private static IUnitOfWork unitOfWork;

        static ProjectService()
        {
            ProjectService.unitOfWork = new UnitOfWork();
            ProjectService.repository =
                RepositoryFactory.GetRepository<IProjectRepository,
                Project>(ProjectService.unitOfWork);
        }

        public static IList<Project> GetAllProjects()
        {
            return ProjectService.repository.FindAll();
        }
```

```
    public static IList<MarketSegment> GetMarketSegments()
    {
        return ProjectService.repository.FindAllMarketSegments();
    }

    public static void SaveProject(Project project)
    {
        ProjectService.repository[project.Key] = project;
        ProjectService.unitOfWork.Commit();
    }
  }
}
```

The first thing to notice about this class is that it is a static class with all static methods. Again, the idea is to make it very easy to use. The next interesting part of the class is its static constructor. This is where the instance to the IProjectRepository is created via the RepositoryFactory. Also note that when the IProjectRepository is created it is injected with a UnitOfWork instance. This is necessary since I will be saving Project instances in this class and want that operation to be wrapped in a transaction.

The rest of the class is just acting as a façade in front of the IProjectRepository instance. The next interesting method is the SaveProject method. Notice how the collection-like functionality of the IProjectRepository instance is utilized by calling the indexer (see Chapter 2 for more information). What's nice about having the indexer is that the RepositoryBase<T> class will figure out whether it is a new Project or an existing one. Also, after updating the IProjectRepository with the newly updated Project instance, the Commit method is called on the UnitOfWork instance to commit the transaction.

The EmployeeService Class

Currently, the only thing that the EmployeeService class does is to wrap the IEmployeeRepository calls for the GetConstructionAdministrators and GetPrincipals methods.

```
using System;
using System.Collections.Generic;
using SmartCA.Infrastructure;
using SmartCA.Infrastructure.RepositoryFramework;

namespace SmartCA.Model.Employees
{
    public static class EmployeeService
    {
        private static IEmployeeRepository repository;
        private static IUnitOfWork unitOfWork;

        static EmployeeService()
        {
            EmployeeService.unitOfWork = new UnitOfWork();
            EmployeeService.repository
                = RepositoryFactory.GetRepository<IEmployeeRepository,
                Employee>(EmployeeService.unitOfWork);
        }

        public static IList<Employee> GetConstructionAdministrators()
```

(continued)

(continued)

```
        {
            return EmployeeService.repository.GetConstructionAdministrators();
        }

        public static IList<Employee> GetPrincipals()
        {
            return EmployeeService.repository.GetPrincipals();
        }
    }
}
```

This code should look very similar to the `ProjectService` class. It literally is acting like a façade for now, but there is plenty of room for it to grow later. Right now, we do not need any additional functionality in it yet.

The Project Information ViewModel Implementation

As I showed in Chapter 2, with the `SelectProjectViewModel` example, the ViewModel class is used for adapting the domain model to the UI, or View.

The ViewModel Class Revisited

Since writing Chapter 2, I went in and did some refactoring on this concept and made an abstract `ViewModel` class for all of the new ViewModel classes to inherit from.

```
using System;
using System.ComponentModel;

namespace SmartCA.Infrastructure.UI
{
    public abstract class ViewModel : INotifyPropertyChanged
    {
        private IView view;
        private DelegateCommand cancelCommand;
        private ObjectState currentObjectState;
        private const string currentObjectStatePropertyName = "CurrentObjectState";

        protected ViewModel()
            : this(null)
        {
        }

        protected ViewModel(IView view)
        {
            this.view = view;
            this.cancelCommand = new DelegateCommand(this.CancelCommandHandler);
            this.currentObjectState = ObjectState.Existing;
        }

        public enum ObjectState
```

```
    {
        New,
        Existing,
        Deleted
    }

    public DelegateCommand CancelCommand
    {
        get { return this.cancelCommand; }
    }

    public ObjectState CurrentObjectState
    {
        get { return this.currentObjectState; }
        set
        {
            if (this.currentObjectState != value)
            {
                this.currentObjectState = value;
                this.OnPropertyChanged(
                    ViewModel.currentObjectStatePropertyName);
            }
        }
    }

    protected virtual void OnPropertyChanged(string propertyName)
    {
        if (this.PropertyChanged != null)
        {
            this.PropertyChanged(this,
                new PropertyChangedEventArgs(propertyName));
        }
    }

    protected virtual void CancelCommandHandler(object sender, EventArgs e)
    {
        this.CloseView();
    }

    protected void CloseView()
    {
        if (this.view != null)
        {
            this.view.Close();
        }
    }

    #region INotifyPropertyChanged Members

    public event PropertyChangedEventHandler PropertyChanged;

    #endregion
    }
}
```

This class implements the INotifyPropertyChanged interface, which tells the WPF UI when certain object properties have changed so that the UI will automatically be updated. Again, this is all part of adapting the domain model to the UI. It also contains properties for a CancelCommand and an ObjectState property, so the View can know whether its domain object is new, deleted, or updated. It can then act appropriately based on those states. I will show an example of this with the ProjectInformationView a little bit later.

The constructor for the ViewModel class takes care of getting a reference to the passed in IView instance, as well as wiring up the CancelCommand's DelegateCommand to the CancelCommandHandler method. This class is very simple, yet it gives me a lot of necessary functionality that I need in all of my ViewModel classes.

The ProjectInformationViewModel Class

Now, I can create my ProjectInformationViewModel class and inherit from the new ViewModel abstract class:

```
using System;
using SmartCA.Presentation.Views;
using SmartCA.Model.Projects;
using SmartCA.Application;
using System.Windows.Data;
using SmartCA.Infrastructure.UI;
using System.ComponentModel;
using SmartCA.Model.Employees;
using SmartCA.Model.Companies;

namespace SmartCA.Presentation.ViewModels
{
    public class ProjectInformationViewModel : ViewModel
    {
        private static class Constants
        {
            public const string CurrentProjectPropertyName = "CurrentProject";
            public const string ProjectAddressPropertyName = "ProjectAddress";
            public const string OwnerHeadquartersAddressPropertyName =
                "ProjectOwnerHeadquartersAddress";
        }

        private Project currentProject;
        private string newProjectNumber;
        private string newProjectName;
        private MutableAddress projectAddress;
        private MutableAddress projectOwnerHeadquartersAddress;
        private CollectionView owners;
        private CollectionView marketSegments;
        private CollectionView constructionAdministrators;
        private CollectionView principals;
        private DelegateCommand saveCommand;
        private DelegateCommand newCommand;

        public ProjectInformationViewModel()
            : this(null)
```

```
{
}

public ProjectInformationViewModel(IView view)
    : base(view)
{
    this.currentProject = UserSession.CurrentProject;
    this.newProjectNumber = string.Empty;
    this.newProjectName = string.Empty;

    this.projectAddress = new MutableAddress
      {
          Street = this.currentProject.Address.Street,
          City = this.currentProject.Address.City,
          State = this.currentProject.Address.State,
          PostalCode = this.currentProject.Address.PostalCode
      };

    this.projectOwnerHeadquartersAddress = new MutableAddress
      {
          Street = this.currentProject.Owner.HeadquartersAddress.Street,
          City = this.currentProject.Owner.HeadquartersAddress.City,
          State = this.currentProject.Owner.HeadquartersAddress.State,
          PostalCode =
          this.currentProject.Owner.HeadquartersAddress.PostalCode
      };

    this.CurrentObjectState =
        (this.currentProject != null ?
        ObjectState.Existing : ObjectState.New);

    this.owners = new CollectionView(CompanyService.GetOwners());

    this.marketSegments =
        new CollectionView(ProjectService.GetMarketSegments());

    this.constructionAdministrators =
        new CollectionView(
            EmployeeService.GetConstructionAdministrators());

    this.principals = new CollectionView(EmployeeService.GetPrincipals());
    this.saveCommand = new DelegateCommand(this.SaveCommandHandler);
    this.newCommand = new DelegateCommand(this.NewCommandHandler);
}

public Project CurrentProject
{
    get { return this.currentProject; }
}

public string NewProjectNumber
{
    get { return this.newProjectNumber; }
    set
```

(continued)

(continued)

```
        {
            if (this.newProjectNumber != value)
            {
                this.newProjectNumber = value;
                this.VerifyNewProject();
            }
        }
    }

    public string NewProjectName
    {
        get { return this.newProjectName; }
        set
        {
            if (this.newProjectName != value)
            {
                this.newProjectName = value;
                this.VerifyNewProject();
            }
        }
    }

    public MutableAddress ProjectAddress
    {
        get { return this.projectAddress; }
    }

    public MutableAddress ProjectOwnerHeadquartersAddress
    {
        get { return this.projectOwnerHeadquartersAddress; }
    }

    public CollectionView Owners
    {
        get { return this.owners; }
    }

    public CollectionView MarketSegments
    {
        get { return this.marketSegments; }
    }

    public CollectionView ConstructionAdministrators
    {
        get { return this.constructionAdministrators; }
    }

    public CollectionView Principals
```

```
{
    get { return this.principals; }
}

public DelegateCommand SaveCommand
{
    get { return this.saveCommand; }
}

public DelegateCommand NewCommand
{
    get { return this.newCommand; }
}

private void SaveCommandHandler(object sender, EventArgs e)
{
    this.currentProject.Address = this.projectAddress.ToAddress();

    this.currentProject.Owner.HeadquartersAddress =
        this.projectOwnerHeadquartersAddress.ToAddress();

    ProjectService.SaveProject(this.currentProject);

    this.OnPropertyChanged(
        Constants.CurrentProjectPropertyName);

    this.CurrentObjectState = ObjectState.Existing;
}

private void NewCommandHandler(object sender, EventArgs e)
{
    this.currentProject = null;
    this.projectAddress = new MutableAddress();

    this.OnPropertyChanged(
        Constants.ProjectAddressPropertyName);

    this.newProjectNumber = string.Empty;
    this.newProjectName = string.Empty;
    this.projectOwnerHeadquartersAddress = new MutableAddress();

    this.OnPropertyChanged(
        Constants.OwnerHeadquartersAddressPropertyName);

    this.CurrentObjectState = ObjectState.New;

    this.OnPropertyChanged(
        Constants.CurrentProjectPropertyName);
}

private void VerifyNewProject()
```

(continued)

(continued)

```
        {
            if (this.newProjectNumber.Length > 0 &&
                this.newProjectName.Length > 0)
            {
                this.currentProject = new Project(this.newProjectNumber,
                                          this.newProjectName);
                this.OnPropertyChanged(
                    Constants.CurrentProjectPropertyName);
            }
        }
    }
}
```

The Constructors

Notice that there is quite a bit going on in the constructor. Just like the `SelectProjectViewModel` class in Chapter 2, the `ProjectInformationViewModel` class is a `Value` class.

```
public ProjectInformationViewModel()
    : this(null)
{
}

public ProjectInformationViewModel(IView view)
    : base(view)
{
    this.currentProject = UserSession.CurrentProject;
    this.newProjectNumber = string.Empty;
    this.newProjectName = string.Empty;
    this.projectAddress = new MutableAddress
      {
          Street = this.currentProject.Address.Street,
          City = this.currentProject.Address.City,
          State = this.currentProject.Address.State,
          PostalCode = this.currentProject.Address.PostalCode
      };
    this.projectOwnerHeadquartersAddress = new MutableAddress
      {
          Street = this.currentProject.Owner.HeadquartersAddress.Street,
          City = this.currentProject.Owner.HeadquartersAddress.City,
          State = this.currentProject.Owner.HeadquartersAddress.State,
          PostalCode =
          this.currentProject.Owner.HeadquartersAddress.PostalCode
      };
    this.CurrentObjectState =
        (this.currentProject != null ?
        ObjectState.Existing : ObjectState.New);

    this.owners = new CollectionView(CompanyService.GetOwners());

    this.marketSegments =
        new CollectionView(ProjectService.GetMarketSegments());
```

```
        this.constructionAdministrators =
            new CollectionView(
                EmployeeService.GetConstructionAdministrators());

        this.principals = new CollectionView(EmployeeService.GetPrincipals());
        this.saveCommand = new DelegateCommand(this.SaveCommandHandler);
        this.newCommand = new DelegateCommand(this.NewCommandHandler);
    }
```

In the constructor code above, all of the read-only properties of the class are being initialized. Probably the most important one is the `Project` instance coming from the `UserSession`'s `CurrentProject` property, since editing the `Project` instance is the whole point of the form. Remember from Chapter 2 that the `CurrentProject` property of the `UserSession` class gets set when you select a Project from the `SelectProjectView`.

The MutableAddress Class

The next thing that should stand out to you is that I am creating an instance of a `MutableAddress` class. This class is a mutable companion to the immutable `Address` class, and it allows the UI to have two-way binding to its read-write properties.

```
using System;
using SmartCA.Model;

namespace SmartCA.Presentation.ViewModels
{
    public class MutableAddress
    {
        private string street;
        private string city;
        private string state;
        private string postalCode;

        public string Street
        {
            get { return this.street; }
            set { this.street = value; }
        }

        public string City
        {
            get { return this.city; }
            set { this.city = value; }
        }

        public string State
        {
            get { return this.state; }
            set { this.state = value; }
        }

        public string PostalCode
```

(continued)

(continued)

```
        {
            get { return this.postalCode; }
            set { this.postalCode = value; }
        }

        public Address ToAddress()
        {
            return new Address(this.street, this.city,
                    this.state, this.postalCode);
        }
    }
}
```

The purpose of this class is to make it easy for the presentation layer to deal with the `Address` Value object, since binding to and setting properties on an immutable class is impossible (believe me, I learned the hard way about that). As you can see, it is also a Value object, but not immutable. The `ToAddress` method actually creates an instance of the `Address` Value object, and this is what we will be using from the `ProjectInformationViewModel`.

Using the C# 3.0 Initializer Features

Going back to the `ProjectInformationViewModel`, notice how the `MutableAddress` class is being initialized; I am taking advantage of the new C# 3.0 object initializer features:

```
this.projectAddress = new MutableAddress
    {
        Street = this.currentProject.Address.Street,
        City = this.currentProject.Address.City,
        State = this.currentProject.Address.State,
        PostalCode = this.currentProject.Address.PostalCode
    };
this.projectOwnerHeadquartersAddress = new MutableAddress
    {
        Street = this.currentProject.Owner.HeadquartersAddress.Street,
        City = this.currentProject.Owner.HeadquartersAddress.City,
        State = this.currentProject.Owner.HeadquartersAddress.State,
        PostalCode =
        this.currentProject.Owner.HeadquartersAddress.PostalCode
    };
```

Transforming the Model Objects into View Objects

The rest of the `ProjectInformationViewModel` is transforming `IList<T>` types from the domain model into WPF-friendly `CollectionView` objects and setting up a few `DelegateCommand` instances.

```
this.CurrentObjectState =
    (this.currentProject != null ?
    ObjectState.Existing : ObjectState.New);

this.owners = new CollectionView(CompanyService.GetOwners());

this.marketSegments =
```

```
            new CollectionView(ProjectService.GetMarketSegments());

        this.constructionAdministrators =
            new CollectionView(
                EmployeeService.GetConstructionAdministrators());

        this.principals = new CollectionView(EmployeeService.GetPrincipals());
        this.saveCommand = new DelegateCommand(this.SaveCommandHandler);
        this.newCommand = new DelegateCommand(this.NewCommandHandler);
```

Notice how I am taking full advantage of the `Service` classes I have created that stand in front of the Company and Employee repositories.

The Properties

All of the properties in the `ProjectInformationViewModel` class are read-only except for two, `ProjectName` and `ProjectNumber`. These properties are actually taking the place of the same properties on the `Project` class, kind of like what I did with the `MutableAddress` class shown earlier.

```csharp
public string NewProjectNumber
{
    get { return this.newProjectNumber; }
    set
    {
        if (this.newProjectNumber != value)
        {
            this.newProjectNumber = value;
            this.VerifyNewProject();
        }
    }
}

public string NewProjectName
{
    get { return this.newProjectName; }
    set
    {
        if (this.newProjectName != value)
        {
            this.newProjectName = value;
            this.VerifyNewProject();
        }
    }
}
```

The setters for these two properties both call the `VerifyNewProject` method, and this method checks to make sure that there is both a valid `ProjectNumber` value set and a valid `ProjectName` value set:

```
private void VerifyNewProject()
{
    if (this.newProjectNumber.Length > 0 &&
        this.newProjectName.Length > 0)
    {
        this.currentProject = new Project(this.newProjectNumber,
                                this.newProjectName);
        this.OnPropertyChanged(
            ProjectInformationViewModel.currentProjectPropertyName);
    }
}
```

If the validation passes, it then sets the `CurrentProject` property value of the `ProjectInformationViewModel` class to an instance of a new `Project` class, passing in the two values to the `Project` constructor. Then, in order to signal the UI to refresh, it raises the `PropertyChanged` event. In the next section, you will see how I deal with this functionality in the UI in order to change the display when a new Project is created.

The Project Information View Implementation

The View that is associated with the `ProjectInformationViewModel`, the `ProjectInformationView` class (which consists of XAML plus code-behind), is very similar to the `SelectProjectView` class, in that it has very little code behind in it:

```
using System;
using System.Windows;
using SmartCA.Presentation.ViewModels;
using SmartCA.Infrastructure.UI;

namespace SmartCA.Presentation.Views
{
 public partial class ProjectInformationView : Window, IView
    {
        public ProjectInformationView()
        {
            this.InitializeComponent();
            this.DataContext = new ProjectInformationViewModel(this);
        }
    }
}
```

In fact it is almost identical to the code in the `SelectProjectView` class, except that it initializes the `DataContext` of the View with a `ProjectInformationViewModel` instead of a `SelectProjectViewModel`. The XAML for the form is fairly complex, so first I want to show what the form looks like at run time. Then, you can get a better picture of what I am building, as shown in Figure 3.9.

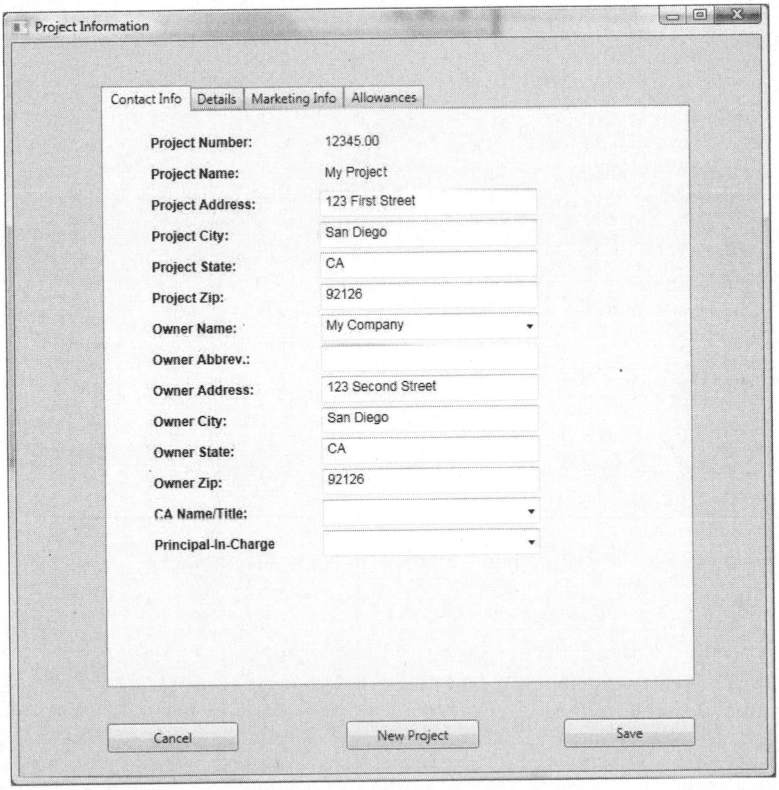

Figure 3.9: The Project Information View

As you can see, it utilizes a tabbed view in order to take better advantage of the screen real estate. Also, notice that the Project Number and Project Name fields are displayed with a label instead of a textbox, thus indicating that they are read-only fields. In this instance of the form, the two fields are bound to the `ProjectNumber` and `ProjectName` properties of the `ProjectInformationViewModel`'s `CurrentProject` property (which is an instance of the `Project` domain object), but when I click on the New Project button, you will see that they both change into textboxes in order to support adding a new Project (see Figure 3.10).

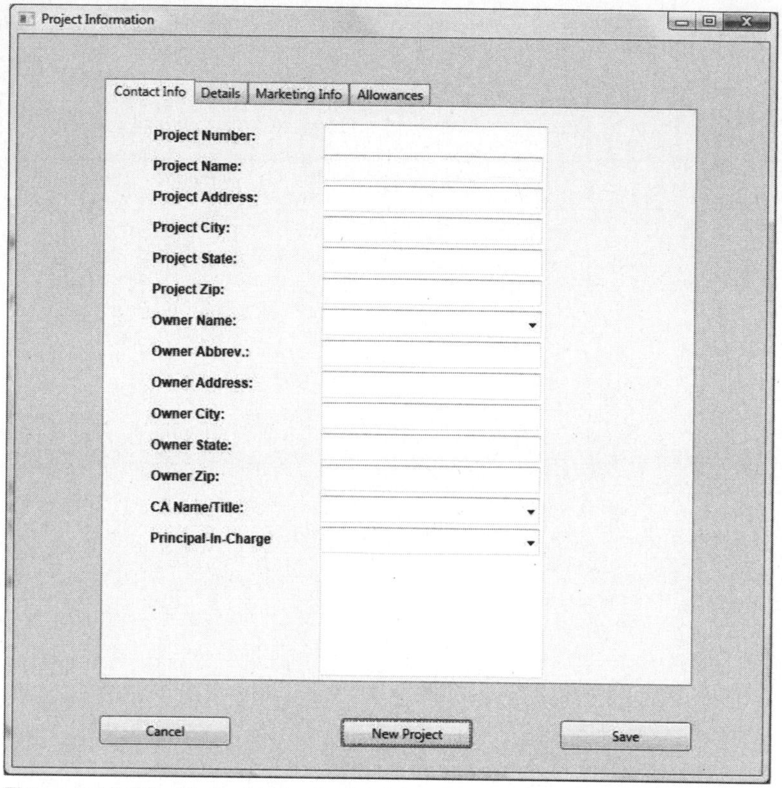

Figure 3.10: The Project Information View for a new Project

This is all made possible through the ProjectInformationViewModel and the XAML of the ProjectInformationView. Specifically, I am using a data template with a data trigger element embedded inside of it, which is bound to properties in the ProjectInformationViewModel.

```
<DataTemplate x:Key="projectNameAndNumber">
<Grid>

        <Label Margin="35,13.04,0,0" Content="Project Number:"
                Style="{StaticResource boldLabelStyle}"/>

        <Label Margin="195,13.04,131,0"
                Content="{Binding Path=CurrentProject.Number}"
                x:Name="projectNumber"
                Style="{StaticResource baseLabelStyle}"/>

        <TextBox Margin="195,13.04,131,0" Visibility="Hidden"
                Text="{Binding Path=NewProjectNumber}"
                x:Name="newProjectNumber"/>
```

```xml
                            <Label Margin="35,41.04,0,0" Content="Project Name:"
                                   Style="{StaticResource boldLabelStyle}"/>

                            <Label Margin="195,41.04,0,0"
                                   Content="{Binding Path=CurrentProject.Name}"
                                   x:Name="projectName"
                                   Style="{StaticResource baseLabelStyle}"/>

                            <TextBox Margin="195,41.04,0,0" Visibility="Hidden"
                                   x:Name="newProjectName"
                                   Text="{Binding Path=NewProjectName}"
                                   Style="{StaticResource baseTextBoxStyle}"/>

                    </Grid>
                    <DataTemplate.Triggers>
                            <DataTrigger Binding="{Binding Path=CurrentObjectState}"
                                   Value="New">

                                    <Setter Property="Visibility" Value="Visible"
                                            TargetName="newProjectNumber" />

                                    <Setter Property="Visibility" Value="Visible"
                                            TargetName="newProjectName" />

                                    <Setter Property="Visibility" Value="Hidden"
                                            TargetName="projectNumber" />

                                    <Setter Property="Visibility" Value="Hidden"
                                            TargetName="projectName" />

                            </DataTrigger>
                    </DataTemplate.Triggers>
```

The data trigger is actually listening for changes to the `CurrentObjectState` property in the `ProjectInformationViewModel`. Based upon the value of that property it either shows textboxes or labels for the Project Name and Project Number fields. Also cool is how this data template is integrated into the rest of the XAML for the tab control:

```xml
    <Grid x:Name="LayoutRoot">
            <TabControl Margin="80,40,64,80" IsSynchronizedWithCurrentItem="True">
                    <TabItem Header="Contact Info">
                            <Grid>
                                    <ContentControl Content="{Binding}"
    ContentTemplate="{StaticResource projectNameAndNumber}"/>
```

All I have to do is place the name of the data template into the `ContentTemplate` attribute of a `ContentControl` element to make it show up in the right place. Setting the `Content` attribute value to `{Binding}` means that the data binding will honor what binding paths I have already set in the `projectNameAndNumber` data template.

I promised earlier to show how I was going to deal with the `Address` Value objects in the XAML code, so here it goes. I already showed how I am handling this in the `ProjectInformationViewModel`, so now it is time to show it in the XAML:

```xml
<Label Margin="35,69.04,0,0" Content="Project Address:"
    Style="{StaticResource boldLabelStyle}"/>

<TextBox Margin="195,69.15,0,0"
    Text="{Binding Path=ProjectAddress.Street}"
    Style="{StaticResource baseTextBoxStyle}"/>

<Label Margin="35,97.04,0,0" Content="Project City:"
    Style="{StaticResource boldLabelStyle}"/>

<TextBox Margin="195,97.15,0,0"
    Text="{Binding Path=ProjectAddress.City}"
    Style="{StaticResource baseTextBoxStyle}"/>

<Label Margin="35,125.04,0,0" Content="Project State:"
    Style="{StaticResource boldLabelStyle}"/>

<TextBox Margin="195,125.15,0,0"
    Text="{Binding Path=ProjectAddress.State}"
    Style="{StaticResource baseTextBoxStyle}"/>

<Label Margin="35,153.04,0,0" Content="Project Zip:"
    Style="{StaticResource boldLabelStyle}"/>

<TextBox Margin="195,153.15,0,0"
    Text="{Binding Path=ProjectAddress.PostalCode}"
    Style="{StaticResource baseTextBoxStyle}"/>
```

The way this works is that I am not actually binding to the `CurrentProject` property of the `ProjectInformationViewModel`; instead I am binding to the properties of the `ProjectAddress` property of the `ProjectInformationViewModel`. Remember, the `ProjectAddress` property is actually an instance of the `MutableAddress` type, so I can change the properties through data binding. The code inside of the `ProjectInformationViewModel` translates this into my immutable `Address` Value object, and the data going into the `Address` Value object's constructor is validated inside of the constructor in order to make sure that I am entering a valid address.

I love the fact that I can bind to my ViewModel and get the type of functionality that I just showed in these examples without having to write any procedural code in my View!

For the sake of brevity, I am not going to show all of the XAML code for the `ProjectInformationView`; there is just too much. There is nothing really special going on with the rest of it; it is the same pattern as I showed in Chapter 2 with the `SelectProjectView` XAML.

Summary

The end result in the UI is not that spectacular, but I certainly covered a lot of ground in getting there. In this chapter, I first defined and modeled all of the objects that make up what a Project is and then started analyzing the classes further in order to define the Aggregate Boundaries. Once the Aggregate Boundaries were defined, the Aggregate Roots were chosen, and then I defined what the various repositories were for the Aggregates. After the repositories were designed and implemented, I then designed and implemented the ViewModel and the View for the use case scenario of editing Projects. I know it may not sound like much, but I actually wrote a lot of code and refactored a lot of code in the process of getting to where I am now. The rest of the way should be well-paved for code reuse in the SmartCA application.

4

Companies and Contacts

Last chapter I showed how both Companies and Contacts were part of the Project Aggregate. Since the focus was on the Project Aggregate, not much was done with these two Entities. This chapter, I will dive in and take a deeper look at the Company and Contact Aggregates, and I will show how they relate to the Project Aggregate.

The Problem

One of the problems with the legacy application is that it does not handle tracking Companies, Contacts, and their associated Addresses very well. The current system does not allow multiple Addresses per Company or Contact, and as a result the users are often entering the same Companies and Contacts into the system as duplicate records in order to show a different Address for the Company or Contact.

With that being said, it sounds like a database issue of having denormalized data. It is not the point of this book to dwell on the database design; I believe that the focus of the problem needs to be on the domain model. If the domain model is designed properly, it can handle this problem. Remember, one of the tenets of Domain-Driven Design, which I discussed in Chapter 2, is *persistence ignorance*. Therefore, the application's data store could be a text file for all I care, because it is abstracted away by the Repository Framework.

The Design

In the SmartCA domain, the purpose of a Project is to bring together and manage all of the people involved in the construction process. In the next few sections, I will be designing the domain model, determining the Project Aggregate and its boundaries, and designing the repository for Projects.

Designing the Domain Model

Companies and Contacts are extremely important in the SmartCA domain, as they ensure that the right construction documents get to the right people in a timely manner. There is a slight distinction between a Contact and a ProjectContact. A ProjectContact is a Contact that happens to be part of a Project, whereas a Contact may or may not be on a Project.

Companies and Contacts both have multiple Addresses, but Companies also must have one of their Addresses designated as their headquarters address. Figure 4.1 is a diagram showing the relationships between Companies, Contacts, ProjectContacts, and Addresses.

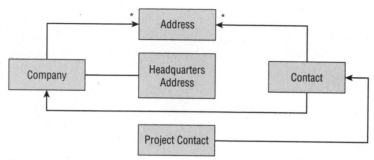

Figure 4.1: Company and Contact Aggregates.

Each contact belongs to a single Company, but people move around, and therefore Contacts often change companies over the course of time. You may notice that in this diagram that a ProjectContact contains a Contact, but does not inherit from a Contact. This is purely my preference to stick with the Gang-of-Four advice by favoring composition over inheritance.

> *The Gang-of-Four, also known as GoF, refers to the four authors who wrote the classic software-engineering book* Design Patterns: Elements of Reusable Object-Oriented Software. *The book's authors are Erich Gamma, Richard Helm, Ralph Johnson, and John Vlissides.*

Defining the Company and Contact Aggregates

Even though the Contact class maintains a relationship to the Company class, both the Company class and the Contact class are the roots of their own Aggregates, with both containing instances of the Address Value class. ProjectContact is not the root of an aggregate; it is an Entity, but it actually belongs to the Project Aggregate (see Figure 4.2).

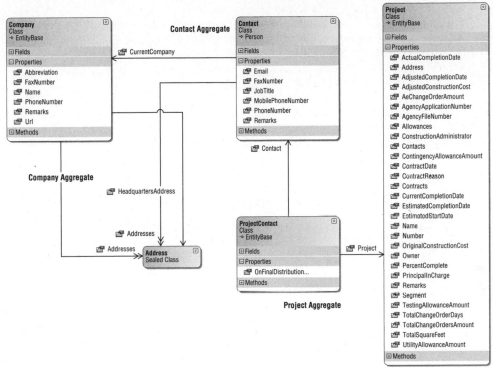

Figure 4.2: Classes composing the Company and Contact Aggregates.

Defining the Aggregate Boundaries

As mentioned before, both the Company and Contact Aggregates share the Address class (see Figure 4.3). Since the Contact class has a Company property, there are two ways to get to a particular company. The first way is to go to the Company Aggregate, and the second way is to go to the Contact Aggregate, navigate to a particular Contact, and then from the Contact navigate to a Company via the CurrentCompany property.

The third Aggregate in the figure is one I have already shown, the Project Aggregate. This time around, I have refactored the domain model to include the ProjectContact class as part of the Project Aggregate and have defined its relationship with the Contact Aggregate to be one of composition.

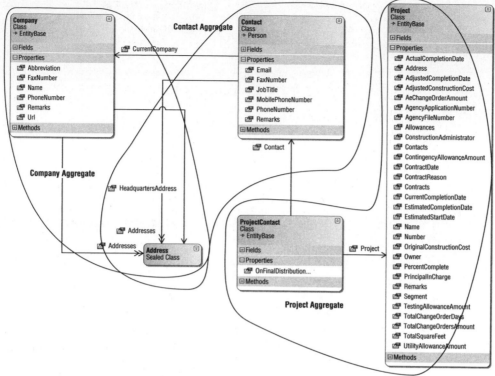

Figure 4.3: The Company and Contact Aggregate boundaries.

Designing the Repositories

Following the one repository per Aggregate rule, there are three repositories to look at in this chapter, the `CompanyRepository`, the `ContactRepository`, and last a revised `ProjectRepository`. Figure 4.4 shows the company and contact repositories.

I did not show the Project Aggregate Repository classes since they are still the same, they will just have some new behavior added to them.

The ICompanyRepository Interface

The `ICompanyRepository` interface is the interface to instances of Company Repositories. Because of the previous refactoring to `IRepository` and `SqlCeRepositoryBase<T>`, the `ICompanyRepository` is currently empty. Here is the `ICompanyRepository` interface:

```
using System;
using SmartCA.Infrastructure.RepositoryFramework;

namespace SmartCA.Model.Companies
{
    public interface ICompanyRepository : IRepository<Company>
    {
    }
}
```

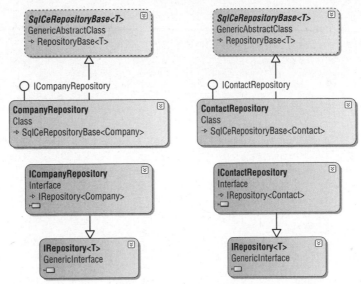

Figure 4.4: The Company and Contact Aggregate Repositories.

The IContactRepository Interface

Just like the ICompanyRepository interface, the IContactRepository interface is also empty. Here is the IContactRepository interface:

```
using System;
using SmartCA.Infrastructure.RepositoryFramework;

namespace SmartCA.Model.Companies
{
    public interface IContactRepository : IRepository<Contact>
    {
    }
}
```

The IProjectRepository Interface Revisited

The IProjectRepository interface has a new method added to it in order to support ProjectContacts:

```
using System;
using System.Collections.Generic;
using SmartCA.Infrastructure.RepositoryFramework;

namespace SmartCA.Model.Projects
{
    public interface IProjectRepository : IRepository<Project>
```

(continued)

113

(continued)

```
    {
        IList<Project> FindBy(IList<MarketSegment> segments, bool completed);
        Project FindBy(string projectNumber);
        IList<MarketSegment> FindAllMarketSegments();
        void SaveContact(ProjectContact contact);

    }
}
```

The new method added is `SaveContact`, which takes an instance of the `ProjectContact` class as its argument. You may be wondering where a `FindProjectContacts` method is, but the fact that `ProjectContact` is not an Aggregate Root and is part of the Project Aggregate means that I must traverse to `ProjectContact` instances from the Project Entity root. This is because the `ProjectContact` class is just an Entity in the Project Aggregate; it is not its own Aggregate Root.

Writing the Unit Tests

Just as in the last chapter, before implementing the solution for managing Companies and Contacts, I am first going to write some unit tests of what I expect of the Company and Contact Repository implementations. It is important to remember that these tests will compile correctly, but they will also fail when run, and that is what I expect. They will pass once I write the code for the Repository implementations in the Solution section.

The ICompanyRepository Unit Tests

I have already created the `CompanyRepositoryTest` class for the `ICompanyRepository` unit tests. I am not going to go over the steps of creating this class, as I covered that in Chapter 3. I am not going to show how I created the instance of the `ICompanyRepository` interface either, as that is explained in the previous chapter.

Since the `ICompanyRepository` interface has no methods in it, and since it does extend the `IRepository<Company>` interface, I am going to test the methods from the `IRepository<Company>` interface.

The FindByKeyTest Method

The purpose of this test is to verify that I can query the `IProjectRepository` interface for all Projects that match the given Market Segments and have not completed.

```
/// <summary>
///A test for FindBy(object key)
///</summary>
[DeploymentItem("SmartCA.sdf"), TestMethod()]
public void FindByKeyTest()
{
    // Set the Key value
    object key = "8b6a05be-6106-45fb-b6cc-b03cfa5ab74b";
```

```
            // Find the Company
            Company company = this.repository.FindBy(key);

            // Verify the Company's name
            Assert.AreEqual("My Company", company.Name);
    }
```

The method first starts out by initializing a unique identifier string value. It then passes that value to the ICompanyRepository interface instance in order to retrieve a Company with that particular Key value. Once the Company instance is returned from the repository, the Company's name is validated.

The FindAllTest Method

The purpose of the FindAllTest method is to validate that the correct number of Company instances have been returned by the Company Repository:

```
/// <summary>
///A test for FindAll()
///</summary>
[DeploymentItem("SmartCA.sdf"), TestMethod()]
public void FindAllTest()
{
    // Get all of the Companies
    IList<Company> companies = this.repository.FindAll();

    // Make sure there are two
    Assert.AreEqual(2, companies.Count);
}
```

This method is pretty short; it simply gets all of the Company instances and checks the total count. What is not seen here is that when the ICompanyRepository interface is implemented, it will test the ability of the repository to map the data correctly from the data store into Company instances. Later in the chapter, when the ICompanyRepository interface is implemented, I can run the test again to see what I messed up when the test fails.

The AddTest Method

The purpose of the AddTest method is to test adding a new Company to the Company Repository:

```
/// <summary>
///A test for Add(Company item)
///</summary>
[DeploymentItem("SmartCA.sdf"), TestMethod()]
public void AddTest()
{
    // Create a new Company and give it a fake name
    Company company = new Company();
    company.Name = "My Test Company";

    // Add the Company to the Repository
    this.repository.Add(company);
```

(continued)

(continued)

```
                // Commit the transaction
                this.unitOfWork.Commit();

                // Reload the Company and verify it's name
                Company savedCompany = this.repository.FindBy(company.Key);
                Assert.AreEqual("My Test Company", savedCompany.Name);

                // Clean up
                this.repository.Remove(savedCompany);
                this.unitOfWork.Commit();
        }
```

This test is a little bit more involved than the previous tests. It starts out by instantiating a new `Company` instance and setting its `Name` property. It then tries to add the Company to the repository, and then commits the transaction by calling the `Commit` method on the `IUnitOfWork` instance.

The `Commit` method is important because that method calls back into the Company Repository to tell it to write the Company's data to the data store.

Once the Company has been saved, it is then reloaded and the Company's `Name` property is checked to verify that the `Add` and `Commit` methods worked properly. The last task that the method needs to perform is to remove the Company. Removing the Company that was just created leaves the data store in the same state as it was in before the method started, which is important for the rest of the tests that may depend on a known state of the data store. Otherwise, some of the other tests may fail because there was data in the data store that was not expected.

The UpdateTest Method

The purpose of the `UpdateTest` method is to find a Company and update it with a different name, and then verify that the change was persisted properly:

```
/// <summary>
///A test for Updating a Company
///</summary>
[DeploymentItem("SmartCA.sdf"), TestMethod()]
public void UpdateTest()
{
    // Set the Key value
    object key = "59427e22-0c9e-4821-95d6-9c9f541bf37a";

    // Find the Company
    Company company = this.repository.FindBy(key);

    // Change the Company's Name
    company.Name = "My Updated Company";

    // Update the Repository
    this.repository[company.Key] = company;
```

```
        // Commit the transaction
        this.unitOfWork.Commit();

        // Verify that the change was saved
        Company savedCompany = this.repository.FindBy(company.Key);
        Assert.AreEqual("My Updated Company", savedCompany.Name);
    }
```

The first few lines of the method should look familiar; I am just using the same Key value I used before to find a Company. Once I have found the Company, I then change its Name property, and then call the indexer method of the ICompanyRepository. After the call to the indexer, I use the IUnitOfWork interface to commit the transaction. Last, I verify that the change actually made it to the data store by reloading the same Company and checking to see whether its Name property value is the same one that I just assigned earlier in the method.

The RemoveTest Method

The purpose of the RemoveTest method is to test the process of removing a Company from the data store:

```
/// <summary>
///A test for Remove(Company item)
///</summary>
[DeploymentItem("SmartCA.sdf"), TestMethod()]
public void RemoveTest()
{
    // Set the Key value
    object key = "8b6a05be-6106-45fb-b6cc-b03cfa5ab74b";

    // Find the Company
    Company company = this.repository.FindBy(key);

    // Remove the Company from the Repository
    this.repository.Remove(company);

    // Commit the transaction
    this.unitOfWork.Commit();

    // Verify that there is now one less Company in the data store
    IList<Company> companies = this.repository.FindAll();
    Assert.AreEqual(1, companies.Count);
}
```

Again, the first few lines of the method should look familiar; I am just using the same Key value I used before to find a Company. Once I have found the Company, I remove it from the repository. After removing it from the repository, I then use the IUnitOfWork interface to commit the transaction. Last, I verify that the change actually made it to the data store by using the repository to find all of the Company instances and making sure that there is now one fewer Company than before.

The IContactRepository Unit Tests

Since the IContactRepository is identical to the ICompanyRepository in that it does not implement any new methods, I have decided not to show any of the unit test code for it. Its test class will have all of the exact same methods tested as the ICompanyRepository test class, only the Entity being passed around will be a Contact instead of a Company.

The IProjectRepository Unit Test

Since the IProjectRepository has been refactored with a new method, the SaveContact method, I will only unit test that method.

I have created a new method in the ProjectRepositoryTest class called SaveProjectContactTest. The purpose of the method is to test creating a new ProjectContact instance that is then saved to the IProjectRepository instance.

```
/// <summary>
///A test for SaveContact(ProjectContact contact)
///</summary>
[DeploymentItem("SmartCA.sdf"), TestMethod()]
public void SaveProjectContactTest()
{
    // The Project Number
    string projectNumber = "12345.00";

    // Try to get the Project
    Project project = this.repository.FindBy(projectNumber);

    // Get the old count of Project Contacts
    int oldCount = project.Contacts.Count;

    // Get a Contact
    IContactRepository contactRepository =
        RepositoryFactory.GetRepository<IContactRepository, Contact>();
    object contactKey = "cae9eb86-5a86-4965-9744-18326fd56a3b";
    Contact contact = contactRepository.FindBy(contactKey);

    // Create a Project Contact
    ProjectContact projectContact = new ProjectContact(project,
        Guid.NewGuid(), contact);

    // Save the Project Contact
    this.repository.SaveContact(projectContact);

    // Commit the transaction
    this.unitOfWork.Commit();

    // Reload the the Project
    Project updatedProject = this.repository.FindBy("12345.00");

    // Verify that there is a new ProjectContact now
    Assert.AreEqual(oldCount, updatedProject.Contacts.Count - 1);
}
```

The first part of the code should remind you of the test code from the last chapter, where I tested finding a Project by a `Project Number` value. The next step is to get the count of `ProjectContact` instances the Project currently contains. Next, I use the `IContactRepository` interface instance to find a Contact, and then I use that contact to create an instance of the `ProjectContact` class. Once I have the new `ProjectContact` instance, I then save it to the `IProjectRepository` instance and commit the transaction on the `IUnitOfWork` instance.

Now that the `ProjectContact` instance is saved, I will reload the same Project from the repository, and make sure that the new count of `ProjectContact` instances is one more than the old count.

The Solution

The design is in place for the Company and Contact domain models, the Company and Contact Aggregates have been defined and their boundaries have been determined, and the repositories have been designed with their associated tests. It is time to start the code implementation. In this section, I will be implementing these designs, as well as implementing the ViewModel and the View for Companies and Contacts.

The Company Class

Like the `Project` class, the `Company` class does not have any behavior yet. I have already shown the `Company` class in Chapter 3, but now I have added some more properties to it:

```
using System;
using SmartCA.Infrastructure.DomainBase;
using System.Collections.Generic;

namespace SmartCA.Model.Companies
{
    public class Company : EntityBase
    {
        private string name;
        private string abbreviation;
        private Address headquartersAddress;
        private List<Address> addresses;
        private string phoneNumber;
        private string faxNumber;
        private string url;
        private string remarks;

        public Company()
            : this(null)
        {
        }

        public Company(object key)
            : base(key)
```

(continued)

(continued)

```csharp
    {
        this.name = string.Empty;
        this.abbreviation = string.Empty;
        this.headquartersAddress = null;
        this.addresses = new List<Address>();
        this.phoneNumber = string.Empty;
        this.faxNumber = string.Empty;
        this.url = string.Empty;
        this.remarks = string.Empty;
    }

    public string Name
    {
        get { return this.name; }
        set { this.name = value; }
    }

    public string Abbreviation
    {
        get { return this.abbreviation; }
        set { this.abbreviation = value; }
    }

    public Address HeadquartersAddress
    {
        get { return this.headquartersAddress; }
        set
        {
            if (this.headquartersAddress != value)
            {
                this.headquartersAddress = value;
                if (!this.addresses.Contains(value))
                {
                    this.addresses.Add(value);
                }
            }
        }
    }

    public IList<Address> Addresses
    {
        get { return this.addresses; }
    }

    public string PhoneNumber
    {
        get { return this.phoneNumber; }
        set { this.phoneNumber = value; }
    }

    public string FaxNumber
```

```
    {
        get { return this.faxNumber; }
        set { this.faxNumber = value; }
    }

    public string Url
    {
        get { return this.url; }
        set { this.url = value; }
    }

    public string Remarks
    {
        get { return this.remarks; }
        set { this.remarks = value; }
    }
  }
}
```

The interesting thing to note about the Company class is its HeadquartersAddress property. The address is really just one of its addresses that has been deemed as a headquarters address. In the setter for this property, I included logic to make sure that the value of the Address being passed in is actually contained in the internal list of Addresses. If it is not present, then the Address is added to the collection. The rest of the properties of the Company class are all very straightforward.

I am not going to go into the detail of the constructors of the Company class; they follow the pattern of having two constructors, a default constructor and a parameterized constructor containing the Key value for the instance. Again, as with the Project class before, this is because sometimes I may need to load an existing Company from a data store and sometimes I may be creating a new Company that does not yet exist in the data store.

The Contact Class

Aside from the names of its properties, the Contact class is almost completely the same as the Company class:

```
using System;
using System.Collections.Generic;
using System.Text;
using SmartCA.Model.Companies;

namespace SmartCA.Model.Contacts
{
    public class Contact : Person
    {
        private string jobTitle;
        private string email;
        private string phoneNumber;
        private string mobilePhoneNumber;
        private string faxNumber;
        private string remarks;
```

(continued)

121

(continued)

```csharp
        private Company currentCompany;
        private IList<Address> addresses;

        public Contact()
            : this(null)
        {
        }

        public Contact(object key)
            : this(key, null, null)
        {
        }

        public Contact(object key, string firstName, string lastName)
            : base(key, firstName, lastName)
        {
            this.jobTitle = string.Empty;
            this.email = string.Empty;
            this.phoneNumber = string.Empty;
            this.mobilePhoneNumber = string.Empty;
            this.faxNumber = string.Empty;
            this.remarks = string.Empty;
            this.currentCompany = null;
            this.addresses = new List<Address>();
        }

        public string JobTitle
        {
            get { return this.jobTitle; }
            set { this.jobTitle = value; }
        }

        public string Email
        {
            get { return this.email; }
            set { this.email = value; }
        }

        public string PhoneNumber
        {
            get { return this.phoneNumber; }
            set { this.phoneNumber = value; }
        }

        public string MobilePhoneNumber
        {
            get { return this.mobilePhoneNumber; }
            set { this.mobilePhoneNumber = value; }
        }
```

```
        public string FaxNumber
        {
            get { return this.faxNumber; }
            set { this.faxNumber = value; }
        }

        public string Remarks
        {
            get { return this.remarks; }
            set { this.remarks = value; }
        }

        public Company CurrentCompany
        {
            get { return this.currentCompany; }
            set { this.currentCompany = value; }
        }

        public IList<Address> Addresses
        {
            get { return this.addresses; }
        }
    }
}
```

The main difference between the `Contact` and `Company` classes is that the `Contact` class's `CurrentCompany` property contains a reference to a `Company` instance. The `Company` class, however, does not contain a reference to any `Contact` instances.

The ProjectContact Class

As I mentioned before, the `ProjectContact` class actually contains a `Contact` instance and then adds one other property to it to distinguish it as a `ProjectContact`:

```
using System;
using SmartCA.Model.Contacts;
using SmartCA.Infrastructure.DomainBase;

namespace SmartCA.Model.Projects
{
    public class ProjectContact : EntityBase
    {
        private Project project;
        private bool onFinalDistributionList;
        private Contact contact;

        public ProjectContact(Project project, object key,
            Contact contact) : base(key)
```

(continued)

(continued)

```
        {
            this.project = project;
            this.contact = contact;
            this.onFinalDistributionList = false;
        }

        public Project Project
        {
            get { return this.project; }
        }

        public Contact Contact
        {
            get { return this.contact; }
        }

        public bool OnFinalDistributionList
        {
            get { return this.onFinalDistributionList; }
            set { this.onFinalDistributionList = value; }
        }
    }
}
```

In fact, you cannot create an instance of the `ProjectContact` class without passing an instance of a `Contact` in its constructor, as well as a `Project` instance and a `Key` value. The property that distinguishes the `ProjectContact` class from the `Contact` class is the `OnFinalDistributionList` property. This property is used to designate which Contacts in a Project are to receive copies of documents for things like Submittal Transmittals, Change Orders, and so on once they become final. The `ProjectContact` class also maintains a reference to the Project to which it belongs via the `Project` property, as well as what Contact it contains via its `Contact` property.

The Repository Implementations

In this section, I will be writing the code for the Company and Contact Repositories, as well as refactoring part of the Project Repository.

The Company Repository

To implement the concrete `CompanyRepository` class, just like the other Repository implementations before, I inherit from the `SqlCeRepositoryBase<T>` class, and also implement the `ICompanyRepository` interface:

```
namespace SmartCA.Infrastructure.Repositories
{
    public class CompanyRepository : SqlCeRepositoryBase<Company>,
        ICompanyRepository
    {
...
```

Public Constructors

Just like the `ProjectRepository` class, there are also two public constructors for the `CompanyRepository` class:

```
#region Public Constructors

public CompanyRepository()
    : this(null)
{
}

public CompanyRepository(IUnitOfWork unitOfWork)
    : base(unitOfWork)
{
}

#endregion
```

All Repository implementations will follow this same pattern.

BuildChildCallbacks

Now that I have finished going over the `IProjectRepository` implementation, it is time to go back to how the `Project` class is actually built. If you recall, this functionality was moved up into the base class, `SqlCeRepositoryBase<T>`, but it does make use of the Template Method pattern, and `BuildChildCallbacks` is one of those abstract template methods that the `ProjectRepository` must implement.

```
#region BuildChildCallbacks

protected override void BuildChildCallbacks()
{
    this.ChildCallbacks.Add("addresses",
        delegate(Company company, object childKeyName)
        {
            this.AppendAddresses(company);
        });
}

#endregion
```

The AppendAddresses Callback

The only entry made in the `ChildCallbacks` dictionary was for the `AppendAddresses` method. This method queries the CompanyAddress table to get the list of addresses for the Company:

```
private void AppendAddresses(Company company)
{
    string sql = string.Format
        ("SELECT * FROM CompanyAddress WHERE CompanyID = '{0}'",
        company.Key);
    using (IDataReader reader = this.ExecuteReader(sql))
```

(continued)

(continued)

```
        {
            Address address = null;
            while (reader.Read())
            {
                address = AddressFactory.BuildAddress(reader);
                company.Addresses.Add(address);
                if (CompanyFactory.IsHeadquartersAddress(reader))
                {
                    company.HeadquartersAddress = address;
                }
            }
        }
    }
```

This method is using the `AddressFactory` static class to build the `Address` instance from the `IDataReader` instance using static field mappings. It then asks the `CompanyFactory` class whether the data for the Address contained in the `IDataReader` contains a Headquarters Address.

```
internal static bool IsHeadquartersAddress(IDataReader reader)
{
    return DataHelper.GetBoolean(reader[FieldNames.IsHeadquarters]);
}
```

If the data does contain a Headquarters Address, the method then sets the `HeadquartersAddress` property of the `Company` instance.

GetBaseQuery

The next abstract Template Method that the `SqlCeRepositoryBase<T>` calls is the `GetBaseQueryMethod`. Here is the `CompanyRepository` class's override of the abstract method:

```
#region GetBaseQuery

protected override string GetBaseQuery()
{
    return "SELECT * FROM Company";
}

#endregion
```

This simply returns the SQL statement for the Company Aggregate. Again, just as I mentioned before, by abstracting this, the `SqlCeRepositryBase<T>` class is able to pull in the two `"FindBy"` methods from the `IRepository<T>` interface, thereby eliminating the code from `CompanyRepository`.

GetBaseWhereClause

This is very similar to the `GetBaseQuery` method just shown, only this time the string returned is just a formatted SQL WHERE clause for the Company Aggregate with a placeholder for the `CompanyID` field:

```
#region GetBaseWhereClause

protected override string GetBaseWhereClause()
{
    return " WHERE CompanyID = '{0}';";
}

#endregion
```

The `SqlCeRepositoryBase<T>` class handles filling in the `CompanyID` placeholder at runtime.

Unit of Work Implementation

As I demonstrated in Chapter 3, in order to implement the Repository Framework's Unit of Work, I only need to override three methods, `PersistNewItem(Company item)`, `PersistUpdatedItem(Company item)`, and `PersistDeletedItem(Company item)`. Here is the code for `PersistNewItem`:

```
protected override void PersistNewItem(Company item)
{
    StringBuilder builder = new StringBuilder(100);
    builder.Append(string.Format("INSERT INTO Company
({0},{1},{2},{3},{4},{5},{6}) ",
        CompanyFactory.FieldNames.CompanyId,
        CompanyFactory.FieldNames.CompanyName,
        CompanyFactory.FieldNames.CompanyShortName,
        CompanyFactory.FieldNames.Phone,
        CompanyFactory.FieldNames.Fax,
        CompanyFactory.FieldNames.Url,
        CompanyFactory.FieldNames.Remarks));
    builder.Append(string.Format("VALUES ({0},{1},{2},{3},{4},{5},{6});",
        DataHelper.GetSqlValue(item.Key),
        DataHelper.GetSqlValue(item.Name),
        DataHelper.GetSqlValue(item.Abbreviation),
        DataHelper.GetSqlValue(item.PhoneNumber),
        DataHelper.GetSqlValue(item.FaxNumber),
        DataHelper.GetSqlValue(item.Url),
        DataHelper.GetSqlValue(item.Remarks)));

    this.Database.ExecuteNonQuery(
        this.Database.GetSqlStringCommand(builder.ToString()));

    // Now do the addresses
    this.InsertAddresses(item);
}
```

The code is building up an insert statement composed of the values from the Company instance and then executing the query using the Microsoft Enterprise Library's Database object. After the insert statement has been executed, the Company's addresses are saved to the database via the InsertAddresses method:

```
private void InsertAddresses(Company company)
{
    foreach (Address address in company.Addresses)
    {
        this.InsertAddress(address, company.Key,
            (company.HeadquartersAddress == address));
    }
}
```

InsertAddresses just iterates the Addresses property of the Company instance and calls InsertAddress on each one. InsertAddress then saves the address to the database:

```
private void InsertAddress(Address address, object key,
    bool isHeadquartersAddress)
{
    StringBuilder builder = new StringBuilder(100);
    builder.Append(string.Format("INSERT INTO CompanyAddress
({0},{1},{2},{3},{4},{5}) ",
        CompanyFactory.FieldNames.CompanyId,
        AddressFactory.FieldNames.Street,
        AddressFactory.FieldNames.City,
        AddressFactory.FieldNames.State,
        AddressFactory.FieldNames.PostalCode,
        CompanyFactory.FieldNames.IsHeadquarters));
    builder.Append(string.Format("VALUES ({0},{1},{2},{3},{4},{5});",
        DataHelper.GetSqlValue(key),
        DataHelper.GetSqlValue(address.Street),
        DataHelper.GetSqlValue(address.City),
        DataHelper.GetSqlValue(address.State),
        DataHelper.GetSqlValue(address.PostalCode),
        DataHelper.GetSqlValue(isHeadquartersAddress)));

    this.Database.ExecuteNonQuery(
        this.Database.GetSqlStringCommand(builder.ToString()));
}
```

InsertAddress is also very similar to the first part of PersistNewItem, in that it builds up its insert statement and executes it against the database in the same manner.

PersistUpdatedItem first does an update to the Company table:

```
protected override void PersistUpdatedItem(Company item)
{
    StringBuilder builder = new StringBuilder(100);
    builder.Append("UPDATE Company SET ");

    builder.Append(string.Format("{0} = {1}",
        CompanyFactory.FieldNames.CompanyName,
```

```
                    DataHelper.GetSqlValue(item.Name)));

        builder.Append(string.Format(",{0} = {1}",
            CompanyFactory.FieldNames.CompanyShortName,
            DataHelper.GetSqlValue(item.Abbreviation)));

        builder.Append(string.Format(",{0} = {1}",
            CompanyFactory.FieldNames.Phone,
            DataHelper.GetSqlValue(item.PhoneNumber)));

        builder.Append(string.Format(",{0} = {1}",
            CompanyFactory.FieldNames.Fax,
            DataHelper.GetSqlValue(item.FaxNumber)));

        builder.Append(string.Format(",{0} = {1}",
            CompanyFactory.FieldNames.Url,
            DataHelper.GetSqlValue(item.Url)));

        builder.Append(string.Format(",{0} = {1}",
            CompanyFactory.FieldNames.Remarks,
            DataHelper.GetSqlValue(item.Remarks)));

        builder.Append(" ");
        builder.Append(this.BuildBaseWhereClause(item.Key));

        this.Database.ExecuteNonQuery(
            this.Database.GetSqlStringCommand(builder.ToString()));

        // Now do the addresses

        // First, delete the existing ones
        this.DeleteAddresses(item);

        // Now, add the current ones
        this.InsertAddresses(item);
    }
```

The second part of the method uses `DeleteAddresses` to delete the existing addresses for the Company and then uses the familiar `InsertAddresses` method to add the addresses from the Company's `Addresses` property to the database. `DeleteAddresses` runs a query against the `CompanyAddress` table to remove all entries with a matching `CompanyID` field value:

```
        private void DeleteAddresses(Company company)
        {
            string query = string.Format("DELETE FROM CompanyAddress {0}",
                this.BuildBaseWhereClause(company.Key));
            this.Database.ExecuteNonQuery(
                this.Database.GetSqlStringCommand(query));
        }
```

The last method in `CompanyRepository` to override, `PersistDeletedItem`, follows the same pattern as `DeleteAddresses`:

```csharp
protected override void PersistDeletedItem(Company item)
{
    // Delete the company addresses first
    this.DeleteAddresses(item);

    // Now delete the company
    string query = string.Format("DELETE FROM Company {0}",
        this.BuildBaseWhereClause(item.Key));
    this.Database.ExecuteNonQuery(
        this.Database.GetSqlStringCommand(query));
}
```

This method actually takes advantage of the `DeleteAddresses` method in the first part of its body in order to remove the entries from the `CompanyAddress` table before deleting a row from the `Company` table. The rest of the code in the method should look very familiar as it is building up a standard delete statement for removing a row from the `Company` table and then executing the statement.

The Contact Repository

To implement the concrete `ContactRepository` class, just as before, I inherit from the `SqlCeRepositoryBase<T>` class, and also implement the `IContactRepository` interface:

```csharp
namespace SmartCA.Infrastructure.Repositories
{
    public class ContactRepository : SqlCeRepositoryBase<Contact>,
        IContactRepository
    {
...
```

Public Constructors

The public constructors for the `ContactRepository` class are exactly the same as the `CompanyRepository` class:

```csharp
#region Public Constructors

public ContactRepository()
    : this(null)
{
}

public ContactRepository(IUnitOfWork unitOfWork)
    : base(unitOfWork)
{
}

#endregion
```

GetBaseQuery

Here is the ContactRepository class's override of the GetBaseQuery abstract method:

```
#region GetBaseQuery

protected override string GetBaseQuery()
{
    return "SELECT * FROM Contact";
}

#endregion
```

This just follows the same Template Method pattern I have shown all along.

GetBaseWhereClause

Again, I am just following the Template Method pattern for implementing the GetBaseWhereClause method:

```
#region GetBaseWhereClause

protected override string GetBaseWhereClause()
{
    return " WHERE ContactID = '{0}';";
}

#endregion
```

Unit of Work Implementation

Since the code for the ContactRepository's Unit of Work implementation is almost identical to the CompanyRepository's implementation, I am not going to show it here. It is follows all of the same patterns, so there is nothing new to see with it.

The Refactored Project Repository Implementation

```
    public void SaveContact(ProjectContact contact)
{

        // Get the list of contacts
        List<ProjectContact> contacts =
            new List<ProjectContact>(
                this.FindBy(contact.Project.Key).Contacts);

        if (contacts.Where(c => c.Key.Equals(contact.Key)).Count() > 0)
        {
            // The contact exists, so update it
            this.UnitOfWork.RegisterChanged(contact, this);
        }
        else
        {
            // The contact is new, so add it
            this.UnitOfWork.RegisterAdded(contact, this);
        }
    }
```

The SaveContact method first uses the FindBy method to find the correct Project based on a Project Key property passed in from the ProjectContact argument. Once the Project is found, I then call the Contacts property getter to get the list of ProjectContact instances for the Project. When the list has been obtained, a LINQ query is performed on the list to see if it contains any ProjectContact instances that match that being passed from the method's argument contact argument. To perform the query, I am using a lambda expression (c => c.Key.Equals(contact.Key)) to find the list of ProjectContacts that meet the criteria, and then using the Count method extension on the IEnumerable interface (which List<ProjectContact> implements) to see whether the results are greater than zero. If the results are greater than zero, then I know that the ProjectContact already exists, and I can go ahead and update it. If not, then I know that the ProjectContact is new and needs to be added.

The way that I am handling the actual changes to the data store is by telling the UnitOfWork property of the RepositoryBase<T> instance to register the items as either changed or added. Then, once the Commit method on the IUnitOfWork instance is called, the items will be properly persisted and the transaction will be committed.

Calling the IUnitOfWork instance directly should look strange, since in every other Repository implementation I just had the RepositoryBase<T> class abstract that away for me. This case is different, because I am not dealing with an object that is an Entity Root. I have to tell the IUnitOfWork instance about the Entity explicitly in order for it to be part of the transaction. I also had to refactor a little bit more of the ProjectRepository in order for the transaction to work. Normally, when Commit is called on the IUnitOfWork instance, the IUnitOfWork instance will cycle through all of the entities in its deleted, added, and changed Entity collections, and call the proper Persist* method on each one (e.g., PersistNewItem). In this case, it's a little bit of a challenge because I want to save one of the Project's ProjectContact items, but not the whole entire Project. In the current implementation of the ProjectRepository, if one of the Persist* overrides is called, it will cause an error because it will try to convert a ProjectContact instance into a Project instance. The way around that was to declare the RepositoryBase<T>'s Persist* methods as virtual and override them, thereby effectively bypassing the RepositoryBase<T>'s translation from EntityBase to Project by casting the Entity to the proper type using the T generic parameter. I then exposed the IUnitOfWork instance as a protected property. Here is what I am talking about on RepositoryBase<T>:

```
#region IUnitOfWorkRepository Members

    public virtual void PersistNewItem(EntityBase item)
    {
        this.PersistNewItem((T)item);
    }

    public virtual void PersistUpdatedItem(EntityBase item)
    {
        this.PersistUpdatedItem((T)item);
    }

    public virtual void PersistDeletedItem(EntityBase item)
    {
        this.PersistDeletedItem((T)item);
    }

#endregion
```

```
protected IUnitOfWork UnitOfWork
{
    get { return this.unitOfWork; }
}
```

```
protected abstract void PersistNewItem(T item);
protected abstract void PersistUpdatedItem(T item);
protected abstract void PersistDeletedItem(T item);
```

By overriding the `PersistNewItem(EntityBase item)`, `PersistUpdatedItem(EntityBase item)`, and `PersistDeletedItem(EntityBase item)` methods, the abstract `PersistNewItem(T item)`, `PersistUpdatedItem(T item)`, and `PersistDeletedItem(T item)` methods never get called. I have to call them myself within the `ProjectRepository`:

```
public override void PersistNewItem(EntityBase item)
{
    Project project = item as Project;
    if (project != null)
    {
        this.PersistNewItem(project);
    }
    else
    {
        ProjectContact contact = item as ProjectContact;
        this.PersistNewItem(contact);
    }
}
```

In the example above, I have to test to see what is getting passed in to the method from the `IUnitOfWork` instance; it could either be a `Project` instance or a `ProjectContact` instance. If it is a `Project` instance, then I just call the existing `PersistNewItem(Project item)` method. If it is a `ProjectContact` instance, then I need to call the new method, `PersistNewItem(ProjectContact item)`.

```
protected void PersistNewItem(ProjectContact contact)
{
    StringBuilder builder = new StringBuilder(100);
    builder.Append(string.Format(
        "INSERT INTO ProjectContact ({0},{1},{2}) ",
    ProjectFactory.FieldNames.ProjectId,
    ContactFactory.FieldNames.ContactId,
    ProjectFactory.FieldNames.OnFinalDistributionList));
    builder.Append(string.Format("VALUES ({0},{1},{2});",
        DataHelper.GetSqlValue(contact.Project.Key),
        DataHelper.GetSqlValue(contact.Contact.Key),
        DataHelper.GetSqlValue(contact.OnFinalDistributionList)));
    this.Database.ExecuteNonQuery(
        this.Database.GetSqlStringCommand(builder.ToString()));
}
```

The other methods, `PersistUpdatedItem` *and* `PersistDeletedItem` *follow the exact same pattern so I am not going to show them.*

133

Everything is still cleanly broken out and easy to maintain. The Repository Framework still works and I now have a pattern for saving Entities off of the aggregate root. That wasn't too painful of a refactoring, and it was actually pretty fun.

The Service Class Implementations

In this application, the only Service classes I have implemented up to this point are those that live in the domain model layer and act as facades to their respective Repository interfaces.

The CompanyService Class

The CompanyService class is responsible for retrieving and saving Company instances.

```
using System;
using System.Collections.Generic;
using SmartCA.Infrastructure;
using SmartCA.Infrastructure.RepositoryFramework;

namespace SmartCA.Model.Companies
{
    public static class CompanyService
    {
        private static ICompanyRepository repository;
        private static IUnitOfWork unitOfWork;

        static CompanyService()
        {
            CompanyService.unitOfWork = new UnitOfWork();
            CompanyService.repository =
                RepositoryFactory.GetRepository<ICompanyRepository,
                Company>(CompanyService.unitOfWork);
        }

        public static IList<Company> GetOwners()
        {
            return CompanyService.GetAllCompanies();
        }

        public static IList<Company> GetAllCompanies()
        {
            return CompanyService.repository.FindAll();
        }

        public static void SaveCompany(Company company)
        {
            CompanyService.repository[company.Key] = company;
            CompanyService.unitOfWork.Commit();
        }
    }
}
```

The first thing to notice about this class is that it is a static class with all static methods. Again, the idea is to make it very easy to use. The next interesting part of the class is its static constructor. This is where the instance to the IProjectRepository is created via the RepositoryFactory. Also note that when the IProjectRepository is created it is injected with a UnitOfWork instance. This is necessary since I will be saving Project instances in this class and want that operation to be wrapped in a transaction.

The rest of the class is just acting as a façade in front of the IProjectRepository instance. The next interesting method is the SaveProject method. Notice how the collection-like functionality of the IProjectRepository instance is utilized by calling the indexer (see Chapter 2 for more information on this). What's nice about having the indexer is that the RepositoryBase<T> class will figure out if it is a new Project or an existing one. Also, after updating the IProjectRepository with the newly updated Project instance, the Commit method is called on the UnitOfWork instance to commit the transaction.

The ContactService Class

Currently, the only thing that the ContactService class does is to wrap the IContactRepository call for saving a Contact:

```
using System;
using SmartCA.Infrastructure;
using SmartCA.Infrastructure.RepositoryFramework;

namespace SmartCA.Model.Contacts
{
    public static class ContactService
    {
        private static IContactRepository repository;
        private static IUnitOfWork unitOfWork;

        static ContactService()
        {
            ContactService.unitOfWork = new UnitOfWork();
            ContactService.repository =
                RepositoryFactory.GetRepository<IContactRepository,
                Contact>(ContactService.unitOfWork);
        }

        public static void SaveContact(Contact contact)
        {
            ContactService.repository[contact.Key] = contact;
            ContactService.unitOfWork.Commit();
        }
    }
}
```

Right now, this code does not need any additional functionality, so I am going to leave it alone for a while.

The ProjectService Class

In order to save a ProjectContact, since it is part of the Project Aggregate, the SaveProjectContact method was added to the ProjectService class:

```
using System;
using System.Collections.Generic;
using SmartCA.Model.Projects;
using SmartCA.Infrastructure.RepositoryFramework;
using SmartCA.Infrastructure;
using SmartCA.Model.Contacts;

namespace SmartCA.Model.Projects
{
    public static class ProjectService
    {
        private static IProjectRepository projectRepository;
        private static IContactRepository contactRepository;
        private static IUnitOfWork unitOfWork;

        static ProjectService()
        {
            ProjectService.unitOfWork = new UnitOfWork();
            ProjectService.projectRepository =
                RepositoryFactory.GetRepository<IProjectRepository,
                Project>(ProjectService.unitOfWork);
            ProjectService.contactRepository =
                RepositoryFactory.GetRepository<IContactRepository,
                Contact>(ProjectService.unitOfWork);
        }

        public static IList<Project> GetAllProjects()
        {
            return ProjectService.projectRepository.FindAll();
        }

        public static IList<MarketSegment> GetMarketSegments()
        {
            return ProjectService.projectRepository.FindAllMarketSegments();
        }

        public static void SaveProject(Project project)
        {
            ProjectService.projectRepository[project.Key] = project;
            ProjectService.unitOfWork.Commit();
        }

        public static void SaveProjectContact(ProjectContact contact)
        {
            ProjectService.contactRepository[contact.Contact.Key]
                = contact.Contact;
```

```
            // Add/Update the project contact
            ProjectService.projectRepository.SaveContact(contact);
            ProjectService.unitOfWork.Commit();
        }
    }
}
```

The method first calls the `IContactRepository` instance's indexer to save the `Contact` instance.
I thought about having this call the `ContactService`'s `SaveContact` method, but then I would
lose my Unit of Work context, so I decided to keep the code here for now. After talking to
the `IContactRepository` instance, the code then calls the `SaveContact` method on the
`IProjectRepository`'s instance. Once both of those calls are made, the Unit of Work is committed.

The Company ViewModel

Following the same patterns as before, the `CompanyViewModel` class adapts the Company Aggregate
from the domain model to the UI. To start out, just like my previous examples, I inherit from the
`ViewModel` abstract class:

```csharp
using System;
using SmartCA.Infrastructure.UI;
using System.Windows.Data;
using SmartCA.Model.Companies;
using System.Collections.Generic;
using SmartCA.Model;
using System.Collections.ObjectModel;
using System.Collections.Specialized;
using System.ComponentModel;
using Xceed.Wpf.DataGrid;

namespace SmartCA.Presentation.ViewModels
{
    public class CompanyViewModel : ViewModel
    {
        #region Constants

        private static class Constants
        {
            public const string CurrentCompanyPropertyName = "CurrentCompany";
            public const string AddressesPropertyName = "Addresses";
            public const string HeadquartersAddressPropertyName =
                "HeadquartersAddress";
        }

        #endregion

        #region Private Fields

        private CollectionView companies;
        private IList<Company> companiesList;
        private Company currentCompany;
```

(continued)

(continued)

```
private BindingList<MutableAddress> addresses;
private MutableAddress headquartersAddress;
private DelegateCommand saveCommand;
private DelegateCommand newCommand;
private DelegateCommand deleteAddressCommand;

#endregion

#region Constructors

public CompanyViewModel()
    : this(null)
{
}

public CompanyViewModel(IView view)
    : base(view)
{
    this.companiesList = CompanyService.GetAllCompanies();
    this.companies = new CollectionView(companiesList);
    this.currentCompany = null;
    this.addresses = new BindingList<MutableAddress>();
    this.headquartersAddress = null;
    this.saveCommand = new DelegateCommand(this.SaveCommandHandler);
    this.saveCommand.IsEnabled = false;
    this.newCommand = new DelegateCommand(this.NewCommandHandler);
    this.deleteAddressCommand =
        new DelegateCommand(this.DeleteAddressCommandHandler);
}

#endregion

#region Public Properties

public CollectionView Companies
{
    get { return this.companies; }
}

public Company CurrentCompany
{
    get { return this.currentCompany; }
    set
    {
        if (this.currentCompany != value)
        {
            this.currentCompany = value;
            this.OnPropertyChanged(Constants.CurrentCompanyPropertyName);
            this.saveCommand.IsEnabled = (this.currentCompany != null);
```

```
                this.PopulateAddresses();
                this.HeadquartersAddress =
                    new MutableAddress(
                        this.currentCompany.HeadquartersAddress);
            }
        }
    }

    public BindingList<MutableAddress> Addresses
    {
        get { return this.addresses; }
    }

    public MutableAddress HeadquartersAddress
    {
        get { return this.headquartersAddress; }
        set
        {
            if (this.headquartersAddress != value)
            {
                this.headquartersAddress = value;
                this.OnPropertyChanged(
                    Constants.HeadquartersAddressPropertyName);
            }
        }
    }

    public DelegateCommand NewCommand
    {
        get { return this.newCommand; }
    }

    public DelegateCommand SaveCommand
    {
        get { return this.saveCommand; }
    }

    public DelegateCommand DeleteAddressCommand
    {
        get { return this.deleteAddressCommand; }
    }

    #endregion

    #region Private Methods

    private void SaveCommandHandler(object sender, EventArgs e)
    {
        this.currentCompany.Addresses.Clear();
        foreach (MutableAddress address in this.addresses)
```

(continued)

(continued)

```
            {
                this.currentCompany.Addresses.Add(address.ToAddress());
            }
            this.currentCompany.HeadquartersAddress =
                this.headquartersAddress.ToAddress();
            CompanyService.SaveCompany(this.currentCompany);
        }

        private void NewCommandHandler(object sender, EventArgs e)
        {
            Company company = new Company();
            company.Name = "{Enter Company Name}";
            this.companiesList.Add(company);
            this.companies.Refresh();
            this.companies.MoveCurrentToLast();
        }

        private void DeleteAddressCommandHandler(object sender,
            DelegateCommandEventArgs e)
        {
            MutableAddress address = e.Parameter as MutableAddress;
            if (address != null)
            {
                this.addresses.Remove(address);
            }
        }

        private void PopulateAddresses()
        {
            if (this.currentCompany != null)
            {
                this.addresses.Clear();
                foreach (Address address in this.currentCompany.Addresses)
                {
                    this.addresses.Add(new MutableAddress(address));
                }
                this.OnPropertyChanged(Constants.AddressesPropertyName);
            }
        }

        #endregion
    }
}
```

Constructor

The interesting thing to note in this class, which is a little different from the other `ViewModel` classes, is the initialization of the `BindingList<MutableAddress>` (the addresses variable) type in the constructor that is used to represent the list of addresses for the Company.

```
#region Constructors

public CompanyViewModel()
    : this(null)
{
}

public CompanyViewModel(IView view)
    : base(view)
{
    this.companiesList = CompanyService.GetAllCompanies();
    this.companies = new CollectionView(companiesList);
    this.currentCompany = null;
    this.addresses = new BindingList<MutableAddress>();
    this.headquartersAddress = null;
    this.saveCommand = new DelegateCommand(this.SaveCommandHandler);
    this.saveCommand.IsEnabled = false;
    this.newCommand = new DelegateCommand(this.NewCommandHandler);
    this.deleteAddressCommand =
        new DelegateCommand(this.DeleteAddressCommandHandler);
}

#endregion
```

The MutableAddress type should look familiar, as I have already used that in last chapter's ProjectInformationViewModel class. The reason I had to use this type of object, and not something like a CollectionView, is because I have decided to display the Company's addresses in the form of a data grid, and the data grid I am using (more on that in the next section) requires that the data bound to it implement the IBindingList interface. Since the BindingList class gives me that implementation for free, I have decided to use it.

You may be wondering why I am maintaining an IList<Company> variable (companiesList) as well as the CollectionView of the list. In the UI form I am going to be displaying a list of Companies to choose from, but I am also supporting adding new Companies, which need to be added the list. Therefore, I need access to the IList interface so that I can add new Companies to the list. Just as when I had to deal with addresses in the previous chapter, I am also maintaining a MutableAddress instance for the Company's HeadquartersAddress property. The rest of the constructor code should look very familiar; I am just doing the standard wire-up code for the DelegateCommand instances.

Properties

The CurrentCompany property indicates the current Company instance that is being edited:

```
public Company CurrentCompany
{
    get { return this.currentCompany; }
    set
    {
        if (this.currentCompany != value)
```

(continued)

(continued)

```
                {
                    this.currentCompany = value;
                    this.OnPropertyChanged(Constants.CurrentCompanyPropertyName);
                    this.saveCommand.IsEnabled = (this.currentCompany != null);
                    this.PopulateAddresses();
                    this.HeadquartersAddress =
                        new MutableAddress(
                            this.currentCompany.HeadquartersAddress);
                }
            }
        }
```

Whenever a new Company is selected in the UI, the `CurrentProperty` setter is called (I will show you how this is done in the XAML in a few paragraphs). Once that has happened, the `PropertyChanged` event for the `CurrentCompany` property is raised, thus letting the UI know to refresh itself. Next, the `SaveCommand`'s `IsEnabled` property is set to the boolean value of the Current Company. Then the `PopulateAddresses` method is called:

```
    private void PopulateAddresses()
    {
        if (this.currentCompany != null)
        {
            this.addresses.Clear();
            foreach (Address address in this.currentCompany.Addresses)
            {
                this.addresses.Add(new MutableAddress(address));
            }
            this.OnPropertyChanged(Constants.AddressesPropertyName);
        }
    }
```

This is necessary because the Addresses contained in the Company's `Addresses` property are the immutable Address types, and in order to be able to edit the Addresses I have to convert them into `MutableAddress` types. Once this is done, then the `PropertyChanged` event for the `Addresses` property is raised so the UI can refresh itself.

The `CurrentCompany` property setter then finishes by resetting the `HeadquartersAddress` property. This is necessary because the `HeadquartersAddress` property is also a converter between the current Company's immutable `Address` type and a `MutableAddress`:

```
    public MutableAddress HeadquartersAddress
    {
        get { return this.headquartersAddress; }
        set
        {
            if (this.headquartersAddress != value)
```

```
        {
            this.headquartersAddress = value;
            this.OnPropertyChanged(
                Constants.HeadquartersAddressPropertyName);
        }
    }
}
```

The code for the property setter ensures that when the property changes the `PropertyChanged` event is fired for the UI to consume.

The rest of the properties in the `CompanyView` class are the read-only `DelegateCommand` properties for creating New Companies, saving Companies, and deleting Addresses from a Company.

Command Handler Methods

The handlers for the `DelegateCommand` properties are pretty interesting. The `NewCommandHandler` method has to do a lot of housekeeping:

```
private void NewCommandHandler(object sender, EventArgs e)
{
    Company company = new Company();
    company.Name = "{Enter Company Name}";
    this.companiesList.Add(company);
    this.companies.Refresh();
    this.companies.MoveCurrentToLast();
}
```

It first has to create a new instance of a `Company`, set its `Name` property to some default text, and then add it to the internal list of companies. Once the internal list has been updated, it then calls `Refresh` on the `CollectionView` companies variable in order to have the UI be refreshed. Finally, by calling the `MoveCurrentToLast` method on the `CollectionView`, the new Company will appear last in the list in the UI.

The `DeleteAddressCommandHandler` method is interesting because it gets the `MutableAddress` that must be deleted passed in to it from the `DelegateCommandEventArgs` parameter.

```
private void DeleteAddressCommandHandler(object sender,
    DelegateCommandEventArgs e)
{
    MutableAddress address = e.Parameter as MutableAddress;
    if (address != null)
    {
        this.addresses.Remove(address);
    }
}
```

It then checks to see whether it is null, and if it is not, it removes it from the `BindingList <MutableAddress>` collection (the addresses are variable). Once this happens, the data grid that is bound to it is automatically updated.

The Company View

The View that is associated with the `CompanyViewModel`, the `CompanyView` class (which consists of XAML plus code-behind), is very similar to the `ProjectInformationView` class, in that it has very little code behind it:

```
using System;
using System.Windows;
using SmartCA.Presentation.ViewModels;
using SmartCA.Infrastructure.UI;

namespace SmartCA.Presentation.Views
{
 public partial class CompanyView : Window, IView
    {
        public CompanyView()
        {
            this.InitializeComponent();
             this.DataContext = new CompanyViewModel(this);
        }
    }
}
```

From this point forward, I will not show the code-behind any more for the Views, since they are almost always going to be identical. Before diving into the XAML for the `CompanyView`, take a look at Figure 4.5, which shows what the form looks like at run time.

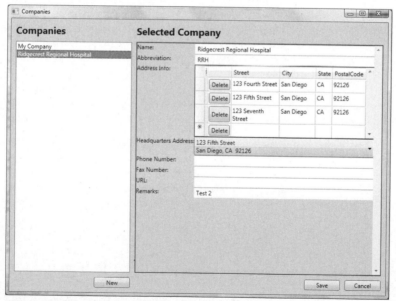

Figure 4.5: The Company View

The form is split into two parts; the one on the left is for selecting a Company to edit, and the one on the right is for actually editing the Company. The New button adds a new Company to the list. The Save and Cancel buttons both deal with the currently selected Company. There are two things that should stand out to you while looking at this form. One, I am using a data grid to display and edit the addresses, and two, the dropdown for the headquarters address looks pretty cool, doesn't it?

For the grid, I am using the Xceed DataGrid for WPF component. Xceed recognized that Microsoft did not include a data grid implementation in WPF, and so they made one themselves. The nice part is that their product is licensed for free, with an unlimited number of licenses per company. Kudos to them, I think that this was a very smart marketing move on their part, since most developers are going to want to use a data grid control at some point when working in WPF.

Using the Xceed Data Grid

Since the XAML code for displaying lists of addresses will be needed for Contacts as well as Companies, I have created the `Addresses` reusable `UserControl` to display editable Address data in a grid. Because I am using the Xceed DataGrid control, it was fairly easy to create the `Addresses` `UserControl` to display the list of editable addresses. In order to get the look and feel shown in Figure 4.5 the `UserControl` contains the following XAML:

```
<UserControl x:Class="SmartCA.Presentation.Views.Addresses"
    xmlns="http://schemas.microsoft.com/winfx/2006/xaml/presentation"
    xmlns:xcdg="http://schemas.xceed.com/wpf/xaml/datagrid"
    xmlns:x="http://schemas.microsoft.com/winfx/2006/xaml">
    <xcdg:DataGridControl ItemsSource="{Binding}">
        <xcdg:DataGridControl.Columns>
            <xcdg:Column Width="50" FieldName="DeleteButton"
                    DisplayMemberBinding="{Binding .}">
                <xcdg:Column.CellContentTemplate>
                    <DataTemplate>
                        <Button Content="Delete"
                                Command="{Binding
                                RelativeSource={RelativeSource
                                FindAncestor, AncestorType={x:Type
Window}},
Path=DataContext.DeleteAddressCommand}">
                            <Button.CommandParameter>
                                <Binding Path="."/>
                            </Button.CommandParameter>
                        </Button>
                    </DataTemplate>
                </xcdg:Column.CellContentTemplate>
            </xcdg:Column>
            <xcdg:Column FieldName="Street" Width="100" TextWrapping="Wrap"/>
            <xcdg:Column FieldName="City" Width="75" TextWrapping="Wrap"/>
            <xcdg:Column FieldName="State"  MaxWidth="35"/>
            <xcdg:Column FieldName="PostalCode" MaxWidth="70"/>
        </xcdg:DataGridControl.Columns>
```

(continued)

(continued)

```
                    <xcdg:DataGridControl.View>
                          <xcdg:TableView HorizontalGridLineThickness="1"
                                VerticalGridLineThickness="1">
                                <xcdg:TableView.HorizontalGridLineBrush>
                                      <SolidColorBrush Color="Orange"/>
                                </xcdg:TableView.HorizontalGridLineBrush>
                                <xcdg:TableView.VerticalGridLineBrush>
                                      <SolidColorBrush Color="Orange"/>
                                </xcdg:TableView.VerticalGridLineBrush>
                                <xcdg:TableView.Footers>
                                      <DataTemplate>
                                            <xcdg:InsertionRow/>
                                      </DataTemplate>
                                </xcdg:TableView.Footers>
                                <xcdg:TableView.FixedHeaders>
                                      <xcdg:ClearHeadersFooters/>
                                      <DataTemplate>
                                            <xcdg:ColumnManagerRow/>
                                      </DataTemplate>
                                </xcdg:TableView.FixedHeaders>
                          </xcdg:TableView>
                    </xcdg:DataGridControl.View>
            </xcdg:DataGridControl>
      </UserControl>
```

The first thing to notice is that, at the top of the XAML, I am setting the `ItemsSource` property of the `DataGridControl` to a value of `"{Binding}"`. This allows the `DataGridControl` to take advantage of the current Window's `DataContext`. The next interesting thing to note is the Delete button that shows up in every row of the addresses grid. The grid column containing repeating Delete buttons has its `DisplayMemberBinding` set to a value of `"{Binding .}"`, and the Button itself has its `Command` property's binding set to `"{Binding RelativeSource={RelativeSource FindAncestor, AncestorType={x:Type Window}}, Path=DataContext.DeleteAddressCommand}"`. These settings allow each Delete Button to traverse up the binding tree to the `Window`, descend from the `Window` to the `DataContext`, and then bind to the `DeleteAddressCommand` property of the `DataContext`, which in this case is the `CompanyViewModel`. The next thing I need, once I get the Delete Button's `Command` property bound, is to have it pass as a parameter to the item that is being deleted. This is done by the following code inside of the Button element:

```
<Button.CommandParameter>
    <Binding Path="."/>
</Button.CommandParameter>
```

This allows the Button's `Command` property to receive the item being deleted; in this case it is an `Address` instance.

The Headquarters Address Addresses Dropdown

As far as the dropdown for the headquarters address, this is made possible by a little refactoring to both the `Address` and `MutableAddress` classes and some WPF magic.

Here is the `ToString` override in the `Address` class:

```
public override string ToString()
{
    StringBuilder builder = new StringBuilder(300);
    builder.Append(this.street);
    builder.Append("\r\n");
    builder.Append(this.city);
    builder.Append(", ");
    builder.Append(this.state);
    builder.Append(" ");
    builder.Append(this.postalCode);
    return builder.ToString();
}
```

In the `MutableAddress` class, it is even easier:

```
public override string ToString()
{
    return this.ToAddress().ToString();
}
```

In WPF, by not specifying the `DisplayMemberPath` property of the `ComboBox` control, what is rendered for the text of the items in the list is the `ToString()` result of each item in the list. In .NET, the default value specified on the `System.Object` class is the type name of the class, that is, "System.Object" or "System.String", and so on, but, if your class overrides the `ToString` method, then WPF will use that for the value of the list item.

Here is the XAML for the Headquarters Address `ComboBox`:

```
<ComboBox Grid.Row="3" Grid.Column="1"
    SelectedItem="{Binding Path=HeadquartersAddress}"
    ItemsSource="{Binding Path=Addresses}">
</ComboBox>
```

This XAML declares that the `SelectedItem` of the `ComboBox` will set the `HeadquartersAddress` property in the `CompanyViewModel` class (remember that a `CompanyViewModel` instance has been set as the `DataContext` for the whole `Window`). It also declares that the `ItemsSource` property is bound to the `Addresses` property in the `CompanyViewModel`, and that property is a `BindingList` `<MutableAddress>` type.

The rest of the XAML for the `CompanyView` is fairly vanilla, so I will not show it here for the sake of brevity.

The Project Contact View Model

The ProjectContactViewModel is very similar to the CompanyViewModel, and is actually a little bit simpler. Because both the CompanyViewModel and ProjectContactViewModel need to contain an Addresses property and the necessary behavior around that property, I was able to factor that functionality out from the CompanyViewModel into a new abstract class called AddressesViewModel.

```csharp
using System;
using System.Collections.Generic;
using SmartCA.Infrastructure.UI;
using System.ComponentModel;

namespace SmartCA.Presentation.ViewModels
{
    public abstract class AddressesViewModel : ViewModel
    {
        #region Constants

        private static class Constants
        {
            public const string AddressesPropertyName = "Addresses";
        }

        #endregion

        #region Private Fields

        private BindingList<MutableAddress> addresses;
        private DelegateCommand deleteAddressCommand;

        #endregion

        #region Constructors

        protected AddressesViewModel()
            : this(null)
        {
        }

        protected AddressesViewModel(IView view)
            : base(view)
        {
            this.addresses = new BindingList<MutableAddress>();
            this.deleteAddressCommand =
                new DelegateCommand(this.DeleteAddressCommandHandler);
        }

        #endregion

        #region Public Properties

        public BindingList<MutableAddress> Addresses
```

```
    {
        get { return this.addresses; }
    }

    public DelegateCommand DeleteAddressCommand
    {
        get { return this.deleteAddressCommand; }
    }

    #endregion

    #region Private Methods

    private void DeleteAddressCommandHandler(object sender,
        DelegateCommandEventArgs e)
    {
        MutableAddress address = e.Parameter as MutableAddress;
        if (address != null)
        {
            this.addresses.Remove(address);
        }
    }

    #endregion

    #region Virtual Methods

    protected virtual void PopulateAddresses()
    {
        this.OnPropertyChanged(Constants.AddressesPropertyName);
    }

    #endregion
    }
}
```

This class should look very similar to the parts of the `CompanyViewModel` that dealt with Addresses. In fact, I copied and pasted most of the code from that class into the `AddressesViewModel`. It is an abstract class, so the `CompanyViewModel` class changed to inherit from `AddressesViewModel` instead of `ViewModel`. The only method that I needed to change was `PopulateAddressses`; I had to change it to raise only the `PropertyChanged` event for the `Addresses` property, and then I marked it as virtual so I could override it and call it from `CompanyViewModel` and `ProjectContactViewModel`.

Here is the code for the `ProjectContactViewModel` using the new `AddressesViewModel` class:

```
using System;
using System.Collections.Generic;
using SmartCA.Infrastructure.UI;
using System.Windows.Data;
using SmartCA.Application;
using SmartCA.Model.Companies;
using SmartCA.Model.Projects;
```

(continued)

149

(continued)

```
using System.ComponentModel;
using SmartCA.Model.Contacts;
using SmartCA.Model;

namespace SmartCA.Presentation.ViewModels
{
    public class ProjectContactViewModel : AddressesViewModel
    {
        #region Constants

        private static class Constants
        {
            public const string CurrentContactPropertyName = "CurrentContact";
        }

        #endregion

        private CollectionView contacts;
        private IList<ProjectContact> contactsList;
        ProjectContact currentContact;
        private CollectionView companies;
        private DelegateCommand saveCommand;
        private DelegateCommand newCommand;

        #region Constructors

        public ProjectContactViewModel()
            : this(null)
        {
        }

        public ProjectContactViewModel(IVicw view)
            : base(view)
        {
            this.contactsList = UserSession.CurrentProject.Contacts;
            this.contacts = new CollectionView(contactsList);
            this.currentContact = null;
            this.companies = new CollectionView(CompanyService.GetAllCompanies());
            this.saveCommand = new DelegateCommand(this.SaveCommandHandler);
            this.newCommand = new DelegateCommand(this.NewCommandHandler);
        }

        #endregion

        public CollectionView Contacts
        {
            get { return this.contacts; }
        }

        public ProjectContact CurrentContact
```

```
{
    get { return this.currentContact; }
    set
    {
        if (this.currentContact != value)
        {
            this.currentContact = value;
            this.OnPropertyChanged(Constants.CurrentContactPropertyName);
            this.saveCommand.IsEnabled = (this.currentContact != null);
            this.PopulateAddresses();
        }
    }
}

public CollectionView Companies
{
    get { return this.companies; }
}

public DelegateCommand SaveCommand
{
    get { return this.saveCommand; }
}

public DelegateCommand NewCommand
{
    get { return this.newCommand; }
}

private void SaveCommandHandler(object sender, EventArgs e)
{
    this.currentContact.Contact.Addresses.Clear();
    foreach (MutableAddress address in this.Addresses)
    {
        this.currentContact.Contact.Addresses.Add(address.ToAddress());
    }
    ProjectService.SaveProjectContact(this.currentContact);
}

private void NewCommandHandler(object sender, EventArgs e)
{
    ProjectContact contact = new ProjectContact(UserSession.CurrentProject,
                            null, new Contact(null,
                                        "{First Name}", "{Last Name}"));
    this.contactsList.Add(contact);
    this.contacts.Refresh();
    this.contacts.MoveCurrentToLast();
}

protected override void PopulateAddresses()
```

(continued)

(continued)

```
        {
            if (this.currentContact != null)
            {
                this.Addresses.Clear();
                foreach (Address address in this.currentContact.Contact.Addresses)
                {
                    this.Addresses.Add(new MutableAddress(address));
                }
                base.PopulateAddresses();
            }
        }
    }
}
```

As you can see, it inherits from the `AddressesViewModel` class, thus eliminating several lines of code from the class.

Constructor

The constructor is almost exactly the same as the `CompanyViewModel` constructor, only this time I am dealing with ProjectContacts instead of Companies. There is a variable and property for Companies, but that is used as a dropdown list in the UI to assign a ProjectContact to a Company.

```
#region Constructors

public ProjectContactViewModel()
    : this(null)
{
}

public ProjectContactViewModel(IView view)
    : base(view)
{
    this.contactsList = UserSession.CurrentProject.Contacts;
    this.contacts = new CollectionView(contactsList);
    this.currentContact = null;
    this.companies = new CollectionView(CompanyService.GetAllCompanies());
    this.saveCommand = new DelegateCommand(this.SaveCommandHandler);
    this.newCommand = new DelegateCommand(this.NewCommandHandler);
}

#endregion
```

Just like the `CompanyView` class, I am also maintaining an `IList<T>` variable (contactsList) as well as the `CollectionView` of the list. There is a `CollectionView` containing `Company` instances, and this is used by the UI to select the Company to which a Contact belongs.

Properties

The CurrentContact property indicates the current ProjectContact instance that is being edited.

```
public ProjectContact CurrentContact
{
    get { return this.currentContact; }
    set
    {
        if (this.currentContact != value)
        {
            this.currentContact = value;
            this.OnPropertyChanged(Constants.CurrentContactPropertyName);
            this.saveCommand.IsEnabled = (this.currentContact != null);
            this.PopulateAddresses();
        }
    }
}
```

Whenever a new ProjectContact is selected in the UI, then this property's setter is called. Once that has happened, then the PropertyChanged event for the CurrentContact property is raised, thus letting the UI know to refresh itself. The next thing to happen is to set the SaveCommand's IsEnabled property to the boolean value of the Current ProjectContact. Then the PopulateAddresses method is called:

```
protected override void PopulateAddresses()
{
    if (this.currentContact != null)
    {
        this.Addresses.Clear();
        foreach (Address address in this.currentContact.Contact.Addresses)
        {
            this.Addresses.Add(new MutableAddress(address));
        }
        base.PopulateAddresses();
    }
}
```

This is now changed to account for the PopulateAddresses method in the AddressesViewModel base class.

The rest of the properties in the ProjectContactView class are the Companies CollectionView property and the read-only DelegateCommand properties for creating New ProjectContacts and saving ProjectContacts.

Command Handler Methods

The handlers for the DelegateCommand properties are pretty interesting. The NewCommandHandler method has to do a lot of housekeeping:

```
private void NewCommandHandler(object sender, EventArgs e)
{
    ProjectContact contact = new ProjectContact(UserSession.CurrentProject,
                                null, new Contact(null,
                                        "{First Name}", "{Last Name}"));
    this.contactsList.Add(contact);
    this.contacts.Refresh();
    this.contacts.MoveCurrentToLast();
}
```

It first has to create a new instance of a ProjectContact, and then add it to the internal list of ProjectContacts. Once the internal list has been updated, it then calls Refresh on the CollectionView contacts variable in order to have the UI refreshed. Finally, by calling the MoveCurrentToLast method on the CollectionView, the ProjectContact will appear last in the list in the UI.

The SaveCommandHandler first has to swap out the addresses from the Addresses property into the Addresses property of the ProjectContact.

```
private void SaveCommandHandler(object sender, EventArgs e)
{
    this.currentContact.Contact.Addresses.Clear();
    foreach (MutableAddress address in this.Addresses)
    {
        this.currentContact.Contact.Addresses.Add(address.ToAddress());
    }
    ProjectService.SaveProjectContact(this.currentContact);
}
```

It then finishes up by using the ProjectService class to save the current ProjectContact instance. Again, it is nice how this Service class makes it very easy for the UI code to concentrate on display rather than the plumbing of saving a ProjectContact.

The Project Contact View

The View that is associated with the ProjectContactViewModel, the ProjectContactView class (which consists of XAML plus code-behind), is almost identical to the CompanyView class shown previously in this chapter. Figure 4.6 shows what the form looks like at run time.

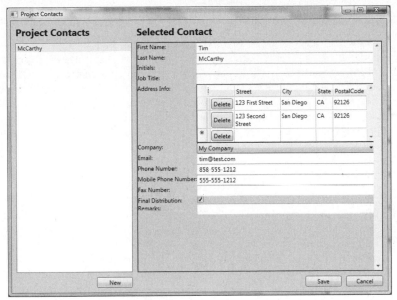

Figure 4.6: The ProjectContact View

The main difference between this form and `CompanyView` form is that now I am dealing with ProjectContacts instead of Companies. Everything else is almost identical, from the selection of items to edit to using the `UserControl` for Addresses to saving and adding new ProjectContacts.

There is one more difference, and that is that this View has a dropdown for choosing what Company a ProjectContact belongs to.

Here is the XAML for the Company `ComboBox`:

```
<ComboBox Grid.Row="5" Grid.Column="1"
    SelectedItem="{Binding Path=CurrentContact.Contact.CurrentCompany}"
    DisplayMemberPath="Name"
    ItemsSource="{Binding Path=Companies}">
</ComboBox>
```

This XAML declares that the `SelectedItem` of the ComboBox will set the `CurrentCompany` property in the `ProjectContactViewModel` class. It also declares that the `ItemsSource` property is bound to the `Companies` property in the `ProjectContactViewModel`, and the property that will be displayed to the user in the `ComboBox` will be the `Name` property on the `Company` instances.

The rest of the XAML for the `ProjectContactView` is so similar to the `CompanyView` that it is not worth showing here.

Summary

In this chapter I defined and modeled Companies, Contacts, and ProjectContacts, and then defined the Aggregate Boundaries for these classes in the domain model. A new concept was added to both the Domain Layer and Infrastructure Layer that allowed saving Entities that are not their own Aggregate Root. This was demonstrated by the techniques I used to save ProjectContacts within the Project Aggregate. Also covered was how to deal with `Address` Value Objects using the Xceed DataGrid control. I showed how to wrap this functionality into a reusable `UserControl` for Addresses. Furthermore, there was also a lot of good refactoring going on with the `ProjectRepository` and the new `ViewModel` classes.

5

Submittal Transmittals

In the last chapter, I took a deep look at Companies and Contacts, mainly because they are building blocks to be used in other parts of the SmartCA domain model. In this chapter, I will show what Submittal Transmittals are and how they also depend on Contacts, Companies, and several other classes in the domain model.

The Problem

In the construction administration world, submittal requirements are part of the project specifications. The book of specifications for construction projects is very large and describes "how the project is to be constructed and what results are to be achieved."

Architects and engineers prepare the specifications. Almost all specifications used in the United States and Canada are based on a format called the "MasterFormat" developed by the Construction Specifications Institute. Some design firms use the 16 division MasterFormat from the 1995 version. Other design firms have adopted the 2004 edition, which has 20 divisions.

As a rule, submittal requirements are set forth in project specifications. Another section lays out specific submittal procedures. At the beginning of a project, the general contractor will prepare a submittal schedule. The schedule, sometimes called a submittal log, indicates the specification sections, due dates, and responsible party for each required submittal. The design firm then approves this schedule.

The specification details the time requirements for the architect's review of each submittal and the type of cover sheets and transmittal memos needed to identify them. Examples of some common submittals for specifications are items such as product data and shop drawings.

The Design

A Submittal Transmittal is made up of many parts, but probably the most important part is the tracking of the status of the specification sections. It is very important for the Smart Design firm to know the status of all of their submittals, such as which have been received and which are still pending.

Designing the Domain Model

Figure 5.1 is a drawing showing the relationships between the classes that combine to make up a Submittal Transmittal.

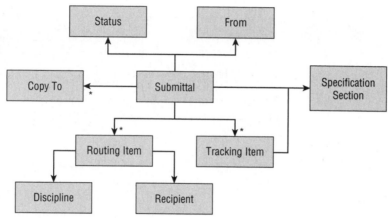

Figure 5.1: Submittal Aggregate.

Obviously, the root of this Aggregate is the Submittal class. Probably its most important relationship is the one to the Specification Section. This is the whole purpose of the submittal transmittal, to track the actual materials and labor against the project specifications. The Status class is used to convey the overall status of the Submittal. Also, notice that each Tracking Item is related to an individual Specification Section: this is how the domain model determines the status of each specification item in the Submittal.

The next important part of the diagram is the Submittal's relationship to the Routing Item. This is how Smart Design determines to whom each Submittal has been routed for action, and that person's Discipline, such as an architect, engineer, or a construction administrator. Also, notice that there is a Copy To relationship from a Submittal; this represents the list of Recipients who need to be copied on all correspondence having to do with the Submittal.

Defining the Submittal Aggregate

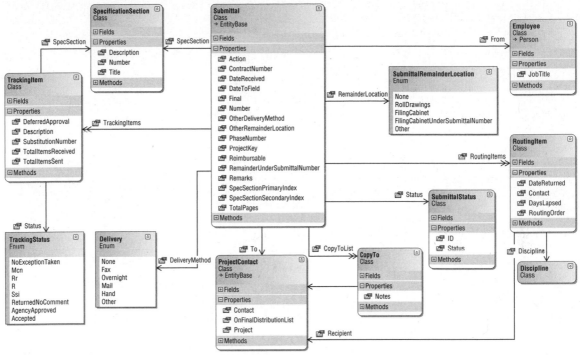

Figure 5.2: Classes composing the Submittal Aggregate.

As you can see from the diagram of the Submittal Aggregate in Figure 5.2, there are a lot of moving parts in this Aggregate. Notice how I am starting to make use of some of the other Entities introduced in previous chapters, such as the ProjectContact class, which is used to represent the To property of the Submittal class, the Recipient property of the RoutingItem class, and the Contact property of the CopyTo class. Also, the Employee class is used in the Submittal's From property to represent the Employee that originated the Submittal.

Defining the Aggregate Boundaries

The Submittal class has its own identity and is definitely the root of its own Aggregate. All of the other classes in the diagram in Figure 5.3, except for ProjectContact and Employee, belong to the Submittal Aggregate. As shown in earlier chapters, ProjectContact belongs to the Project Aggregate, and Employee is the root of its own Aggregate.

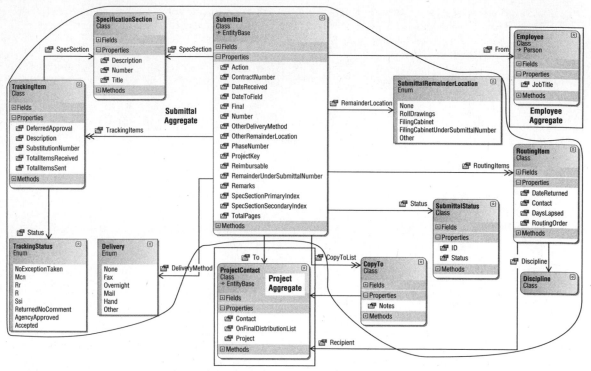

Figure 5.3: Submittal Aggregate boundaries.

Designing the Repository

Since Submittal is its own Aggregate root, it will have its own repository, as shown in Figure 5.4.

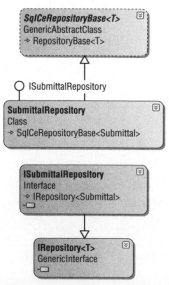

Figure 5.4: Submittal Aggregate repository.

Although the Project Aggregate and the Employee Aggregate are part of the Submittal Aggregate, I will not be covering their respective repositories here because they have already been covered in Chapter 3. I will only be covering the Submittal repository in this chapter.

The ISubmittalRepository interface is the interface into instances of Submittal repositories. Here is the ISubmittalRepository interface:

```
using System.Collections.Generic;
using SmartCA.Infrastructure.RepositoryFramework;
using SmartCA.Model.Projects;

namespace SmartCA.Model.Submittals
{
    public interface ISubmittalRepository : IRepository<Submittal>
    {
        IList<Submittal> FindBy(Project project);
        IList<SpecificationSection> FindAllSpecificationSections();
        IList<SubmittalStatus> FindAllSubmittalStatuses();
        IList<Discipline> FindAllDisciplines();
    }
}
```

The first method, FindBy, will be called fairly often, as most Submittals will only be looked at on a per-project basis. The FindAllSpecificationSections, FindAllSubmittalStatuses, and FindAllDisciplines methods all return lists of their respective Value objects from the data store. These lists will be used later in the UI for lookup purposes.

Writing the Unit Tests

In this section, I will be writing some unit tests of what I expect of the Submittal repository implementation. As noted before, these tests will compile correctly, but they will also fail until I write the code for the Repository implementation later on in the Solution section.

There will be more unit tests in the accompanying code for this chapter, but for brevity's sake I am showing the tests that I think are important here.

The FindSubmittalsByProjectTest Method

The purpose of the FindSubmittalsByProjectTest method is to validate that the correct number of Submittal instances have been returned by the Submittal repository for a given Project:

```
/// <summary>
/// A test for FindBy(Project project)
/// </summary>
[DeploymentItem("SmartCA.sdf"), TestMethod()]
public void FindSubmittalsByProjectTest()
{
    // Get a Project reference
    Project project =
        ProjectService.GetProject("5704f6b9-6ffa-444c-9583-35cc340fce2a");
```

(continued)

(continued)

```
        // FIns all of the Submittals for the Project
        IList<Submittal> submittals = this.repository.FindBy(project);

        // Verify that at least one Submittal was returned
        Assert.IsTrue(submittals.Count > 0);
    }
```

This method starts out by getting a `Project` instance from the `ProjectService` class. It then calls the `FindBy` method on the repository to get the list of Submittals for the given `Project` instance. The method finishes by checking that the repository returned at least one `Submittal`.

The AddSubmittalTest Method

The purpose of the `AddSubmittalTest` method is to test adding a new Submittal to the Submittal repository:

```
/// <summary>
///A test for Add(Submittal item)
///</summary>
[DeploymentItem("SmartCA.sdf"), TestMethod()]
public void AddSubmittalTest()
{
    // Create a new Submittal
    IList<SpecificationSection> specSections =
        this.repository.FindAllSpecificationSections();
    Guid projectKey = new Guid("5704f6b9-6ffa-444c-9583-35cc340fce2a");
    Submittal submittal = new Submittal(specSections[0], projectKey);
    submittal.To = ProjectService.GetProject(projectKey).Contacts[0];
    submittal.From = EmployeeService.GetEmployees()[0];
    IList<SubmittalStatus> statuses =
        this.repository.FindAllSubmittalStatuses();
    submittal.Status = statuses[0];

    // Add the Submittal to the Repository
    this.repository.Add(submittal);

    // Commit the transaction
    this.unitOfWork.Commit();

    // Reload the Submittal and verify it's number
    Submittal savedSubmittal = this.repository.FindBy(submittal.Key);
    Assert.AreEqual("00 11 13.01.00", savedSubmittal.Number);

    // Clean up
    this.repository.Remove(savedSubmittal);
    this.unitOfWork.Commit();
}
```

This test is a little bit more involved than the previous test. It starts out by getting the list of all `SpecificationSection` instances. It then creates a Project Key value, and then passes the first `SpecificationSection` from the `specSections` list variable as well as the Project Key value into the constructor of the Submittal class. The next step is to initialize the To and From properties of the Submittal instance with a ProjectContact instance and an Employee instance. Once those properties are set, the next property that needs to be set is the Status property. The Status property is set the value of the first SubmittalStatus in the list of all SubmittalStatus instances.

The next step is to add the Submittal to the repository, and then to commit the transaction by calling the Commit method on the IUnitOfWork instance. The Commit method is important because that method calls back into the Submittal repository to tell it to write the Submittal's data to the data store.

Once the Submittal has been saved, it is then reloaded, and the Submittal's Number property is checked to verify that the Add and Commit methods worked properly. The last task that the method needs to perform is to remove the Submittal. Removing the Submittal that was just created leaves the data store in the same state it was in before the method started, which is important for the rest of the tests that may depend on a known state of the data store. Otherwise, some of the other tests may fail because there was unexpected Submittal's data in the data store.

The UpdateSubmittalTest Method

The purpose of the UpdateTest method is to find a Submittal and update it with a different DateReceived property value and then verify that the change was persisted properly:

```
/// <summary>
///A test for Updating a Submittal
///</summary>
[DeploymentItem("SmartCA.sdf"), TestMethod()]
public void UpdateSubmittalTest()
{
    // Get the list of all Submittals
    IList<Submittal> submittals = this.repository.FindAll();

    // Change the first Submittal's DateReceived value
    DateTime dateReceived = DateTime.Now;
    submittals[0].DateReceived = dateReceived;

    // Update the Repository
    this.repository[submittals[0].Key] = submittals[0];

    // Commit the transaction
    this.unitOfWork.Commit();

    // Verify that the change was saved
    IList<Submittal> refreshedSubmittals = this.repository.FindAll();
    Assert.AreEqual(dateReceived.Date,
        refreshedSubmittals[0].DateReceived.Value.Date);
}
```

In this method I start out by getting the entire list of Submittals from the data store. I then proceed to change the DateReceived property value on the first Submittal in the list, and then call the indexer method of the ISubmittalRepository. After the call to the indexer, I then use the IUnitOfWork interface to commit the transaction. Last, I verify that the change actually made it to the data store by reloading the same Submittal and checking to see if its DateReceived property value is the same calendar date that I just assigned to the Submittal earlier in the method.

The RemoveSubmittalTest Method

The purpose of the `RemoveTest` method is to test the process of removing a Submittal from the data store:

```
/// <summary>
///A test for Remove(Submittal item)
///</summary>
[DeploymentItem("SmartCA.sdf"), TestMethod()]
public void RemoveSubmittalTest()
{
    // Get the list of all Submittals
    IList<Submittal> submittals = this.repository.FindAll();

    // Remove the Submittal from the Repository
    this.repository.Remove(submittals[0]);

    // Commit the transaction
    this.unitOfWork.Commit();

    // Verify that there is now one less Submittal in the data store
    IList<Submittal> refreshedSubmittals = this.repository.FindAll();
    Assert.AreEqual(0, refreshedSubmittals.Count);

    // Reset the state
    this.AddSubmittalTest();
}
```

The first line of this method should look familiar; I am getting the entire list of Submittals from the data store. I then remove the first Submittal in the list from the repository. After removing the Submittal from the repository, I then use the `IUnitOfWork` interface to commit the transaction. Last, I verify that the change actually made it to the data store by using the repository to find all of the Submittal instances and making sure there is now one less Submittal than before. Last, I call the `AddSubmittalTest` method to add the Submittal I just deleted back into the data store in order to reset the original state of the data store.

The Solution

Now that the design is in place for the Submittal domain model, the Submittal Aggregate has been defined and its boundaries have been determined, and the repository has been designed with its associated tests, it is time to start the code implementation. In this section, I will be implementing these designs, as well as implementing the ViewModel and the View for Submittals.

Implementing the Submittal Class Private Fields and Constructors

There are two constructors for the `Submittal` class, and they both take a `projectKey` parameter of type `System.Object` and a `specSection` parameter of type `SpecificationSection`. Every Submittal must be associated with a Specification Section. That is why it is in both constructors. The `projectKey` parameter links the Submittal with a particular Project.

I decided to use a key value for a Project instead of a full blown `Project` instance, since I can always get to the Project via the `ProjectService` class. The second constructor takes a key argument of type `System.Object`, thus following the pattern I have laid out before for creating instances of existing Entity classes.

```
using System;
using System.Collections.Generic;
using System.Text;
using SmartCA.Infrastructure.DomainBase;
using SmartCA.Model.Employees;
using SmartCA.Model.Projects;

namespace SmartCA.Model.Submittals
{
    public class Submittal : EntityBase
    {
        private object projectKey;
        private SpecificationSection specSection;
        private string specSectionPrimaryIndex;
        private string specSectionSecondaryIndex;
        private ProjectContact to;
        private DateTime transmittalDate;
        private Employee from;
        private int totalPages;
        private Delivery deliveryMethod;
        private string otherDeliveryMethod;
        private string phaseNumber;
        private bool reimbursable;
        private bool final;
        private List<CopyTo> copyToList;
        private DateTime? dateReceived;
        private string contractNumber;
        private List<TrackingItem> trackingItems;
        private List<RoutingItem> routingItems;
        private string remarks;
        private ActionStatus action;
        private SubmittalStatus status;
        private DateTime? dateToField;
        private SubmittalRemainderLocation remainderLocation;
        private string remainderUnderSubmittalNumber;
        private string otherRemainderLocation;

        public Submittal(SpecificationSection specSection, object projectKey)
            : this(null, specSection, projectKey)
        {
        }

        public Submittal(object key, SpecificationSection specSection,
            object projectKey) : base(key)
        {
            this.projectKey = projectKey;
```

(continued)

(continued)

```
        this.specSection = specSection;
        this.specSectionPrimaryIndex = "01";
        this.specSectionSecondaryIndex = "00";
        this.to = null;
        this.transmittalDate = DateTime.Now;
        this.from = null;
        this.totalPages = 1;
        this.deliveryMethod = Delivery.None;
        this.otherDeliveryMethod = string.Empty;
        this.phaseNumber = string.Empty;
        this.reimbursable = false;
        this.final = false;
        this.copyToList = new List<CopyTo>();
        this.dateReceived = null;
        this.contractNumber = string.Empty;
        this.trackingItems = new List<TrackingItem>();
        this.routingItems = new List<RoutingItem>();
        this.remarks = string.Empty;
        this.action = ActionStatus.NoExceptionTaken;
        this.status = null;
        this.dateToField = null;
        this.remainderLocation = SubmittalRemainderLocation.None;
        this.remainderUnderSubmittalNumber = string.Empty;
        this.otherRemainderLocation = string.Empty;
        this.Validate();
    }
```

All of the data for the `Submittal` class are initialized and validated in the second constructor, which gets called by the first constructor. The default value for `specSectionPrimaryIndex` is "01"; this signifies the first submittal associated with a particular Specification Section. The default value for `specSectionSecondaryIndex` is "00"; the default value is retained unless another Submittal is created for the same Specification Section.

The Submittal Properties

The `Submittal` class does not have much behavior yet, aside from the getter for the `Number` property, which concatenates values in the submittal in order to produce a Submittal Number:

```
public object ProjectKey
    {
        get { return this.projectKey; }
    }

    public SpecificationSection SpecSection
    {
        get { return this.specSection; }
        set { this.specSection = value; }
    }

    public string SpecSectionPrimaryIndex
```

```
{
    get { return this.specSectionPrimaryIndex; }
    set { this.specSectionPrimaryIndex = value; }
}

public string SpecSectionSecondaryIndex
{
    get { return this.specSectionSecondaryIndex; }
    set { this.specSectionSecondaryIndex = value; }
}

public string Number
{
    get
    {
        return string.Format("{0}.{1}.{2}",
            this.specSection.Number, this.specSectionPrimaryIndex,
            this.specSectionSecondaryIndex);
    }
}

public ProjectContact To
{
    get { return this.to; }
    set { this.to = value; }
}

public DateTime TransmittalDate
{
    get { return this.transmittalDate; }
    set { this.transmittalDate = value; }
}

public Employee From
{
    get { return this.from; }
    set { this.from = value; }
}

public int TotalPages
{
    get { return this.totalPages; }
    set { this.totalPages = value; }
}

public Delivery DeliveryMethod
{
    get { return this.deliveryMethod; }
    set { this.deliveryMethod = value; }
}

public string OtherDeliveryMethod
```

(continued)

(continued)

```
    {
        get { return this.otherDeliveryMethod; }
        set { this.otherDeliveryMethod = value; }
    }

    public string PhaseNumber
    {
        get { return this.phaseNumber; }
        set { this.phaseNumber = value; }
    }

    public bool Reimbursable
    {
        get { return this.reimbursable; }
        set { this.reimbursable = value; }
    }

    public bool Final
    {
        get { return this.final; }
        set { this.final = value; }
    }

    public IList<CopyTo> CopyToList
    {
        get { return this.copyToList; }
    }

    public DateTime? DateReceived
    {
        get { return this.dateReceived; }
        set { this.dateReceived = value; }
    }

    public string ContractNumber
    {
        get { return this.contractNumber; }
        set { this.contractNumber = value; }
    }

    public IList<TrackingItem> TrackingItems
    {
        get { return this.trackingItems; }
    }

    public IList<RoutingItem> RoutingItems
    {
        get { return this.routingItems; }
    }
```

```
public string Remarks
{
    get { return this.remarks; }
    set { this.remarks = value; }
}

public ActionStatus Action
{
    get { return this.action; }
    set { this.action = value; }
}

public SubmittalStatus Status
{
    get { return this.status; }
    set { this.status = value; }
}

public DateTime? DateToField
{
    get { return this.dateToField; }
    set { this.dateToField = value; }
}

public SubmittalRemainderLocation RemainderLocation
{
    get { return this.remainderLocation; }
    set { this.remainderLocation = value; }
}

public string RemainderUnderSubmittalNumber
{
    get { return this.remainderUnderSubmittalNumber; }
    set { this.remainderUnderSubmittalNumber = value; }
}

public string OtherRemainderLocation
{
    get { return this.otherRemainderLocation; }
    set { this.otherRemainderLocation = value; }
}
```

Actually, this code could be simplified considerably because the properties currently do nothing other than setting or getting the backing field. In C# 3.0 the backing field can be created automatically by the compiler in these situations; however, I do actually want the private fields in this class because later I intend to add more behavior to this class and that behavior will be acting on the private fields.

The SpecSection Property

The `SpecSection` property represents a `SpecificationSection` class instance. The `SpecificationSection` class is a value class composed of a number, a title, and a description:

```
using System;

namespace SmartCA.Model.Projects
{
    public class SpecificationSection
    {
        private string number;
        private string title;
        private string description;

        public SpecificationSection(string number, string title,
            string description)
        {
            this.number = number;
            this.title = title;
            this.description = description;
        }

        public string Number
        {
            get { return this.number; }
        }

        public string Title
        {
            get { return this.title; }
        }

        public string Description
        {
            get { return this.description; }
        }
    }
}
```

Although the concept of a Specification Section is very important to Submittals, it is still a value class because it is only representing values. This may change later, but, for now, it makes things simple to keep this as a `Value` class.

The DeliveryMethod Property

The `DeliveryMethod` property of the Submittal class is represented by the `Delivery` enumeration:

```
using System;

namespace SmartCA.Model.Submittals
{
    [Flags]
    public enum Delivery
```

```
    {
        None = 0,
        Fax = 1,
        Overnight = 2,
        Mail = 4,
        Hand = 8,
        Other = 16
    }
}
```

Take a look at the `Flags` attribute on the enumeration. This means that the values of this enumeration can be combined, and when `ToString()` is called on the enumeration, it will render a comma-separated list of enumeration values, such as "Fax, Mail."

This is very handy when displaying the combination of values selected. I could do the same thing without the `Flags` attribute, but then the `ToString()` method would only render the value 5.

Using the enumeration in this way shows that the same Submittal can be delivered in a combination of ways, such as Fax and Mail, or Hand and Overnight.

The CopyToList Property

The `CopyToList` property represents all of the people that get a copy of the Submittal once it is transmitted. It is actually a `List` of type `CopyTo`. The `CopyTo` class is also a value class, containing read-only properties for a `ProjectContact` and notes about the `ProjectContact` being copied:

```csharp
using SmartCA.Model.Projects;

namespace SmartCA.Model.Submittals
{
    public class CopyTo
    {
        private ProjectContact contact;
        private string notes;

        public CopyTo(ProjectContact contact, string notes)
        {
            this.contact = contact;
            this.notes = notes;
        }

        public ProjectContact Contact
        {
            get { return this.contact; }
        }

        public string Notes
        {
            get { return this.notes; }
        }

        public override bool Equals(object obj)
```

(continued)

(continued)

```
        {
            return obj != null
                && obj.GetType() == typeof(CopyTo)
                && this == (CopyTo)obj;
        }

        public static bool operator ==(CopyTo one, CopyTo other)
        {
            // check for both null (cast to object to avoid recursive loop)
            if ((object)one == null && (object)other == null)
            {
                return true;
            }

            // check for either of them equal to null
            if ((object)one == null || (object)other == null)
            {
                return false;
            }

            if (one.Contact != other.Contact
                || one.Notes != other.Notes)
            {
                return false;
            }

            return true;
        }

        public static bool operator !=(CopyTo one, CopyTo other)
        {
            return !(one == other);
        }

        public override int GetHashCode()
        {
            return this.contact.GetHashCode()
                ^ this.notes.GetHashCode();
        }

        public override string ToString()
        {
            return string.Format("{0} - {1}",
                this.contact.Contact.LastName, this.notes);
        }
    }
}
```

As you will see in later chapters, it makes sense to have this class as a Value class, especially since it will be reused later in other parts of the domain model.

The TrackingItems Property

The TrackingItems property represents a List of type TrackingItem. The TrackingItem class is not a Value class, but it must be constructed with a SpecificationSection instance.

```
namespace SmartCA.Model.Submittals
{
    public class TrackingItem
    {
        private int totalItemsReceived;
        private int totalItemsSent;
        private int deferredApproval;
        private int substitutionNumber;
        private string description;
        private ActionStatus status;

        public TrackingItem()
        {
            this.totalItemsReceived = 0;
            this.totalItemsSent = 0;
            this.deferredApproval = 0;
            this.description = string.Empty;
            this.status = ActionStatus.NoExceptionTaken;
        }

        public int TotalItemsReceived
        {
            get { return this.totalItemsReceived; }
            set
            {
                if (value != this.totalItemsReceived)
                {
                    this.totalItemsReceived = value;
                    // Default to making the total number
                    // of items sent equal to what was received
                    this.totalItemsSent = value;
                }
            }
        }

        public int TotalItemsSent
        {
            get { return this.totalItemsSent; }
            set { this.totalItemsSent = value; }
        }

        public int DeferredApproval
        {
            get { return this.deferredApproval; }
            set { this.deferredApproval = value; }
        }

        public int SubstitutionNumber
```

(continued)

(continued)

```
            {
                get { return this.substitutionNumber; }
                set { this.substitutionNumber = value; }
            }

        public string Description
            {
                get { return this.description; }
                set { this.description = value; }
            }

        public ActionStatus Status
            {
                get { return this.status; }
                set { this.status = value; }
            }
        }
    }
```

The Constructor

The reason the `TrackingItem` class must be passed a `SpecificationSection` instance in its constructor is because that is what the `TrackingItem` class is providing information about, and it must have a value in order to do that.

The TotalItemsSent and TotalItemsReceived Properties

The `TotalItemsSent` property has logic in its setter to update automatically the `TotalItemsReceived` property to the same value as was received. This is a business rule specified by the Smart Design firm, and one that used to reside in the user interface code of the legacy application.

The DeferredApproval Property

There is nothing special, codewise, about this property, except that I need to explain the concept of Deferred Approval. The Deferred Approvals are documents that are prepared by others that are "deferred" agency submittal until the manufacturer is selected. These could be things like fire sprinkler systems, bleachers, and elevator guide rails. Once those plans are approved they become part of the Contract Documents.

They are typically listed on the General Sheet of the Smart Design firm's Drawings under a Deferred Approval section and are listed like:

1. Fire Sprinkler System
2. Bleachers
3. Elevator Guide Rails

The number they assign follows the number listed on the General Sheet. So, in this case, Fire Sprinkler System would have a Deferred Approval value of 1, Bleachers would have a value of 2, and so on.

The Status Property

The `Status` property is using the `ActionStatus` enumeration type. This type is fairly self-evident:

```
using System;

namespace SmartCA.Model.Submittals
{
    public enum ActionStatus
    {
        Accepted,
        AgencyApproved,
        MakeCorrectionsNoted,
        NoExceptionTaken,
        ReceiptAcknowledgedNoActionTaken,
        Rejected,
        ReturnedNoComment,
        ReviseResubmit,
        SubmitSpecificItem,
    }
}
```

The RoutingItems Property

The `RoutingItems` property represents a `List` of type `RoutingItem`. The `RoutingItem` class keeps track of who has seen a particular document, when the document was seen, and how long the document was held before it was returned. The `RoutingItem` class is not a `Value` class, but it must be constructed with the discipline of the person being routed to, who the person is and in what order they are in the routing, and when the item was sent to them.

```
using System;
using SmartCA.Model.Projects;

namespace SmartCA.Model.Submittals
{
    public class RoutingItem
    {
        private object key;
        private Discipline discipline;
        private int routingOrder;
        private ProjectContact recipient;
        private DateTime dateSent;
        private DateTime? dateReturned;
        private int daysLapsed;

        public RoutingItem(object key, Discipline discipline,
            int routingOrder, ProjectContact recipient,
            DateTime dateSent)
        {
            this.key = key;
            this.discipline = discipline;
            this.routingOrder = routingOrder;
            this.recipient = recipient;
```

(continued)

(continued)

```
            this.dateSent = dateSent;
            this.dateReturned = null;
            this.daysLapsed = 0;
    }

    public object Key
    {
        get { return this.key; }
    }

    public Discipline Discipline
    {
        get { return this.discipline; }
    }

    public int RoutingOrder
    {
        get { return this.routingOrder; }
    }

    public ProjectContact Recipient
    {
        get { return this.recipient; }
    }

    public DateTime DateSent
    {
        get { return this.dateSent; }
    }

    public DateTime? DateReturned
    {
        get { return this.dateReturned; }
        set
        {
            if (value != this.dateReturned && value.HasValue)
            {
                this.dateReturned = value;
                this.CalculateDaysLapsed();
            }
        }
    }

    public int DaysLapsed
    {
        get { return this.daysLapsed; }
    }

    private void CalculateDaysLapsed()
    {
        if (this.dateReturned.HasValue &&
            this.dateReturned.Value > this.dateSent)
```

```
                {
                    this.daysLapsed =
                        this.dateReturned.Value.Subtract(this.dateSent).Days;
                }
            }
        }
    }
```

The Constructor

The reason that the `RoutingItem` class must pass a `Discipline` instance, a `RoutingOrder` value, a `ProjectContact` instance, and a `DateTime` value in its constructor is that the `RoutingItem` class needs to know who the item is being routed to (`ProjectContact recipient`), what that person's discipline (`Discipline discipline`) is, and when (`DateTime dateSent`) it was sent to them. Without these values, the `RoutingItem` instance is useless.

The Properties

The `Discipline`, `RoutingOrder`, `Recipient`, and `DateSent` properties are all read-only, as their values can only be set in the constructor. In order to change these values, you must construct a new `RoutingItem` instance. The `DateReturned` value is the only property in the class that is not read-only, and when it is changed, it calls the `CalculateDaysLapsed` method if the value being passed to it is different from the original value. The `CalculateDaysLapsed` method figures out the number of days between when the item was sent and when it was returned, and then updates the value for the read-only `DaysLapsed` property.

The Status Property

The `Status` property indicates the overall status of the Submittal, such as whether it is complete or whether it has even been accepted yet. The `Status` property is represented by a `SubmittalStatus` instance. The `SubmittalStatus` class is a `Value` class, composed of an integer identification value and a status value of type `string`.

```
using System;

namespace SmartCA.Model.Submittals
{
    public class SubmittalStatus
    {
        private int id;
        private string status;

        public SubmittalStatus(int id, string status)
        {
            this.id = id;
            this.status = status;
        }

        public int Id
        {
            get { return this.id; }
        }

        public string Status
```

(continued)

(continued)

```
        {
            get { return this.status; }
        }
    }
}
```

The values for the `SubmittalStatus` class will come from the database.

The RemainderLocation Property

The `RemainderLocation` property is represented by the `SubmittalRemainderLocation` enumeration:

```
using System;

namespace SmartCA.Model.Submittals
{
    [Flags]
    public enum SubmittalRemainderLocation
    {
        None,
        RollDrawings,
        FilingCabinet,
        FilingCabinetUnderSubmittalNumber,
        Other
    }
}
```

This property indicates the location of the rest of the items associated with the Submittal. This is for Smart Design's use only and is not to be seen by third parties. This property allows Smart Design to tie together papers associated with the electronic Submittal in a timely fashion. They are not ready to go paperless just yet, and so this process is one way to allow them at least to track the location of their Submittal paper documents.

The Submittal Repository Implementation

After going over the `ISubmittalRepository` interface in the Design section, it is now time to explain how the `Submittal` class actually gets persisted to and from the data store by the Submittal repository. In this section, I will be writing the code for the Submittal repository.

Most of the work for building a Submittal instance from the data store is done in the `SqlCeReposiotryBase<T>` class. If you recall, the Template Method pattern I have been using in the repositories for getting Entity Root instances, the `BuildChildCallbacks` method, must be overridden in the `SubmittalRepository`.

```
        #region BuildChildCallbacks

        protected override void BuildChildCallbacks()
        {
            this.ChildCallbacks.Add(SubmittalFactory.FieldNames.EmployeeId,
                this.AppendFrom);
```

```
        this.ChildCallbacks.Add(SubmittalFactory.FieldNames.ProjectContactId,
            this.AppendTo);
    this.ChildCallbacks.Add("CopyToList",
        delegate(Submittal submittal, object childKeyName)
        {
            this.AppendCopyToList(submittal);
        });
    this.ChildCallbacks.Add("TrackingItems",
        delegate(Submittal submittal, object childKeyName)
        {
            this.AppendTrackingItems(submittal);
        });
    this.ChildCallbacks.Add("RoutingItems",
        delegate(Submittal submittal, object childKeyName)
        {
            this.AppendRoutingItems(submittal);
        });
}

#endregion
```

The AppendFrom Callback

The first entry made in the ChildCallbacks dictionary is for the AppendFrom method. Thanks to the EmployeeService class's GetEmployee method, this method's code is very simple:

```
private void AppendFrom(Submittal submittal, object fromEmployeeId)
{
    submittal.From = EmployeeService.GetEmployee(fromEmployeeId);
}
```

You may recall the GetEmployee private method in the ProjectRepository class from Chapter 3. I have since refactored the code from the GetEmployee method into the EmployeeService class where it really belongs:

```
public static Employee GetEmployee(object employeeKey)
{
    return EmployeeService.repository.FindBy(employeeKey);
}
```

This method simply delegates to the IEmployeeRepository interface instance to find an Employee by the method's employeeKey argument.

The AppendTo Callback

This method is very similar to the AppendFrom method; instead of retrieving an Employee, however, it retrieves and adds a ProjectContact to the Submittal:

```
private void AppendTo(Submittal submittal, object fromProjectContactKey)
{
    submittal.To = ProjectService.GetProjectContact(submittal.ProjectKey,
        fromProjectContactKey);
}
```

This uses the `ProjectContactService`'s class newly added `GetProjectContact` method to find the right `ProjectContact` based on the key value:

```
public static ProjectContact GetProjectContact(object projectKey,
    object projectContactKey)
{

    // Get the list of contacts for the project
    List<ProjectContact> contacts = new List<ProjectContact>(
            ProjectService.projectRepository.FindBy(projectKey).Contacts);
    // Return the one that matches the key
    return contacts.Where(c => c.Key.Equals(projectContactKey)).Single();
}
```

The `GetProjectContact` method first uses the ProjectRepository's `FindBy` method to get the correct Project instance, and it then gets the `Contacts` property (which is an `IList<ProjectContact>` type) of the found Project. I then take the `IList<ProjectContact>` instance and use it to initialize a `List<ProjectContact>` type. I then turn the `IList<ProjectContact>` type into a `List<ProjectContact>` type. The reason why I do this is so that I can use a LINQ query on the `List<ProjectContact>` instance to easily find the ProjectContact I am trying to traverse to:

```
// Return the one that matches the key
return contacts.Where(c => c.Key.Equals(projectContactKey)).Single();
```

The above code uses a lambda expression (`c => c.Key.Equals(projectContactKey)`) as an argument for the `Where` extension method on the `List<T>` class to return a type of `IEnumerable<ProjectContactContact>`. The `Single` extension method of the `IEnumerable<T>` class is then used to return a single ProjectContact instance. Pretty cool, huh? That LINQ query saved me several lines of code, and I think that it makes the intent of what I am trying to do much more obvious.

The AppendCopyToList Callback

The `AppendCopyToList` method has to perform a query on the database to get a list of `CopyTo` instances and then adds the items from the list to the `CopyToList` property on the `Submittal` class:

```
private void AppendCopyToList(Submittal submittal)
{
    StringBuilder builder = new StringBuilder(100);
    builder.Append("SELECT * FROM SubmittalCopyList");
    builder.Append(string.Format(" WHERE SubmittalID = '{0}';",
        submittal.Key));
    using (IDataReader reader = this.ExecuteReader(builder.ToString()))
    {
        while (reader.Read())
        {
            submittal.CopyToList.Add(SubmittalFactory.BuildCopyTo(
                submittal.ProjectKey, reader));
        }
    }
}
```

As the code iterates through the IDataReader results of the query, I use the SubmittalFactory's BuildCopyTo method to build the CopyTo instance from the IDataReader's current position. The BuildCopyTo method is also fairly interesting, as it uses the ProjectContactService class to help it get its job done:

```
internal static CopyTo BuildCopyTo(object projectKey, IDataReader reader)
{
    ProjectContact contact = ProjectService.GetProjectContact(projectKey,
        reader[FieldNames.ProjectContactId]);
    return new CopyTo(contact, reader[FieldNames.Notes].ToString());
}
```

The GetProjectContact method being called should look familiar, since I just showed that earlier in the chapter. Notice, also, that the CopyTo class is a Value class, as evidenced by having to supply all of the data for the class to its constructor.

The AppendTrackingItems Callback

This method is very similar to the AppendCopyToList method just shown:

```
private void AppendTrackingItems(Submittal submittal)
{
    StringBuilder builder = new StringBuilder(100);
    builder.Append("SELECT * FROM SubmittalTrackingItem");
    builder.Append(string.Format(" WHERE SubmittalID = '{0}';",
        submittal.Key));
    using (IDataReader reader = this.ExecuteReader(builder.ToString()))
    {
        while (reader.Read())
        {
            submittal.TrackingItems.Add(
                SubmittalFactory.BuildTrackingItem(reader));
        }
    }
}
```

It also uses a StringBuilder to build up a SQL statement, and then uses SqlCeRepositoryBase<T> to get an IDataReader instance. While iterating through the IDataReader, it also uses the SubmittalFactory, this time calling the BuildTrackingItem method.

```
private void AppendTrackingItems(Submittal submittal)
{
    StringBuilder builder = new StringBuilder(100);
    builder.Append("SELECT * FROM SubmittalTrackingItem sti");
    builder.Append(" INNER JOIN SpecificationSection ss");
    builder.Append(" ON sti.SpecificationSectionID =");
    builder.Append( "ss.SpecificationSectionID");
    builder.Append(string.Format(" WHERE SubmittalID = '{0}';",
        submittal.Key));
    using (IDataReader reader = this.ExecuteReader(builder.ToString()))
    {
        while (reader.Read())
```

(continued)

181

(continued)

```
            {
                submittal.TrackingItems.Add(
                    SubmittalFactory.BuildTrackingItem(reader));
            }
        }
    }
```

The `BuildTrackingItem` method first builds a `SpecificationSection` object to pass in to the `TrackingItem` class's constructor, and then it populates the rest of the class's properties:

```
internal static TrackingItem BuildTrackingItem(IDataReader reader)
{
    TrackingItem item = new TrackingItem(
                        SubmittalFactory.BuildSpecSection(reader));
    item.TotalItemsReceived = DataHelper.GetInteger(
        reader[FieldNames.TotalItemsReceived]);
    item.TotalItemsSent = DataHelper.GetInteger(
        reader[FieldNames.TotalItemsSent]);
    item.DeferredApproval = DataHelper.GetInteger(
        reader[FieldNames.DeferredApproval]);
    item.SubstitutionNumber = DataHelper.GetInteger(
        reader[FieldNames.SubstitutionNumber]);
    item.Description = reader[FieldNames.Description].ToString();
    item.Status = DataHelper.GetEnumValue<ActionStatus>(
        reader[FieldNames.Status].ToString());
    return item;
}
```

I get some nice code reuse when building the `SpecificationSection` instance via the `BuildSpecSection` method of the factory. The rest of this factory method is just setting properties on the `TrackingItem` from the `IDataReader` instance.

The AppendRoutingItems Callback

This method is also similar to the previous callback methods, following the same pattern of executing a SQL statement and delegating to the factory to build `RoutingItem` instances:

```
private void AppendRoutingItems(Submittal submittal)
{
    StringBuilder builder = new StringBuilder(100);
    builder.Append("SELECT * FROM SubmittalRoutingItem sri ");
    builder.Append(" INNER JOIN RoutingItem ri ON");
    builder.Append(" sri.RoutingItemID = ri.RoutingItemID");
    builder.Append(" INNER JOIN Discipline d ON");
    builder.Append(" ri.DisciplineID = d.DisciplineID");
    builder.Append(string.Format(" WHERE sri.SubmittalID = '{0}';",
        submittal.Key));
    using (IDataReader reader = this.ExecuteReader(builder.ToString()))
```

```
        {
            while (reader.Read())
            {
                submittal.RoutingItems.Add(SubmittalFactory.BuildRoutingItem(
                    submittal.ProjectKey, reader));
            }
        }
    }
```

This code should look very familiar to you by now, except for the SQL statement requiring a few more joins to get all of the necessary data into the `IDataReader` instance. I am not going to show the `BuildRoutingItem` method of the `SubmittalFactory` class, since it is very similar to the `BuildCopyTo` method just shown.

Unit of Work Implementation

Following the same steps that I have shown before to implement the Unit of Work pattern, I only need to override three methods, `PersistNewItem(Submittal item)`, `PersistUpdatedItem(Submittal item)`, and `PersistDeletedItem(Submittal item)`.

The PersistNewItem Method

The first method override for the `SubmittalRepository`'s Unit of Work implementation is the `PersistNewItem` method:

```
protected override void PersistNewItem(Submittal item)
        {
            StringBuilder builder = new StringBuilder(100);
            builder.Append(string.Format("INSERT INTO Submittal
({0},{1},{2},{3},{4},{5},{6},{7},{8},{9},{10},{11},{12},{13},{14},{15},{16},{17},
{18},{19},{20},{21}) ",
                SubmittalFactory.FieldNames.SubmittalId,
                ProjectFactory.FieldNames.ProjectId,
                SubmittalFactory.FieldNames.SpecificationSectionId,
                SubmittalFactory.FieldNames.SpecificationSectionPrimaryIndex,
                SubmittalFactory.FieldNames.SpecificationSectionSecondaryIndex,
                SubmittalFactory.FieldNames.ProjectContactId,
                SubmittalFactory.FieldNames.EmployeeId,
                SubmittalFactory.FieldNames.TotalPages,
                SubmittalFactory.FieldNames.DeliveryMethod,
                SubmittalFactory.FieldNames.OtherDeliveryMethod,
                SubmittalFactory.FieldNames.PhaseNumber,
                SubmittalFactory.FieldNames.Reimbursable,
                SubmittalFactory.FieldNames.Final,
                SubmittalFactory.FieldNames.DateReceived,
                SubmittalFactory.FieldNames.ContractNumber,
                SubmittalFactory.FieldNames.Remarks,
                SubmittalFactory.FieldNames.Action,
                SubmittalFactory.FieldNames.SubmittalStatusId,
                SubmittalFactory.FieldNames.DateToField,
                SubmittalFactory.FieldNames.RemainderLocation,
                SubmittalFactory.FieldNames.RemainderUnderSubmittalNumber,
```

(continued)

(continued)

```
                SubmittalFactory.FieldNames.OtherRemainderLocation));
        builder.Append(string.Format("VALUES ({0},{1},{2},{3},{4},{5},{6},{7},
    {8},{9},{10},{11},{12},{13},{14},{15},{16},{17},{18},{19},{20},{21});",
                DataHelper.GetSqlValue(item.Key),
                DataHelper.GetSqlValue(item.ProjectKey),
                DataHelper.GetSqlValue(item.SpecSection.Key),
                DataHelper.GetSqlValue(item.SpecSectionPrimaryIndex),
                DataHelper.GetSqlValue(item.SpecSectionSecondaryIndex),
                DataHelper.GetSqlValue(item.To.Key),
                DataHelper.GetSqlValue(item.From.Key),
                DataHelper.GetSqlValue(item.TotalPages),
                DataHelper.GetSqlValue(item.DeliveryMethod),
                DataHelper.GetSqlValue(item.OtherDeliveryMethod),
                DataHelper.GetSqlValue(item.PhaseNumber),
                DataHelper.GetSqlValue(item.Reimbursable),
                DataHelper.GetSqlValue(item.Final),
                DataHelper.GetSqlValue(item.DateReceived),
                DataHelper.GetSqlValue(item.ContractNumber),
                DataHelper.GetSqlValue(item.Remarks),
                DataHelper.GetSqlValue(item.Action),
                DataHelper.GetSqlValue(item.Status.Id),
                DataHelper.GetSqlValue(item.DateToField),
                DataHelper.GetSqlValue(item.RemainderLocation),
                DataHelper.GetSqlValue(item.RemainderUnderSubmittalNumber),
                DataHelper.GetSqlValue(item.OtherRemainderLocation)));

        this.Database.ExecuteNonQuery(
            this.Database.GetSqlStringCommand(builder.ToString()));

        // Now do the child objects
        this.InsertCopyToList(item);
        this.InsertRoutingItems(item);
        this.InsertTrackingItems(item);
    }
```

The code builds up a large insert statement composed of the values from the `Submittal` instance, and then executes the query using the Microsoft Enterprise Library's `Database` object. After the insert statement has been executed, I also need to insert the `CopyTo`, `RoutingItem`, and `TrackingItem` instances for the Submittal. I do this by calling the `InsertCopyToList`, `InsertRoutingItems`, and `InsertTrackingItems` methods, which all take a Submittal instance as an argument. The `InsertCopyToList` method saves all of the Submittal's `CopyTo` items in the database:

```
    private void InsertCopyToList(Submittal submittal)
    {
        foreach (CopyTo copyTo in submittal.CopyToList)
        {
            this.InsertCopyTo(copyTo, submittal.Key);
        }
    }
```

The `InsertCopyToList` method just iterates the `CopyToList` property of the `Submittal` instance and calls `InsertCopyTo` on each item in the list. `InsertCopyTo` then saves the `CopyTo` instance to the database:

```
private void InsertCopyTo(CopyTo copyTo, object key)
{
    StringBuilder builder = new StringBuilder(100);
    builder.Append(string.Format("INSERT INTO SubmittalCopyList
({0},{1},{2}) ",
        SubmittalFactory.FieldNames.SubmittalId,
        SubmittalFactory.FieldNames.ProjectContactId,
        SubmittalFactory.FieldNames.Notes));
    builder.Append(string.Format("VALUES ({0},{1},{2});",
        DataHelper.GetSqlValue(key),
        DataHelper.GetSqlValue(copyTo.Contact.Key),
        DataHelper.GetSqlValue(copyTo.Notes)));

    this.Database.ExecuteNonQuery(
        this.Database.GetSqlStringCommand(builder.ToString()));
}
```

The code for `InsertCopyTo` should look very familiar; it follows the same pattern of building a SQL insert string and then executing it against the database.

I am not going to show the code for the `InsertRoutingItems` and `InsertTrackingItems` methods because they and their helper methods are almost identical to the `InsertCopyToList` method and its helper methods.

The PersistUpdatedItem Method

`PersistUpdatedItem` first does an update to the Submittal table:

```
protected override void PersistUpdatedItem(Submittal item)
{
    StringBuilder builder = new StringBuilder(100);
    builder.Append("UPDATE Submittal SET ");

    builder.Append(string.Format("{0} = {1}",
        SubmittalFactory.FieldNames.SpecificationSectionId,
        DataHelper.GetSqlValue(item.SpecSection.Key)));

    builder.Append(string.Format(",{0} = {1}",
        SubmittalFactory.FieldNames.SpecificationSectionPrimaryIndex,
        DataHelper.GetSqlValue(item.SpecSectionPrimaryIndex)));

    *******************************************************************

    builder.Append(string.Format(",{0} = {1}",
        SubmittalFactory.FieldNames.OtherRemainderLocation,
        DataHelper.GetSqlValue(item.OtherRemainderLocation)));
```

(continued)

(continued)

```
        builder.Append(" ");
        builder.Append(this.BuildBaseWhereClause(item.Key));

        this.Database.ExecuteNonQuery(
            this.Database.GetSqlStringCommand(builder.ToString()));

        // Now do the child objects

        // First, delete the existing ones
        this.DeleteCopyToList(item);
        this.DeleteRoutingItems(item);
        this.DeleteTrackingItems(item);

        // Now, add the current ones
        this.InsertCopyToList(item);
        this.InsertRoutingItems(item);
        this.InsertTrackingItems(item);
    }
```

I have omitted several lines of repetitive code building the SQL update statement in the middle of the code in order save you from the boring code. The omitted lines are represented by the stars (**********).

The second part of the method uses the `DeleteCoyToList`, `DeleteRoutingItems`, and `DeleteTrackingItems` helper methods to delete all of the child objects of the Submittal, and then uses the familiar `InsertCopyToList`, `InsertRoutingItems`, and `InsertTrackingItems` helper methods to add the existing child objects from the Submittal to the database. `DeleteCopyToList` runs a query against the `SubmittalCopyList` table to remove all entries with a matching `SubmittalID` field value.

```
        private void DeleteCopyToList(Submittal submittal)
        {
            string query = string.Format("DELETE FROM SubmittalCopyList {0}",
                this.BuildBaseWhereClause(submittal.Key));
            this.Database.ExecuteNonQuery(
                this.Database.GetSqlStringCommand(query));
        }
```

The `DeleteRoutingItems` and `DeleteTrackingItems` are very similar to the `DeleteCopyToList` method, so I will not show the code for those methods here.

The PersistDeletedItem Method

The last method in `SubmittalRepository` to override, `PersistDeletedItem`, follows the same pattern that I have shown for the `PersistDeletedItem` override in the other Repository classes:

```
        protected override void PersistDeletedItem(Submittal item)
        {
            // Delete the child objects first
            this.DeleteCopyToList(item);
            this.DeleteRoutingItems(item);
```

```
                    this.DeleteTrackingItems(item);

                    // Now delete the submittal
                    string query = string.Format("DELETE FROM Submittal {0}",
                        this.BuildBaseWhereClause(item.Key));
                    this.Database.ExecuteNonQuery(
                        this.Database.GetSqlStringCommand(query));
            }
```

This code deletes all of the child objects from the Submittal first, and then deletes the Submittal record from the database.

The Submittal Service Implementation

The only Service classes I have implemented up to this point are the Service classes that live in the domain model layer and act as facades for their respective Repository interfaces.

The SubmittalService class is responsible for retrieving and saving Submittal instances:

```
using System.Collections.Generic;
using SmartCA.Infrastructure;
using SmartCA.Infrastructure.RepositoryFramework;
using SmartCA.Model.Projects;

namespace SmartCA.Model.Submittals
{
    public static class SubmittalService
    {
        private static ISubmittalRepository repository;
        private static IUnitOfWork unitOfWork;

        static SubmittalService()
        {
            SubmittalService.unitOfWork = new UnitOfWork();
            SubmittalService.repository =
                RepositoryFactory.GetRepository<ISubmittalRepository,
                Submittal>(SubmittalService.unitOfWork);
        }

        public static IList<Submittal> GetSubmittals(Project project)
        {
            return SubmittalService.repository.FindBy(project);
        }

        public static IList<SpecificationSection> GetSpecificationSections()
        {
            return SubmittalService.repository.FindAllSpecificationSections();
        }
```

(continued)

187

(continued)

```
        public static IList<SubmittalStatus> GetSubmittalStatuses()
        {
            return SubmittalService.repository.FindAllSubmittalStatuses();
        }

        public static void SaveSubmittal(Submittal submittal)
        {
            SubmittalService.repository[submittal.Key] = submittal;
            SubmittalService.unitOfWork.Commit();
        }

        public static IList<Discipline> GetDisciplines()
        {
            return SubmittalService.repository.FindAllDisciplines();
        }
    }
}
```

This class, like the other `Service` classes in the application, is just acting as a façade for the `ISubmittalRepository` instance. All of the methods from the `ISubmittalRepository` interface are now exposed as static methods, which, as you will see in the next section covering the `SubmittalViewModel` class, make it very easy to interact with the repository.

The Submittal View Model

Following the same patterns as before, the `SubmittalViewModel` class adapts the Submittal Aggregate from the domain model to the UI. Like all previously shown `ViewModel` classes, I start out by inheriting from the `ViewModel` abstract class:

```
using System;
using System.Collections.Generic;
using SmartCA.Infrastructure.UI;
using SmartCA.Model.Submittals;
using System.Windows.Data;
using SmartCA.Application;
using SmartCA.Model.Employees;
using System.ComponentModel;
using SmartCA.Model.Projects;

namespace SmartCA.Presentation.ViewModels
{
    public class SubmittalViewModel : ViewModel
    {
```

The Constructor

As you have already seen in the `CompanyViewModel` and `ProjectContactViewModel` classes, anywhere that there is a parent-child relationship in the Aggregate, such as Company and Addresses, a `BindingList<T>` must be used to represent the child list in the ViewModel. This is because the Xceed DataGrid needs to bind to the `IBindingList<T>` interface to be able to add records to the grid dynamically. In the `SubmittalViewModel`, that means I need to use a `BindingList<T>` for the `CopyToList`, `RoutingItems`, and `TrackingItems` Submittal properties.

```
#region Constructors

public SubmittalViewModel()
    : this(null)
{
}

public SubmittalViewModel(IView view)
    : base(view)
{
    this.currentSubmittal = null;
    this.submittalsList = new List<Submittal>(
                            SubmittalService.GetSubmittals(
                            UserSession.CurrentProject));
    this.submittals = new CollectionView(this.submittalsList);
    this.specificationSections
        = SubmittalService.GetSpecificationSections();
    this.submittalStatuses = SubmittalService.GetSubmittalStatuses();
    this.toList = UserSession.CurrentProject.Contacts;
    this.mutableCopyToList = new BindingList<MutableCopyTo>();
    this.routingItems = new BindingList<RoutingItem>();
    this.trackingItems = new BindingList<TrackingItem>();
    this.fromList = EmployeeService.GetEmployees();
    this.trackingStatusValues = new CollectionView(
                                    Enum.GetNames(typeof(ActionStatus)));
    this.deliveryMethods = new CollectionView(
                                Enum.GetNames(typeof(Delivery)));
    this.disciplines = SubmittalService.GetDisciplines();
    this.saveCommand = new DelegateCommand(this.SaveCommandHandler);
    this.newCommand = new DelegateCommand(this.NewCommandHandler);
    this.deleteCopyToCommand =
        new DelegateCommand(this.DeleteCopyToCommandHandler);
    this.deleteRoutingItemCommand =
        new DelegateCommand(this.DeleteRoutingItemCommandHandler);
    this.deleteTrackingItemCommand =
        new DelegateCommand(this.DeleteTrackingItemCommandHandler);
}

#endregion
```

The MutableCopyTo type is very similar to the MutableAddress type shown in previous chapters, and it is used to edit the values for the CopyTo Value type. Remember, in WPF, I cannot use two-way binding with read-only objects, so the MutableCopyTo gives me that flexibility without changing any of my domain objects.

Similarly to what I did to maintain the list of Contacts and Companies in the last chapter, I am again maintaining both a List<Submittal> variable (submittalsList) and the CollectionView variable (submittals) of the list. This allows me the benefit of using the CollectionView to know when a Submittal has been selected from the CollectionView (without having to write any code) and to be able to add new Submittals, which need to be added to the list. Using the List<Submittal> type, I am easily able to add new Submittal instances and then subsequently refresh the CollectionView. The other pattern I am following in this constructor is to initialize all of my property data, such as the data used to display all of the dropdowns in the UI (i.e., Employees, ProjectContacts, etc.). The rest of the constructor code is the standard wire-up code for the DelegateCommand instances.

The Properties

The CurrentSubmittal property indicates the current Submittal instance that is being edited:

```
public Submittal CurrentSubmittal
{
    get { return this.currentSubmittal; }
    set
    {
        if (this.currentSubmittal != value)
        {
            this.currentSubmittal = value;
            this.OnPropertyChanged(Constants.CurrentSubmittalPropertyName);
            this.saveCommand.IsEnabled = (this.currentSubmittal != null);
            this.PopulateSubmittalChildren();
        }
    }
}
```

Just as with Contacts and Companies, whenever a Submittal is selected from the list box in the UI, the property's setter is called. Once that has happened, the PropertyChanged event for the CurrentSubmittal property is raised, letting the UI know to refresh itself. The next thing to happen is to set the SaveCommand's IsEnabled property to true if the current Submittal is null; otherwise, it is set to false. Then the PopulateSubmittalChildren method is called:

```
private void PopulateSubmittalChildren()
{
    this.PopulateMutableCopyToList();
    this.PopulateRoutingItems();
    this.PopulateTrackingItems();
}
```

This is essentially a controller method, as it calls three more methods to populate the collections representing the children of the Submittal Aggregate.

The PopulateMutableCopyToList method is very similar to the PopulateAddresses method used in the last chapter:

```
private void PopulateMutableCopyToList()
{
    if (this.currentSubmittal != null)
    {
        this.mutableCopyToList.Clear();
        foreach (CopyTo copyTo in this.currentSubmittal.CopyToList)
        {
            this.mutableCopyToList.Add(new MutableCopyTo(copyTo));
        }
        this.OnPropertyChanged(Constants.MutableCopyToListPropertyName);
    }
}
```

This is necessary because the `CopyTo` instances contained in the Submittal's `CopyToList` property are the immutable `CopyTo` types, and in order to be able to edit the `CopyToList`, I have to convert them into `MutableCopyTo` types. Once this is done, the `PropertyChanged` event for the `MutableCopyToList` property is raised so that the UI can refresh itself.

The `PopulateRoutingItems` and `PopulateTrackingItems` methods are almost identical, so I will just show `PopulateRoutingItems` method:

```csharp
private void PopulateRoutingItems()
{
    if (this.currentSubmittal != null)
    {
        this.routingItems.Clear();
        foreach (RoutingItem item in this.currentSubmittal.RoutingItems)
        {
            this.routingItems.Add(item);
        }
        this.OnPropertyChanged(Constants.RoutingItemsPropertyName);
    }
}
```

You may be asking yourself, "Why can't we just use the `RoutingItems` property of the Submittal class? Why do we have to create a whole new separate property for that and have to maintain the state between the two?" That's a good question, and the answer is because I need the `RoutingItems` property to be in the form of a `BindingList<RoutingItem>` rather than an `IList<RoutingItem>`. The reason I need it to be in that form is because that is the type that my data grid (Xceed Data Grid for WPF) is looking for in order to get the nice functionality of adding rows to the grid at run time without writing any code.

The rest of the properties in the `SubmittalViewModel` class are simple read-only properties representing lookup lists, and the `DelegateCommand` instances for creating New Submittals, saving Submittals, and deleting `RoutingItems`, `TrackingItems`, and `CopyTo` instances from the Submittal Aggregate.

Command Handler Methods

The handlers for the `DelegateCommand` properties are pretty interesting. The `NewCommandHandler` method has to do a lot of housekeeping:

```csharp
private void NewCommandHandler(object sender, EventArgs e)
{
    Submittal newSubmittal = new Submittal(
                                this.currentSubmittal.SpecSection,
                                this.currentSubmittal.ProjectKey);
    newSubmittal.SpecSectionSecondaryIndex = "01";

    this.currentSubmittal = null;
    this.mutableCopyToList.Clear();
    this.routingItems.Clear();
    this.trackingItems.Clear();
```

(continued)

(continued)

```
            this.CurrentObjectState = ObjectState.New;
            this.OnPropertyChanged(
                Constants.CurrentSubmittalPropertyName);

            this.submittalsList.Add(newSubmittal);
            this.submittals.Refresh();
            this.submittals.MoveCurrentToLast();
        }
```

It first has to create a new instance of a `Submittal` and initialize its `SpecSection` constructor argument to be the same as the current Submittal, as well as feed it the same Project key as the current Submittal. This is necessary because a Submittal cannot be created without knowing the Specification Section or to what Project it belongs. The Specification Section value can be changed via a property setter later, but to start I need to put something there. As far as the Project key, that cannot be changed unless a different project is selected altogether. Once the Submittal has been created, it is given a default Specification Section Secondary Index of "01". This is to prevent any duplicate entries, and once again, can be changed via property setters later.

The next steps are to clear the current Submittal data and then to clear out the `MutableCopyToList`, `RoutingItems`, and `TrackingItems` lists. Once that is done, the state of the ViewModel is set to `New`, and the `PropertyChanged` event is raised for the UI to refresh itself.

Next, the newly created Submittal is added to the current list of Submittals, and then the `Refresh` method is called on the `CollectionView` submittals variable in order to have the UI refreshed. Finally, by calling the `MoveCurrentToLast` method on the `CollectionView`, the Submittal will appear last in the list in the UI.

The `DeleteCopyToCommandHandler` method is interesting because it gets the `MutableCopyTo` instance that must be deleted passed to it from the `DelegateCommandEventArgs` parameter:

```
        private void DeleteCopyToCommandHandler(object sender,
            DelegateCommandEventArgs e)
        {
            MutableCopyTo copyTo = e.Parameter as MutableCopyTo;
            if (copyTo != null)
            {
                this.mutableCopyToList.Remove(copyTo);
            }
        }
```

It then checks to see whether the `MutableCopyTo` instance is null, and if it is not, it removes it from the `BindingList<MutableCopyTo>` collection (the `mutableCopyToList` variable). Once this happens, the data grid that is bound to it is automatically updated. The `DeleteCopyToCommandHandler` and `DeleteCopyToCommandHandler` methods are almost identical to the `DeleteCopyToCommandHandler` method, so I will not show them here.

The Submittal View

The View for Submittals is the most complicated view encountered so far, because it has to manage all of the parent-child relationships in the Aggregate. Before diving into the XAML for the `SubmittalView`, take a look at Figure 5.5, which shows what the form looks like at run time:

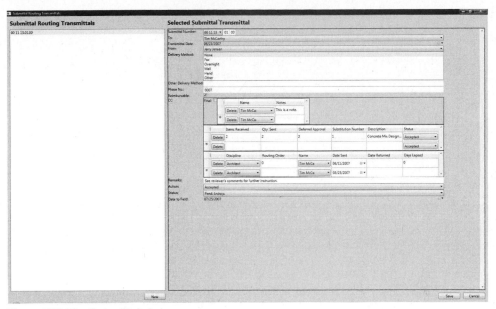

Figure 5.5: The Submittal view.

The form is not the most elegant looking in the world, but it is functional.

Like the form for Companies and Contacts, this form is split into two parts: the one on the left is for selecting a Submittal to edit and the one on the right is for editing the selected Submittal. The New button adds a new Submittal to the list. The Save and Cancel buttons both deal with the currently selected Submittal.

In the form, you will see three grid areas, one for the `CopyToList`, one for `TrackingItems`, and one for `RoutingItems`. These have all been implemented as separate user controls, so that they may be reused in other parts of the UI that require routing, tracking, and copying.

The XAML for this form is pretty large, so I am only going to show the sections that are implemented differently from what has been done so far in the UI.

Using the StackPanel Element

The first interesting part WPF-wise is the very top field, the Submittal Number field:

```
<Label Grid.Row="0" Grid.Column="0" Content="Submittal Number:"
Style="{StaticResource baseLabelStyle}"/>

<StackPanel Orientation="Horizontal" Grid.Row="0" Grid.Column="1">
    <ComboBox SelectedItem="{Binding Path=CurrentSubmittal.SpecSection}"
        IsSynchronizedWithCurrentItem="True"
        DisplayMemberPath="Number"
        ItemsSource="{Binding Path=SpecificationSections}">
    </ComboBox>
```

(continued)

(continued)

```
<TextBox
    Text="{Binding Path=CurrentSubmittal.SpecSectionPrimaryIndex}"/>
<TextBox
    Text="{Binding Path=CurrentSubmittal.SpecSectionSecondaryIndex}"/>
</StackPanel>
```

The first part is just the label for the field. The second part needs to squeeze a combo box and two textboxes right next to each other. In WPF, this is not possible to do in a single cell of a `Grid`, but the way around that limitation is to wrap a `StackPanel` around the three elements, and then the `StackPanel` becomes the only child element in the grid cell. `StackPanel` elements allow you to group more than one element together. This is a good thing to remember when building WPF applications.

Using the Xceed DatePicker Control

In order to allow users to edit date fields, I am using the Xceed DatePicker control, which comes for free with the free WPF Data Grid control. The first occasion I need to use it is for the Transmittal Date field:

```
<Label Grid.Row="2" Grid.Column="0" Content="Transmittal Date:"
    Style="{StaticResource baseLabelStyle}"/>
<xcdg:DatePicker Grid.Row="2" Grid.Column="1"
    SelectedDate="{Binding Path=CurrentSubmittal.TransmittalDate}"
    SyncCalendarWithSelectedDate="True" />
```

The first part of the XAML is just for the label, but the second part contains the `DatePicker` element, which supports binding to `DateTime` properties (in this case, I am binding to the `TransmittalDate` property of the Submittal). Also, it has a nice feature that syncs the calendar with the selected date, which looks like Figure 5.6.

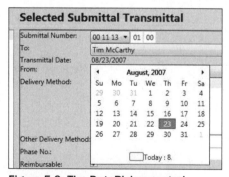

Figure 5.6: The DatePicker control.

This is great, because once again, I do not have to write that UI plumbing code, Xceed has already done a great job for me.

The CopyToList Section

The next interesting part of the XAML for the form is the section that displays the `CopyTo` child items, as shown in Figure 5.7.

Figure 5.7: The CopyToList section.

This requires using a `StackPanel` element again in order to stack the Final checkbox field next to the grid:

```
<Border BorderBrush="Black" Padding="1" BorderThickness="1"
 Grid.Row="8" Grid.Column="1">
    <StackPanel Orientation="Horizontal">
        <Label Content="Final: " Style="{StaticResource baseLabelStyle}"/>
        <CheckBox IsChecked="{Binding Path=CurrentSubmittal.Final}" />
        <presentation:CopyToList DataContext="{Binding Path=MutableCopyToList}"/>
    </StackPanel>
</Border>
```

Also included in the mix for this section is the `Border` element that wraps the `StackPanel`. This is what gives the border line around the controls. Then, inside of the `StackPanel` is the label for the checkbox, the actual checkbox itself, and then the `CopyTo` grid. The `CopyTo` grid is actually a new user control, the `CopyToList` user control. Here is the XAML for the `CopyToList` control:

```
<UserControl x:Class="SmartCA.Presentation.Views.CopyToList"
    xmlns="http://schemas.microsoft.com/winfx/2006/xaml/presentation"
    xmlns:xcdg="http://schemas.xceed.com/wpf/xaml/datagrid"
    xmlns:x="http://schemas.microsoft.com/winfx/2006/xaml">
    <xcdg:DataGridControl ItemsSource="{Binding}">
        <xcdg:DataGridControl.Columns>
            <xcdg:Column Width="50" FieldName="DeleteButton"
                    DisplayMemberBinding="{Binding .}">
                <xcdg:Column.CellContentTemplate>
                    <DataTemplate>
                        <Button Content="Delete"
                            Command="{Binding
                            RelativeSource=
                            {RelativeSource FindAncestor,
                            AncestorType={x:Type Window}},
                            Path=DataContext.DeleteCopyToCommand}">
                            <Button.CommandParameter>
                                <Binding Path="."/>
                            </Button.CommandParameter>
                        </Button>
                    </DataTemplate>
                </xcdg:Column.CellContentTemplate>
            </xcdg:Column>
```

(continued)

(continued)

```xml
                        <xcdg:Column FieldName="ProjectContact" Title="Name">
                            <xcdg:Column.CellContentTemplate>
                                <DataTemplate>
                                    <ComboBox
                                            ItemsSource="{Binding
                                            RelativeSource=
                                            {RelativeSource FindAncestor,
                                            AncestorType={x:Type Window}},
                                            Path=DataContext.ToList}"
                                            SelectedItem="{Binding .}"
                                            IsSynchronizedWithCurrentItem="True">
                                        <ComboBox.ItemTemplate>
                                            <DataTemplate>
                                                <Grid>

<Grid.ColumnDefinitions>

<ColumnDefinition />

<ColumnDefinition />

<ColumnDefinition />

</Grid.ColumnDefinitions>

            <TextBlock Grid.Column="0" Text="{Binding Path=Contact.FirstName}"/>
            <TextBlock Grid.Column="1" Text=" " />
            <TextBlock Grid.Column="2" Text="{Binding Path=Contact.LastName}"/>
                                                </Grid>
                                            </DataTemplate>
                                        </ComboBox.ItemTemplate>
                                    </ComboBox>
                                </DataTemplate>
                            </xcdg:Column.CellContentTemplate>
                        </xcdg:Column>
                        <xcdg:Column FieldName="Notes"
                                Title="Notes" Width="100" TextWrapping="Wrap"/>
                    </xcdg:DataGridControl.Columns>
                    <xcdg:DataGridControl.View>
                        <xcdg:TableView HorizontalGridLineThickness="1"
                                VerticalGridLineThickness="1">
                            <xcdg:TableView.HorizontalGridLineBrush>
                                <SolidColorBrush Color="Orange"/>
                            </xcdg:TableView.HorizontalGridLineBrush>
                            <xcdg:TableView.VerticalGridLineBrush>
                                <SolidColorBrush Color="Orange"/>
                            </xcdg:TableView.VerticalGridLineBrush>
                            <xcdg:TableView.Footers>
                                <DataTemplate>
                                        <xcdg:InsertionRow/>
                                </DataTemplate>
                            </xcdg:TableView.Footers>
```

```
            <xcdg:TableView.FixedHeaders>
                    <xcdg:ClearHeadersFooters/>
                    <DataTemplate>
                            <xcdg:ColumnManagerRow/>
                    </DataTemplate>
            </xcdg:TableView.FixedHeaders>
        </xcdg:TableView>
    </xcdg:DataGridControl.View>
  </xcdg:DataGridControl>
</ UserControl>
```

The XAML for this control is very similar to the XAML for the Addresses user control shown in the previous chapter. Probably the most important things to pay attention to here are the bindings for the various elements in the control. The Delete button is pretty much the same as the Addresses control's delete button, but this is the first time that I have had to use a nested combo box inside of the Xceed DataGrid. I have to say that it handled it very well, with the only caveat that you have to make sure that you specify the binding for the SelectedItem property like this: SelectedItem="{Binding .}". Other than having to figure that out, it was pretty easy to put together and use.

The Routing Items and Tracking Items sections both follow the same pattern used for the CopyToList section, so I am not going to show the code for those here.

Summary

In this chapter, I introduced the concept of a Submittal Transmittal in the construction industry, and then I used that concept to model the Submittal Aggregate. I then defined the boundaries for the Submittal Aggregate, as well as implemented all of the necessary domain model and Infrastructure classes necessary to work with those classes. A new concept was added to the both the domain layer and infrastructure layer, and that was how to deal with saving child collections from the Entity Root repository. The concept was demonstrated by the techniques I used to save CopyTo, RoutingItem, and TrackingItem instances of the Submittal Aggregate. I also covered how to deal with CopyTo Value objects using the Xceed DataGrid control, and I showed how to wrap this functionality up into a reusable UserControl for the CopyToList, RoutingItems and Tacking Items. On top of those items, I threw in a few little WPF UI tricks. There was also some refactoring again in this chapter, particularly with the service classes being used almost like a façade in front of the repositories from all of the ViewModel classes.

6

Requests for Information

In the last chapter, I dove into some of the important domain logic for the SmartCA application by covering Submittal Transmittals. In this chapter, I will continue that trend by introducing another important new concept to the domain, the Request for Information (RFI). As you will see, the RFI is similar to a Submittal Transmittal in that they share a lot of the same classes: this will also prompt some refactoring.

The Problem

Contractors can have many questions throughout a project that may concern documents, construction, materials, and so on. In the old days, these questions were answered with a phone call or an informal conversation with the architect in charge. Nowadays, however, it is necessary to document every request and reply between project contractors and the firm that is running the project, which in this case is Smart Design. This documentation is necessary because significant costs and complications may arise during the question/answer process, and the RFI can be used as a tool to shape the project's direction.

Some of the uses of RFIs do not have cost implications, such as a simple non-change request for more information about something shown in the specifications. They can also be used to let the architect know about an occurrence of something on the job site, or to let the architect know about latent or unknown conditions. The most important rule for an RFI is that it must contain all of the necessary information and not be too brief. If a contractor has a question for the architect, the architect needs to know exactly what the question is so that it may be answered properly.

Each RFI needs to be numbered in the sequence issued, per project. The RFI number is later used as a reference for members of the project when the architect answers the questions or resolves the issues. The RFI is a time-sensitive document, and it must include the date that it was sent, as well as the date that a response is needed. It is important that there are no duplicate RFI numbers per project and that there are no gaps between RFI numbers. RFI numbers can be reused across other projects.

The Design

In the SmartCA domain, an RFI contains several important business concepts that must be closely followed. In the next few sections, I will be designing the domain model, determining the RFI Aggregate and its boundaries, and designing the Repository for RFIs.

Designing the Domain Model

As stated earlier, the most important parts of the RFI are the Date Received, Date Requested By, Date to Field, Question, and Answer properties. Since these are properties, it is a little bit difficult to model their expected behavior in a diagram. This can be remedied by using a Specification (Evans, *Domain-Driven Design, Tackling Complexity in the Heart of Software*, 225) class to specify the rules for these properties, and actually make the specification part of the domain. This helps convey to the business domain experts what the intended logic is instead of burying it inside of the Request for Information class.

Figure 6.1 shows a drawing showing the relationships among the classes that combine to make up a Request for Information.

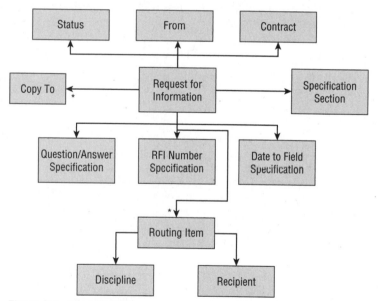

Figure 6.1: RFI Aggregate.

Obviously, the root of this aggregate is the Request for Information class. Note the relationships to the Question/Answer Specification, Date to Field Specification, and RFI Number Specification. These relationships make it very clear to the domain experts that there are rules being modeled for these important concepts.

The relationship to the Status class shows exactly what state the RFI is in, such as completed, pending an architect review, and so on. The relationship to the "From" class represents who the RFI is from, and to go along with who it is from is what Contract is associated with the RFI. The relationship to the

Specification Section is not as important for an RFI as it was for a Submittal Transmittal. It is quite possible that the RFI may not require a reference to a Specification Section, as the RFI could be requesting information about something else that may have nothing to do with a Specification Section, such as an incident.

The next important part of the diagram is the RFI's relationship to the Routing Item. This is how Smart Design knows to whom each RFI has been routed for action, and the Discipline of that person, such as architect, engineer, or construction administrator. Just like the Submittal Transmittal Aggregate, there is a Copy To relationship from an RFI which represents the list of Recipients who need to be copied on all correspondence having to do with the RFI.

Defining the RFI Aggregate

As you can see from the diagram of the RFI Aggregate in Figure 6.2, there are a lot of moving parts.

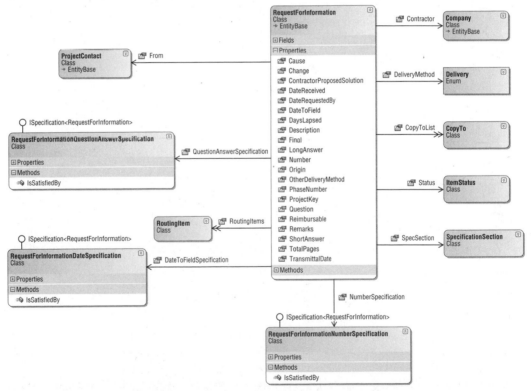

Figure 6.2: Classes constituting the RFI Aggregate.

Notice how I am starting to make use of some of the other Entities introduced in previous chapters, such as the `ProjectContact` class, which is used to represent the To property of the Submittal class, the Recipient property of the RoutingItem class, and the Contact property of the CopyTo class. Also, the `ProjectContact` class is used in the RFI's From property to represent the person originating the RFI.

Defining the Aggregate Boundaries

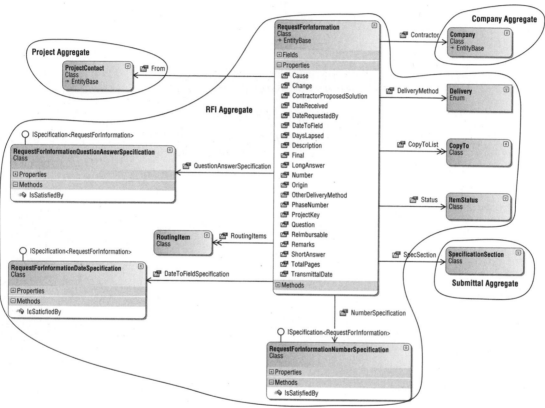

Figure 6.3: RFI Aggregate boundaries.

The RequestForInformation class has its own identity and is definitely the root of its own Aggregate (see Figure 6.3). All of the other classes in the diagram, except for ProjectContact, Company, and SpecificationSection, belong to the RFI Aggregate. As shown in earlier chapters, ProjectContact belongs to the Project Aggregate, Company is the root of its own Aggregate, and the SpecificationSection class is part of the Submittal Aggregate.

Designing the Repository

Since the RequestForInformation class is its own Aggregate root, it will have its own Repository, as shown in Figure 6.4.

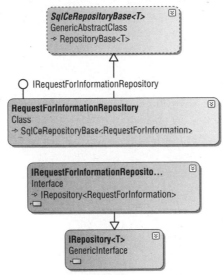

Figure 6.4: RFI Aggregate Repository.

Although the Project Aggregate, Company Aggregate, and Submittal Aggregate are part of the RFI Aggregate, I will not be covering their respective Repositories here because they have already been covered in the previous chapters. I will only be covering the RFI Repository in this chapter.

The IRequestForInformationRepository interface provides access to instances of RFI Repositories. Here is the IRequestForInformationRepository interface:

```
using System;
using System.Collections.Generic;
using SmartCA.Infrastructure.RepositoryFramework;
using SmartCA.Model.Projects;

namespace SmartCA.Model.RFI
{
    public interface IRequestForInformationRepository
        : IRepository<RequestForInformation>
    {
        IList<RequestForInformation> FindBy(Project project);
    }
}
```

Its only unique method, FindBy, should be called fairly often, as almost all of the time RFIs will only be looked at on a per-project basis.

Writing the Unit Tests

In this section, I will be writing some unit tests of what I expect of the Submittal Repository implementation. As noted before, these tests will compile correctly, but they will also fail until I write the code for the Repository implementation later on in the Solution section.

Please note that there will be more unit tests in the accompanying code for this chapter, but for brevity's sake I am showing the tests that I think are important here.

The FindRfisByProjectTest Method

The purpose of the `FindSubmittalsByProjectTest` method is to validate that the correct number of `Submittal` instances have been returned by the Submittal Repository for a given Project.

```
/// <summary>
/// A test for FindBy(Project project)
/// </summary>
[DeploymentItem("SmartCA.sdf"), TestMethod()]
public void FindRfisByProjectTest()
{
    // Get a Project reference
    Project project =
        ProjectService.GetProject("5704f6b9-6ffa-444c-9583-35cc340fce2a");

    // Find all of the RFI's for the Project
    IList<RequestForInformation> rfis = this.repository.FindBy(project);

    // Verify that at least one RFI was returned
    Assert.IsTrue(rfis.Count > 0);
}
```

This method starts out by getting a `Project` instance from the `ProjectService` class. It then calls the `FindBy` method on the repository to get the list of RFI's for the given `Project` instance. The method finishes by checking that the repository returned at least one `RequestForInformation`.

The AddRfiTest Method

The purpose of the `AddRfiTest` method is to test adding a new RFI to the RFI Repository:

```
/// <summary>
///A test for Add(RequestForInformation item)
///</summary>
[DeploymentItem("SmartCA.sdf"), TestMethod()]
public void AddRfiTest()
{
    // Create a new RequestForInformation
    Guid projectKey = new Guid("5704f6b9-6ffa-444c-9583-35cc340fce2a");
    RequestForInformation rfi = new RequestForInformation(projectKey, 2);
    IList<ItemStatus> statuses = SubmittalService.GetItemStatuses();
    rfi.From = ProjectService.GetProject(projectKey).Contacts[0];
    rfi.Status = statuses[0];
    rfi.Contractor = CompanyService.GetAllCompanies()[0];
    IList<SpecificationSection> specSections =
```

```
            SubmittalService.GetSpecificationSections();
        rfi.SpecSection = specSections[0];

        // Add the RFI to the Repository
        this.repository.Add(rfi);

        // Commit the transaction
        this.unitOfWork.Commit();

        // Reload the RFI and verify it's number
        RequestForInformation savedRfi = this.repository.FindBy(rfi.Key);
        Assert.AreEqual(2, savedRfi.Number);

        // Clean up
        this.repository.Remove(savedRfi);
        this.unitOfWork.Commit();
    }
```

This test is a little more complicated than the last test. It starts out by creating a Project Key value, and then passes the Project Key value as well as an RFI number into the constructor of the RequestForInformation class. Now that I have an initialized the RequestForInformation instance, the next step is to set the From property of the RequestForInformation instance with a ProjectContact instance. The next property that needs to be set is the Status property. The Status property is set to the value of the first ItemStatus in the list of all ItemStatus instances. I then set the Contractor property with a Company instance that is retrieved by the CompanyService class. Last, I get the list of all Specification Sections from the SubmittalService class and set the RFI's SpecSection property to the first value in the list of Specification Sections.

The next step is to add the RFI to the repository, and then to commit the transaction by calling the Commit method on the IUnitOfWork instance. The Commit method is important because that method calls back into the RFI Repository to tell it to write the RFI's data to the data store.

Once the RFI has been saved, it is then reloaded and the RFI's Number property is checked to verify that the Add and Commit methods worked properly. The last task that the method needs to perform is to remove the RFI. Removing the RFI that was just created leaves the data store in the same state as it was in before the method started, which is important for the rest of the tests that may depend on a known state of the data store.

The UpdateRfiTest Method

The purpose of the UpdateTest method is to find an RFI and update it with a different DateReceived property value, and then verify that the change was persisted properly.

```
/// <summary>
///A test for Updating an RFI
///</summary>
[DeploymentItem("SmartCA.sdf"), TestMethod()]
public void UpdateRfiTest()
{
    IList<RequestForInformation> rfis = this.repository.FindAll();

    // Change the RFI's DateReceived value
```

(continued)

(continued)

```
                    DateTime dateReceived = DateTime.Now;
                    rfis[0].DateReceived = dateReceived;

                    // Update the Repository
                    this.repository[rfis[0].Key] = rfis[0];

                    // Commit the transaction
                    this.unitOfWork.Commit();

                    // Verify that the change was saved
                    IList<RequestForInformation> refreshedRfis = this.repository.FindAll();
                    Assert.AreEqual(dateReceived.Date,
                        refreshedRfis[0].DateReceived.Value.Date);
            }
```

In this method I start out by getting the entire list of RFIs from the data store. I then proceed to change the `DateReceived` property value on the first RFI in the list, and then call the indexer method of the `IRequestForInformationRepository`. After the call to the indexer, I then use the `IUnitOfWork` interface to commit the transaction. Last, I verify that the change actually made it to the data store by reloading the same RFI and checking to see if its `DateReceived` property value is the same calendar date that I just assigned to the RFI earlier in the method.

The RemoveRfiTest Method

The purpose of the `RemoveRfiTest` method is to test the process of removing an RFI from the data store.

```
            /// <summary>
            ///A test for Remove(RequestForInformation item)
            ///</summary>
            [DeploymentItem("SmartCA.sdf"), TestMethod()]
            public void RemoveRfiTest()
            {
                IList<RequestForInformation> rfis = this.repository.FindAll();

                // Remove the RFI from the Repository
                this.repository.Remove(rfis[0]);

                // Commit the transaction
                this.unitOfWork.Commit();

                // Verify that there is now one less RFI in the data store
                IList<RequestForInformation> refreshedRfis = this.repository.FindAll();
                Assert.AreEqual(0, refreshedRfis.Count);

                // Reset the state
                this.AddRfiTest();
            }
```

The first line of this method should look familiar; I am getting the entire list of RFIs from the data store. I then remove the first RFI in the list from the repository. After removing the RFI from the repository, I then use the `IUnitOfWork` interface to commit the transaction. Next, I verify that the change actually made it to the data store by using the repository to find all of the RFI instances and making sure there is now one less RFI than before. Last, I call the AddRfiTest method to add the RFI I just deleted back into the data store in order to reset the original state of the data store.

The Solution

Now that I have finished going over the design the RFI domain model, Aggregate, and repository, it's time to do my favorite thing: write some code! In this section I will be implementing these designs, as well as implementing the ViewModel and the View for RFIs.

The RFI Class Private Fields and Constructors

There are two constructors for the RFI class, and they both take a projectKey parameter of type System.Object and a number (integer) parameter. Every RFI must have a number and belong to a Project, so that is why those arguments are in both constructors.

Again, as in the last chapter, I am using a key value for a Project instead of a full blown Project instance, since I can always get to the Project via the ProjectService class. The second constructor takes a key argument of type System.Object, thus following the existing pattern for creating instances of existing Entity classes.

```
using System;
using SmartCA.Infrastructure.DomainBase;
using SmartCA.Model.Submittals;
using SmartCA.Model.Employees;
using SmartCA.Model.Projects;
using System.Collections.Generic;
using System.Text;
using SmartCA.Model.Companies;

namespace SmartCA.Model.RFI
{
    public class RequestForInformation : EntityBase
    {
        private object projectKey;
        private int number;
        private DateTime transmittalDate;
        private ProjectContact from;
        private int totalPages;
        private Delivery deliveryMethod;
        private string otherDeliveryMethod;
        private string phaseNumber;
        private bool reimbursable;
        private bool final;
        private List<CopyTo> copyToList;
        private DateTime? dateReceived;
        private DateTime? dateRequestedBy;
        private Company contractor;
```

(continued)

207

(continued)

```csharp
        private SpecificationSection specSection;
        private List<RoutingItem> routingItems;
        private string question;
        private string description;
        private string contractorProposedSolution;
        private bool change;
        private int cause;
        private int origin;
        private ItemStatus status;
        private DateTime? dateToField;
        private string shortAnswer;
        private string longAnswer;
        private string remarks;
        private RequestForInformationNumberSpecification numberSpecification;
        private RequestForInformationDateSpecification dateToFieldSpecification;
        private RequestForInformationQuestionAnswerSpecification
questionAnswerSpecification;

        public RequestForInformation(object projectKey, int number)
            : this(null, projectKey, number)
        {
        }

        public RequestForInformation(object key, object projectKey,
            int number) : base(key)
        {
            this.projectKey = projectKey;
            this.number = number;
            this.transmittalDate = DateTime.Now;
            this.from = null;
            this.totalPages = 1;
            this.deliveryMethod = Delivery.None;
            this.otherDeliveryMethod = string.Empty;
            this.phaseNumber = string.Empty;
            this.reimbursable = false;
            this.final = false;
            this.copyToList = new List<CopyTo>();
            this.dateReceived = null;
            this.dateRequestedBy = null;
            this.contractor = null;
            this.specSection = null;
            this.routingItems = new List<RoutingItem>();
            this.question = string.Empty;
            this.description = string.Empty;
            this.contractorProposedSolution = string.Empty;
            this.change = false;
            this.cause = 0;
            this.origin = 0;
            this.status = null;
            this.dateToField = null;
            this.shortAnswer = string.Empty;
            this.longAnswer = string.Empty;
```

```
            this.remarks = string.Empty;
            this.numberSpecification = new
RequestForInformationNumberSpecification();
            this.dateToFieldSpecification = new
RequestForInformationDateSpecification();
            this.questionAnswerSpecification = new
RequestForInformationQuestionAnswerSpecification();
            this.Validate();
        }
```

All of the data for the RequestForInformation class is initialized and validated in the second constructor, which is called by the first constructor.

The RFI Properties

The properties of the RequestForInformation class are very similar to those of the Submittal class, so I am only going to show the differences here. Most of the properties in this class are fairly straightforward.

```
        public DateTime? DateRequestedBy
        {
            get { return this.dateRequestedBy; }
            set { this.dateRequestedBy = value; }
        }

        public int DaysLapsed
        {
            get
            {
                int daysLapsed = 0;
                if (this.dateReceived.HasValue &&
                    this.dateToField.HasValue)
                {
                    daysLapsed =
this.dateToField.Value.Subtract(this.dateReceived.Value).Days;
                }
                return daysLapsed;
            }
        }

        public Company Contractor
        {
            get { return this.contractor; }
            set { this.contractor = value; }
        }

        public string Question
        {
            get { return this.question; }
            set { this.question = value; }
        }
```

(continued)

209

(continued)

```csharp
public string Description
{
    get { return this.description; }
    set { this.description = value; }
}

public string ContractorProposedSolution
{
    get { return this.contractorProposedSolution; }
    set { this.contractorProposedSolution = value; }
}

public bool Change
{
    get { return this.change; }
    set { this.change = value; }
}

public int Cause
{
    get { return this.cause; }
    set { this.cause = value; }
}

public int Origin
{
    get { return this.origin; }
    set { this.origin = value; }
}

public string ShortAnswer
{
    get { return this.shortAnswer; }
    set { this.shortAnswer = value; }
}

public string LongAnswer
{
    get { return this.longAnswer; }
    set { this.longAnswer = value; }
}

public RequestForInformationNumberSpecification NumberSpecification
{
    get { return this.numberSpecification; }
}

public RequestForInformationDateSpecification DateToFieldSpecification
{
    get { return this.dateToFieldSpecification; }
}
```

```
        public RequestForInformationQuestionAnswerSpecification
QuestionAnswerSpecification
        {
            get { return this.questionAnswerSpecification; }
        }
```

The DaysLapsed Property

This read-only property represents the difference in time from when the RFI was received to when it was sent to the field.

The NumberSpecification Property

This property is designed to model the business rules about the proper numbering of RFIs. The NumberSpecification property is represented by the RequestForInformationNumberSpecification class. Its only job is to validate that the RFI adheres to the numbering rules, which are, if you remember, that all RFIs must be numbered consecutively within a Project, and there cannot be duplicate RFI numbers within a Project.

```
using System;
using SmartCA.Infrastructure.Specifications;
using System.Collections.Generic;
using SmartCA.Model.Projects;
using System.Linq;

namespace SmartCA.Model.RFI
{
    public class RequestForInformationNumberSpecification
        : Specification<RequestForInformation>
    {
        public override bool IsSatisfiedBy(RequestForInformation candidate)
        {
            bool isSatisfiedBy = true;

            // Make sure that the same RFI number has not been used for the
            // current project, and that there are no gaps between RFI numbers

            // First get the project associated with the RFI
            Project project = ProjectService.GetProject(candidate.ProjectKey);

            // Next get the list of RFIs for the project
            IList<RequestForInformation> requests =
RequestForInformationService.GetRequestsForInformation(project);

            // Determine if the RFI number has been used before
            isSatisfiedBy = (requests.Where(rfi =>
rfi.Number.Equals(candidate.Number)).Count() < 1);

            // See if the candidate passed the first test
            if (isSatisfiedBy)
```

(continued)

(continued)

```
            {
                // First test passed, now make sure that there are no gaps
                isSatisfiedBy = (candidate.Number - requests.Max(rfi =>
    rfi.Number) == 1);
            }

            return isSatisfiedBy;
        }
    }
}
```

This code starts out by getting the list of RFIs for the current Project, which is the Project that is associated with the RFI. Once it has the list of RFIs, it then uses a LINQ query to determine whether the count of RFIs in the list that matches the candidate RFI's Number property is less than one. If the count is less than one, then the test passes.

The next test is to make sure that the candidate RFI will not introduce any numbering gaps within RFIs of the current Project. This is done with another LINQ query to get the highest RFI number (Max) in the list; then that number is subtracted from the candidate RFI's Number property. If the result equals one, then the test passes.

The DateToFieldSpecification Property

This property is designed to model the business rule about the dates associated with RFIs. The DateToFieldSpecification property is represented by the RequestForInformationDateSpecification class. Its only job is to validate that the RFI has both a date received value and a date requested by value.

```
using System;
using SmartCA.Infrastructure.Specifications;

namespace SmartCA.Model.RFI
{
    public class RequestForInformationDateSpecification
        : Specification<RequestForInformation>
    {
        public override bool IsSatisfiedBy(RequestForInformation candidate)
        {
            // Each RFI must have a date received and a date
            // that the response is needed
            return (candidate.DateReceived.HasValue &&
                candidate.DateRequestedBy.HasValue);
        }
    }
}
```

This code is much simpler than the first Specification class, as it only needs to perform two simple Boolean checks for the two dates.

The QuestionAnswerSpecification Property

This property is designed to model the business rule question and answer associated with RFIs. The QuestionAnswerSpecification property is represented by the RequestForInformationQuestionAnswerSpecification class. Its only job is to validate that the RFI has a question entered and either a short answer or a long answer entered.

```
using System;
using SmartCA.Infrastructure.Specifications;

namespace SmartCA.Model.RFI
{
    public class RequestForInformationQuestionAnswerSpecification
        : Specification<RequestForInformation>
    {
        public override bool IsSatisfiedBy(RequestForInformation candidate)
        {
            // The RFI must have a question and answer

            // The answer could be the short answer or
            // the long answer
            return (!string.IsNullOrEmpty(candidate.Question) &&
                (!string.IsNullOrEmpty(candidate.ShortAnswer) ||
                !string.IsNullOrEmpty(candidate.LongAnswer)));
        }
    }
}
```

This code is also performing Boolean comparisons by ensuring that the Question property is valid and that either the ShortAnswer or the LongAnswer property is valid.

The RFI Repository Implementation

After going over the IRequestForInformationRepository interface in the Design section, it is now time to explain how the RequestForInformation class is actually persisted to and from the data store by the RFI Repository. In this section, I will be writing the code for the RFI Repository.

The BuildChildCallbacks Method

If you have been following along, you know that the application's Template Method pattern implementation that I have been using in the repositories for getting Entity Root instances, the BuildChildCallbacks method, must be overridden in the RequestForInformationRepository.

```
#region BuildChildCallbacks

protected override void BuildChildCallbacks()
{
    this.ChildCallbacks.Add(ProjectFactory.FieldNames.ProjectContactId,
        this.AppendFrom);
    this.ChildCallbacks.Add("CopyToList",
        delegate(RequestForInformation rfi, object childKeyName)
```

(continued)

213

(continued)

```
                        {
                                this.AppendCopyToList(rfi);
                        });
                this.ChildCallbacks.Add("RoutingItems",
                        delegate(RequestForInformation rfi, object childKeyName)
                        {
                                this.AppendRoutingItems(rfi);
                        });
        }

        #endregion
```

The AppendFrom Callback

The first entry made in the `ChildCallbacks` dictionary is for the `AppendFrom` method. Thanks to the `ProjectService` class's `GetProjectContact` method, this method's code is very simple:

```
private void AppendFrom(RequestForInformation rfi, object fromProjectContactKey)
{
    rfi.From = ProjectService.GetProjectContact(rfi.ProjectKey,
        fromProjectContactKey);
}
```

The AppendCopyToList and AppendRoutingItems Callbacks

You have probably noticed that the `AppendCopyToList` and `AppendRoutingItems` callbacks look identical to those from the Submittal Repository. Well, you are right! This signals me that I need to do some refactoring of classes and methods. In order to prevent code duplication, I have identified the "area" that needs refactoring, and that "area" is any code that deals with the transmittal aspect of a Submittal or an RFI. I will cover this refactoring in the next few paragraphs.

The Transmittal Refactoring

The whole reason for needing to do a refactoring was the RFI Repository was just about ready to have the same code as the Submittal Repository, and that code was for handling the `CopyTo` list and the `RoutingItems` list associated with the RFI. Looking at this a little bit further, it seems as if there is more in common between Submittals and RFIs. They both happen to be a document transmittal, and there is certain data around that transmittal that is common. The first step to refactor this was to put everything they have in common into an interface, and I decided to name this interface the `ITransmittal` interface.

```
using System;
using System.Collections.Generic;
using SmartCA.Model;

namespace SmartCA.Model.Transmittals
{
    public interface ITransmittal
    {
        object ProjectKey { get; }
        DateTime TransmittalDate { get; set; }
        int TotalPages { get; set; }
        Delivery DeliveryMethod { get; set; }
```

```
        string OtherDeliveryMethod { get; set; }
        string PhaseNumber { get; set; }
        bool Reimbursable { get; set; }
        bool Final { get; set; }
        IList<CopyTo> CopyToList { get; }
    }
}
```

This interface contains all of the common properties associated with a document Transmittal, including the associated Project.

You may have noticed that there are no Routing Items in this interface, and that is because when I did my analysis of the existing application, I noticed that not all transmittals were always routable. To account for transmittals that could be routed, I created another interface, the `IRoutableTransmittal` interface:

```
using System;
using System.Collections.Generic;

namespace SmartCA.Model.Transmittals
{
    public interface IRoutableTransmittal : ITransmittal
    {
        IList<RoutingItem> RoutingItems { get; }
    }
}
```

This interface simply adds to the existing `ITransmittal` interface and adds a property for the Routing Items. The next step in the refactoring was to modify the `Submittal` and `RequestForInformation` classes to implement these interfaces. Luckily, these classes already contain all of these properties, so it was a very simple refactoring to change the class signatures:

```
public class RequestForInformation : EntityBase, IRoutableTransmittal
```

```
public class Submittal : EntityBase, IRoutableTransmittal
```

Remember, in the .NET Framework, you can only inherit from one base class, but you can implement as many interfaces as you like.

The next step was to add a new Repository to the inheritance chain so that the Transmittal-related behavior could be shared by both the `SubmittalRepository` and the `RequestForInformationRepository` classes. So I made a new Repository and called it `SqlCeTransmittalRepository<T>`. This Repository is an abstract class that inherits from `SqlCeRepositoryBase<T>`.

Here is the signature for the Repository:

```
public abstract class SqlCeTransmittalRepository<T> : SqlCeRepositoryBase<T>
        where T : EntityBase, ITransmittal
```

The next thing to add to this new class was the pass-through constructors to the
`SqlCeRepositoryBase<T>` class:

```
#region Constructors

protected SqlCeTransmittalRepository()
    : this(null)
{
}

protected SqlCeTransmittalRepository(IUnitOfWork unitOfWork)
    : base(unitOfWork)
{
}

#endregion
```

Figure 6.5 shows a diagram of what the new RFI Aggregate Repository inheritance chain looks like now.

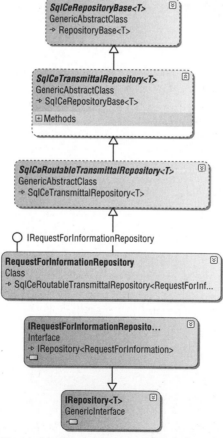

Figure 6.5: Newly refactored RFI Aggregate
Repository.

The next function that I needed to perform was splitting out the code that deals with the `CopyTo` instances.

The AppendCopyToList Method

This method is now refactored to take a type of `EntityBase` and `ITransmittal` for its arguments:

```
protected void AppendCopyToList(T transmittal)
{
    StringBuilder builder = new StringBuilder(100);
    builder.Append(string.Format("SELECT * FROM {0}CopyList",
        this.EntityName));
    builder.Append(string.Format(" WHERE {0} = '{1}';",
        this.KeyFieldName,
        transmittal.Key));
    using (IDataReader reader = this.ExecuteReader(builder.ToString()))
    {
        while (reader.Read())
        {
            transmittal.CopyToList.Add(TransmittalFactory.BuildCopyTo(
                transmittal.ProjectKey, reader));
        }
    }
}
```

This code is essentially the same as the code from the old version of the `SubmittalRepository`, but instead of being hard-coded to a `Submittal` instance or a `RequestForInformation` instance, it now only relies upon `EntityBase` and `ITransmittal`. The queries have been changed to be more generic as well. An important thing to note about this change is that I needed also to refactor the `SqlCeRepositoryBase<T>` class a little bit, with the addition of the `EntityName` and `KeyFieldName` properties. Also, all classes deriving from `SqlCeRepositoryBase<T>` now need to implement the following new abstract methods:

```
protected abstract string GetEntityName();
protected abstract string GetKeyFieldName();
```

Here is an example of how the `RequestForInformationRepository` class is implementing the methods:

```
#region GetEntityName

protected override string GetEntityName()
{
    return "RequestForInformation";
}

#endregion

#region GetKeyFieldName

protected override string GetKeyFieldName()
```

(continued)

(continued)

```
    {
        return RequestForInformationFactory.FieldNames.RequestForInformationId;
    }

    #endregion
```

These follow the same Template Method Pattern that the SqlCeRepositoryBase<T> class has been implementing all along, as two more calls have been added to its constructor:

```
protected SqlCeRepositoryBase(IUnitOfWork unitOfWork)
    : base(unitOfWork)
{
    this.database = DatabaseFactory.CreateDatabase();
    this.entityFactory = EntityFactoryBuilder.BuildFactory<T>();
    this.childCallbacks = new Dictionary<string, AppendChildData>();
    this.BuildChildCallbacks();
    this.baseQuery = this.GetBaseQuery();
    this.baseWhereClause = this.GetBaseWhereClause();
    this.entityName = this.GetEntityName();
    this.keyFieldName = this.GetKeyFieldName();
}
```

The DeleteCopyToList Method

This method has been refactored very similarly to the AppendCopyToList method.

```
protected void DeleteCopyToList(T transmittal)
{
    string query = string.Format("DELETE FROM {0}CopyList {1}",
        this.EntityName, this.BuildBaseWhereClause(transmittal.Key));
    this.Database.ExecuteNonQuery(
        this.Database.GetSqlStringCommand(query));
}
```

The only change in this method is that, just like the AppendCopyToList method, it has been made more generic and relies upon the EntityBase class as well as the ITransmittal interface in order to build its SQL query.

The InsertCopyToList and InsertCopyTo Methods

These methods keep following the same pattern in their refactoring as the others:

```
protected void InsertCopyToList(T transmittal)
{
    foreach (CopyTo copyTo in transmittal.CopyToList)
    {
        this.InsertCopyTo(copyTo, transmittal.Key);
    }
}
private void InsertCopyTo(CopyTo copyTo, object key)
```

```
    {
        StringBuilder builder = new StringBuilder(100);
        builder.Append(string.Format("INSERT INTO {0}CopyList ({1},{2},{3}) ",
            this.EntityName,
            this.KeyFieldName,
            TransmittalFactory.FieldNames.ProjectContactId,
            TransmittalFactory.FieldNames.Notes));
        builder.Append(string.Format("VALUES ({0},{1},{2});",
            DataHelper.GetSqlValue(key),
            DataHelper.GetSqlValue(copyTo.Contact.Key),
            DataHelper.GetSqlValue(copyTo.Notes)));

        this.Database.ExecuteNonQuery(
            this.Database.GetSqlStringCommand(builder.ToString()));
    }
```

Like the other methods, these methods are also aided by the new interface and the new properties and abstract methods of the `SqlCeRepositoryBase<T>` class.

The next piece of functionality that needed refactoring was the notion of routable Transmittals. As shown earlier, the `IRoutableTransmital` interface shows that a routable Transmittal is one that has `RoutingItems` associated with it.

```
public interface IRoutableTransmittal : ITransmittal
{
    IList<RoutingItem> RoutingItems { get; }
}
```

So the next logical step was to add a new abstract Repository to house the necessary code for `RoutingItems`. That class is the `SqlCeRoutableTransmittalRepository<T>` class, and its signature is shown here:

```
public abstract class SqlCeRoutableTransmittalRepository<T> :
        SqlCeTransmittalRepository<T>
        where T : EntityBase, IRoutableTransmittal
```

I am not going to show its pass-through constructors, since they are almost identical to the constructors in the `SqlCeTransmittalRepository<T>` class. As you might expect, this class is intended to isolate the code that deals with `RoutingItem` instances. It has three protected methods in it, `AppendRoutingItems`, `DeleteRoutingItems`, and `InsertRoutingItems`, and two private methods, `DeleteRoutingItem` and `InsertRoutingItem`. I am not going to show the code for these methods, as they are nearly identical to the old methods, and they have simply been modified, like all of the other newly refactored methods, to be more generic. Instead of depending upon the `ITransmittal` interface, the new methods in the `SqlCeRoutableTransmittalRepository<T>` class depend upon the `IRoutableTransmittal` interface.

Unit of Work Implementation

Following the same steps that I have shown before to implement the Unit of Work pattern, I need to override the following three methods: `PersistNewItem(RequestForInformation item)`, `PersistUpdatedItem(RequestForInformation item)`, and `PersistDeletedItem(RequestForInformation item)`.

The PersistNewItem Method

The first method override for the `RequestForInformationRepository`'s Unit of Work implementation is the `PersistNewItem` method:

```
        protected override void PersistNewItem(RequestForInformation item)
        {
            StringBuilder builder = new StringBuilder(100);
            builder.Append(string.Format("INSERT INTO RequestForInformation
({0},{1},{2},{3},{4},{5},{6},{7},{8},{9},{10},{11},{12},{13},{14},{15},{16},{17},
{18},{19},{20},{21},{22},{23},{24},{25}) ",
                RequestForInformationFactory.FieldNames.RequestForInformationId,
                ProjectFactory.FieldNames.ProjectId,
                RequestForInformationFactory.FieldNames.RequestForInformationNumber,
                RequestForInformationFactory.FieldNames.TransmittalDate,
                RequestForInformationFactory.FieldNames.ProjectContactId,
                RequestForInformationFactory.FieldNames.TotalPages,
                RequestForInformationFactory.FieldNames.DeliveryMethod,
                RequestForInformationFactory.FieldNames.OtherDeliveryMethod,
                RequestForInformationFactory.FieldNames.PhaseNumber,
                RequestForInformationFactory.FieldNames.Reimbursable,
                RequestForInformationFactory.FieldNames.Final,
                RequestForInformationFactory.FieldNames.DateReceived,
                RequestForInformationFactory.FieldNames.DateRequestedBy,
                CompanyFactory.FieldNames.CompanyId,
                SubmittalFactory.FieldNames.SpecificationSectionId,
                RequestForInformationFactory.FieldNames.Question,
                RequestForInformationFactory.FieldNames.Description,
                RequestForInformationFactory.FieldNames.ContractorProposedSolution,
                RequestForInformationFactory.FieldNames.NoChange,
                RequestForInformationFactory.FieldNames.Cause,
                RequestForInformationFactory.FieldNames.Origin,
                RequestForInformationFactory.FieldNames.ItemStatusId,
                RequestForInformationFactory.FieldNames.DateToField,
                RequestForInformationFactory.FieldNames.ShortAnswer,
                RequestForInformationFactory.FieldNames.LongAnswer,
                RequestForInformationFactory.FieldNames.Remarks
            ));
            builder.Append(string.Format("VALUES
({0},{1},{2},{3},{4},{5},{6},{7},{8},{9},{10},{11},{12},{13},{14},{15},{16},{17},
{18},{19},{20},{21},{22},{23},{24},{25});",
                DataHelper.GetSqlValue(item.Key),
                DataHelper.GetSqlValue(item.ProjectKey),
                DataHelper.GetSqlValue(item.Number),
                DataHelper.GetSqlValue(item.TransmittalDate),
                DataHelper.GetSqlValue(item.From.Key),
                DataHelper.GetSqlValue(item.TotalPages),
                DataHelper.GetSqlValue(item.DeliveryMethod),
                DataHelper.GetSqlValue(item.OtherDeliveryMethod),
                DataHelper.GetSqlValue(item.PhaseNumber),
                DataHelper.GetSqlValue(item.Reimbursable),
                DataHelper.GetSqlValue(item.Final),
                DataHelper.GetSqlValue(item.DateReceived),
                DataHelper.GetSqlValue(item.DateRequestedBy),
```

```
                    DataHelper.GetSqlValue(item.Contractor),
                    DataHelper.GetSqlValue(item.SpecSection),
                    DataHelper.GetSqlValue(item.Question),
                    DataHelper.GetSqlValue(item.Description),
                    DataHelper.GetSqlValue(item.ContractorProposedSolution),
                    DataHelper.GetSqlValue(item.Change),
                    DataHelper.GetSqlValue(item.Cause),
                    DataHelper.GetSqlValue(item.Origin),
                    DataHelper.GetSqlValue(item.Status.Id),
                    DataHelper.GetSqlValue(item.DateToField),
                    DataHelper.GetSqlValue(item.ShortAnswer),
                    DataHelper.GetSqlValue(item.LongAnswer),
                    DataHelper.GetSqlValue(item.Remarks)));

            this.Database.ExecuteNonQuery(
                this.Database.GetSqlStringCommand(builder.ToString()));

            // Now do the child objects
            this.InsertCopyToList(item);
            this.InsertRoutingItems(item);
        }
```

The code builds up a large insert statement composed of the values from the `RequestForInformation` instance and then executes the query using the Microsoft Enterprise Library's `Database` object. After the insert statement has been executed, I have to account for inserting the `CopyTo` and `RoutingItem` instances for the RFI. I do this by calling the newly refactored `InsertCopyToList` and `InsertRoutingItems` methods, which all take an `IRoutableTransmittal` instance (which the RFI class implements) as their only argument.

The PersistUpdatedItem Method

`PersistUpdatedItem` first does an update to the `RequestForInformation` table:

```
        protected override void PersistUpdatedItem(RequestForInformation item)
        {
            StringBuilder builder = new StringBuilder(100);
            builder.Append("UPDATE RequestForInformation SET ");

            builder.Append(string.Format("{0} = {1}",
                RequestForInformationFactory.FieldNames
.RequestForInformationNumber,
                DataHelper.GetSqlValue(item.Number)));

            builder.Append(string.Format(",{0} = {1}",
                RequestForInformationFactory.FieldNames.TransmittalDate,
                DataHelper.GetSqlValue(item.TransmittalDate)));
*************************************************************************
builder.Append(string.Format(",{0} = {1}",
                RequestForInformationFactory.FieldNames.Remarks,
                DataHelper.GetSqlValue(item.Remarks)));

            builder.Append(" ");
```

(continued)

(continued)

```
                    builder.Append(this.BuildBaseWhereClause(item.Key));

                    this.Database.ExecuteNonQuery(
                        this.Database.GetSqlStringCommand(builder.ToString()));

                    // Now do the child objects

                    // First, delete the existing ones
                    this.DeleteCopyToList(item);
                    this.DeleteRoutingItems(item);

                    // Now, add the current ones
                    this.InsertCopyToList(item);
                    this.InsertRoutingItems(item);
                }
```

I have omitted several lines of repetitive code building the SQL update statement in the middle of the code in order save you from the boring code. The removed lines are represented by a single line of asterisks.

The second part of the method then uses the newly refactored `DeleteCopyToList` and `DeleteRoutingItems` helper methods to delete all of the child objects of the RFI, and then uses the also newly refactored `InsertCopyToList` and `InsertRoutingItems` helper methods to add the existing child objects from the RFI to the database.

PersistDeletedItem

As I was writing the last method in `RequestForInformationRepository` to override, `PersistDeletedItem`, I realized that I could refactor that back into the base classes as well. Originally, the code I wrote looked like this:

```
        protected override void PersistDeletedItem(RequestForInformation item)
        {
            // Delete the child objects first
            this.DeleteCopyToList(item);
            this.DeleteRoutingItems(item);

            // Now delete the RFI
            string query = string.Format("DELETE FROM RequestForInformation {0}",
                this.BuildBaseWhereClause(item.Key));
            this.Database.ExecuteNonQuery(
                this.Database.GetSqlStringCommand(query));
        }
```

After analyzing the code, I saw another opportunity to refactor it back into the `SqlCeRepositoryBase<T>` and `SqlCeRoutableTransmittalRepository<T>` classes. I will start with the `SqlCeRepositoryBase<T>` implementation:

```
        protected override void PersistDeletedItem(T item)
        {
            // Delete the Entity
            string query = string.Format("DELETE FROM {0} {1}",
```

```
            this.entityName,
            this.BuildBaseWhereClause(item.Key));
    this.Database.ExecuteNonQuery(
        this.Database.GetSqlStringCommand(query));
}
```

This was made possible by the Template Method Pattern implemented in the earlier refactoring for the `EntityName` and `EntityKey` properties of the `SqlCeRepositoryBase<T>` class. This method is now generic enough to delete any Entity from the database. So the logical question now is, "what about when the Entity has children that must be deleted first?" The answer comes in overriding the `PersistDeletedItem` method in derived classes. I took this a step further with the concept of deleting Transmittals and added functionality in the `SqlCeRoutableTransmittalRepository<T>` class to do just this:

```
protected override void PersistDeletedItem(T transmittal)
{
    // Delete the child objects first
    this.DeleteCopyToList(transmittal);
    this.DeleteRoutingItems(transmittal);

    // Delete the transmittal entity
    base.PersistDeletedItem(transmittal);
}
```

This is great because now I can delete whatever child objects I want to delete first, and then call the base class, in this case `SqlCeRepositoryBase<T>`, to do the rest. So in the `SubmittalRepository`, the implementation now becomes:

```
protected override void PersistDeletedItem(Submittal item)
{
    // Delete the child objects first
    this.DeleteTrackingItems(item);

    // Now delete the submittal and its associated
    // transmittal objects
    base.PersistDeletedItem(item);
}
```

Because Tracking Items are not part of the `ITransmittal` interface, I needed to delete these first, and then by calling the base class, in this case the `SqlCeRoutableTransmittalRepository<T>` class, I am able to delete the rest of the child objects (the `CopyToList` and the `RoutingItems`) as well as the Entity itself. What is even better is that in the `RequestForInformationRepository` class (and in a few other repositories), the need to override the `PersistDeletedItem` method goes away completely!

The RFI Service Implementation

Still in this application, the only `Service` classes I have implemented up to this point are all `Service` classes that live in the domain model layer and are acting as facades to their respective Repository interfaces.

The `RequestForInformationService` class is responsible for retrieving and saving `RequestForInformation` instances.

```
using System;
using SmartCA.Infrastructure;
using SmartCA.Infrastructure.RepositoryFramework;
using SmartCA.Model.Projects;
using System.Collections.Generic;

namespace SmartCA.Model.RFI
{
    public static class RequestForInformationService
    {
        private static IRequestForInformationRepository repository;
        private static IUnitOfWork unitOfWork;

        static RequestForInformationService()
        {
            RequestForInformationService.unitOfWork = new UnitOfWork();
            RequestForInformationService.repository =
                RepositoryFactory.GetRepository<IRequestForInformationRepository,
                RequestForInformation>(RequestForInformationService.unitOfWork);
        }

        public static IList<RequestForInformation>
            GetRequestsForInformation(Project project)
        {
            return RequestForInformationService.repository.FindBy(project);
        }

        public static void SaveRequestForInformation(RequestForInformation rfi)
        {
            RequestForInformationService.repository[rfi.Key] = rfi;
            RequestForInformationService.unitOfWork.Commit();
        }
    }
}
```

This class is mainly just acting as a façade in front of the `IRequestForInformationRepository` instance. There is nothing really new in this `Service` class compared to the other ones.

The RFI ViewModel Classes

Following the same patterns for all `ViewModel` classes as before, the `RequestForInformationViewModel` class adapts the RFI Aggregate from the domain model to the UI. When I started coding the ViewModel for the RFI I noticed that there was a lot in common between the `SubmittalViewModel` and the `RequestForInformationViewModel`, so I did another major refactoring and created a new abstract `ViewModel` class called, you guessed it, the `TransmittalViewModel<T>` class.

The TransmittalViewModel<T> Class

This class is very similar to the `SqlCeTransmittalRepository<T>` and `SqlCeRoutableTransmittalRepository<T>` classes that I showed earlier. It is the same concept again, which is to refactor common functionality into an abstract base class and have future classes that share the same functionality inherit them from the new base class. In this case, just like with the `Repository` classes and the `SqlCeRepositoryBase<T>` class, there is already an abstract base class that my `ViewModel` classes inherit from, and that is the `ViewModel` class. The `TransmittalViewModel<T>` class will be extending this class and it will be abstract as well. Here is the signature for the class:

```
public abstract class TransmittalViewModel<T> : ViewModel
        where T : EntityBase, IRoutableTransmittal
```

This is following the same pattern as the `SqlCeTransmittalRepository<T>` and `SqlCeRoutableTransmittalRepository<T>` classes, since it is a generic class and is using constraints to make sure that the generic class is an `EntityBase` that implements the `IRoutableTransmittal` interface.

The Constructor

My goal with this class was to lift all of the Transmittal behavior out of the `SubmittalViewModel` class and put it into this class. Therefore, the constructor code you see below should look very much like the old `SubmittalViewModel` code, with all references to anything named "submittal" changed to "transmittal."

```
#region Constructors

public TransmittalViewModel()
    : this(null)
{
}

public TransmittalViewModel(IView view)
    : base(view)
{
    this.currentTransmittal = null;
    this.transmittalList = this.GetTransmittals();
    this.transmittals = new CollectionView(this.transmittalList);
    this.specificationSections
        = SubmittalService.GetSpecificationSections();
    this.itemStatuses = SubmittalService.GetItemStatuses();
    this.mutableCopyToList = new BindingList<MutableCopyTo>();
    this.routingItems = new BindingList<RoutingItem>();
    this.deliveryMethods = new CollectionView(
                            Enum.GetNames(typeof(Delivery)));
    this.disciplines = SubmittalService.GetDisciplines();
    this.saveCommand = new DelegateCommand(this.SaveCommandHandler);
    this.newCommand = new DelegateCommand(this.NewCommandHandler);
    this.deleteCopyToCommand =
        new DelegateCommand(this.DeleteCopyToCommandHandler);
    this.deleteRoutingItemCommand =
        new DelegateCommand(this.DeleteRoutingItemCommandHandler);
}

#endregion
```

I was able to reuse almost everything in the old constructor, except for the Tracking Items, which are not part of what I have defined for a Transmittal. I decided for now to leave the calls in to the SubmittalService, although that class is also a candidate for refactoring.

Notice how the GetTransmittals method is called in order to initialize the list of Transmittals. This is an abstract method of the TransmittalViewModel<T> class, and thus I am once again using the Template Method pattern. I will show more on this method later.

The Properties

The CurrentTransmittal property is extremely similar to the old CurrentSubmittal property of the SubmitalViewModel class:

```
public T CurrentTransmittal
{
    get { return this.currentTransmittal; }
    set
    {
        if (this.currentTransmittal != value)
        {
            this.currentTransmittal = value;
            this.OnPropertyChanged(Constants
.CurrentTransmittalPropertyName);
            this.OnPropertyChanged("Status");
            this.saveCommand.IsEnabled = (this.currentTransmittal != null);
            this.PopulateTransmittalChildren();
        }
    }
}
```

The only difference between this code and the SubmitalViewModel CurrentTransmittal property code is that this code is more generic. Don't you just love Generics? I bet you can't tell that I do!

The PopulateSubmittalChildren method has been changed to the PopulateSubmittalChildren method. Here is the old method:

```
private void PopulateSubmittalChildren()
{
    this.PopulateMutableCopyToList();
    this.PopulateRoutingItems();
    this.PopulateTrackingItems();
}
```

And here is the new method:

```
protected virtual void PopulateTransmittalChildren()
{
    this.PopulateMutableCopyToList();
    this.PopulateRoutingItems();
}
```

The only difference in this method is that it no longer tries to populate the Tracking Items data, and that is exactly why I made it virtual, because derived classes may need to override this method in order to populate their own child objects as necessary.

The `PopulateMutableCopyToList` method has been changed from this:

```
private void PopulateMutableCopyToList()
{
    if (this.currentSubmittal != null)
    {
        this.mutableCopyToList.Clear();
        foreach (CopyTo copyTo in this.currentSubmittal.CopyToList)
        {
            this.mutableCopyToList.Add(new MutableCopyTo(copyTo));
        }
        this.OnPropertyChanged(Constants.MutableCopyToListPropertyName);
    }
}
```

To this:

```
private void PopulateMutableCopyToList()
{
    if (this.currentTransmittal != null)
    {
        this.mutableCopyToList.Clear();
        foreach (CopyTo copyTo in this.currentTransmittal.CopyToList)
        {
            this.mutableCopyToList.Add(new MutableCopyTo(copyTo));
        }
        this.OnPropertyChanged(Constants.MutableCopyToListPropertyName);
    }
}
```

I am not going to show the `PopulateRoutingItems` method because it follows the exact same pattern as the `PopulateMutableCopyToList` method.

The Command Handler Methods

Refactoring the Command Handler methods was a little bit trickier than some of the other methods in the `TransmittalViewModel` class. The `SaveCommandHandler` and the `NewCommandHandler` methods both had to be marked as virtual, and that is because I could only pull so much out of them into this, and the rest that is specific to the derived class must be overridden.

For example, the `NewCommandHandler` went from this:

```
private void NewCommandHandler(object sender, EventArgs e)
{
    Submittal newSubmittal = new Submittal(
                        this.currentSubmittal.SpecSection,
                        this.currentSubmittal.ProjectKey);
```

(continued)

227

(continued)

```
            newSubmittal.SpecSectionSecondaryIndex = "01";

            this.currentSubmittal = null;
            this.mutableCopyToList.Clear();
            this.routingItems.Clear();
            this.trackingItems.Clear();
            this.CurrentObjectState = ObjectState.New;
            this.OnPropertyChanged(
                Constants.CurrentSubmittalPropertyName);

            this.submittalsList.Add(newSubmittal);
            this.submittals.Refresh();
            this.submittals.MoveCurrentToLast();
        }
```

To this:

```
            protected virtual void NewCommandHandler(object sender, EventArgs e)
            {
                this.currentTransmittal = null;
                this.mutableCopyToList.Clear();
                this.routingItems.Clear();
                this.CurrentObjectState = ObjectState.New;
                this.OnPropertyChanged(
                    Constants.CurrentTransmittalPropertyName);
            }
```

The code that initializes the new Entity (i.e., the `Submittal` class in the first example above) had to be removed and must be overridden in the derived `ViewModel`. I also needed to remove the code that added the Submittal to the list of Submittals because I needed that to happen last in the derived class, after this code executes.

The GetTransmittals Template Pattern Method

As seen in the constructor, the `GetTransmittals` abstract method is called in order to initialize the list of Transmittals for the class. Here is the signature of this method:

```
    protected abstract List<T> GetTransmittals();
```

This is great because by doing this I am delegating the derived class to get the right list of objects, yet I can still code against that list in my base class. Combining the Template Method pattern with Generics is a great thing!

The RequestForInformationViewModel Class

Now the fruits of our ViewModel refactoring labor start to pay off. The code inside of the `RequestForInformationViewModel` and `SubmittalViewModel` classes has been reduced significantly. Here is what the signature of the `RequestForInformationViewModel` class looks like when deriving from the `TransmittalViewModel<T>` class:

```
    public class RequestForInformationViewModel
        : TransmittalViewModel<RequestForInformation>
```

Notice how the generic parameter from the `TransmittalViewModel<T>` class is replaced by the `RequestForInformation` class.

The Constructor

The constructors for the `RequestForInformationViewModel` class now are mostly pass-through. Here is the old `SubmittalViewModel` constructor:

```
#region Constructors

public SubmittalViewModel()
    : this(null)
{
}

public SubmittalViewModel(IView view)
    : base(view)
{
    this.currentSubmittal = null;
    this.submittalsList = new List<Submittal>(
                            SubmittalService.GetSubmittals(
                            UserSession.CurrentProject));
    this.submittals = new CollectionView(this.submittalsList);
    this.specificationSections
        = SubmittalService.GetSpecificationSections();
    this.submittalStatuses = SubmittalService.GetSubmittalStatuses();
    this.toList = UserSession.CurrentProject.Contacts;
    this.mutableCopyToList = new BindingList<MutableCopyTo>();
    this.routingItems = new BindingList<RoutingItem>();
    this.trackingItems = new BindingList<TrackingItem>();
    this.fromList = EmployeeService.GetEmployees();
    this.trackingStatusValues = new CollectionView(
                                    Enum.GetNames(typeof(ActionStatus)));
    this.deliveryMethods = new CollectionView(
                                Enum.GetNames(typeof(Delivery)));
    this.disciplines = SubmittalService.GetDisciplines();
    this.saveCommand = new DelegateCommand(this.SaveCommandHandler);
    this.newCommand = new DelegateCommand(this.NewCommandHandler);
    this.deleteCopyToCommand =
        new DelegateCommand(this.DeleteCopyToCommandHandler);
    this.deleteRoutingItemCommand =
        new DelegateCommand(this.DeleteRoutingItemCommandHandler);
    this.deleteTrackingItemCommand =
        new DelegateCommand(this.DeleteTrackingItemCommandHandler);
}

#endregion
```

Here are the new constructors for the `RequestForInformationViewModel` class:

```
#region Constructors

public RequestForInformationViewModel()
    : this(null)
{
}

public RequestForInformationViewModel(IView view)
    : base(view)
{
    this.toList = UserSession.CurrentProject.Contacts;
    this.fromList = UserSession.CurrentProject.Contacts;
}

#endregion
```

That's quite a reduction in code! The `toList` and `fromList` private fields are not contained in the base class and therefore need to be initialized here.

The Properties

There are not many properties left to implement in the `RequestForInformationViewModel` class. Here is all of the code for the properties:

```
#region Properties

public IList<ProjectContact> ToList
{
    get { return this.toList; }
}

public IList<ProjectContact> FromList
{
    get { return this.fromList; }
}

#endregion
```

The Command Handler Methods

The only command handler methods that I need to override in the `RequestForInformationViewModel` class are the `NewCommandHandler` and `SaveCommandHandler` methods. The `DeleteCommandHandler` method is completely taken care of by the base class.

Because the `NewCommandHandler` method in the base class was marked as virtual, I am still able to use it as well as add my own functionality:

```
protected override void NewCommandHandler(object sender, EventArgs e)
{
    base.NewCommandHandler(sender, e);
    RequestForInformation newRfi = new RequestForInformation(
                            this.CurrentTransmittal.ProjectKey,
                            this.CurrentTransmittal.Number + 1);
    this.TransmittalList.Add(newRfi);
    this.Transmittals.Refresh();
    this.Transmittals.MoveCurrentToLast();
}
```

Notice how on the first line of the method I call the same method in the base class. This allows me to reuse the common code yet gives me the flexibility to do my own housekeeping when creating the new `RequestForInformation` instance.

The GetTransmittals Template Pattern Method

As I mentioned before, the `GetTransmittals` method is overridden in the derived classes because only they know where to get their data; the base class does not need to know about that:

```
#region GetTransmittals

    protected override List<RequestForInformation> GetTransmittals()
    {
        return new
List<RequestForInformation>(RequestForInformationService.GetRequestsForInformation(
                            UserSession.CurrentProject));
    }

    #endregion
```

In this case of the `RequestForInformationViewModel` class's override, I am simply calling out to the `RequestForInformationService` to get the list of `RequestForInformation` instances.

The RFI View

The View for RFIs is almost exactly identical to that for Submittals. Figure 6.6 shows what the form looks like at run time.

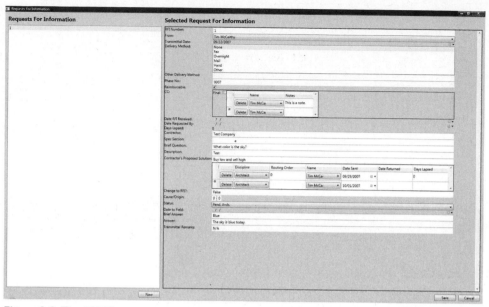

Figure 6.6: The RFI View.

Following the same pattern as before, the form is split into two parts: the one on the left is for selecting an RFI to edit, and the one on the right is for editing the selected RFI. The New button adds a new RFI to the list. The Save and Cancel buttons both deal with the currently selected RFI.

I really do not need to show any of the XAML code for this form because there is really not much in it that is different from the Submittal form.

Summary

In this chapter, I introduced the concept of a Request for Information (RFI) in the construction industry and then used that concept to model the RFI Aggregate. I also introduced a new concept into the domain, called the Specification Pattern. This made some of the business rule modeling very clear by bringing business rules out from underneath class methods and placing them into their own Specification classes. I then defined the boundaries for the RFI Aggregate, as well as implementing all of the necessary domain model and Infrastructure classes necessary to work with those classes. I also did some major refactoring in this chapter for the repositories and ViewModels dealing with the new concept of Transmittals.

7

Proposal Requests

In the last chapter, I covered the ins and outs of the Request for Information (RFI) document. In this chapter, I will cover another concept that is similar to an RFI but has a different intent. That concept is the Proposal Request.

The Problem

In the construction industry, just like the software industry, projects rarely finish exactly as planned; there are usually changes that have to be made along the way. In software, it could be that the application you are working on has some features that the business no longer needs, or doesn't have new features discovered while the application is still in development. Likewise, in the construction industry, there are many factors in a project that may necessitate a change to the original contract.

A Contractor can discover physical or economic situations, usually unanticipated, that may make it impossible to follow the contract documents. Architects could find it necessary to recommend changes in the contract documents because of errors in the contract documents. Other sources of changes could be weather damage such as wind and rain, natural disasters such as an earthquake, labor and material shortages, and fire and explosion.

When these types of events occur, it means that there needs to be a Change Order issued for the project. In the construction industry, there is an action that must occur before the Change Order is drafted. That action is known officially as the Work Changes Proposal Request. For the purposes of this chapter, I will refer to this as a Proposal Request.

A Proposal Request is a one page form that identifies the change and all the parties involved in the contract. The form is prepared by the architect and is directed to the Contractor. It is essentially a request for a price and time proposal for carrying out the proposed change. A copy of it should be sent to all parties involved and a record kept of all recipients. A Proposal Request is not an authorization to do the work. It is not a Change Order. It is only a special type of request for information that will be needed by the owner and architect to decide whether to make the change, modify it, or to cancel it.

The form includes a time limit for the Contractor's submission of the proposal or for a commitment of the date on which the completed Proposal Request will be submitted. Like the RFI, each Proposal Request should be serially numbered by project.

The Design

In the SmartCA domain, an RFI contains several important business concepts that must be closely followed. In the next few sections, I will be designing the domain model, determining the RFI Aggregate and its boundaries, and designing the Repository for RFIs.

Designing the Domain Model

As stated earlier, the most important parts of the Proposal Request are the Expected Return Date from the Contractor, the Description of the Proposal Request, and the proper ordering of the Proposal Request Number. Just as in the last chapter, I will be using the Specification pattern to specify the rules for these properties, and the specifications that I create will also be part of the domain model.

Below is a drawing showing the relationships between the classes that combine to make up a Proposal Request:

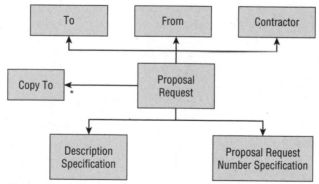

Figure 7.1: **Proposal Request Aggregate.**

In the diagram, it should be pretty clear that the Proposal Request class is the root of the Aggregate. The relationships to the Description Specification and Proposal Request Number Specification classes help model the important rules of the Proposal Request.

The relationship to the "From" class represents from whom the Proposal Request came, and with which Contractor it is associated. The "To" class represents for what Project Contact the Proposal Request is intended.

Just as with the Submittal Transmittal and RFI Aggregates, there is a Copy To relationship from a Proposal Request, which represents the list of Recipients who need to be copied on all correspondence having to do with the Proposal Request.

Designing the Proposal Request Aggregate

You may have expected this, but as I was analyzing the Proposal Request class from Figure 7.1, I noticed that it had a lot of the same properties as the `RequestForInformation` and `Submittal` classes. Namely, all of the properties that make up the `ITransmittal` interface that I introduced in the last chapter. Instead of having all of these classes implement the `ITransmittal` interface and have all of that duplicate code, I decided to refactor the common code into a new abstract class, the `Transmittal` class.

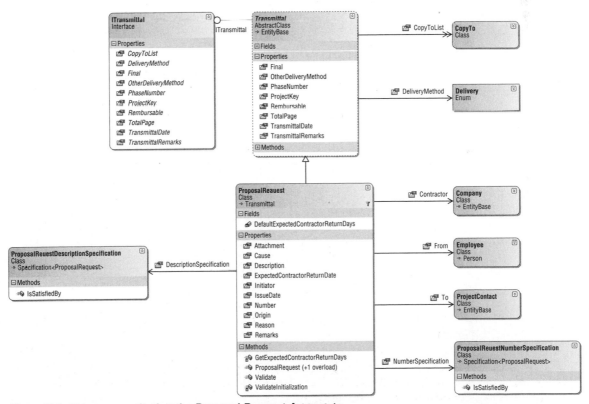

Figure 7.2: Classes constituting the Proposal Request Aggregate.

As shown in Figure 7.2, the `ProposalRequest` class inherits from the `Transmittal` class. Since `ProposalRequest` Transmittals do not have Routing Items, and the `RequestForInformation` and `Submittal` classes do, I made another abstract class for those classes to inherit from, and that class is the `RoutableTransmittal` class. I refactored the `RequestForInformation` and `Submittal` classes to inherit from the `RoutableTransmittal` class. Figure 7.3 details the relationships and hierarchy between the Transmittal and Routable Transmittal interfaces and abstract classes.

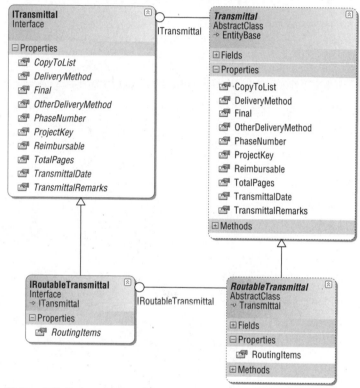

Figure 7.3: Transmittal and RoutableTransmittal classes.

Since the Transmittal and `RoutableTransmittal` classes respectively implement the `ITransmittal` and `IRoutableTransmittal` interfaces, everything will still work as before with their associated repositories.

Defining the Aggregate Boundaries

The `ProposalRequest` class has its own identity and is definitely the root of its own Aggregate. All of the other classes in Figure 7.4, except for `ProjectContact`, `Company`, and `Employee`, belong to the

Proposal Request Aggregate. As shown in earlier chapters, `ProjectContact` belongs to the Project Aggregate, `Company` is the root of its own Aggregate, and the `Employee` class is part of the Employee Aggregate.

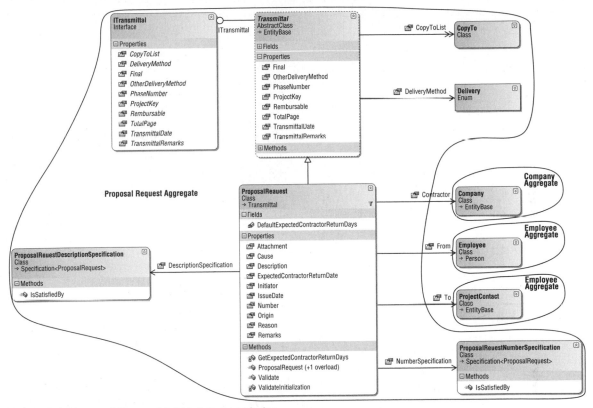

Figure 7.4: Proposal Request Aggregate boundaries.

Designing the Repository

This should be getting familiar by now, but I will say it again: since the `ProposalRequest` class is its own Aggregate root, it will have its own Repository (as shown in Figure 7.5).

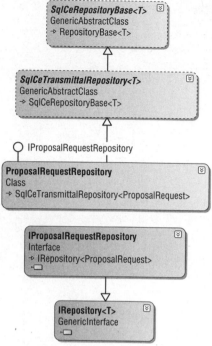

Figure 7.5: Proposal Request Repository.

The IProposalRequestRepository interface is the interface for instances of Proposal Request Repositories. Here is the IProposalRequestRepository interface:

```
using System;
using System.Collections.Generic;
using SmartCA.Infrastructure.RepositoryFramework;
using SmartCA.Model.Projects;

namespace SmartCA.Model.ProposalRequests
{
    public interface IProposalRequestRepository
        : IRepository<ProposalRequest>
    {
        IList<ProposalRequest> FindBy(Project project);
        int GetExpectedContractorReturnDays();
    }
}
```

Like the Repository interfaces for Submittals and RFIs, this Repository interface also has a FindBy method. In addition, it has the GetExpectedContractorReturnDays method, which I will go over in detail later in the chapter.

Writing the Unit Tests

In this section, I will be writing some unit tests for what I expect of the Proposal Request Repository implementation. As noted before, these tests will compile correctly, but they will also fail until I write the code for the Repository implementation later on, in the Solution section.

There will be more unit tests in the accompanying code for this chapter, but for brevity's sake I am showing the tests that I think are important here.

The FindProposalRequestsByProjectTest Method

The purpose of the `FindProposalRequestsByProjectTest` method is to validate that the correct number of `ProposalRequest` instances have been returned by the Proposal Request Repository for a given Project.

```
/// <summary>
/// A test for FindBy(Project project)
/// </summary>
[DeploymentItem("SmartCA.sdf"), TestMethod()]
public void FindProposalRequestsByProjectTest()
{
    // Get a Project reference
    Project project =
        ProjectService.GetProject("5704f6b9-6ffa-444c-9583-35cc340fce2a");

    // Finds all of the Proposal Requests for the Project
    IList<ProposalRequest> proposalRequests =
        ProposalRequestRepositoryUnitTest.repository.FindBy(project);

    // Verify that at least one ProposalRequest was returned
    Assert.IsTrue(proposalRequests.Count > 0);
}
```

This method starts out by getting a `Project` instance from the `ProjectService` class. It then calls the `FindBy` method on the Repository to get the list of Proposal Requests for the given `Project` instance. The method finishes by checking that the repository returned at least one `ProposalRequest`.

The AddProposalRequestTest Method

The purpose of the `AddProposalRequestTest` method is to test adding a new Proposal Request to the Proposal Request Repository.

```
/// <summary>
///A test for Add(ProposalRequest item)
///</summary>
[DeploymentItem("SmartCA.sdf"), TestMethod()]
public void AddProposalRequestTest()
{
    IList<ProposalRequest> proposalRequests =
        ProposalRequestRepositoryUnitTest.repository.FindAll();

    // Create a new ProposalRequest
```

(continued)

(continued)

```
        Guid projectKey = new Guid("5704f6b9-6ffa-444c-9583-35cc340fce2a");
        ProposalRequest pr = new ProposalRequest(projectKey, 2);
        pr.From = EmployeeService.GetEmployees()[0];
        pr.Contractor = CompanyService.GetAllCompanies()[0];
        pr.To = ProjectService.GetProject(projectKey).Contacts[0];

        // Add the ProposalRequest to the Repository
        ProposalRequestRepositoryUnitTest.repository.Add(pr);

        // Commit the transaction
        ProposalRequestRepositoryUnitTest.unitOfWork.Commit();

        // Reload the ProposalRequest and verify it's number
        ProposalRequest savedPr =
            ProposalRequestRepositoryUnitTest.repository.FindBy(pr.Key);
        Assert.AreEqual(2, savedPr.Number);
    }
```

This test is a little more complicated than the last test. It starts out by creating a Project Key value, and then passes the Project Key value as well as a Proposal Request number into the constructor of the ProposalRequest class. Now that I have an initialized ProposalRequest instance, the next step is to set the From property of the ProposalRequest instance with an Employee instance. I then set the Contractor property with a Company instance that is retrieved by the CompanyService class. After those steps, I assign the To property value to the first ProjectContact instance for the Project.

The next step is to add the Proposal Request to the Repository and then to commit the transaction by calling the Commit method on the IUnitOfWork instance. The Commit method is important because that method calls back into the Proposal Request Repository to tell it to write the Proposal Request's data to the data store.

Once the Proposal Request has been saved, it is then reloaded and the Proposal Request's Number property is checked to verify that the Add and Commit methods worked properly.

The UpdateProposalRequestTest Method

The purpose of the UpdateProposalRequestTest method is to find a Proposal Request and update it with a different Description property value, and then verify that the change was persisted properly.

```
    /// <summary>
    ///A test for Updating a Proposal Request
    ///</summary>
    [DeploymentItem("SmartCA.sdf"), TestMethod()]
    public void UpdateProposalRequestTest()
    {
        IList<ProposalRequest> proposalRequests =
            ProposalRequestRepositoryUnitTest.repository.FindAll();

        // Change the Proposal Request's Description value
        proposalRequests[0].Description = "Test Description";

        // Update the Repository
```

```
        ProposalRequestRepositoryUnitTest.repository[proposalRequests[0].Key]
            = proposalRequests[0];

        // Commit the transaction
        ProposalRequestRepositoryUnitTest.unitOfWork.Commit();

        // Verify that the change was saved
        IList<ProposalRequest> refreshedProposalRequests =
            ProposalRequestRepositoryUnitTest.repository.FindAll();
        Assert.AreEqual("Test Description",
            refreshedProposalRequests[0].Description);
    }
```

In this method, I start by getting the entire list of Proposal Requests from the data store. I then change the `Description` property value on the first Proposal Request in the list, and then call the indexer method of the `IProposalRequestRepository`. After the call to the indexer, I then use the `IUnitOfWork` interface to commit the transaction. Finally, I verify that the change actually made it to the data store by reloading the same Proposal Request and checking to see whether its `Description` property value is the same value as the one I assigned to the Proposal Request earlier in the method.

The RemoveProposalRequestTest Method

The purpose of the `RemoveProposalRequestTest` method is to test the process of removing a Proposal Request from the data store.

```
/// <summary>
///A test for Remove(ProposalRequest item)
///</summary>
[DeploymentItem("SmartCA.sdf"), TestMethod()]
public void RemoveProposalRequestTest()
{
    IList<ProposalRequest> proposalRequests =
        ProposalRequestRepositoryUnitTest.repository.FindAll();

    int expectedCount = proposalRequests.Count - 1;

    // Remove the Proposal Request from the Repository
    ProposalRequestRepositoryUnitTest.repository.Remove(
        proposalRequests[0]);

    // Commit the transaction
    ProposalRequestRepositoryUnitTest.unitOfWork.Commit();

    // Verify that there is now one less Proposal Request in the data store
    IList<ProposalRequest> refreshedProposalRequests =
        ProposalRequestRepositoryUnitTest.repository.FindAll();
    Assert.AreEqual(expectedCount, refreshedProposalRequests.Count);
}
```

The first line of this method should look familiar; I am getting the entire list of Proposal Requests from the data store. I then remove the first Proposal Request in the list from the repository. After removing the Proposal Request from the repository, I use the `IUnitOfWork` interface to commit the transaction. Finally, I verify that the change actually made it to the data store by using the repository to find all of the Proposal Request instances and making sure that there is now one fewer Proposal Request.

The Solution

Now for the fun part! I have just shown some very interesting refactoring taking place in the Proposal Request domain model, and now I get to show you how those designs are going to be implemented, as well as how they affect the Proposal Request Repository implementation. In this section, I will also be implementing the ViewModel and the View for Proposal Requests.

The Proposal Request Class Private Fields and Constructors

The `ProposalRequest` class inherits from the `Transmittal` class, and passes its values from its constructors straight through to the Transmittal base class.

```
using System;
using SmartCA.Infrastructure.DomainBase;
using SmartCA.Model.Transmittals;
using SmartCA.Model.Projects;
using System.Collections.Generic;
using SmartCA.Model.Companies;
using SmartCA.Model.Submittals;
using SmartCA.Model.Employees;
using System.Text;

namespace SmartCA.Model.ProposalRequests
{
    public class ProposalRequest : Transmittal
    {
        private int number;
        private ProjectContact to;
        private Employee from;
        private DateTime? issueDate;
        private DateTime expectedContractorReturnDate;
        private Company contractor;
        private string description;
        private string attachment;
        private string reason;
        private string initiator;
        private int cause;
        private int origin;
        private string remarks;
        private ProposalRequestNumberSpecification numberSpecification;
        private ProposalRequestDescriptionSpecification descriptionSpecification;
        private int expectedContractorReturnDays;

        private const int DefaultExpectedContractorReturnDays = 7;

        public ProposalRequest(object projectKey, int number)
            : this(null, projectKey, number)
        {
        }

        public ProposalRequest(object key, object projectKey,
```

```
                      int number) : base(key, projectKey)
        {
            this.number = number;
            this.to = null;
            this.from = null;
            this.issueDate = null;
            this.GetExpectedContractorReturnDays();
            this.expectedContractorReturnDate =
                this.TransmittalDate.AddDays(this.expectedContractorReturnDays);
            this.contractor = null;
            this.description = string.Empty;
            this.attachment = string.Empty;
            this.reason = string.Empty;
            this.initiator = string.Empty;
            this.cause = 0;
            this.origin = 0;
            this.remarks = string.Empty;
            this.numberSpecification =
                new ProposalRequestNumberSpecification();
            this.descriptionSpecification =
                new ProposalRequestDescriptionSpecification();
            this.ValidateInitialization();
        }
```

Just as in the `Submittal` and `RequestForInformation` classes, all of the data for the
`ProposalRequest` class is initialized and validated in the second constructor, which is called by the first
constructor.

The GetExpectedContractorReturnDays Method

On the fifth line of the second constructor, there is a call to the `GetExpectedContractorReturnDays`
method. This private method determines the threshold for how long a Contractor has before he or she
must return the Proposal Request to the issuer:

```
private void GetExpectedContractorReturnDays()
{
    // First go with the default value
    this.expectedContractorReturnDays =
        ProposalRequest.DefaultExpectedContractorReturnDays;

    // Now try to get the real value from the service
    int expectedContractorReturnDays =
        ProposalRequestService.GetExpectedContractorReturnDays();

    // If the service returned a valid value, then use it instead
    // of the default value
    if (expectedContractorReturnDays > 0)
    {
        this.expectedContractorReturnDays =
            expectedContractorReturnDays;
    }
}
```

To start with, the method sets the class variable, expectedContractorReturnDays, to whatever default value is defined for it, by accessing the DefaultExpectedContractorReturnDays class constant value.

```
private const int DefaultExpectedContractorReturnDays = 7;
```

In this case, the class default value is seven days. After getting the default value, the next step is to use the ProposalRequestService class's GetExpectedContractorReturnDays method. I'll cover that method later in this chapter. For now, I don't really care where the value comes from, as long as I know that I have a Service method that I can call to get the value.

After getting the value from the ProposalRequestService class, I then check to see whether it has a value greater than zero; if it does, then I reset the expectedContractorReturnDays class variable to use that value. If it does not, then I do nothing, and the class uses the default value.

Initializing the expectedContractorReturnDate Class Variable

Now that I have just shown how the expectedContractorReturnDays class variable is set, it is time to use it to set the value of the expectedContractorReturnDays class variable. That happens in this line of the second constructor:

```
this.expectedContractorReturnDate =
                this.TransmittalDate.AddDays(this.expectedContractorReturnDays);
```

This line of code sets the expectedContractorReturnDays class variable value to the TransmittalDate property value of the base class and adds to it the number from the expectedContractorReturnDays class variable value. Here is the TransmittalDate property from the Transmittal base class:

```
public DateTime TransmittalDate
{
    get { return this.transmittalDate; }
    set { this.transmittalDate = value; }
}
```

Here is the code that initializes the TransmittalDate value in the Transmittal base class:

```
protected Transmittal(object key, object projectKey)
    : base(key)
{
    this.projectKey = projectKey;
    this.transmittalDate = DateTime.Now;
    this.totalPages = 1;
    this.deliveryMethod = Delivery.None;
    this.otherDeliveryMethod = string.Empty;
    this.phaseNumber = string.Empty;
    this.reimbursable = false;
    this.final = false;
    this.copyToList = new List<CopyTo>();
    this.transmittalRemarks = string.Empty;
}
```

As you can see, the highlighted second line of the `Transmittal` constructor initializes the `TransmittalDate` property.

The ValidateInitialization Method

The last action that happens in the `ProposalRequest` class initialization process is validation. A check is made via the `ValidateInitialization` method to ensure either that the class is passed a key value or that the class has a valid Proposal Request number and is associated with a Project.

```
private void ValidateInitialization()
{
    if (this.Key == null &&
        (this.number < 1 || this.ProjectKey == null))
    {
        StringBuilder builder = new StringBuilder(100);
        builder.Append("Invalid Proposal Request. ");
        builder.Append("The Proposal Request must have ");
        builder.Append("a valid Proposal Request number ");
        builder.Append("and be associated with a Project.");
        throw new InvalidOperationException(builder.ToString());
    }
}
```

The ProposalRequest Properties

The properties of the `ProposalRequest` class are very similar to those covered in previous Domain Model classes, so I am only going to show the differences here. Most of the properties in this class are fairly straightforward.

```
public DateTime? IssueDate
{
    get { return this.issueDate; }
    set { this.issueDate = value; }
}

public DateTime ExpectedContractorReturnDate
{
    get { return this.expectedContractorReturnDate; }
}

public string Description
{
    get { return this.description; }
    set { this.description = value; }
}

public string Attachment
{
    get { return this.attachment; }
    set { this.attachment = value; }
}

public string Reason
```

(continued)

(continued)

```
    {
        get { return this.reason; }
        set { this.reason = value; }
    }

    public string Initiator
    {
        get { return this.initiator; }
        set { this.initiator = value; }
    }

    public int Cause
    {
        get { return this.cause; }
        set
        {
            // Cause must be a positive number
            if (value > 0)
            {
                this.cause = value;
            }
        }
    }

    public int Origin
    {
        get { return this.origin; }
        set
        {
            // Origin must be a positive number
            if (value > 0)
            {
                this.origin = value;
            }
        }
    }

    public ProposalRequestNumberSpecification NumberSpecification
    {
        get { return this.numberSpecification; }
    }

    public ProposalRequestDescriptionSpecification DescriptionSpecification
    {
        get { return this.descriptionSpecification; }
    }
```

The Cause and Origin Properties

Both of these properties have a check in their setter to make sure that any value entered must be a positive number. Slowly, I am starting to put more behavior into the Domain Model classes. More behavior will come with this class in the next few sections.

The NumberSpecification Property

This property is designed to model the business rules about the proper numbering of Proposal Requests. The NumberSpecification property is represented by the ProposalRequestNumberSpecification class. Its only job is to validate that the Proposal Request adheres to the numbering rules, which are, if you remember, that all Proposal Requests must be numbered consecutively within a Project, and there cannot be duplicate Proposal Request numbers within a Project.

```csharp
using System;
using SmartCA.Infrastructure.Specifications;
using System.Collections.Generic;
using SmartCA.Model.Projects;
using System.Linq;

namespace SmartCA.Model.ProposalRequests
{
    public class ProposalRequestNumberSpecification
        : Specification<ProposalRequest>
    {
        public override bool IsSatisfiedBy(ProposalRequest candidate)
        {
            bool isSatisfiedBy = true;

            // Make sure that the same Proposal Request number has not
            // been used for the current project, and that there are no
            // gaps between Proposal Request numbers

            // First get the project associated with the Proposal Request
            Project project = ProjectService.GetProject(candidate.ProjectKey);

            // Next get the list of Proposal Requests for the project
            IList<ProposalRequest> requests =
                ProposalRequestService.GetProposalRequests(project);

            // Determine if the Proposal Request number has been used before
            isSatisfiedBy =
                (requests.Where(pr => pr.Number.Equals(candidate.Number)).Count() <
1);

            // See if the candidate passed the first test
            if (isSatisfiedBy)
            {
                // First test passed, now make sure that there are no gaps
                isSatisfiedBy =
                    (candidate.Number - requests.Max(pr => pr.Number) == 1);
            }

            return isSatisfiedBy;
        }
    }
}
```

This code starts out by getting the list of Proposal Requests for the current Project, which is the Project that is associated with the Proposal Request. Once I have the list of Proposal Requests, I then use a LINQ query to determine whether the count of Proposal Requests in the list that match the candidate Proposal Request's Number property is less than one. If the count is less than one, then the test passes.

The next test is to make sure that the candidate Proposal Request will not introduce any numbering gaps within Proposal Requests of the current Project. This is done with another LINQ query to get the highest Proposal Requests number (Max) in the list, and then subtract that from the candidate Proposal Request's Number property. If the result equals one, then the test passes.

The DescriptionSpecification Property

This property is designed to model the business rule about the dates associated with RFIs. The DateToFieldSpecification property is represented by the RequestForInformationDateSpecification class. Its only job is to validate that the RFI has both a date received value and a date requested by value.

```
using System;
using SmartCA.Infrastructure.Specifications;

namespace SmartCA.Model.ProposalRequests
{
    public class ProposalRequestDescriptionSpecification
        : Specification<ProposalRequest>
    {
        public override bool IsSatisfiedBy(ProposalRequest candidate)
        {
            // The Proposal Request must have a description
            return (!string.IsNullOrEmpty(candidate.Description));
        }
    }
}
```

This code is much simpler than the first Specification class, as it only needs to perform two simple Boolean checks for the two dates.

The Validate Method

Since I have been starting to add more behavior to the Domain Model classes, one of the things that I really need to add is some type of validation before trying to save an Entity. In the ProposalRequest class I have added a Validate method to do just this:

```
protected override void Validate()
{
    if (!this.numberSpecification.IsSatisfiedBy(this))
    {
        this.AddBrokenRule(
            ProposalRequestRuleMessages.MessageKeys.InvalidNumber);
    }
    if (!this.descriptionSpecification.IsSatisfiedBy(this))
    {
```

```
                        this.AddBrokenRule(
                            ProposalRequestRuleMessages.MessageKeys.InvalidDescription);
                    }
                    if (this.to == null)
                    {
                        this.AddBrokenRule(
                            ProposalRequestRuleMessages.MessageKeys.InvalidProjectContact);
                    }
                    if (this.from == null)
                    {
                        this.AddBrokenRule(
                            ProposalRequestRuleMessages.MessageKeys.InvalidEmployee);
                    }
                    if (this.contractor == null)
                    {
                        this.AddBrokenRule(
                            ProposalRequestRuleMessages.MessageKeys.InvalidContractor);
                    }
                    base.Validate();
                }
```

Wait a second, why is it an override, and where is the `Boolean` return value? Ok, I admit it, I did some more refactoring. I made an abstract method in the `EntityBase` class called `Validate`. I also came up with a little mini-framework for dealing with the concept of Broken Rules, which I am borrowing (although simplifying it a bit here) from Rocky Lhotka's CSLA Framework (CSLA). Here is the `BrokenRule` class:

```
using System;

namespace SmartCA.Infrastructure.DomainBase
{
    public class BrokenRule
    {
        private string name;
        private string description;

        public BrokenRule(string name, string description)
        {
            this.name = name;
            this.description = description;
        }

        public string Name
        {
            get { return this.name; }
        }

        public string Description
        {
            get { return this.description; }
        }
    }
}
```

The `BrokenRule` class is a `Value` class for holding information about a broken business rule. Next, I needed some way for my Domain Model classes to get at the list of possible `BrokenRule` instances, so I made another class to capture that functionality:

```csharp
using System;
using System.Collections.Generic;

namespace SmartCA.Infrastructure.DomainBase
{
    public abstract class BrokenRuleMessages
    {
        private Dictionary<string, string> messages;

        protected Dictionary<string, string> Messages
        {
            get { return this.messages; }
        }

        protected BrokenRuleMessages()
        {
            this.messages = new Dictionary<string, string>();
            this.PopulateMessages();
        }

        protected abstract void PopulateMessages();

        public string GetRuleDescription(string messageKey)
        {
            string description = string.Empty;
            if (this.messages.ContainsKey(messageKey))
            {
                description = this.messages[messageKey];
            }
            return description;
        }
    }
}
```

This class is fairly simple; its job is to hold a key-value dictionary of messages, and to provide a way to get messages out of the dictionary via the `GetRuleDescription` method. It also calls the abstract `PopulateMessages` method in its constructor, which means that the deriving class is responsible for putting the messages into the dictionary.

The `BrokenRuleMessages` abstract class is then used inside the `EntityBase` class, and here are the parts of the `EntityBase` class that have been refactored to accommodate this new functionality:

```csharp
    public abstract class EntityBase
    {
        private object key;
        private List<BrokenRule> brokenRules;

        /// <summary>
```

```
/// Default Constructor.
/// </summary>
protected EntityBase()
    : this (null)
{
}

/// <summary>
/// Overloaded constructor.
/// </summary>
/// <param name="key">An <see cref="System.Object"/> that
/// represents the primary identifier value for the
/// class.</param>
protected EntityBase(object key)
{
    this.key = key;
    if (this.key == null)
    {
        this.key = EntityBase.NewKey();
    }
    this.brokenRules = new List<BrokenRule>();
}

protected List<BrokenRule> BrokenRules
{
    get { return this.brokenRules; }
}

protected abstract void Validate();

public ReadOnlyCollection<BrokenRule> GetBrokenRules()
{
    this.Validate();
    return this.brokenRules.AsReadOnly();
}
}
```

So now the EntityBase class holds a list of broken business rules and has a public method for consumers of Entity classes to call, which is the GetBrokenRules method. Notice how the Validate method is declared as abstract; this is because it is the responsibility of the derived Entity class to validate itself. The GetBrokenRules method calls the abstract Validate method (which is the very method in the ProposalRequest class that brought us into this refactoring rant of mine), which will be implemented in the derived class, and then it returns the list of broken business rules as a read-only collection.

So what this design implies is that I can set up a special class in my domain model to hold all of the particular business rules for a particular Entity, and normally that Entity will be an Aggregate Root.

In the case of Proposal Requests, the Aggregate Root is the `ProposalRequest` class, and therefore I have a `ProposalRequestRuleMessages` class:

```
using System;
using System.Collections.Generic;
using SmartCA.Infrastructure.DomainBase;

namespace SmartCA.Model.ProposalRequests
{
    internal class ProposalRequestRuleMessages : BrokenRuleMessages
    {
        internal static class MessageKeys
        {
            public const string InvalidNumber = "Invalid Proposal Request Number";
            public const string InvalidDescription = "Invalid Proposal Request " +
                "Description";
            public const string InvalidProjectContact = "Must Have " +
                "ProjectContact Assigned";
            public const string InvalidEmployee = "Must Have Employee Assigned";
            public const string InvalidContractor = "Must Have Contractor " +
                "Assigned";
        }

        protected override void PopulateMessages()
        {
            // Add the rule messages
            this.Messages.Add(MessageKeys.InvalidNumber,
                "The same Proposal Request number cannot be used for the " +
                "current project, and there cannot be any gaps between " +
                "Proposal Request numbers.");

            this.Messages.Add(MessageKeys.InvalidDescription,
                "The Proposal Request must have a description");

            this.Messages.Add(MessageKeys.InvalidProjectContact,
                "The Proposal Request must have a ProjectContact assigned " +
                "to the To property.");

            this.Messages.Add(MessageKeys.InvalidEmployee,
                "The Proposal Request must have an Employee assigned to the " +
                "From property.");

            this.Messages.Add(MessageKeys.InvalidContractor,
                "The Proposal Request must have a Company assigned to the " +
                "Contractor property.");
        }
    }
}
```

This class helps build all of the messages that I will use to represent the broken business rules of a Proposal Request. This brings us full circle back to the `ProposalRequest` class's `Validate` method:

```
protected override void Validate()
{
    if (!this.numberSpecification.IsSatisfiedBy(this))
    {
        this.AddBrokenRule(
            ProposalRequestRuleMessages.MessageKeys.InvalidNumber);
    }
    if (!this.descriptionSpecification.IsSatisfiedBy(this))
    {
        this.AddBrokenRule(
            ProposalRequestRuleMessages.MessageKeys.InvalidDescription);
    }
    if (this.to == null)
    {
        this.AddBrokenRule(
            ProposalRequestRuleMessages.MessageKeys.InvalidProjectContact);
    }
    if (this.from == null)
    {
        this.AddBrokenRule(
            ProposalRequestRuleMessages.MessageKeys.InvalidEmployee);
    }
    if (this.contractor == null)
    {
        this.AddBrokenRule(
            ProposalRequestRuleMessages.MessageKeys.InvalidContractor);
    }
    base.Validate();
}
```

This method makes use of the mini-validation framework that I have just shown. It first uses the Specification classes and tests to see whether the `ProposalRequest` instance satisfies its criteria. If not, the broken rules are added to the class instance. The rest of the validation is making sure that there are values for the `To`, `From`, and `Contractor` properties. I also added a little helper method to make adding broken rules a little less repetitive:

```
private void AddBrokenRule(string messageKey)
{
    this.BrokenRules.Add(new BrokenRule(messageKey,
        this.brokenRuleMessages.GetRuleDescription(messageKey)));
}
```

This method just allows me not to have to repeat the same verbose code in each of the validations.

The Proposal Request Repository Implementation

After going over the `IProposalRequestRepository` interface in the Design section, it is now time to explain how the `ProposalRequest` class is actually persisted to and from the data store by the Proposal Request Repository. In this section, I will be writing the code for the Proposal Request Repository.

The BuildChildCallbacks Method

As expected from the previous chapters, the `BuildChildCallbacks` method must be overridden as part of the Template Method pattern implementation in the `RequestForInformationRepository`.

```
#region BuildChildCallbacks

protected override void BuildChildCallbacks()
{
    this.ChildCallbacks.Add(
        ProposalRequestFactory.FieldNames.ProjectContactId,
        this.AppendTo);
    this.ChildCallbacks.Add(
        ProposalRequestFactory.FieldNames.EmployeeId,
        this.AppendFrom);
    base.BuildChildCallbacks();
}

#endregion
```

The AppendTo Callback

The first entry made in the `ChildCallbacks` dictionary is for the `AppendFrom` method. Thanks to the `ProjectService` class's `GetProjectContact` method, this method's code is very simple:

```
private void AppendTo(ProposalRequest proposalRequest,
    object toProjectContactKey)
{
    proposalRequest.To = ProjectService.GetProjectContact(
        proposalRequest.ProjectKey, toProjectContactKey);
}
```

The AppendFrom Callback

The first entry made in the `ChildCallbacks` dictionary is for the `AppendFrom` method. Thanks to the `EmployeeService` class's `GetEmployee` method, this method's code is also very simple:

```
private void AppendFrom(ProposalRequest proposalRequest,
    object fromEmployeeKey)
{
    proposalRequest.From =
        EmployeeService.GetEmployee(fromEmployeeKey);
}
```

Unit of Work Implementation

Following the same steps that I have shown before to implement the Unit of Work pattern, I need to override the following three methods: `PersistNewItem(ProposalRequest item)`, `PersistUpdatedItem(ProposalRequest item)`, and `PersistDeletedItem(ProposalRequest item)`.

The PersistNewItem Method

The first method override for the Proposal Request's Unit of Work implementation is the `PersistNewItem` method:

```
protected override void PersistNewItem(ProposalRequest item)
{
    StringBuilder builder = new StringBuilder(100);
    builder.Append(string.Format("INSERT INTO RequestForInformation ({0},
{1},{2},{3},{4},{5},{6},{7},{8},{9},{10},{11},{12},{13},{14},{15},{16},{17},{18},
{19},{20},{21},{22}) ",
        ProposalRequestFactory.FieldNames.ProposalRequestId,
        ProjectFactory.FieldNames.ProjectId,
        ProposalRequestFactory.FieldNames.ProposalRequestNumber,
        ProposalRequestFactory.FieldNames.TransmittalDate,
        ProposalRequestFactory.FieldNames.ProjectContactId,
        ProposalRequestFactory.FieldNames.EmployeeId,
        ProposalRequestFactory.FieldNames.TotalPages,
        ProposalRequestFactory.FieldNames.DeliveryMethod,
        ProposalRequestFactory.FieldNames.OtherDeliveryMethod,
        ProposalRequestFactory.FieldNames.PhaseNumber,
        ProposalRequestFactory.FieldNames.Reimbursable,
        ProposalRequestFactory.FieldNames.Final,
        ProposalRequestFactory.FieldNames.IssueDate,
        CompanyFactory.FieldNames.CompanyId,
        ProposalRequestFactory.FieldNames.Description,
        ProposalRequestFactory.FieldNames.Attachment,
        ProposalRequestFactory.FieldNames.Reason,
        ProposalRequestFactory.FieldNames.Initiator,
        ProposalRequestFactory.FieldNames.Cause,
        ProposalRequestFactory.FieldNames.Origin,
        ProposalRequestFactory.FieldNames.Remarks,
        ProposalRequestFactory.FieldNames.TransmittalRemarks
        ));
    builder.Append(string.Format("VALUES ({0},{1},{2},{3},{4},{5},{6},{7},
{8},{9},{10},{11},{12},{13},{14},{15},{16},{17},{18},{19},{20},{21},{22});",
        DataHelper.GetSqlValue(item.Key),
        DataHelper.GetSqlValue(item.ProjectKey),
        DataHelper.GetSqlValue(item.Number),
        DataHelper.GetSqlValue(item.TransmittalDate),
        DataHelper.GetSqlValue(item.To.Key),
        DataHelper.GetSqlValue(item.From.Key),
        DataHelper.GetSqlValue(item.TotalPages),
        DataHelper.GetSqlValue(item.DeliveryMethod),
        DataHelper.GetSqlValue(item.OtherDeliveryMethod),
        DataHelper.GetSqlValue(item.PhaseNumber),
        DataHelper.GetSqlValue(item.Reimbursable),
        DataHelper.GetSqlValue(item.Final),
        DataHelper.GetSqlValue(item.IssueDate),
        DataHelper.GetSqlValue(item.Contractor.Key),
        DataHelper.GetSqlValue(item.Description),
        DataHelper.GetSqlValue(item.Attachment),
        DataHelper.GetSqlValue(item.Reason),
        DataHelper.GetSqlValue(item.Initiator),
        DataHelper.GetSqlValue(item.Cause),
```

(continued)

(continued)

```
                    DataHelper.GetSqlValue(item.Origin),
                    DataHelper.GetSqlValue(item.Remarks),
                    DataHelper.GetSqlValue(item.TransmittalRemarks)));

            this.Database.ExecuteNonQuery(
                this.Database.GetSqlStringCommand(builder.ToString()));

            // Now do the child objects
            this.InsertCopyToList(item);
        }
```

The code builds up a large insert statement composed of the values from the `ProposalRequest` instance and then executes the query using the Microsoft Enterprise Library's `Database` object. After the insert statement has been executed, I have to account for inserting the `CopyTo` instances for the `ProposalRequest`. I do this by calling the base class `InsertCopyToList` method, which takes an `ITransmittal` instance (which the `ProposalRequest`'s base class, `Transmittal`, implements) as its only argument.

The PersistUpdatedItem Method

`PersistUpdatedItem` first does an update to the `ProposalRequest` table:

```
        protected override void PersistUpdatedItem(ProposalRequest item)
        {
            StringBuilder builder = new StringBuilder(100);
            builder.Append("UPDATE ProposalRequest SET ");

            builder.Append(string.Format("{0} = {1}",
                ProposalRequestFactory.FieldNames.ProposalRequestNumber,
                DataHelper.GetSqlValue(item.Number)));

            builder.Append(string.Format(",{0} = {1}",
                ProposalRequestFactory.FieldNames.TransmittalDate,
                DataHelper.GetSqlValue(item.TransmittalDate)));

            ************************************************************

            builder.Append(string.Format(",{0} = {1}",
                ProposalRequestFactory.FieldNames.Remarks,
                DataHelper.GetSqlValue(item.Remarks)));

            builder.Append(string.Format(",{0} = {1}",
                ProposalRequestFactory.FieldNames.TransmittalRemarks,
                DataHelper.GetSqlValue(item.TransmittalRemarks)));

            builder.Append(" ");
            builder.Append(this.BuildBaseWhereClause(item.Key));

            this.Database.ExecuteNonQuery(
                this.Database.GetSqlStringCommand(builder.ToString()));

            // Now do the child objects

            // First, delete the existing ones
```

```
                    this.DeleteCopyToList(item);

                    // Now, add the current ones
                    this.InsertCopyToList(item);
                }
```

I have omitted several lines of repetitive code building the SQL update statement in the middle of the code in order save you from the boring code.

The second part of the method uses the newly refactored `DeleteCopyToList` helper method to delete all of the `CopyTo` child objects of the Proposal Request and then uses the also newly refactored `InsertCopyToList` helper method to add the existing `CopyTo` child objects from the Proposal Request to the database.

The Proposal Request Service Implementation

Like the other Service classes shown in the domain model so far, the `ProposalRequestService` class is responsible for retrieving and wrapping the methods of its associated Repository interface, in this case the `IProposalRequestRepository` instance.

```
using System;
using System.Collections.Generic;
using SmartCA.Infrastructure;
using SmartCA.Infrastructure.RepositoryFramework;
using SmartCA.Model.Projects;

namespace SmartCA.Model.ProposalRequests
{
    public static class ProposalRequestService
    {
        private static IProposalRequestRepository repository;
        private static IUnitOfWork unitOfWork;

        static ProposalRequestService()
        {
            ProposalRequestService.unitOfWork = new UnitOfWork();
            ProposalRequestService.repository =
                RepositoryFactory.GetRepository<IProposalRequestRepository,
                ProposalRequest>(ProposalRequestService.unitOfWork);
        }

        public static IList<ProposalRequest>
            GetProposalRequests(Project project)
        {
            return ProposalRequestService.repository.FindBy(project);
        }

        public static void SaveProposalRequest(ProposalRequest proposalRequest)
        {
            ProposalRequestService.repository[proposalRequest.Key] =
                proposalRequest;
```

(continued)

(continued)

```
            ProposalRequestService.unitOfWork.Commit();
    }

    public static int GetExpectedContractorReturnDays()
    {
        return ProposalRequestService.repository
.GetExpectedContractorReturnDays();
    }
  }
}
```

The Proposal Request View Model Class

Following the same patterns as before for all `ViewModel` classes, the `ProposalRequestViewModel` class adapts the Proposal Request Aggregate from the domain model to the UI. In the last chapter, I did some major refactoring and created the `TransmittalViewModel<T>` class for adapting Transmittal Entities to the UI, and now I get to use it again.

Just like the code for the RFI and Submittal ViewModels, the code inside of the `ProposalRequestViewModel` class has been reduced significantly. Here is what the signature of the `ProposalRequestViewModel` class looks like when deriving from the `TransmittalViewModel<T>` class:

```
public class ProposalRequestViewModel
    : TransmittalViewModel<ProposalRequest>
```

Notice how the generic parameter from the `TransmittalViewModel<T>` class is replaced with the `ProposalRequest` class.

The Constructor

Because of the recent refactoring, the constructors for the `ProposalRequestViewModel` class now are very small. Here are the constructors for the `ProposalRequestViewModel` class:

```
        #region Constructors

        public ProposalRequestViewModel()
            : this(null)
        {
        }

        public ProposalRequestViewModel(IView view)
            : base(view)
        {
            this.toList = UserSession.CurrentProject.Contacts;
            this.fromList = EmployeeService.GetEmployees();
        }

        #endregion
```

Just like with the `RequestForInformationViewModel` class, the `toList` and `fromList` private fields are not contained in the base class and therefore need to be initialized here.

The Properties

There are not many properties left to implement in the `ProposalRequestViewModel` class. Here is all of the code for the properties:

```
#region Properties

public IList<ProjectContact> ToList
{
    get { return this.toList; }
}

public IList<Employee> FromList
{
    get { return this.fromList; }
}

#endregion
```

The Command Handler Methods

The only command handler methods that I need to override in the `ProposalRequestViewModel` class are the `SaveCommandHandler` and `NewCommandHandler` methods. Again, if you remember from before, the `DeleteCommandHandler` method is completely taken care of by the base class.

The NewCommandHandler Method

Here is the code for the `NewCommandHandler` method:

```
protected override void NewCommandHandler(object sender, EventArgs e)
{
    base.NewCommandHandler(sender, e);
    ProposalRequest newProposalRequest = new ProposalRequest(
                            this.CurrentTransmittal.ProjectKey,
                            this.CurrentTransmittal.Number + 1);
    this.TransmittalList.Add(newProposalRequest);
    this.Transmittals.Refresh();
    this.Transmittals.MoveCurrentToLast();
}
```

On the first line of the method, I call the same method of the base class. This allows me to reuse the common code for managing the new Transmittal state and yet it still gives me the flexibility to do my own housekeeping for creating the new `ProposalRequest` instance.

The SaveCommandHandler Method

This method is much simpler, since it first calls the same method on the base class, and then proceeds to save the `ProposalRequest` instance:

```
protected override void SaveCommandHandler(object sender, EventArgs e)
{
    base.SaveCommandHandler(sender, e);
    ProposalRequestService.SaveProposalRequest(this.CurrentTransmittal);
}
```

Now, one thing that I am not taking advantage of here is the new validation functionality that I just built. Here is what the call will look like now:

```
protected override void SaveCommandHandler(object sender, EventArgs e)
{
    if (this.CurrentTransmittal.GetBrokenRules().Count == 0)
    {
        base.SaveCommandHandler(sender, e);
        ProposalRequestService.SaveProposalRequest(
            this.CurrentTransmittal);
    }
}
```

This really needs to be refactored a little bit more in order to display the list of broken rules to the user in an easily consumable manner. I will leave this as an exercise to do later.

The GetTransmittals Template Pattern Method

Here is the `GetTransmittals` method override:

```
#region GetTransmittals

protected override List<ProposalRequest> GetTransmittals()
{
    return new List<ProposalRequest>(
            ProposalRequestService.GetProposalRequests(
            UserSession.CurrentProject));
}

#endregion
```

In this method, just as in the last chapter, I am simply calling out to the `Service` class (the `ProposalRequestService` class) to get the list of instances (`ProposalRequest` instances).

The Proposal Request View

The View for Proposal Requests is almost exactly identical to the ones for Submittals and RFIs. Figure 7.6 shows what the form looks like at run time:

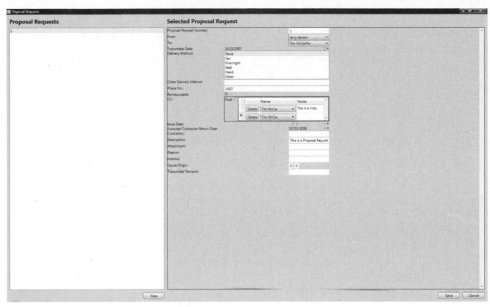

Figure 7.6: Proposal Request View.

Well, I have been doing a lot of refactoring lately regarding the common functionality of Transmittals and Routable Transmittals, and there is no reason that refactoring cannot continue in the UI. So, instead of having to repeat the same XAML over and over for Submittals, RFIs, and now Proposal Requests, I have decided to refactor the XAML that makes up the Transmittal sections of those Entities into some WPF UserControls. These are very similar to the UserControls that I created for Addresses, CopyToList, RoutingItems, and TrackingItems; in fact it is the same concept once again.

The Transmittal User Control

Once again, there is no code for this User Control, only XAML. The XAML for the `Transmittal` User Control is just a `Grid` element with all of the fields that are part of a Transmittal:

```
<UserControl
  x:Class="SmartCA.Presentation.Views.Transmittal"
  xmlns:presentation="clr-namespace:SmartCA.Presentation.Views"
    xmlns="http://schemas.microsoft.com/winfx/2006/xaml/presentation"
    xmlns:xcdg="http://schemas.xceed.com/wpf/xaml/datagrid"
    xmlns:x="http://schemas.microsoft.com/winfx/2006/xaml">

  <Grid>

      <Grid.RowDefinitions>
            <RowDefinition Height="Auto" />
            <RowDefinition Height="Auto" />
            <RowDefinition Height="Auto" />
            <RowDefinition Height="Auto" />
            <RowDefinition Height="Auto" />
            <RowDefinition Height="Auto" />
```

(continued)

(continued)

```
        </Grid.RowDefinitions>

        <Grid.ColumnDefinitions>
                <ColumnDefinition Width="200" />
                <ColumnDefinition Width="Auto" />
        </Grid.ColumnDefinitions>

        <Label Grid.Row="0" Grid.Column="0" Content="Transmittal Date:"
                Style="{StaticResource baseLabelStyle}"/>
        <xcdg:DatePicker Grid.Row="0" Grid.Column="1"
                SelectedDate="{Binding Path=CurrentTransmittal.TransmittalDate}"
                SyncCalendarWithSelectedDate="True" />

        <Label Grid.Row="1" Grid.Column="0" Content="Delivery Method:"
                Style="{StaticResource baseLabelStyle}"/>
        <ListBox Grid.Row="1" Grid.Column="1"
                SelectedItem="{Binding Path=CurrentTransmittal.DeliveryMethod}"
                IsSynchronizedWithCurrentItem="True"
                ItemsSource="{Binding Path=DeliveryMethods}"
                SelectionMode="Multiple"/>

        <Label Grid.Row="2" Grid.Column="0" Content="Other Delivery Method:"
                Style="{StaticResource baseLabelStyle}"/>
        <TextBox Grid.Row="2" Grid.Column="1"
                Text="{Binding Path=CurrentTransmittal.OtherDeliveryMethod}"/>

        <Label Grid.Row="3" Grid.Column="0" Content="Phase No.:"
                Style="{StaticResource baseLabelStyle}"/>
        <TextBox Grid.Row="3" Grid.Column="1"
                Text="{Binding Path=CurrentTransmittal.PhaseNumber}"/>

        <Label Grid.Row="4" Grid.Column="0" Content="Reimbursable:"
                Style="{StaticResource baseLabelStyle}"/>
        <CheckBox Grid.Row="4" Grid.Column="1"
                IsChecked="{Binding Path=CurrentTransmittal.Reimbursable}"/>

        <Label Content="CC:" Grid.Row="5" Grid.Column="0"
                                Style="{StaticResource baseLabelStyle}"/>
        <Border BorderBrush="Black" Padding="1" BorderThickness="1"
                Grid.Row="5" Grid.Column="1">
                <StackPanel Orientation="Horizontal">
                        <Label Content="Final: "
                                Style="{StaticResource baseLabelStyle}"/>
                        <CheckBox IsChecked=
                                "{Binding Path=CurrentTransmittal.Final}" />
                        <presentation:CopyToList
                                DataContext="{Binding Path=MutableCopyToList}"/>
                </StackPanel>
        </Border>

    </Grid>

</UserControl>
```

The RoutableTransmittal User Control

Since a Routable Transmittal is just a Transmittal that contains Routing Items, it should follow that I should be able to use the `Transmittal` User Control shown above, plus the `RoutingItems` User Control from a few chapters back to make one composite User Control. In fact, that is exactly what I did for the `RoutableTransmittal` UserControl:

```xml
<UserControl
  x:Class="SmartCA.Presentation.Views.RoutableTransmittal"
  xmlns:presentation="clr-namespace:SmartCA.Presentation.Views"
    xmlns="http://schemas.microsoft.com/winfx/2006/xaml/presentation"
    xmlns:x="http://schemas.microsoft.com/winfx/2006/xaml">
    <Grid>

        <Grid.RowDefinitions>
            <RowDefinition Height="Auto" />
            <RowDefinition Height="Auto" />
        </Grid.RowDefinitions>

        <Grid.ColumnDefinitions>
            <ColumnDefinition Width="200"/>
            <ColumnDefinition Width="Auto" />
        </Grid.ColumnDefinitions>

        <presentation:Transmittal Grid.Row="0"
            Grid.Column="0" Grid.ColumnSpan="2"
            DataContext="{Binding Path= .}"/>

        <Label Grid.Row="1" Grid.Column="0" Content="Routing:"
            Style="{StaticResource baseLabelStyle}"/>
        <presentation:RoutingItems Grid.Row="1" Grid.Column="1"
            DataContext="{Binding Path=RoutingItems}"/>

    </Grid>
</UserControl>
```

Nothing really new here, I am just enjoying the fact that not only can I get good code re-use out of my domain model, but now I can also get it in my UI code as well!

Summary

In this chapter, I introduced the concept of a Proposal Request in the construction industry, and then I used that concept to model the Proposal Request Aggregate. Up until this point, the classes in the domain model had been a little bit anemic, but by adding lots of behavior to them in this chapter, they are starting to become rich Domain Model classes. I also introduced a new concept into the domain this chapter in regard to handling broken business rules inside my Domain Model classes. Then I put in some validation to exercise both the broken rule functionality as well as the Specification functionality, showing how the two can play nicely together. I also continued my constant refactoring in this chapter, only this time I showed how to refactor some of the UI UserControls to handle some of the Transmittal concepts.

8

Change Orders

In the last chapter, I covered Proposal Requests, which must precede Change Orders in the construction industry. In this chapter, I am going to cover the actual Change Order itself.

The Problem

If it turns out that a Proposal Request that was submitted was acceptable to the owner, or becomes acceptable after adjustment of the scope, negotiation of the price, and/or the adjustment of the Contract time, then a Change Order can be prepared. After execution by the Owner and Contractor, and countersignature by the Architect, it becomes a modification of the construction Contract. It authorizes the Contractor to do the work and obligates the Owner to pay for it.

There are two types of Change Orders:

1. **Change in Contract Price** — Any change, up or down, in the Contract price should be agreed and entered into the Change Order form.

2. **Change in Contract Time** — Any change, up or down, in the Contract time should be agreed on and entered into the Change Order form. If there is no change in time, then the change order should state that there is no change in Contract time. It is a big mistake to leave the time blank, as this will often result in a dispute. The Owner will assume that the blank means no change in time, while the Contractor reasons that the blank means that it will be discussed later.

When there is to be a change in Contract time only, but with no change in Contract price, it is good practice to handle it as a Change Order complete with a Change Order form and signatures of the Owner and Contractor. The form should clearly state the change in Contract time and that the Contract price is unchanged.

Like RFIs and Proposal Requests, each Change Order should be serially numbered by Project.

The Design

In the SmartCA domain, a Change Order is one of the most important concepts for the entire application, and it also contains several important business concepts that must be closely tracked. In the next few sections I will be designing the domain model, determining the Change Order Aggregate and its boundaries, and designing the Repository for Change Orders.

Designing the Domain Model

As stated earlier, the most important parts of the Change Order are the changes in Contract time or price, as well as the proper ordering of the Change Order Number. I will be using the Specification pattern to govern the rules for the Number property, and the Specification that I create will also be part of the domain model. It is very important that the logic inside of the Change Order be correct for calculating the total price or time whenever one of those items is changed.

Figure 8.1 shows a drawing showing the relationships between the classes that combine to make up a Change Order:

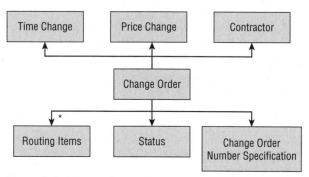

Figure 8.1: Change Order Aggregate.

In the diagram, the Change Order class is clearly the root of the Aggregate. The two most important attributes of the Change Order are the amount of time being changed and the amount of money being added. These are both represented in the diagram by the Time Change and Price Change relationships, respectively. The relationship to the Contractor class shows what Contractor has requested the Change Order.

The next important part of the diagram is the Change Order's relationship to the Routing Items. It is important for Smart Design to know to whom each Change Order has been routed internally for action, and that person's Discipline, such as architect, engineer, or construction administrator. This was already created and used in Chapter 6; I am just reusing the same concept in this Aggregate.

The relationship to the `Status` class shows exactly the state of the Change Order, such as completed or pending an architect review. The relationship to the Change Order Number Specification helps model the numbering rules of the Change Order.

Designing the Change Order Aggregate

The Change Order Aggregate does not have as many classes in it as some of the other Aggregates, but it does contain some important concepts that I will show later in the Solution section (see Figure 8.2).

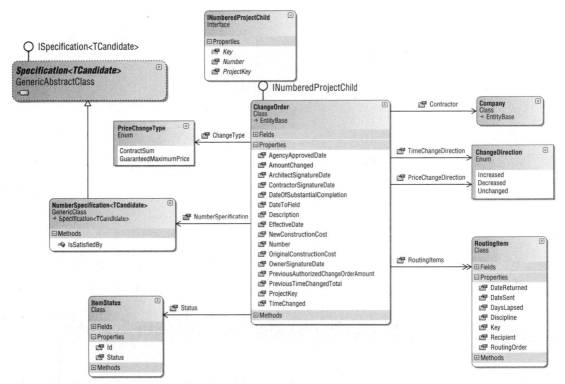

Figure 8.2: Classes Constituting the Change Order Aggregate.

As shown in the diagram, the `ChangeOrder` class inherits from the `EntityBase` class and implements the `INumberedProjectChild` interface. I will talk more about this interface and how it is used in relation to the other parts of the domain model later in the chapter.

Defining the Aggregate Boundaries

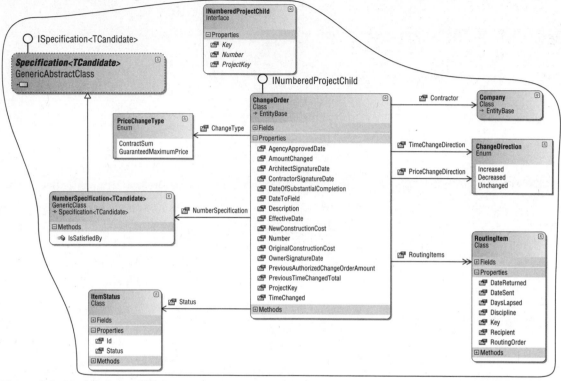

Figure 8.3: Change Order Aggregate boundaries.

The `ChangeOrder` class has its own identity and is definitely the root of its own Aggregate (see Figure 8.3). All of the other classes in the diagram, except for the `Company` class, belong to the Change Order Aggregate. The `Company` class is the root of its own Aggregate.

Designing the Repository

Since the `ChangeOrder` class is its own Aggregate root, it will have its own repository (see Figure 8.4).

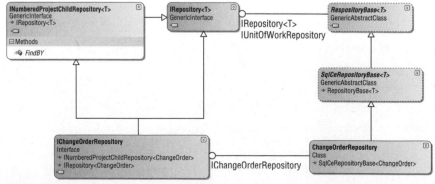

Figure 8.4: The Change Order Repository.

Designing the IChangeOrderRepository Interface

The `IChangeOrderRepository` interface is the interface into instances of Change Order Repositories. Here is the `IChangeOrderRepository` interface:

```
using System;
using System.Collections.Generic;

namespace SmartCA.Model.ChangeOrders
{
    public interface IChangeOrderRepository :
        INumberedProjectChildRepository<ChangeOrder>
    {
        decimal GetPreviousAuthorizedAmountFrom(ChangeOrder co);
        int GetPreviousTimeChangedTotalFrom(ChangeOrder co);
    }
}
```

The `GetPreviousAuthorizedAmountFrom` and the `GetPreviousTimeChangedTotal` methods should look pretty familiar as the `ChangeOrder` class implementation has been calling these methods indirectly via the `ChangeOrderService` class.

The most interesting thing to notice about this interface is that it extends the `INumberedProjectChildRepository<T>` interface, as previously shown in Figure 8.4.

Designing the INumberedProjectChild Interface

You probably saw this coming, since I had the `INumberedProjectChild` interface already. It turned out that all created instances of the `INumberedProjectChild` interface were usually a result of the `FindBy(Project project)` method, so I put this method into its own interface and factored it out of the `IChangeOrderRepository` interface. As a result, I factored this method out of the `IProposalRequestRepository` and `IRequestForInformationRepository` interfaces as well. Here is the `INumberedProjectChildRepository<T>` interface:

```
using System;
using System.Collections.Generic;
using SmartCA.Infrastructure.RepositoryFramework;
using SmartCA.Model.Projects;
using SmartCA.Infrastructure.DomainBase;

namespace SmartCA.Model
{
    public interface INumberedProjectChildRepository<T>
        : IRepository<T> where T : IAggregateRoot, INumberedProjectChild
    {
        IList<T> FindBy(Project project);
    }
}
```

Notice how it is extending the `IRepository<T>` interface; that is expected, but the constraints on the Generic parameter should look different. I am actually able to constrain the Entity (the `T` Generic parameter) that has to implement the `INumberedProjectChild` interface, as well as the `IAggregateRoot` interface, which I will cover next.

I thought about using a custom attribute instead of an empty interface, but I decided I really like the use of interfaces more. They seem to me to be much more explicit, and they allow me to use Generic constraints on them, which I will explain later.

Designing the IAggregateRoot Interface

This should really jump out at you. What is this IAggregateRoot interface? Here is what it looks like:

```
using System;

namespace SmartCA.Infrastructure.DomainBase
{
    /// <summary>
    /// This is a marker interface that indicates that an
    /// Entity is an Aggregate Root.
    /// </summary>
    public interface IAggregateRoot : IEntity
    {
    }
}
```

It does not look like much—it is just a marker interface that simply extends the IEntity interface—but conceptually, this is huge. By using this interface as a constraint on a repository, I can now enforce the DDD rule that only the Aggregate Root is allowed to have a repository associated with it. This is huge from a DDD standpoint! I refactored the IRepository<T> interface to make sure that it uses this constraint as well:

```
using System;
using SmartCA.Infrastructure.DomainBase;
using System.Collections.Generic;

namespace SmartCA.Infrastructure.RepositoryFramework
{
    public interface IRepository<T> where T : IAggregateRoot
    {
        T FindBy(object key);
        IList<T> FindAll();
        void Add(T item);
        T this[object key] { get; set; }
        void Remove(T item);
    }
}
```

I also refactored all of the classes that have been deemed Aggregate Root classes to extend this interface. I did not mention it earlier in the chapter, but some of you may have noticed that the signature of the ChangeOrder class also extends this interface:

```
public class ChangeOrder : EntityBase, IAggregateRoot, INumberedProjectChild
```

I also refactored the RepositoryFactory class to honor this new concept.

```
public static TRepository GetRepository<TRepository, TEntity>(IUnitOfWork
unitOfWork)
            where TRepository : class, IRepository<TEntity>
            where TEntity : IAggregateRoot
```

This new interface and subsequent refactoring really helps clarify the domain model and enforce the DDD concepts that I have been implementing.

Writing the Unit Tests

I am not going to show the unit tests here in this section because they are essentially the same as most of the unit tests written in previous chapters. The main point is that they are there to guide me along my way as I refactor the code; every time I refactor I try to make sure to run my unit tests in order to make sure that I do not break any pieces in the application.

The Solution

The classes used to make up the Change Order Aggregate should look very familiar to you; I am at the point in the application architecture where I am starting to reuse many of the classes. The thing that is a little bit different from previous chapters is that now there is much more business logic to implement inside of the classes. Change Orders deal with money and time, and these types of documents may literally be dealing with millions of dollars.

The Change Order Class Private Fields and Constructors

The `ChangeOrder` class inherits from the `Transmittal` class and passes its values from its constructors straight through to the `Transmittal` base class.

```
using System;
using SmartCA.Model.Companies;
using SmartCA.Infrastructure.DomainBase;
using System.Collections.Generic;
using SmartCA.Model.Transmittals;
using System.Text;
using SmartCA.Model.Projects;

namespace SmartCA.Model.ChangeOrders
{
    public class ChangeOrder : EntityBase, INumberedProjectChild
    {
        #region Private Fields

        private object projectKey;
        private int number;
        private DateTime effectiveDate;
        private Company contractor;
        private string description;
        private Project currentProject;
        private PriceChangeType? changeType;
```

(continued)

271

(continued)

```
            private ChangeDirection priceChangeDirection;
            private decimal? previousAuthorizedChangeOrderAmount;
            private decimal amountChanged;
            private ChangeDirection timeChangeDirection;
            private int? previousTimeChangedTotal;
            private int timeChanged;
            private List<RoutingItem> routingItems;
            private ItemStatus status;
            private DateTime? agencyApprovedDate;
            private DateTime? dateToField;
            private DateTime? ownerSignatureDate;
            private DateTime? architectSignatureDate;
            private DateTime? contractorSignatureDate;
            private NumberSpecification<ChangeOrder> numberSpecification;
            private BrokenRuleMessages brokenRuleMessages;

            #endregion

            #region Constructors

            public ChangeOrder(object projectKey, int number)
                : this(null, projectKey, number)
            {
            }

            public ChangeOrder(object key, object projectKey,
                int number) : base(key)
            {
                this.projectKey = projectKey;
                this.number = number;
                this.effectiveDate = DateTime.Now;
                this.contractor = null;
                this.description = string.Empty;
                this.changeType = null;
                this.priceChangeDirection = ChangeDirection.Unchanged;
                this.previousAuthorizedChangeOrderAmount = 0;
                this.previousTimeChangedTotal = 0;
                this.amountChanged = 0;
                this.timeChangeDirection = ChangeDirection.Unchanged;
                this.timeChanged = 0;
                this.routingItems = new List<RoutingItem>();
                this.status = null;
                this.agencyApprovedDate = null;
                this.dateToField = null;
                this.ownerSignatureDate = null;
                this.architectSignatureDate = null;
                this.contractorSignatureDate = null;
                this.numberSpecification =
                    new NumberSpecification<ChangeOrder>();
                this.ValidateInitialization();
                this.brokenRuleMessages = new ChangeOrderRuleMessages();
            }

            #endregion
```

Just like the `Submittal` and `RequestForInformation` classes, all of the data for the `ChangeOrder` class is initialized and validated in the second constructor, which is called by the first constructor.

The ValidateInitialization Method

The last action that happens in the `ChangeOrder` class initialization process is validation. A check is made via the `ValidateInitialization` method to ensure that, if the class is not passed in a key value, then the class has a valid Change Order number and is associated with a Project.

```
private void ValidateInitialization()
{
    NumberedProjectChildValidator.ValidateInitialState(this,
        "Change Order");
}
```

The old code for this method would have looked like this:

```
private void ValidateInitialization()
{
    if (this.Key == null &&
        (this.number < 1 || this.ProjectKey == null))
    {
        StringBuilder builder = new StringBuilder(100);
        builder.Append("Invalid Change Order. ");
        builder.Append("The Change Order must have ");
        builder.Append("a valid Change Order number ");
        builder.Append("and be associated with a Project.");
        throw new InvalidOperationException(builder.ToString());
    }
}
```

This method's code has been factored out into a new class, the `NumberedProjectChildValidator` class. This new static class has one method, `ValidateInitialState`, which helps reduce the repetitive initialization validation code that I implemented in some of the other Entity classes:

```
using System;
using System.Text;

namespace SmartCA.Model
{
    public static class NumberedProjectChildValidator
    {
        /// <summary>
        /// This method throws an exception if the initial state is not valid.
        /// </summary>
        /// <param name="child">The Entity instance, which must implement the
        /// INumberedProjectChild interface.</param>
        /// <param name="entityFriendlyName">The friendly name of the Entity,
        /// such as "Change Order".</param>
        public static void ValidateInitialState(INumberedProjectChild child,
            string entityFriendlyName)
        {
            if (child.Key == null &&
```

(continued)

(continued)

```
                                (child.Number < 1 || child.ProjectKey == null))
                {
                    StringBuilder builder = new StringBuilder(100);
                    builder.Append(string.Format("Invalid {0}. ",
                        entityFriendlyName));
                    builder.Append(string.Format("The {0} must have ",
                        entityFriendlyName));
                    builder.Append(string.Format("a valid {0} number ",
                        entityFriendlyName));
                    builder.Append("and be associated with a Project.");
                    throw new InvalidOperationException(builder.ToString());
                }
            }
        }
    }
```

The logic is exactly the same as before, but this method takes as its arguments an instance of the INumberedProjectChild interface and the friendly name of the Entity to validate. By factoring this logic out into a separate class, I am now able to reuse it across several of the Entity classes that fall into this category, such as Proposal Requests or RFIs.

The INumberedProjectChild interface is a nice way to represent all Entities that belong to a Project and have a Number property. Here is what its signature looks like:

```
using System;
using SmartCA.Infrastructure.DomainBase;

namespace SmartCA.Model
{
    public interface INumberedProjectChild : IEntity
    {
        object ProjectKey { get; }
        int Number { get; set; }
    }
}
```

Something that should catch your eye right away is that this interface implements the IEntity interface. The IEntity interface represents an Entity:

```
using System;

namespace SmartCA.Infrastructure.DomainBase
{
    public interface IEntity
    {
        object Key { get; }
    }
}
```

This is something I probably should have done before, but I was not quite sure about it. After working with this domain model for a while now, this just feels like the right thing to do. I have also refactored the `EntityBase` class to implement the `IEntity` interface as well.

```
public abstract class EntityBase : IEntity
```

I did not have to change any of the other code in the `EntityBase` class, since it already implements the `Key` property required by the `IEntity` interface.

I also changed a lot of other places in the code where an `EntityBase` class was used, in any part of any method argument or class property, to an `IEntity` interface instead. When I was first pondering this change, I thought it might be a risky move, especially since the `EntityBase` class is referred to almost everywhere in the code, but it turned out that really the dependency was only on the `EntityBase` class's `Key` property. When I decided to make the changes, it really was not too big a deal; once I was able to get everything to compile, I re-ran all of the unit tests until each one passed.

Making the change to `IEntity` actually makes the domain model a lot better; for example, when I cover how to synchronize with the server in Chapter 10, I introduce a `Transaction` class that does not need a lot of validation logic in it. So instead of the `Transaction` class inheriting from the `EntityBase` class and having to implement required functionality for `BrokenRule` logic, it can simply implement the `IEntity` interface and avoid all of that code that does not quite fit with what it is trying to represent.

The ChangeOrder Properties

A lot of the properties of the `ChangeOrder` class are very similar to those covered in previous Domain Model classes, so I am only going to cover those that contain behavior here.

The OriginalConstructionCost Property

The first property I will cover, the `OriginalConstructionCost` property, represents the original cost of the Project from the time it started. It is used as a baseline to compare against the sum of the current Change Orders to date.

```
public decimal OriginalConstructionCost
{
    get
    {
        this.GetCurrentProject();
        return this.currentProject.OriginalConstructionCost;
    }
}
```

This is a read-only property, and it uses the private `currentProject` field to get the value from the Project instance. Before doing so, it calls the `GetCurrentProject` private method to make sure that the `currentProject` field has been populated:

```
private void GetCurrentProject()
{
    if (this.currentProject == null)
    {
        this.currentProject = ProjectService.GetProject(this.projectKey);
    }
}
```

This method implements lazy-load functionality on the `currentProject` field; if it is a null value, then it uses the `ProjectService` class to load it up via its `GetProject` method.

The PreviousAuthorizedAmount Property

The `PreviousAuthorizedAmount` property is another read-only property that represents what has been previously authorized from all of the previous Change Orders before the date of the current Change Order.

```
public decimal PreviousAuthorizedAmount
{
    get
    {
        this.GetPreviousAuthorizedAmount();
        return this.previousAuthorizedAmount.HasValue ?
            this.previousAuthorizedAmount.Value : 0;
    }
}
```

Very similar to the `OriginalConstructionCost` property, this property also calls a private method to get the value in a lazy-load type manner. The `previousAuthorizedAmount` field is a Nullable type, so if it has a value, then the value is used; otherwise, the property returns a value of zero. The private method the property calls is the `GetPreviousAuthorizedAmount` method:

```
private void GetPreviousAuthorizedAmount()
{
    if (!this.previousAuthorizedAmount.HasValue)
    {
        this.previousAuthorizedAmount =
            ChangeOrderService.GetPreviousAuthorizedAmountFrom(this);
    }
}
```

This method implements its lazy-load functionality by checking to see whether the `previousAuthorizedAmount` field has a value; if it does not have a value, then it sets its value using the `GetPreviousAuthorizedAmountFrom` method of the `ChangeOrderService`.

The NewConstructionCost Property

This property is read-only and represents what the new construction cost is as of the date of the current Change Order.

```
public decimal NewConstructionCost
{
    get
    {
        this.GetPreviousAuthorizedAmount();
        return this.OriginalConstructionCost +
            this.PreviousAuthorizedAmount +
            this.amountChanged;
    }
}
```

This property starts out by calling the method I just showed, the `GetPreviousAuthorizedAmount` method. It then adds up the value of the `OriginalConstructionCost` property, the `PreviousAuthorizedAmount` property, and the `amountChanged` private field. The `amountChanged` private field is changed by the setter on the `AmountChanged` property. These values added together represent the new construction cost of a Project at the particular point in time of the current Change Order.

The PreviousTimeChangedTotal Property

This is another read-only property that represents the total amount of days that have been added or subtracted from the Project as of the date of the current Change Order.

```
public int PreviousTimeChangedTotal
{
    get
    {
        this.GetPreviousTimeChangedTotal();
        return this.previousTimeChangedTotal.HasValue ?
            this.previousTimeChangedTotal.Value : 0;
    }
}
```

The logic for this property is pretty much the same as for the `PreviousAuthorizedAmount` property. It also calls a private method to get the value in a lazy-load type manner. The `previousTimeChangedTotal` field is a Nullable type, so if it has a value, then the value is used; otherwise, the property returns a value of zero. The private method the property calls is the `GetPreviousTimeChangedTotal` method:

```
private void GetPreviousTimeChangedTotal()
{
    if (!this.previousTimeChangedTotal.HasValue)
    {
        this.previousTimeChangedTotal =
            ChangeOrderService.GetPreviousTimeChangedTotalFrom(this);
    }
}
```

As you would expect, the logic for this method is very similar to the logic for the `GetPreviousAuthorizedAmount` method. This method also implements lazy-load functionality by checking to see whether the `previousTimeChangedTotal` field has a value; if it does not have a value, then it sets its value using the `GetPreviousTimeChangedTotalFrom` method of the `ChangeOrderService`.

The DateOfSubstantialCompletion Property

This read-only property represents the date that the Project will be completed as of the current Change order. This takes into account all of the days added or subtracted from the Project by previous Change Orders.

```
            public DateTime? DateOfSubstantialCompletion
            {
                get
                {
                    DateTime? completionDate = null;
                    this.GetCurrentProject();
                    if (this.currentProject.EstimatedCompletionDate.HasValue)
                    {
                        this.GetPreviousTimeChangedTotal();
                        completionDate =
                            this.currentProject.EstimatedCompletionDate.Value.AddDays(
                            this.PreviousTimeChangedTotal + this.timeChanged);
                    }
                    return completionDate;
                }
            }
```

This getter starts by setting up a `Nullable DateTime` variable to use as the return value and sets it to null. The next step is to check whether the `currentProject` instance's `EstimatedCompletionDate` property value has a value, but before doing that, I have to call the `GetCurrentProject` method to make sure that the `currentProject` field is properly initialized. If the Project has an `EstimatedCompletionDate` value, I then call the `GetPreviousTimeChangedTotal` method to get the number of days that have been added to or subtracted from the current Project as of the date of the current Change Order. I then add the value of the `PreviousTimeChangedTotal` property and the `timeChanged` class field value to add the right number of days to the Project's `EstimatedCompletionDate` property and then return that value. The `timeChanged` field value is set via the `TimeChanged` property.

The NumberSpecification Property

This property is designed to model the business rules about the proper numbering of Change Orders. The `NumberSpecification` property is represented by the `ChangeOrderNumberSpecification` class. Its only job is to validate that the Change Order adheres to the numbering rules, which are, if you remember, that all Change Orders must be numbered consecutively within a Project and that there cannot be duplicate Change Order numbers within a Project.

```
            public NumberSpecification<ChangeOrder> NumberSpecification
            {
                get { return this.numberSpecification; }
            }
```

This is very similar to the other Number Specification implementations in the last two chapters, so, seeing that, I felt this needed some more refactoring in order to eliminate the duplicate code. As a result, I created a generic Number Specification class; actually it is a .NET Generic `NumberSpecification<TCandidate>` class.

```csharp
using System;
using System.Collections.Generic;
using System.Linq;
using SmartCA.Infrastructure.Specifications;
using SmartCA.Model.Projects;
using SmartCA.Infrastructure.RepositoryFramework;
using SmartCA.Infrastructure.DomainBase;

namespace SmartCA.Model
{
    public class NumberSpecification<TCandidate>
        : Specification<TCandidate> where TCandidate : IAggregateRoot,
        INumberedProjectChild
    {
        public override bool IsSatisfiedBy(TCandidate candidate)
        {
            bool isSatisfiedBy = true;

            // Make sure that the same entity number has not
            // been used for the current project, and that there are no
            // gaps between entity numbers

            // First get the project associated with the entity
            Project project = ProjectService.GetProject(candidate.ProjectKey);

            // Next get the list of items for the project

            // First get the correct Repository
            INumberedProjectChildRepository<TCandidate> repository =
                RepositoryFactory.GetRepository
                <INumberedProjectChildRepository<TCandidate>, TCandidate>();

            // Now use the Repository to find all of the items by the Project
            IList<TCandidate> items = repository.FindBy(project);

            // Use a LINQ query to determine if the entity number has been
            // used before
            isSatisfiedBy =
                (items.Where(item => item.Number.Equals(candidate.Number)).Count()
                    < 1);

            // See if the candidate passed the first test
            if (isSatisfiedBy)
            {
                // First test passed, now use another LINQ query to make sure that
                // there are no gaps
                isSatisfiedBy =
                    (candidate.Number - items.Max(item => item.Number) == 1);
            }

            return isSatisfiedBy;
        }
    }
}
```

This code is almost the same as the other Number Specification implementations, only it uses .NET Generics to give it reusability. Let me start out by comparing the signature of this class to the non-Generic class that would have been created.

Here is the old way of implementing this:

```
public class ChangeOrderNumberSpecification : Specification<ChangeOrder>
```

Here, again, is the new way:

```
public class NumberSpecification<TCandidate> : Specification<TCandidate> where
    TCandidate : IAggregateRoot, INumberedProjectChild
```

The trick here is using the constraints on the TCandidate Generic parameter. By declaring that the TCandidate Generic parameter has to implement the INumberedProjectChild interface, I now have strongly typed access to its properties (via the TCandidate candidate argument) in the IsSatisfied method. I then proceed to use the ProjectKey property to get the correct Project instance via the ProjectService class. I get an instance of the INumberedProjectChildRepository interface and then use that to get the list of all of the items (in this case, it would be ChangeOrder instances) for the given Project. Finally, in the LINQ queries I use the Number property of the INumberedProjectChild interface instance to make sure that the Number has not been used before and that there are no gaps between the last item (in this case ChangeOrder) Number and this item (again, ChangeOrder) Number.

I also went back and refactored the NumberSpecification properties on the ProposalRequest and RequestForInformation classes to use the new NumberSpecification<TCandidate> class.

The Validate Method

Taking advantage of the mini-validation framework that was built in the last chapter, here is the Validate method override for the ChangeOrder class:

```
protected override void Validate()
{
    if (!this.numberSpecification.IsSatisfiedBy(this))
    {
        this.AddBrokenRule(
            ChangeOrderRuleMessages.MessageKeys.InvalidNumber);
    }
    if (this.contractor == null)
    {
        this.AddBrokenRule(
            ChangeOrderRuleMessages.MessageKeys.InvalidContractor);
    }
}
```

If you remember in the last chapter, there was a little bit more to this implementation than just overriding the Validate method of the EntityBase class. Well, I know this is hard to believe, but I did a little bit more refactoring since then. I moved the brokenRuleMessages field into the EntityBase class, as well as the AddBrokenRule method.

Here are the new changes to the EntityBase class:

```
public abstract class EntityBase : IEntity
{
    private object key;
    private List<BrokenRule> brokenRules;
    private BrokenRuleMessages brokenRuleMessages;

    /// <summary>
    /// Overloaded constructor.
    /// </summary>
    /// <param name="key">An <see cref="System.Object"/> that
    /// represents the primary identifier value for the
    /// class.</param>
    protected EntityBase(object key)
    {
        this.key = key;
        if (this.key == null)
        {
            this.key = EntityBase.NewKey();
        }
        this.brokenRules = new List<BrokenRule>();
        this.brokenRuleMessages = this.GetBrokenRuleMessages();
    }

    #region Validation and Broken Rules

    protected abstract void Validate();

    protected abstract BrokenRuleMessages GetBrokenRuleMessages();

    protected List<BrokenRule> BrokenRules
    {
        get { return this.brokenRules; }
    }

    public ReadOnlyCollection<BrokenRule> GetBrokenRules()
    {
        this.Validate();
        return this.brokenRules.AsReadOnly();
    }

    protected void AddBrokenRule(string messageKey)
    {
        this.brokenRules.Add(new BrokenRule(messageKey,
            this.brokenRuleMessages.GetRuleDescription(messageKey)));
    }

    #endregion
```

There is also a new abstract method in the `EntityBase` class, the `GetBrokenRulesMessages` method. This allows the `EntityBase` class to separate the `brokenRuleMessages` field completely from the derived classes; all they have to do is implement the `GetBrokenRuleMessages` method and return a `BrokenRuleMessages` instance. Here is how it is implemented in the `ChangeOrder` class:

```
protected override BrokenRuleMessages GetBrokenRuleMessages()
{
    return new ChangeOrderRuleMessages();
}
```

This is another implementation of the Template Method pattern, and as you can see it really helps to encapsulate the logic of managing `BrokenRule` instances. Here is the `ChangeOrderRuleMessages` class:

```
using System;
using SmartCA.Infrastructure.DomainBase;

namespace SmartCA.Model.ChangeOrders
{
    public class ChangeOrderRuleMessages : BrokenRuleMessages
    {
        internal static class MessageKeys
        {
            public const string InvalidNumber = "Invalid Change Order Number";
            public const string InvalidDescription = "Invalid Change Order " +
                "Description";
            public const string InvalidStatus = "Must Have " +
                "Status Assigned";
            public const string InvalidContractor = "Must Have Contractor " +
                "Assigned";
        }

        protected override void PopulateMessages()
        {
            // Add the rule messages
            this.Messages.Add(MessageKeys.InvalidNumber,
                "The same Change Order number cannot be used for the " +
                "current project, and there cannot be any gaps between " +
                "Change Order numbers.");

            this.Messages.Add(MessageKeys.InvalidDescription,
                "The Change Order must have a description");

            this.Messages.Add(MessageKeys.InvalidContractor,
                "The Change Order must have a Company assigned to the " +
                "Contractor property.");
        }
    }
}
```

The main idea to take away from this class is that it inherits the `BrokenRuleMessages` class, and because of this I am able to return an instance of it from the `ChangeOrder` class's `GetBrokenRuleMessages` method override.

The end result of this refactoring is that now my Entity classes can be validated with even less code in them, and they are even more focused on nothing but the business logic.

The Change Order Repository Implementation

After going over the `IChangeOrderRepository` interface in the Design section, it is now time to explain how the `ChangeOrder` class is actually persisted to and from the data store by the Change Order Repository. In this section, I will be writing the code for the Change Order Repository.

The BuildChildCallbacks Method

It should be like clockwork now: it is time to implement the Template Method pattern that I have been using in the repositories for getting Entity Root instances, and that means that the `BuildChildCallbacks` method has to be overridden in the `ChangeOrderRepository`.

```
#region BuildChildCallbacks

protected override void BuildChildCallbacks()
{
    this.ChildCallbacks.Add(CompanyFactory.FieldNames.CompanyId,
        this.AppendContractor);
    this.ChildCallbacks.Add("RoutingItems",
        delegate(ChangeOrder co, object childKeyName)
        {
            this.AppendRoutingItems(co);
        });
}

#endregion
```

The AppendContractor Callback

The first entry made in the `ChildCallbacks` dictionary is for the `AppendContractor` method. Thanks to the `CompanyService` class's `GetCompany` method, this method's code is very simple:

```
private void AppendContractor(ChangeOrder co, object contractorKey)
{
    co.Contractor = CompanyService.GetCompany(contractorKey);
}
```

The AppendRoutingItems Callback

The last entry made in the `ChildCallbacks` dictionary is for the `AppendRoutingItems` method. Thanks to the `ProjectService` class's `GetProjectContact` method, this method's code is very simple:

```
private void AppendRoutingItems(ChangeOrder co)
{
    StringBuilder builder = new StringBuilder(100);
    builder.Append(string.Format("SELECT * FROM {0}RoutingItem tri ",
        this.EntityName));
    builder.Append(" INNER JOIN RoutingItem ri ON");
    builder.Append(" tri.RoutingItemID = ri.RoutingItemID");
```

(continued)

(continued)

```
            builder.Append(" INNER JOIN Discipline d ON");
            builder.Append(" ri.DisciplineID = d.DisciplineID");
            builder.Append(string.Format(" WHERE tri.{0} = '{1}';",
                this.KeyFieldName, co.Key));
            using (IDataReader reader = this.ExecuteReader(builder.ToString()))
            {
                while (reader.Read())
                {
                    co.RoutingItems.Add(TransmittalFactory.BuildRoutingItem(
                        co.ProjectKey, reader));
                }
            }
        }
    }
```

This code is almost identical to the code for the `AppendRoutingItems` in the `SqlCeRoutableTransmittalRepository` class. In fact, it actually uses the `TransmittalFactory` class to build the instances of the `RoutingItem` class from the `IDataReader` instance.

The FindBy Method

The `FindBy` method is very similar to the other `FindBy` methods in the other Repository implementations. The only part that is really different is the SQL query that is being used.

```
        public IList<ChangeOrder> FindBy(Project project)
        {
            StringBuilder builder = this.GetBaseQueryBuilder();
            builder.Append(string.Format(" WHERE ProjectID = '{0}';",
                project.Key));
            return this.BuildEntitiesFromSql(builder.ToString());
        }
```

This method should also probably be refactored into a separate class, but I will leave that as an exercise to be done later.

The GetPreviousAuthorizedAmountFrom Method

The purpose of this method is to get the total number of Change Orders for the particular Project that occurred before the current Change Order being passed in.

```
        public decimal GetPreviousAuthorizedAmountFrom(ChangeOrder co)
        {
            StringBuilder builder = new StringBuilder(100);
            builder.Append("SELECT SUM(AmountChanged) FROM ChangeOrder ");
            builder.Append(string.Format("WHERE ProjectID = '{0}' ",
                co.ProjectKey.ToString()));
            builder.Append(string.Format("AND ChangeOrderNumber < '{1}';",
                co.Number));
            object previousAuthorizedAmountResult =
                this.Database.ExecuteScalar(
                this.Database.GetSqlStringCommand(builder.ToString()));
            return previousAuthorizedAmountResult != null ?
                Convert.ToDecimal(previousAuthorizedAmountResult) : 0;
        }
```

It builds an SQL statement to get the total amount from the `ChangeOrder` table, and then uses the Microsoft Enterprise Library's `ExecuteScalar` method to retrieve the value from the query. It then checks to see whether the value is null, and if it is null, it returns a value of zero instead.

The GetPreviousTimeChangedTotalFrom Method

This method is very similar in implementation to the previous method. Its purpose is to get the total number of days that have been added or subtracted from the Project before the current Change Order being passed in.

```
public int GetPreviousTimeChangedTotalFrom(ChangeOrder co)
{
    StringBuilder builder = new StringBuilder(100);
    builder.Append("SELECT SUM(TimeChangedDays) FROM ChangeOrder ");
    builder.Append(string.Format("WHERE ProjectID = '{0}' ",
        co.ProjectKey.ToString()));
    builder.Append(string.Format("AND ChangeOrderNumber < '{0}';",
        co.Number));
    object previousTimeChangedTotalResult =
        this.Database.ExecuteScalar(
        this.Database.GetSqlStringCommand(builder.ToString()));
    return previousTimeChangedTotalResult != null ?
        Convert.ToInt32(previousTimeChangedTotalResult) : 0;
}
```

It also builds an SQL query, only this query is to get the total number of days that have been added or subtracted, and it also uses the Microsoft Enterprise Library's `ExecuteScalar` method to get the result of the query. As before, I make a check to see whether the value is null, and if the value is null, then I return a value of zero.

Unit of Work Implementation

Following the same steps that I have shown before to implement the Unit of Work pattern, I only need to override the `PersistNewItem(ChangeOrder item)` and `PersistUpdatedItem(ChangeOrder item)` methods.

The `PersistNewItem` Method

The first method override for the Change Order's Unit of Work implementation is the `PersistNewItem` method:

```
protected override void PersistNewItem(ChangeOrder item)
{
    StringBuilder builder = new StringBuilder(100);
    builder.Append(string.Format("INSERT INTO ChangeOrder
({0},{1},{2},{3},{4},{5},{6},{7},{8},{9},{10},{11},{12},{13},{14},{15},{16}) ",
        ChangeOrderFactory.FieldNames.ChangeOrderId,
        ProjectFactory.FieldNames.ProjectId,
        ChangeOrderFactory.FieldNames.ChangeOrderNumber,
        ChangeOrderFactory.FieldNames.EffectiveDate,
        CompanyFactory.FieldNames.CompanyId,
        ChangeOrderFactory.FieldNames.Description,
        ChangeOrderFactory.FieldNames.PriceChangeType,
```

(continued)

(continued)

```
                    ChangeOrderFactory.FieldNames.PriceChangeTypeDirection,
                    ChangeOrderFactory.FieldNames.AmountChanged,
                    ChangeOrderFactory.FieldNames.TimeChangeDirection,
                    ChangeOrderFactory.FieldNames.TimeChangedDays,
                    ChangeOrderFactory.FieldNames.ItemStatusId,
                    ChangeOrderFactory.FieldNames.AgencyApprovedDate,
                    ChangeOrderFactory.FieldNames.DateToField,
                    ChangeOrderFactory.FieldNames.OwnerSignatureDate,
                    ChangeOrderFactory.FieldNames.ArchitectSignatureDate,
                    ChangeOrderFactory.FieldNames.ContractorSignatureDate
                    ));
            builder.Append(string.Format("VALUES
({0},{1},{2},{3},{4},{5},{6},{7},{8},{9},{10},{11},{12},{13},{14},{15},{16});",
                    DataHelper.GetSqlValue(item.Key),
                    DataHelper.GetSqlValue(item.ProjectKey),
                    DataHelper.GetSqlValue(item.Number),
                    DataHelper.GetSqlValue(item.EffectiveDate),
                    DataHelper.GetSqlValue(item.Contractor.Key),
                    DataHelper.GetSqlValue(item.Description),
                    DataHelper.GetSqlValue(item.ChangeType),
                    DataHelper.GetSqlValue(item.PriceChangeDirection),
                    DataHelper.GetSqlValue(item.AmountChanged),
                    DataHelper.GetSqlValue(item.TimeChangeDirection),
                    DataHelper.GetSqlValue(item.TimeChanged),
                    DataHelper.GetSqlValue(item.Status.Id),
                    DataHelper.GetSqlValue(item.AgencyApprovedDate),
                    DataHelper.GetSqlValue(item.DateToField),
                    DataHelper.GetSqlValue(item.OwnerSignatureDate),
                    DataHelper.GetSqlValue(item.ArchitectSignatureDate),
                    DataHelper.GetSqlValue(item.ContractorSignatureDate)));

            this.Database.ExecuteNonQuery(
                this.Database.GetSqlStringCommand(builder.ToString()));

            // Now do the child objects
            this.InsertRoutingItems(item);
        }
```

The code builds up a large insert statement composed of the values from the `ChangeOrder` instance and then executes the query using the Microsoft Enterprise Library's `Database` object. After the insert statement has been executed, I then have to account for inserting the `RoutingItem` instances for the `ChangeOrder`. I do this by calling the `InsertRoutingItems` method, which is almost identical to the same method in the `SqlCeRoutableTransmittalRepository` class:

```
        private void InsertRoutingItems(ChangeOrder co)
        {
            foreach (RoutingItem item in co.RoutingItems)
            {
                this.InsertRoutingItem(item, co.Key);
            }
        }
```

And this code does a basic loop through all of the `RoutingItem` instances in the list and calls the `InsertRoutingItem` method for each one. I am not going to show the code for that method as it is identical to the one in the `SqlCeRoutableTransmittalRepository` class. This definitely signals to me that this code needs to be refactored, but for now I will just flag it to be refactored at a later time.

The `PersistUpdatedItem` Method

`PersistUpdatedItem` first does an update to the `ChangeOrder` table:

```
protected override void PersistUpdatedItem(ChangeOrder item)
    {
        StringBuilder builder = new StringBuilder(100);
        builder.Append("UPDATE ChangeOrder SET ");

        builder.Append(string.Format("{0} = {1}",
            ChangeOrderFactory.FieldNames.ChangeOrderNumber,
            DataHelper.GetSqlValue(item.Number)));

        builder.Append(string.Format(",{0} = {1}",
            ChangeOrderFactory.FieldNames.EffectiveDate,
            DataHelper.GetSqlValue(item.EffectiveDate)));

        builder.Append(string.Format(",{0} = {1}",
            ChangeOrderFactory.FieldNames.OwnerSignatureDate,
            DataHelper.GetSqlValue(item.OwnerSignatureDate)));

        /**************************************************************/

        builder.Append(string.Format(",{0} = {1}",
            ChangeOrderFactory.FieldNames.ArchitectSignatureDate,
            DataHelper.GetSqlValue(item.ArchitectSignatureDate)));

        builder.Append(string.Format(",{0} = {1}",
            ChangeOrderFactory.FieldNames.ContractorSignatureDate,
            DataHelper.GetSqlValue(item.ContractorSignatureDate)));

        builder.Append(" ");
        builder.Append(this.BuildBaseWhereClause(item.Key));

        this.Database.ExecuteNonQuery(
            this.Database.GetSqlStringCommand(builder.ToString()));

        // Now do the child objects

        // First, delete the existing ones
        this.DeleteRoutingItems(item);

        // Now, add the current ones
        this.InsertRoutingItems(item);
    }
```

I have omitted several lines of repetitive code building the SQL update statement in the middle of the code in order to try to save you from the boring code.

287

The second part of the method then uses the `DeleteRoutingItems` helper method to delete all of the `RoutingItem` child objects of the Change Order and then uses the also newly refactored `InsertRoutingItems` helper method to add the existing `RoutingItem` child objects from the Change Order to the database.

The Change Order Service Implementation

Like the other Service classes shown in the domain model so far, the `ChangeOrderService` class is responsible for retrieving and wrapping the methods of its associated Repository interface, in this case the `IChangeOrderRepository` instance:

```
using System;
using System.Collections.Generic;
using SmartCA.Model.Projects;
using SmartCA.Infrastructure;
using SmartCA.Infrastructure.RepositoryFramework;

namespace SmartCA.Model.ChangeOrders
{
    public static class ChangeOrderService
    {
        private static IChangeOrderRepository repository;
        private static IUnitOfWork unitOfWork;

        static ChangeOrderService()
        {
            ChangeOrderService.unitOfWork = new UnitOfWork();
            ChangeOrderService.repository =
                RepositoryFactory.GetRepository<IChangeOrderRepository,
                ChangeOrder>(ChangeOrderService.unitOfWork);
        }

        public static IList<ChangeOrder>
            GetChangeOrders(Project project)
        {
            return ChangeOrderService.repository.FindBy(project);
        }

        public static void SaveChangeOrder(ChangeOrder co)
        {
            ChangeOrderService.repository[co.Key] = co;
            ChangeOrderService.unitOfWork.Commit();
        }

        public static decimal GetPreviousAuthorizedAmountFrom(ChangeOrder co)
        {
            return
                ChangeOrderService.repository.GetPreviousAuthorizedAmountFrom(co);
        }

        public static int GetPreviousTimeChangedTotalFrom(ChangeOrder co)
        {
            return
```

```
                               ChangeOrderService.repository.GetPreviousTimeChangedTotalFrom(co);
            }
        }
    }
```

These are the only methods needed for now, but others could easily be added later, such as a method for removing Change Orders.

The Change Order View Model Class

Following the same patterns for all `ViewModel` classes as before, the `ChangeOrderViewModel` class adapts the Change Order Aggregate from the domain model to the UI. It follows the usual pattern of inheriting from the `ViewModel` class introduced previously:

```
using System;
using System.Collections.Generic;
using SmartCA.Infrastructure.UI;
using SmartCA.Model.ChangeOrders;
using System.Windows.Data;
using SmartCA.Model;
using SmartCA.Model.Transmittals;
using System.ComponentModel;
using SmartCA.Application;
using SmartCA.Model.Submittals;
using SmartCA.Model.Companies;

namespace SmartCA.Presentation.ViewModels
{
    public class ChangeOrderViewModel : ViewModel
```

The Constructor

Again, there are not any new concepts being introduced in the constructor code for this class, I am just following the same patterns as laid out in the previous chapters. Here are the constructors for the `ChangeOrderViewModel` class:

```
        #region Constructors

        public ChangeOrderViewModel()
            : this(null)
        {
        }

        public ChangeOrderViewModel(IView view)
            : base(view)
        {
            this.currentChangeOrder = null;
            this.changeOrderList = new List<ChangeOrder>(
                ChangeOrderService.GetChangeOrders(UserSession.CurrentProject));
            this.changeOrders = new CollectionView(this.changeOrderList);
            this.contractors = CompanyService.GetAllCompanies();
```

(continued)

(continued)

```
            this.priceChangeTypesView = new
                CollectionView(Enum.GetNames(typeof(PriceChangeType)));
        string[] changeDirections = Enum.GetNames(typeof(ChangeDirection));
        this.priceChangeDirections = new CollectionView(changeDirections);
        this.timeChangeDirections = new CollectionView(changeDirections);
        this.itemStatuses = SubmittalService.GetItemStatuses();
        this.routingItems = new BindingList<RoutingItem>();
        this.disciplines = SubmittalService.GetDisciplines();
        this.saveCommand = new DelegateCommand(this.SaveCommandHandler);
        this.newCommand = new DelegateCommand(this.NewCommandHandler);
        this.deleteRoutingItemCommand =
            new DelegateCommand(this.DeleteRoutingItemCommandHandler);
    }

    #endregion
```

I am making good use of the `ChangeOrderService` and the `SubmittalService` classes to retrieve the necessary data for the dropdowns in the UI. Note how I am also exposing the enumeration data types as `CollectionView` instances here. You may wonder why I am using two different `CollectionView` objects to represent the `ChangeDirection` enumeration. I am using them to represent two different properties, `PriceChangeDirection` and `TimeChangeDirection`, and because of the synchronization that WPF uses, if I do not use two separate instances, whenever one is changed, the other will change its value to be the same as the first.

The Properties

All of the properties in the `ChangeOrderViewModel` class are read-only, except for the `CurrentChangeOrder` property:

```
    public ChangeOrder CurrentChangeOrder
    {
        get { return this.currentChangeOrder; }
        set
        {
            if (this.currentChangeOrder != value)
            {
                this.currentChangeOrder = value;
                this.OnPropertyChanged(
                    Constants.CurrentChangeOrderPropertyName);
                this.saveCommand.IsEnabled =
                    (this.currentChangeOrder != null);
                this.PopulateRoutingItems();
            }
        }
    }
```

The getter for the property is pretty simple, but the property's setter is a little bit more interesting. It is following the same pattern as before, by first checking to see whether the value being set is actually a different `ChangeOrder` instance. If it is, then the `currentChangeOrder` field is set to the setter's value, and the `PropertyChanged` event is raised. Also, the `saveCommand` field's `IsEnabled` property is set to true if the `currentChangeOrder` field's value is not null. Last, the `RoutingItems` property value is initialized based on the `currentChangeOrder` field's `RoutingItems` property value via the `PopulateRoutingItems` private method.

The Command Handler Methods

The only command handler methods that I need to override in the ChangeOrderViewModel class are the SaveCommandHandler and NewCommandHandler methods. Again, I do not have to worry about deletes because the DeleteCommandHandler method is completely taken care of by the base class.

The NewCommandHandler method

Here is the code for the NewCommandHandler method:

```
protected void NewCommandHandler(object sender, EventArgs e)
{
    object projectKey = this.currentChangeOrder.ProjectKey;
    this.currentChangeOrder = null;
    this.routingItems.Clear();
    this.CurrentObjectState = ObjectState.New;
    this.OnPropertyChanged(
        Constants.CurrentChangeOrderPropertyName);
    ChangeOrder newChangeOrder = new ChangeOrder(
                                projectKey,
                                this.currentChangeOrder.Number + 1);
    this.changeOrderList.Add(newChangeOrder);
    this.changeOrders.Refresh();
    this.changeOrders.MoveCurrentToLast();
}
```

This method starts out by obtaining the ProjectKey property value of the old Change Order instance (the currentChangeOrder field). It then sets the currentChangeOrder field to null, clears the RoutingItems property, and sets the state of the ViewModel to New. Next, it raises the PropertyChanged event so the UI can clear its screen. Then, a new ChangeOrder instance is created and initialized with the old ProjectKey property value saved on the first line of the method, and the current Change Order Number plus one. Finally, the new ChangeOrder instance is added to the list of Change Orders (the changeOrdersList field), and the wrapping changeOrders CollectionView field is then refreshed and directed to move the current Change Order to the last position.

The SaveCommandHandler Method

This method is responsible for validating and saving the currently selected Change Order instance.

```
protected void SaveCommandHandler(object sender, EventArgs e)
{
    if (this.currentChangeOrder != null &&
        this.currentChangeOrder.GetBrokenRules().Count == 0)
    {
        foreach (RoutingItem item in this.routingItems)
        {
            this.currentChangeOrder.RoutingItems.Add(item);
        }
        ChangeOrderService.SaveChangeOrder(this.currentChangeOrder);
    }
    this.CurrentObjectState = ObjectState.Existing;
}
```

It begins by making sure that the current Change Order is not null, and also calls the `GetBrokenRules` method to validate the state of the Change Order. Currently, I do not have anything wired up to handle any of the broken rules, but the hook is there for it. I probably would add another property to the ViewModel for the broken rules so the XAML could easily bind to it.

The next step after passing validation is to add all of the `RoutingItem` instances into the current Change Order, and then finally, to save the Change Order.

The Change Order View

The View for Change Orders is very similar to what has been seen in the past few chapters, where the list of Change Orders is on the left, and the currently selected Change Order is on the right. Following is what the form looks like at run time (see Figure 8.5).

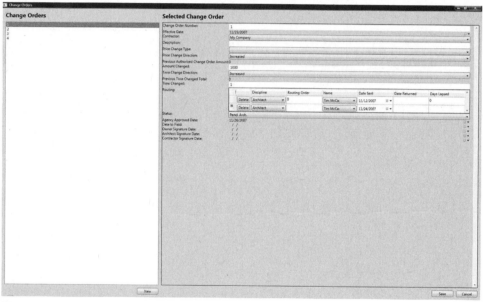

Figure 8.5: Change Order View.

There certainly is a lot more that I could be doing in the UI regarding validation, but that really is not the focus of this chapter or book. I want to keep the focus on the domain model, but at some point this application will definitely need to wire the validation for the domain model into the UI in an elegant way. The Microsoft Patterns and Practices team has actually built a Validation application block that I have not really tapped into in this book, but I imagine that I will later in the life of this code base.

Summary

In this chapter, I introduced the concept of a Change Order in the construction industry, and then I used this concept to model the Change Order Aggregate. I added quite a bit more behavior to my classes in this chapter, and the current Domain Model classes are certainly starting to get much richer than they were before. I also created a nice way of distinguishing the Aggregate Roots in the domain model by way of the `IAggregateRoot` interface. This concept is also heavily reinforced in the various Repository classes through the use of Generic Constraints constraining the repositories to use the `IAggregateRoot` interface for the Entity Roots that they are supporting. While I was refactoring again, I changed a good portion of the code base to rely on the `IEntity` interface instead of the `EntityBase` class. In fact, the `EntityBase` class itself implements the `IEntity` interface. Also involved in the refactoring was the creation of the new Generic `NumberSpecification<TCandidate>` class, which made nice use of the new `INumberedProjectChild` interface.

Construction Change Directives

In the last two chapters, I covered Proposal Requests and Change Orders, and in this chapter I will be showing you the last of the Change Order–related concepts, the Construction Change Directive.

The Problem

Sometimes a Change Order will be approved and signed off on by the Architect and the Owner, but not by the Contractor. The Contractor may not agree with the change in work, contract price, contract time, or both. This type of Change Order will be signed by the Owner and Architect but not by the Contractor. When this happens, the Contractor is obligated to go ahead with the work, with the price and time adjustments to be determined later by the Architect, utilizing standard industry guidelines.

The means to capture this type of change is the Construction Change Directive. At any time that the contractor later agrees to its terms or mutual agreement is obtained by adjustment of its terms, it is then turned into a Change Order. In the event that the contractor finds it impossible to accept the Architect's determination of changed cost and time, the Contractor's only other alternative at that point is mediation and arbitration.

Like RFIs, Proposal Requests, and Change Orders, each Construction Change Directive should also be serially numbered by Project.

The Design

In the SmartCA domain, a Change Order is one of the most important concepts for the entire application, and it also contains several important business concepts that must be closely tracked. In the next few sections, I will be designing the domain model, determining the Change Order Aggregate and its boundaries, and designing the Repository for Change Orders.

Designing the Domain Model

As stated earlier, the most important parts of the Construction Change Directive are the changes in contract time or price, as well as the proper ordering of the Construction Change Directive Number. I again will be using the Specification pattern to define the rules for the Number property, and the Specification that I create will also be part of the domain model. It is very important that the logic inside of the Construction Change Directive be correct for calculating the total price and time whenever one of those items is changed from the Construction Change Directive.

Figure 9.1 shows a drawing showing the relationships between the classes that combine to make up a Construction Change Directive.

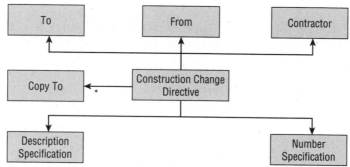

Figure 9.1: Construction Change Directive Aggregate.

In the diagram, the Construction Change Directive class is clearly the root of the Aggregate. The two most important attributes of the Construction Change Directive are the amount of time being changed and the amount of money being added. These are represented in the diagram by the Time Change and Price Change relationships, respectively. The relationship to the Contractor class shows the Contractor that has requested the Construction Change Directive.

The next important part of the diagram is the Construction Change Directive's relationship to the Routing Items. It is important for Smart Design to know to whom each Construction Change Directive has been routed internally, and the Discipline of that person, such as architect, engineer, or construction administrator. This was already created and used in Chapter 6; I am just reusing the same concept again in this Aggregate.

The relationship to the Status class shows exactly the state of the Construction Change Directive, such as completed or pending an architect review. The relationship to the Construction Change Directive Number Specification helps model the numbering rules of the Construction Change Directive.

Designing the Construction Change Directive Aggregate

The Construction Change Directive Aggregate does not have as many classes in it as some of the other Aggregates, but it definitely uses a lot of interfaces (see Figure 9.2)!

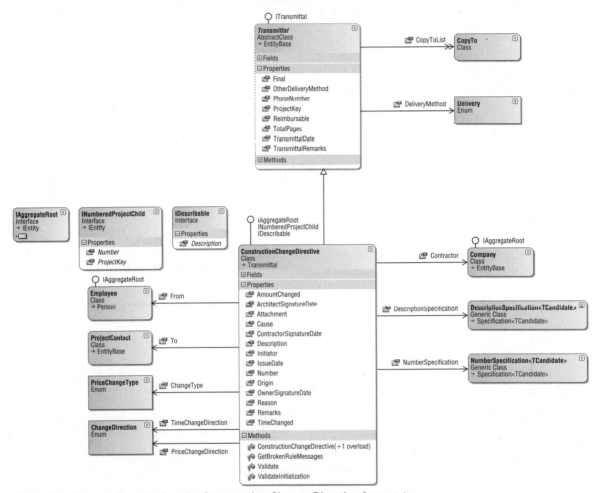

Figure 9.2: Classes Constituting the Construction Change Directive Aggregate.

As shown in the diagram, the ConstructionChangeDirective class inherits from the Transmittal class and implements the IAggregateRoot, INumberedProjectChild, and IDescribable interfaces. I have already covered what all of these interfaces are for, except for the IDescribable interface. This interface goes hand in hand with the DescriptionSpecification<TCandidate> class, and I will cover both of these later in the chapter.

Defining the Aggregate Boundaries

The `ConstructionChangeDirective` class has its own identity and is definitely the root of its own Aggregate (see Figure 9.3).

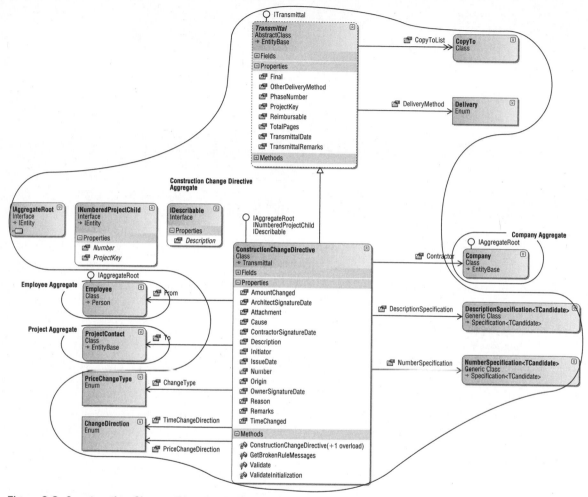

Figure 9.3: Construction Change Directive Aggregate Boundaries.

All of the other classes in the diagram, except for `Company`, `Employee`, and `ProjectContact` classes, belong to the Construction Change Directive Aggregate. The `Company` and `Employee` classes are actually the root of their own Aggregates, and the `ProjectContact` class is part of the Project Aggregate.

Designing the Repository

As you should definitely know by now, since the `ConstructionChangeDirective` class is its own Aggregate root, it will have its own repository.

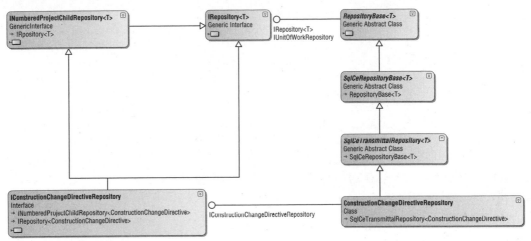

Figure 9.4: Construction Change Directive Repository.

Figure 9.4 should look familiar to you, as it is very similar to the Change Order Repository diagram from the last chapter.

The `IConstructionChangeDirectiveRepository` interface is the interface into instances of Construction Change Directive Repositories. Here is the `IConstructionChangeDirectiveRepository` interface:

```
using System;
using SmartCA.Model.NumberedProjectChildren;

namespace SmartCA.Model.ConstructionChangeDirectives
{
    public interface IConstructionChangeDirectiveRepository
        : INumberedProjectChildRepository<ConstructionChangeDirective>
    {
    }
}
```

As you can see, since the `ConstructionChangeDirective` class implements the `INumberedProjectChild` interface, it follows that the `IConstructionChangeDirectiveRepository` interface extends the `INumberedProjectChildRepository` interface. There are no methods in the `IConstructionChangeDirectiveRepository` interface, as you can see it is just merely extending the `INumberedProjectChildRepository` interface.

Writing the Unit Tests

Again, in this chapter, I am not going to show the unit tests in this section because they are essentially the same as most of the unit tests written in previous chapters. They are important; in fact I rely upon them very much as I refactor the code.

The Solution

The classes used to make up the Construction Change Directive Aggregate should look very familiar to you; I am at the point in the application architecture where I am starting to reuse many of the classes. The thing that is a little bit different from previous chapters is that now there is much more business logic to implement inside of the classes. This is because the Construction Change Directives deal with money, and these types of documents may literally be dealing with millions of dollars.

The Construction Change Directive Class Private Fields and Constructors

The `ConstructionChangeDirective` class inherits from the `Transmittal` class and passes its values from its constructors straight through to the `Transmittal` base class.

```
using System;
using SmartCA.Model.Transmittals;
using SmartCA.Infrastructure.DomainBase;
using SmartCA.Model.Companies;
using SmartCA.Model.Employees;
using SmartCA.Model.Projects;
using SmartCA.Model.ChangeOrders;
using SmartCA.Model.Description;
using SmartCA.Model.NumberedProjectChildren;

namespace SmartCA.Model.ConstructionChangeDirectives
{
    public class ConstructionChangeDirective
        : Transmittal, IAggregateRoot, INumberedProjectChild, IDescribable
    {
        private int number;
        private ProjectContact to;
        private Employee from;
        private DateTime? issueDate;
        private Company contractor;
        private string description;
        private string attachment;
        private string reason;
        private string initiator;
        private int cause;
        private int origin;
        private string remarks;
        private PriceChangeType? changeType;
        private ChangeDirection priceChangeDirection;
```

```
        private decimal amountChanged;
        private ChangeDirection timeChangeDirection;
        private int timeChanged;
        private DateTime? ownerSignatureDate;
        private DateTime? architectSignatureDate;
        private DateTime? contractorSignatureDate;
        private NumberSpecification<ConstructionChangeDirective>
numberSpecification;
        private DescriptionSpecification<ConstructionChangeDirective>
descriptionSpecification;
        private object changeOrderKey;
        private BrokenRuleMessages brokenRuleMessages;

        public ConstructionChangeDirective(object projectKey, int number)
            : this(null, projectKey, number)
        {
        }

        public ConstructionChangeDirective(object key, object projectKey,
            int number) : base(key, projectKey)
        {
            this.number = number;
            this.to = null;
            this.from = null;
            this.issueDate = null;
            this.contractor = null;
            this.description = string.Empty;
            this.attachment = string.Empty;
            this.reason = string.Empty;
            this.initiator = string.Empty;
            this.cause = 0;
            this.origin = 0;
            this.remarks = string.Empty;
            this.changeType = null;
            this.priceChangeDirection = ChangeDirection.Unchanged;
            this.amountChanged = 0;
            this.timeChangeDirection = ChangeDirection.Unchanged;
            this.timeChanged = 0;
            this.ownerSignatureDate = null;
            this.architectSignatureDate = null;
            this.contractorSignatureDate = null;
            this.numberSpecification =
                new NumberSpecification<ConstructionChangeDirective>();
            this.descriptionSpecification =
                new DescriptionSpecification<ConstructionChangeDirective>();
            this.changeOrderKey = null;
            this.ValidateInitialization();
            this.brokenRuleMessages =
                new ConstructionChangeDirectiveRuleMessages();
        }
```

Just like the Submittal and RequestForInformation classes, all of the data for the ConstructionChangeDirective class is initialized and validated in the second constructor, which is called by the first constructor.

The ValidateInitialization Method

The last action that happens in the `ConstructionChangeDirective` class initialization process is validation. A check is made via the `ValidateInitialization` method to ensure that, if the class is not passed in a `key` value, it contains a valid Construction Change Directive `number` and is associated with a `Project`.

```
private void ValidateInitialization()
{
    NumberedProjectChildValidator.ValidateInitialState(this,
        "Construction Change Directive");
}
```

The ConstructionChangeDirective Properties

A lot of the properties of the `ConstructionChangeDirective` class are very similar to those covered in previous Domain Model classes, so I am only going to cover those that are new here and also those that contain behavior.

The DescriptionSpecification Property

This property is designed to make sure that Construction Change Directives have a description associated with them. The `DescriptionSpecification` property is represented by the `DescriptionSpecification<T>` Generic class.

```
public DescriptionSpecification<ConstructionChangeDirective>
DescriptionSpecification
    {
        get { return this.descriptionSpecification; }
    }
```

Just as with the previously refactored `NumberSpecification< TCandidate>` class in last chapter, I have another situation with Description Specification implementations repeating themselves in the last couple of chapters, so I decided to refactor it, as well. As a result, I created the Generic Description Specification class; actually it is a .NET Generic `DescriptionSpecification<TCandidate>` class.

```
using System;
using SmartCA.Infrastructure.Specifications;
using SmartCA.Infrastructure.DomainBase;
using SmartCA.Model.Description;

namespace SmartCA.Model.Description
{
    public class DescriptionSpecification<TCandidate>
        : Specification<TCandidate> where TCandidate : IDescribable
    {
        public override bool IsSatisfiedBy(TCandidate candidate)
        {
            // The candidate must have a description
            return (!string.IsNullOrEmpty(candidate.Description));
        }
    }
}
```

This code is almost the same as the other Description Specification implementations, but again, I am using .NET Generics to make it reusable. I will compare the signature of this class to the non-Generic class that would have been created. Here is the old way of implementing this:

```
public class ConstructionChangeDirectiveDescriptionSpecification :
Specification<ConstructionChangeDirective>
```

Here is the new way:

```
public class DescriptionSpecification<TCandidate> : Specification<TCandidate> where
    TCandidate : IDescribable
```

Again, just like the NumberSpecification<TCandidate> class, the trick here is using the constraints on the TCandidate Generic parameter. By declaring that the TCandidate Generic parameter has to implement the IDescribable interface, I now have strongly typed access to its properties (via the TCandidate candidate argument) in the IsSatisfied method. All I want is access to the Description property so that I can validate it, and the IDescribable interface gives me exactly that:

```
using System;

namespace SmartCA.Model.Description
{
    public interface IDescribable
    {
        string Description { get; set; }
    }
}
```

The signature for the ConstructionChangeDirective class shows that it now implements this interface:

```
public class ConstructionChangeDirective
        : Transmittal, IAggregateRoot, INumberedChild, IDescribable
```

I also went back and refactored the DescriptionSpecification properties on the ProposalRequest and RequestForInformation classes to use the new DescriptionSpecification<TCandidate> class.

The HasBeenTransformedToChangeOrder Property

This property signifies whether the ConstructionChangeDirective has been converted to a ChangeOrder instance. If you remember from the beginning of the chapter, one of the interesting characteristics of a Construction Change Directive is that once the Contractor agrees with the terms of the Construction Change Directive, it can then be turned into a Change Order. This property represents whether or not that transformation has happened.

```
public bool HasBeenTransformedToChangeOrder
{
    get { return (this.changeOrderKey != null); }
}
```

The way I am keeping track of this is by using the `changeOrderKey` field; this field will get populated once the `ConstructionChangeDirective` has been transformed into a `ChangeOrder`, and it will contain the value of the key for the `ChangeOrder`.

The Validate Method

Taking advantage of the mini-validation framework that was built in the last chapter, here is the `Validate` method override for the `ConstructionChangeDirective` class:

```
protected override void Validate()
{
    if (!this.numberSpecification.IsSatisfiedBy(this))
    {
        this.AddBrokenRule(
            NumberedProjectChildrenRuleMessageKeys.InvalidNumber);
    }
    if (!(this.descriptionSpecification.IsSatisfiedBy(this)))
    {
        this.AddBrokenRule(
            DescriptionRuleMessageKeys.InvalidDescription);
    }
    if (this.contractor == null)
    {
        this.AddBrokenRule(

ConstructionChangeDirectiveRuleMessages.MessageKeys.InvalidContractor);
    }
}
```

You may notice in the code block above that I am now putting the rule constants classes with their respective class families, that is, the description messages are now centralized in the `DescriptionRuleMessageKeys` class:

```
using System;

namespace SmartCA.Model.Description
{
    internal static class DescriptionRuleMessageKeys
    {
        public const string InvalidDescription =
            "Invalid Description property value";
    }
}
```

Here is the `ConstructionChangeDirectiveRuleMessages` class:

```
using System;
using SmartCA.Infrastructure.DomainBase;
using SmartCA.Model.NumberedProjectChildren;
using SmartCA.Model.Description;

namespace SmartCA.Model.ConstructionChangeDirectives
{
```

```
public class ConstructionChangeDirectiveRuleMessages
    : BrokenRuleMessages
{
    internal static class MessageKeys
    {
        public const string InvalidContractor = "Must Have Contractor " +
            "Assigned";
    }

    protected override void PopulateMessages()
    {
        // Add the rule messages
        this.Messages.Add(DescriptionRuleMessageKeys.InvalidDescription,
            "The Construction Change Directive must have a description");

        this.Messages.Add(MessageKeys.InvalidContractor,
            "The Construction Change Directive must have a Company assigned " +
            "to the Contractor property.");
    }
}
```

Just as in the last chapter, this class inherits from the `BrokenRuleMessages` class, and because of this I am able to return an instance of it from the `ConstructionChangeDirective` class's `GetBrokenRuleMessages` method override.

The TransformToChangeOrder Method

As mentioned already, this method essentially promoted the `ConstructionChangeDirective` up to a `ChangeOrder` instance:

```
public ChangeOrder TransformToChangeOrder()
{
    ChangeOrder co = null;

    // See if it has already been transformed into a
    // Change Order...it can only be changed once!
    if (!this.HasBeenTransformedToChangeOrder)
    {
        Project project = ProjectService.GetProject(this.ProjectKey);
        co = NumberedProjectChildFactory.CreateNumberedProjectChild
            <ChangeOrder>(project);
        co.AmountChanged = this.amountChanged;
        co.ArchitectSignatureDate = this.architectSignatureDate;
        co.ChangeType = this.changeType;
        co.Contractor = this.contractor;
        co.ContractorSignatureDate = this.contractorSignatureDate;
        co.Description = this.description;
        co.OwnerSignatureDate = this.ownerSignatureDate;
        co.PriceChangeDirection = this.priceChangeDirection;
        co.TimeChanged = this.timeChanged;
        co.TimeChangeDirection = this.timeChangeDirection;
    }
```

(continued)

(continued)

```
                else
                {
                    // It was already changed, so get the Change Order that it was
                    // changed into
                    co = ChangeOrderService.GetChangeOrder(this.changeOrderKey);
                }

                // Get the key of the Change Order
                this.changeOrderKey = co.Key;

                // Return the instance
                return co;
            }
```

This method starts out by first testing whether the ConstructionChangeDirective has already been transformed. If it has not, then a new instance is created, and if it has, then it uses the changeOrderKey field to pass into the ChangeOrderService's GetChangeOrder method to get the existing ChangeOrder instance.

The interesting part about the method is where it has to create a new instance of the ChangeOrder. Specifically, it uses a new Factory class to get a correctly initialized ChangeOrder instance with the correct Number value applied to it. This class is the NumberedProjectChildFactory class.

The NumberedProjectChildFactory Class

The sole responsibility of this class is to create instances of classes that implement the INumberedProjectChild interface that are properly numbered:

```
using System;
using SmartCA.Infrastructure.DomainBase;
using SmartCA.Infrastructure.RepositoryFramework;
using System.Collections.Generic;
using System.Linq;
using SmartCA.Model.Projects;

namespace SmartCA.Model.NumberedProjectChildren
{
    public static class NumberedProjectChildFactory
    {
        public static T CreateNumberedProjectChild<T>(Project project)
            where T : EntityBase, IAggregateRoot, INumberedProjectChild
        {
            // Initialize the NumberedProjectChild return value
            T newNumberedProjectChild = default(T);

            // Get the correct repository using the Repository Factory
            INumberedProjectChildRepository<T> repository =
                RepositoryFactory.GetRepository
                <INumberedProjectChildRepository<T>, T>();

            // Get all of the items in the Aggregate from the FindBy method
```

```
        IList<T> numberedProjectChildren = repository.FindBy(project);

        // Use LINQ to get the last numbered item in the list
        // and increment it by 1
        int newNumber = numberedProjectChildren.Last().Number + 1;

        // Create the instance, passing in the projectKey value as well
        // as the new number to the constructor of the INumberedProjectChild
        // instance, and then casting it to the correct type (T)
        newNumberedProjectChild = Activator.CreateInstance(typeof(T),
            new object[] { project.Key, newNumber }) as T;

        // Return the newly initialized object
        return newNumberedProjectChild;
    }
  }
}
```

Notice that the `CreateNumberedProjectChild` method is a Generic method and that it is using constraints on the Generic parameter `T` to ensure that the parameter is an `EntityBase` type that implements the `IAggregateRoot` and `INumberedProjectChild` interfaces. It has to implement `IAggregateRoot` in order to have a repository associated with it, and it must implement the `INumberedProjectChild` interface in order to be able to call the `FindBy(Project project)` method on the repository.

The method starts out by declaring and initializing the `newNumberedProjectChild` variable to its default value. It then uses the `RepositoryFactory` to get the correct `INumberedProjectChildRepository` instance. Once the repository is retrieved, then it uses it to get the list of all items in the repository by Project. I next use a LINQ extension method (`Last`) on the `List<T>` class to find the last item in the list, then get the `Number` property of the item and add one to its value to create the new number for the soon-to-be-created `INumberedProjectChild` instance. I then use Reflection to create the `INumberedProjectChild` instance, and pass the new number value as well as the `Key` value of the `Project` instance to the `INumberedProjectChild` instance's constructor in the `CreateInstance` method. Finally, the newly created and initialized `INumberedProjectChild` instance, represented by the `newNumberedProjectChild` variable, is returned.

The Construction Change Directive Repository Implementation

After going over the `IConstructionChangeDirectiveRepository` interface in the Design section, it is now time to show in code how the `ConstructionChangeDirective` class actually gets persisted to and from the data store by the Construction Change Directive Repository. In this section, I will be writing the code for the Construction Change Directive Repository.

The BuildChildCallbacks Method

Now that I have finished going over the `IConstructionChangeDirectiveRepository` interface, it is time to build the `ConstructionChangeDirective` class. Again, most of the work is done in the `SqlCeRepositoryBase<T>` class. If you have been following along, you know that from the application's Template Method pattern implementation that I have been using in the Repositories for getting Entity Root instances, the `BuildChildCallbacks` method must be overridden in the `ConstructionChangeDirectiveRepository`.

```
#region BuildChildCallbacks

protected override void BuildChildCallbacks()
{
    this.ChildCallbacks.Add(
        ProposalRequestFactory.FieldNames.ProjectContactId,
        this.AppendTo);
    this.ChildCallbacks.Add(
        ProposalRequestFactory.FieldNames.EmployeeId,
        this.AppendFrom);
    this.ChildCallbacks.Add(CompanyFactory.FieldNames.CompanyId,
        this.AppendContractor);
    base.BuildChildCallbacks();
}

#endregion
```

There is nothing really new in this method; it is just following the same pattern as laid out in earlier chapters.

The AppendTo Callback

```
private void AppendTo(ConstructionChangeDirective ccd,
    object toProjectContactKey)
{
    ccd.To = ProjectService.GetProjectContact(
        ccd.ProjectKey, toProjectContactKey);
}
```

Again, this method is very similar to the other `AppendTo` methods from some of the other Repositories.

The AppendFrom Callback

```
private void AppendFrom(ConstructionChangeDirective ccd,
    object fromEmployeeKey)
{
    ccd.From =
        EmployeeService.GetEmployee(fromEmployeeKey);
}
```

Same thing here with the `AppendFrom` method—it is nice that all of this stuff is already built for me!

The AppendContractor Callback

The last entry made in the `ChildCallbacks` dictionary is for the `AppendContractor` method. Thanks to the `CompanyService` class's `GetCompany` method, this method's code is also very simple:

```
private void AppendContractor(ConstructionChangeDirective ccd,
    object contractorKey)
{
    ccd.Contractor = CompanyService.GetCompany(contractorKey);
}
```

The FindBy Method

I talked about refactoring this method in the last chapter. The same code is repeated for it in different repositories, so here is the newly refactored method.

```
public IList<ConstructionChangeDirective> FindBy(Project project)
{
    return
        NumberedProjectChildRepositoryHelper.FindBy
        <ConstructionChangeDirective>(this, project);
}
```

As you can see, all of the functionality of the method has been factored out into the `NumberedProjectChildRepositoryHelper` class. This class is a static class with one Generic method, `FindBy`:

```
using System;
using System.Collections.Generic;
using SmartCA.Model.Projects;
using System.Text;
using SmartCA.Infrastructure.DomainBase;
using SmartCA.Model.NumberedProjectChildren;

namespace SmartCA.Infrastructure.Repositories.NumberedProjectChildren
{
    public static class NumberedProjectChildRepositoryHelper
    {
        public static IList<T> FindBy<T>(SqlCeRepositoryBase<T> repository,
            Project project) where T : IAggregateRoot, INumberedProjectChild
        {
            StringBuilder builder = new StringBuilder(100);
            builder.Append(repository.BaseQuery);
            builder.Append(string.Format(" WHERE ProjectID = '{0}';",
                project.Key));
            return repository.BuildEntitiesFromSql(builder);
        }
    }
}
```

This code looks pretty similar to the `CreateNumberedProjectChild` method of the `NumberedProjectChildFactory` class. They are both Generic methods and make heavy use of constraints, and both are constraining the Generic parameter to implement the `IAggregateRoot` and `INumberedProjectChild` interfaces.

This method actually takes an instance of the `SqlCeRepositoryBase<T>` class, as well as a `Project` instance. The body of the method should look pretty familiar; it is just factoring out the code that would have been in the `ConstructionChangeDirectiveRepository` implementation. This method was made possible by the `SqlCeRepositoryBase<T>` instance, an argument of the method, and this pattern is known as inversion of control.

Unit of Work Implementation

Following the same steps that I have shown before to implement the Unit of Work pattern, I now need to override the `PersistNewItem(ConstructionChangeDirective item)` and `PersistUpdatedItem(ConstructionChangeDirective item)` methods.

The PersistNewItem Method

The first method override for the `ConstructionChangeDirective`'s Unit of Work implementation is the `PersistNewItem` method.

```
        protected override void PersistNewItem(ConstructionChangeDirective item)
        {
            StringBuilder builder = new StringBuilder(100);
            builder.Append(string.Format("INSERT INTO ConstructionChangeDirective
({0},{1},{2},{3},{4},{5},{6},{7},{8},{9},{10},{11},{12},{13},{14},{15},{16},{17},
{18},{19},{20},{21},{22},{23},{24},{25},{26},{27},{28},{29}) ",

ConstructionChangeDirectiveFactory.FieldNames.ConstructionChangeDirectiveId,
                ProjectFactory.FieldNames.ProjectId,
ConstructionChangeDirectiveFactory.FieldNames.ConstructionChangeDirectiveNumber,
                TransmittalFactory.FieldNames.TransmittalDate,
                ProjectFactory.FieldNames.ProjectContactId,
                EmployeeFactory.FieldNames.EmployeeId,
                TransmittalFactory.FieldNames.TotalPages,
                TransmittalFactory.FieldNames.DeliveryMethod,
                TransmittalFactory.FieldNames.OtherDeliveryMethod,
                TransmittalFactory.FieldNames.PhaseNumber,
                TransmittalFactory.FieldNames.Reimbursable,
                TransmittalFactory.FieldNames.Final,
                ConstructionChangeDirectiveFactory.FieldNames.IssueDate,
                CompanyFactory.FieldNames.CompanyId,
                ConstructionChangeDirectiveFactory.FieldNames.Description,
                ConstructionChangeDirectiveFactory.FieldNames.Attachment,
                ConstructionChangeDirectiveFactory.FieldNames.Reason,
                ConstructionChangeDirectiveFactory.FieldNames.Initiator,
                ConstructionChangeDirectiveFactory.FieldNames.Cause,
                ConstructionChangeDirectiveFactory.FieldNames.Origin,
                ConstructionChangeDirectiveFactory.FieldNames.Remarks,
                TransmittalFactory.FieldNames.TransmittalRemarks,
                ConstructionChangeDirectiveFactory.FieldNames.PriceChangeType,
ConstructionChangeDirectiveFactory.FieldNames.PriceChangeTypeDirection,
                ConstructionChangeDirectiveFactory.FieldNames.AmountChanged,
                ConstructionChangeDirectiveFactory.FieldNames.TimeChangeDirection,
                ConstructionChangeDirectiveFactory.FieldNames.TimeChangedDays,
                ConstructionChangeDirectiveFactory.FieldNames.OwnerSignatureDate,
ConstructionChangeDirectiveFactory.FieldNames.ArchitectSignatureDate,
ConstructionChangeDirectiveFactory.FieldNames.ContractorSignatureDate
                ));
            builder.Append(string.Format("VALUES
({0},{1},{2},{3},{4},{5},{6},{7},{8},{9},{10},{11},{12},{13},{14},{15},{16},{17},
{18},{19},{20},{21},{22},{23},{24},{25},{26},{27},{28},{29});",
                DataHelper.GetSqlValue(item.Key),
                DataHelper.GetSqlValue(item.ProjectKey),
                DataHelper.GetSqlValue(item.Number),
```

```
            DataHelper.GetSqlValue(item.TransmittalDate),
            DataHelper.GetSqlValue(item.To.Key),
            DataHelper.GetSqlValue(item.From.Key),
            DataHelper.GetSqlValue(item.TotalPages),
            DataHelper.GetSqlValue(item.DeliveryMethod),
            DataHelper.GetSqlValue(item.OtherDeliveryMethod),
            DataHelper.GetSqlValue(item.PhaseNumber),
            DataHelper.GetSqlValue(item.Reimbursable),
            DataHelper.GetSqlValue(item.Final),
            DataHelper.GetSqlValue(item.IssueDate),
            DataHelper.GetSqlValue(item.Contractor.Key),
            DataHelper.GetSqlValue(item.Description),
            DataHelper.GetSqlValue(item.Attachment),
            DataHelper.GetSqlValue(item.Reason),
            DataHelper.GetSqlValue(item.Initiator),
            DataHelper.GetSqlValue(item.Cause),
            DataHelper.GetSqlValue(item.Origin),
            DataHelper.GetSqlValue(item.Remarks),
            DataHelper.GetSqlValue(item.TransmittalRemarks),
            DataHelper.GetSqlValue(item.ChangeType),
            DataHelper.GetSqlValue(item.PriceChangeDirection),
            DataHelper.GetSqlValue(item.AmountChanged),
            DataHelper.GetSqlValue(item.TimeChangeDirection),
            DataHelper.GetSqlValue(item.TimeChanged),
            DataHelper.GetSqlValue(item.OwnerSignatureDate),
            DataHelper.GetSqlValue(item.ArchitectSignatureDate),
            DataHelper.GetSqlValue(item.ContractorSignatureDate)));

        this.Database.ExecuteNonQuery(
            this.Database.GetSqlStringCommand(builder.ToString()));

        // Now do the child objects
        this.InsertCopyToList(item);
    }
```

The code builds up a large insert statement composed of the values from the
ConstructionChangeDirective instance and then executes the query using the Microsoft Enterprise
Library's Database object. After the main insert statement has been executed, I then need to insert the
CopyTo instances for the ConstructionChangeDirective.

PersistUpdatedItem

The PersistUpdatedItem method first does an update to the ConstructionChangeDirective table:

```
        protected override void PersistUpdatedItem(ConstructionChangeDirective item)
        {
            StringBuilder builder = new StringBuilder(100);
            builder.Append("UPDATE ConstructionChangeDirective SET ");

            builder.Append(string.Format("{0} = {1}",

ConstructionChangeDirectiveFactory.FieldNames.ConstructionChangeDirectiveNumber,
            DataHelper.GetSqlValue(item.Number)));
```

(continued)

(continued)

```
        builder.Append(string.Format(",{0} = {1}",
            TransmittalFactory.FieldNames.TransmittalDate,
            DataHelper.GetSqlValue(item.TransmittalDate)));

        builder.Append(string.Format(",{0} = {1}",
            ProjectFactory.FieldNames.ProjectContactId,
            DataHelper.GetSqlValue(item.To.Key)));

        builder.Append(string.Format(",{0} = {1}",
            EmployeeFactory.FieldNames.EmployeeId,
            DataHelper.GetSqlValue(item.From.Key)));

        builder.Append(string.Format(",{0} = {1}",
            TransmittalFactory.FieldNames.TotalPages,
            DataHelper.GetSqlValue(item.TotalPages)));

        builder.Append(string.Format(",{0} = {1}",
            TransmittalFactory.FieldNames.DeliveryMethod,
            DataHelper.GetSqlValue(item.DeliveryMethod)));

        builder.Append(string.Format(",{0} = {1}",
            TransmittalFactory.FieldNames.OtherDeliveryMethod,
            DataHelper.GetSqlValue(item.OtherDeliveryMethod)));

        /************************************************************/

        builder.Append(string.Format(",{0} = {1}",
            ConstructionChangeDirectiveFactory.FieldNames.PriceChangeType,
            DataHelper.GetSqlValue(item.ChangeType)));

        builder.Append(string.Format(",{0} = {1}",

ConstructionChangeDirectiveFactory.FieldNames.PriceChangeTypeDirection,
            DataHelper.GetSqlValue(item.PriceChangeDirection)));

        builder.Append(string.Format(",{0} = {1}",
            ConstructionChangeDirectiveFactory.FieldNames.AmountChanged,
            DataHelper.GetSqlValue(item.AmountChanged)));

        builder.Append(string.Format(",{0} = {1}",
            ConstructionChangeDirectiveFactory.FieldNames.TimeChangeDirection,
            DataHelper.GetSqlValue(item.TimeChangeDirection)));

        builder.Append(string.Format(",{0} = {1}",
            ConstructionChangeDirectiveFactory.FieldNames.TimeChangedDays,
            DataHelper.GetSqlValue(item.TimeChanged)));

        builder.Append(string.Format(",{0} = {1}",
            ConstructionChangeDirectiveFactory.FieldNames.OwnerSignatureDate,
            DataHelper.GetSqlValue(item.OwnerSignatureDate)));

        builder.Append(string.Format(",{0} = {1}",
```

```
ConstructionChangeDirectiveFactory.FieldNames.ArchitectSignatureDate,
        DataHelper.GetSqlValue(item.ArchitectSignatureDate)));

        builder.Append(string.Format(",{0} = {1}",

ConstructionChangeDirectiveFactory.FieldNames.ContractorSignatureDate,
        DataHelper.GetSqlValue(item.ContractorSignatureDate)));

        builder.Append(" ");
        builder.Append(this.BuildBaseWhereClause(item.Key));

        this.Database.ExecuteNonQuery(
            this.Database.GetSqlStringCommand(builder.ToString()));

        // Now do the child objects

        // First, delete the existing ones
        this.DeleteCopyToList(item);

        // Now, add the current ones
        this.InsertCopyToList(item);
    }
```

I have omitted several lines of repetitive code building the SQL update statement in the middle of the code in order to try to save you from the boring code.

The second part of the method then uses the `DeleteCopyToList` helper method to delete all of the `CopyTo` child objects of the Construction Change Directive, and then uses the `InsertCopyToList` helper method to add the existing `CopyTo` child objects from the Construction Change Directive to the database.

The Construction Change Directive Service Implementation

Like the other `Service` classes shown in the domain model so far, the `ConstructionChangeDirectiveService` class is responsible for retrieving and wrapping the methods of its associated Repository interface, in this case the `IConstructionChangeDirectiveRepository` instance.

```
using System;
using SmartCA.Infrastructure;
using SmartCA.Infrastructure.RepositoryFramework;
using System.Collections.Generic;
using SmartCA.Model.Projects;
using System.Linq;

namespace SmartCA.Model.ConstructionChangeDirectives
{
    public class ConstructionChangeDirectiveService
```

(continued)

(continued)

```
    {
        private static IConstructionChangeDirectiveRepository repository;
        private static IUnitOfWork unitOfWork;

        static ConstructionChangeDirectiveService()
        {
            ConstructionChangeDirectiveService.unitOfWork = new UnitOfWork();
            ConstructionChangeDirectiveService.repository =
                RepositoryFactory.GetRepository
                <IConstructionChangeDirectiveRepository,
                ConstructionChangeDirective>(
                ConstructionChangeDirectiveService.unitOfWork);
        }

        public static IList<ConstructionChangeDirective>
            GetConstructionChangeDirectives(Project project)
        {
            return
                ConstructionChangeDirectiveService.repository.FindBy(
                project);
        }

        public static void SaveConstructionChangeDirective(
            ConstructionChangeDirective ccd)
        {
            ConstructionChangeDirectiveService.repository[ccd.Key] = ccd;
            ConstructionChangeDirectiveService.unitOfWork.Commit();
        }
    }
}
```

These are the only methods needed for now, but others could easily be added later, such as a method for removing Construction Change Directives.

The Construction Change Directive ViewModel Class

Following the same patterns for all ViewModel classes as before, the ConstructionChangeDirectiveViewModel class adapts the Construction Change Directive Aggregate from the domain model to the UI. Just like the ProposalRequestViewModel class, it inherits from the TransmittalViewModel<T> class introduced previously:

```
using System;
using SmartCA.Model.ConstructionChangeDirectives;
using System.Collections.Generic;
using SmartCA.Model.Projects;
using SmartCA.Model.Employees;
using SmartCA.Model.Companies;
using SmartCA.Application;
using SmartCA.Infrastructure.UI;
using SmartCA.Infrastructure.DomainBase;
```

```
using SmartCA.Model.NumberedProjectChildren;

namespace SmartCA.Presentation.ViewModels
{
    public class ConstructionChangeDirectiveViewModel :
        TransmittalViewModel <ConstructionChangeDirective>
```

The Constructor

Here are the constructors for the `ConstructionChangeDirectiveViewModel` class:

```
#region Constructors

public ConstructionChangeDirectiveViewModel()
    : this(null)
{
}

public ConstructionChangeDirectiveViewModel(IView view)
    : base(view)
{
    this.toList = UserSession.CurrentProject.Contacts;
    this.fromList = EmployeeService.GetEmployees();
    this.contractors = CompanyService.GetAllCompanies();
}

#endregion
```

On the surface, this looks to be just like all of the other View Model implementations so far, but I have actually done some major refactoring to all of the `ViewModel` classes that I will show you shortly.

The Properties

All of the properties in the `ConstructionChangeDirectiveViewModel` class are read-only:

```
#region Properties

public IList<ProjectContact> ToList
{
    get { return this.toList; }
}

public IList<Employee> FromList
{
    get { return this.fromList; }
}

public IList<Company> Contractors
{
    get { return this.contractors; }
}

#endregion
```

One thing you may have picked up on already is that there is no `CurrentConstructionChangeDirective` property in this class. That is due to the intense refactoring of the View Model base classes that I just did!

The ViewModel Class Refactoring

I have refactored a lot of the functionality out of the `ViewModel` class and into a new class called the `EditableViewModel<T>` class. Here is what the new `ViewModel` class looks like:

```
using System;

namespace SmartCA.Infrastructure.UI
{
    public abstract class ViewModel
    {
        private IView view;
        private DelegateCommand cancelCommand;

        protected ViewModel()
            : this(null)
        {
        }

        protected ViewModel(IView view)
        {
            this.view = view;
            this.cancelCommand = new DelegateCommand(this.CancelCommandHandler);
        }

        public DelegateCommand CancelCommand
        {
            get { return this.cancelCommand; }
        }

        protected virtual void CancelCommandHandler(object sender, EventArgs e)
        {
            this.CloseView();
        }

        protected void CloseView()
        {
            if (this.view != null)
            {
                this.view.Close();
            }
        }
    }
}
```

All I have really done here is pared this class down to what it used to be like back in Chapter 3, although it no longer implements the `INotifyPropertyChanged` interface. This is because the intent of this class is to serve only enough functionality for read-only user interfaces, such as dialog boxes. The `SelectProjectView` is a perfect example of the read-only user interface that I am talking about.

The EditableViewModel<T> Class

The next step was to put all of the functionality for editing objects into the EditableViewModel<T> class. It extends the ViewModel class, and adds a lot more functionality to it:

```
using System;
using SmartCA.Infrastructure.DomainBase;
using System.Collections.ObjectModel;
using System.Collections.Generic;
using System.Windows.Data;
using System.ComponentModel;

namespace SmartCA.Infrastructure.UI
{
    public abstract class EditableViewModel<T>
        : ViewModel, INotifyPropertyChanged where T : EntityBase
```

The first thing to note is that it is now a Generic class with a constraint on the type passed in. I had so much success with the Generic TransmittalViewModel<T> class that I decided to embrace that concept here!

The next thing to note about the EditableViewModel<T> class is that it is extending the ViewModel class and implementing the INotifyPropertyChanged interface. It is also responsible for maintaining the state of the current Entity that is being edited. This is done via the ObjectState enumeration:

```
#region ObjectState Enum

public enum ObjectState
{
    New,
    Existing,
    Deleted
}

#endregion
```

The Constructors and Private Fields

Here are the private fields and constructors for the class:

```
#region Private Fields

private ObjectState currentObjectState;
private IList<BrokenRule> brokenRules;
private T currentEntity;
private List<T> entitiesList;
private CollectionView entitiesView;
private DelegateCommand saveCommand;
private DelegateCommand newCommand;

#endregion

#region Constructors

protected EditableViewModel()
```

(continued)

(continued)

```
            : this(null)
        {
        }

        protected EditableViewModel(IView view)
            : base(view)
        {
            this.currentObjectState = ObjectState.Existing;
            this.brokenRules = new List<BrokenRule>();
            this.currentEntity = default(T);
            this.entitiesList = this.GetEntitiesList();
            this.entitiesView = new CollectionView(this.entitiesList);
            this.saveCommand = new DelegateCommand(this.SaveCommandHandler);
            this.newCommand = new DelegateCommand(this.NewCommandHandler);
        }

        #endregion
```

Notice is that I am fully embracing the concept of treating Broken Rules as a first-class citizen in this class. The derived `ViewModel` classes no longer have to worry about them as this class will take care of all of that infrastructure-type code. The next important concept that should jump out at you is that I have made the current object being edited and the list of available objects to edit generic enough to fit into this class. This really opens up a lot of possibilities for code reduction as you will see later in the derived classes. Also, since I know that every object I an editing is going to have a `Save` command and a `New` command, I have centralized them into this class as well.

The interesting thing to note about the constructor is how it initializes the `entitiesList` private field. It is calling the `GetEntitiesList` method, which is actually an abstract method:

```
    protected abstract List<T> GetEntitiesList();
```

This is great; I can now let the derived `ViewModel` class know how to get their list of Entities. I love the Template Method pattern; it just gives me so much flexibility, especially when combined with Generics!

The Properties

I will only show the read-write properties here. Suffice it to say that all private fields not shown here are exposed as read-only properties.

The CurrentObjectState Property

This property represents the state of the object currently being edited:

```
        public ObjectState CurrentObjectState
        {
            get { return this.currentObjectState; }
            set
            {
                if (this.currentObjectState != value)
                {
                    this.currentObjectState = value;
                    this.OnPropertyChanged(
```

```
                                  EditableViewModel<T>.currentObjectStatePropertyName);
                    }
               }
          }
```

The interesting part of this property is its setter. The setter is actually raising the `PropertyChanged` event if the state of the current object has changed. This is important for the WPF UI, as WPF is smart about knowing how to handle this event automatically.

The CurrentEntity Property

This property used to be in the derived classes, and you probably knew it before from such names as `CurrentCompany`, `CurrentTransmittal`, and so on. Now it has been made appropriately generic to eliminate that code in the derived classes:

```
public T CurrentEntity
{
    get { return this.currentEntity; }
    set
    {
        if (this.currentEntity != value)
        {
            this.currentEntity = value;
            this.SetCurrentEntity(value);
            this.saveCommand.IsEnabled = (this.currentEntity != null);
            this.OnPropertyChanged(
                EditableViewModel<T>.currentEntityPropertyName);
        }
    }
}
```

The property setter again makes use of another abstract method, the `SetCurrentEntity` method:

```
protected abstract void SetCurrentEntity(T entity);
```

This method is made abstract in order to give the derived class some freedom on what must happen when the `CurrentEntity` being edited changes. It may need to do things such as create new mutable objects based on the values of some of the Value objects in the `CurrentEntity`.

The last thing the property setter does is to raise the `PropertyChanged` event to let the UI know that it has a new object to display and edit now.

The ValidateCurrentObject Method

This method makes use of the previous refactoring on the `EntityBase` class to keep track of Broken Rules:

```
#region ValidateCurrentObject

protected bool ValidateCurrentObject()
{
    this.brokenRules.Clear();
```

(continued)

(continued)

```
        ReadOnlyCollection<BrokenRule> currentObjectBrokenRules =
            this.currentEntity.GetBrokenRules();
        foreach (BrokenRule rule in currentObjectBrokenRules)
        {
            this.brokenRules.Add(rule);
        }
        return (this.brokenRules.Count == 0);
    }

    #endregion
```

The first thing it does is to clear the `brokenRules` private field. It then asks the `CurrentEntity` for all of its Broken Rules (via the functionality in the `EntityBase` class) and then adds the Broken Rules returned by the `CurrentEntity` to the `brokenRules` private field. Now, the UI can bind to the `BrokenRules` property and do whatever it wants with that property when the property changes. The last thing the method does is to return a `Boolean` value indicating whether there were any Broken Rules.

The Command Handler Methods

In order to separate `New` and `Save` algorithms from the derived classes, the `SaveCommandHandler` and `NewCommandHandler` methods have been placed into this class.

The NewCommandHandler method

Here is the code for the `NewCommandHandler` method:

```
protected virtual void NewCommandHandler(object sender, EventArgs e)
{
    this.CurrentObjectState = ObjectState.New;
    this.brokenRules.Clear();
    this.entitiesList.Add(this.BuildNewEntity());
    this.currentEntity = null;
    this.entitiesView.Refresh();
    this.entitiesView.MoveCurrentToLast();
}
```

As you can see, this method does a lot of generic housekeeping duties, such as changing the state of the object being edited, clearing the Broken Rules, and resetting the `CurrentEntity`. It also uses another abstract class to build the new Entity that is being added:

```
protected abstract T BuildNewEntity();
```

This lets the derived class do whatever it needs to do to build the Entity, as long as the Entity conforms to the constraints placed on the generic `T` parameter.

The last thing the method does is to refresh the `CollectionView` and make sure that the new Entity is the last item in the `CollectionView`.

The SaveCommandHandler Method

This method is responsible for validating and saving the `CurrentEntity` instance.

```
    protected void SaveCommandHandler(object sender, EventArgs e)
    {
        if (this.ValidateCurrentObject())
        {
            this.SaveCurrentEntity(sender, e);
            this.CurrentObjectState = ObjectState.Existing;
        }
    }
```

It begins by validating the `CurrentEntity` via the `ValidateCurrentObject` method. If that validation passes, it then calls another abstract method, `SaveCurrentEntity`, in order to save the Entity.

```
    protected abstract void SaveCurrentEntity(object sender, EventArgs e);
```

Again, I am delegating down to the derived class here to figure out what it needs to do to save the Entity.

The last thing the method does is to change the state of `CurrentEntity` to that of Existing.

The Newly Refactored TransmittalViewModel Class

The signature of this class has changed a little bit; here is what it looks like now:

```
using System;
using SmartCA.Infrastructure.UI;
using SmartCA.Infrastructure.DomainBase;
using SmartCA.Model.Transmittals;
using SmartCA.Model.Submittals;
using System.Collections.Generic;
using SmartCA.Model;
using System.ComponentModel;
using System.Windows.Data;
using System.Collections.ObjectModel;

namespace SmartCA.Presentation.ViewModels
{
    public abstract class TransmittalViewModel<T> : EditableViewModel<T>
        where T : EntityBase, ITransmittal
```

Instead of inheriting from the `ViewModel` class, it now inherits from the `EditableViewModel<T>` class.

The Constructor and Private Fields

The number of private fields and the amount of code in the constructor have been significantly reduced:

```
    #region Private Fields

    private IList<SpecificationSection> specificationSections;
    private IList<ItemStatus> itemStatuses;
    private BindingList<MutableCopyTo> mutableCopyToList;
    private CollectionView deliveryMethods;
    private IList<Discipline> disciplines;
```

(continued)

(continued)

```
            private DelegateCommand deleteCopyToCommand;

        #endregion

        #region Constructors

        public TransmittalViewModel()
            : this(null)
        {
        }

        public TransmittalViewModel(IView view)
            : base(view)
        {
            this.specificationSections
                = SubmittalService.GetSpecificationSections();
            this.itemStatuses = SubmittalService.GetItemStatuses();
            this.mutableCopyToList = new BindingList<MutableCopyTo>();
            this.deliveryMethods = new CollectionView(
                                    Enum.GetNames(typeof(Delivery)));
            this.disciplines = SubmittalService.GetDisciplines();
            this.deleteCopyToCommand =
                new DelegateCommand(this.DeleteCopyToCommandHandler);
        }

        #endregion
```

As you can see, it is not doing anything really special. In fact, a lot of the code that would have been in this constructor is now handled by the constructor in the base class, the `EditableViewModel<T>` class.

The Properties

There is really nothing interesting to look at for the properties, they are all just read-only representations of their respective private fields.

The NewCommandHandler Method

This method has really been reduced:

```
        protected override void NewCommandHandler(object sender, EventArgs e)
        {
            this.mutableCopyToList.Clear();
            base.NewCommandHandler(sender, e);
        }
```

It simply clears the `mutableCopyToList` private field and then calls the base method for `NewCommandHandler`.

The SaveCurrentEntity Method Override

This method takes care of the Transmittal-specific action of clearing and resetting the `CopyTo` list:

```
protected override void SaveCurrentEntity(object sender, EventArgs e)
{
    this.CurrentEntity.CopyToList.Clear();
    foreach (MutableCopyTo copyTo in this.mutableCopyToList)
    {
        this.CurrentEntity.CopyToList.Add(copyTo.ToCopyTo());
    }
}
```

It does not need to do anything else, as the derived class will take care of actually saving the `Transmittal`.

The SetCurrentEntity Method Override

This method simply raises the `PropertyChanged` event for the `Status` property as well as calling down to the `PopulateTransmittalChildren` method.

```
protected override void SetCurrentEntity(T entity)
{
    this.OnPropertyChanged("Status");
    this.PopulateTransmittalChildren();
}
```

The ConstructionChangeDirectiveViewModel Class Method Overrides

Ok, it is time to get back to the `ConstructionChangeDirectiveViewModel` class! The last thing to look at in this class is the methods that it needs to override from the base classes.

The BuildNewEntity Method Override

This method makes use of the previously shown `NumberedProjectChildFactory` class to build a new `ConstructionChangeDirective` instance:

```
protected override ConstructionChangeDirective BuildNewEntity()
{
    return NumberedProjectChildFactory.CreateNumberedProjectChild
        <ConstructionChangeDirective>(UserSession.CurrentProject);
}
```

All it needs to do is to pass in the `Project` instance and specify that it wants a type of `ConstructionChangeDirective` returned.

The SaveCurrentEntity Method Override

This method just needs to call the base method first, and then it simply calls its associated `Service` class to save the `ConstructionChangeDirective`:

```
protected override void SaveCurrentEntity(object sender, EventArgs e)
{

    base.SaveCurrentEntity(sender, e);
    ConstructionChangeDirectiveService.SaveConstructionChangeDirective(
        this.CurrentEntity);

}
```

Notice how it is passing the `CurrentEntity` property value, and that value is coming from the base class, but is typed as a `ConstructionChangeDirective`.... Man, I love Generics!

The GetEntitiesList Method Override

The signature on this method is also typed properly, because of Generics again:

```
protected override List<ConstructionChangeDirective> GetEntitiesList()
{
    return new List<ConstructionChangeDirective>(

ConstructionChangeDirectiveService.GetConstructionChangeDirectives(
            UserSession.CurrentProject));
}
```

It simply delegates the `ConstructionChangeDirectiveService` class to get the list of `ConstructionChangeDirective` instances for the current Project.

The Construction Change Directive View

The View for Construction Change Directives is very similar to that seen in the past few chapters, where the list of Construction Change Directives is on the left, and the currently selected Construction Change Directive is on the right. Figure 9.5 shows what the form looks like at run time.

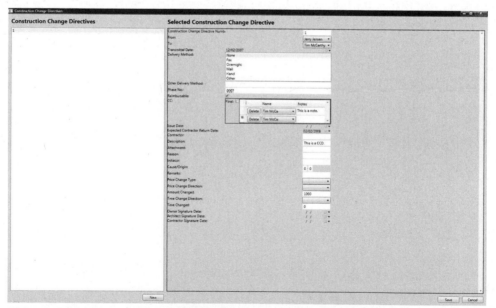

Figure 9.5: Construction Change Directive View.

324

One of the last things left to do in the UI is to hook up the `BrokenRules` property from the `EditableViewModel<T>` class to the UI. That could actually get pretty interesting, especially using WPF Triggers. Again, I am focusing on the domain model here, so I am not going to go into that; I am just going to suggest that the framework is there to do whatever you want to do with the `BrokenRule` instances in the UI.

Summary

In this chapter, I introduced the concept of a Construction Change Directive in the construction industry, and then I used that concept to model the Construction Change Directive Aggregate. As you may have noticed, I did a ton of refactoring in this chapter. Most of the refactoring was focused on the various `ViewModel` classes. A lot of the refactoring was made possible by using interfaces and Generics together. This proved to be quite a powerful combination in making the code base more maintainable, more robust, and also in making the domain model that much richer.

Synchronizing With the Server

In Chapter 1, Introducing the Project: The SmartCA Application, I stated that one of the requirements for the SmartCA application was that it must be offline capable. Now, when I say offline capable, the best example that comes to mind is Microsoft Outlook. In Microsoft Outlook versions 2003 and above, you can work connected to or disconnected from your email server and still have a good user experience. During this chapter, I would like you to keep in mind how Microsoft Outlook works in order to understand some of the design decisions presented later in the chapter.

The Problem

Thanks to using a local data store on the client, the SmartCA is definitely offline capable. Now, the challenge is to get it online and connected to the server. I am going to be calling this process of connecting to the server and transferring application data back and forth the Synchronization process.

What the SmartCA application needs is an intelligent, service-based way of synchronizing its data with the server. The user should not be bothered with any silly errors because they are not connected to the network or the Internet, they should be able to do their work, and the application should gracefully handle the transactions and pushing the data back and forth.

The Design

I also mentioned in Chapter 1 that I would be using Microsoft Synchronization Services for ADO.NET for this synchronization, but I have since changed my mind. After analyzing the problem domain further, I really feel that what the SmartCA application needs is a way to keep some type of running log of all of the transactions that the user performs on the client domain model, and then to send that in some message form to the server and have the server try to execute all of the messages on its own domain model.

Although Microsoft Synchronization Services for ADO.NET is a great piece of work, I did not feel it met the requirements that I had. I really do not want to get backed into a low-level database replication corner, and it seemed like that was really what Microsoft Synchronization Services for ADO.NET was doing, although it is doing it in an n-tier way.

Redesigning the Unit of Work

The more I thought about it, the more I liked the idea of encapsulating all of the client-side transactions into messages. I really want to make the synchronization a business-level process rather than a data-level process. As it turns out, I have already implemented a pattern in the SmartCA application that will lend itself very well to this type of architecture, and that is the Unit of Work pattern.

So after coming to this conclusion, I have decided to refactor my Unit of Work implementation a little bit in order to handle creating and storing transaction messages as it sends them to the various repositories for processing.

What is also needed is some type of process (or background thread) running that can take all of the messages created by the Unit of Work instances and send them to the server, as well as taking messages from the server and handing them to the SmartCA domain model.

The diagram in Figure 10.1 shows the modification to the Unit of Work implementation that allows me to use it for persisting transaction messages on the client:

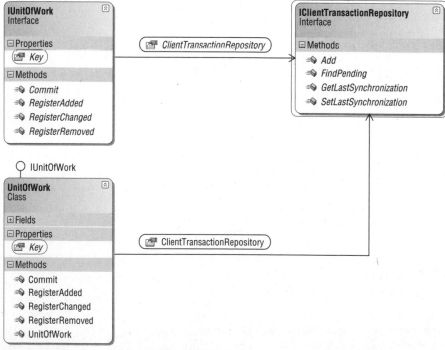

Figure 10.1: Unit of Work modifications.

What this diagram shows is that a Key property has been added to the IUnitOfWork interface, and that value represents a unique identifier for a Unit of Work. Also, the diagram shows a relationship to an IClientTransactionRepository, which implies that a Unit of Work message can be persisted. I will talk more about the Client Transaction Repository implementation later in this chapter.

The Refactored IUnitOfWork Interface

```
using System;
using SmartCA.Infrastructure.DomainBase;
using SmartCA.Infrastructure.RepositoryFramework;
using SmartCA.Infrastructure.Transactions;

namespace SmartCA.Infrastructure
{
    public interface IUnitOfWork
    {
        void RegisterAdded(EntityBase entity, IUnitOfWorkRepository repository);
        void RegisterChanged(EntityBase entity, IUnitOfWorkRepository repository);
        void RegisterRemoved(EntityBase entity, IUnitOfWorkRepository repository);
        void Commit();
        object Key { get; }
        IClientTransactionRepository ClientTransactionRepository { get; }
    }
}
```

The new IClientTransactionRepository Interface

Since I want to be flexible in how these messages are persisted, I have created an interface for the repository, called the IClientTransactionRepository. This Repository interface contains all of the methods necessary to save and retrieve client transactions.

```
using System;
using SmartCA.Infrastructure.DomainBase;
using System.Collections.Generic;

namespace SmartCA.Infrastructure.Transactions
{
    public interface IClientTransactionRepository
    {
        DateTime? GetLastSynchronization();
        void SetLastSynchronization(DateTime? lastSynchronization);
        void Add(ClientTransaction transaction);
        IList<ClientTransaction> FindPending();
    }
}
```

The Transaction Class Implementations

You may have noticed the reference to the `ClientTransaction` class in the `IClientTransactionRepository` interface in the above code sample. For the purposes of synchronization, there are two types of transactions, Client Transactions and Server Transactions (see Figure 10.2).

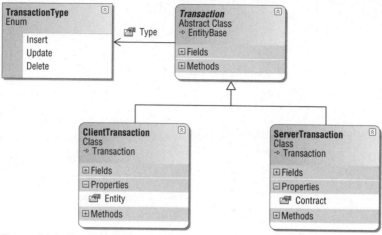

Figure 10.2: The Transaction classes.

Both of these types of Transactions inherit from the `Transaction` abstract class. Notice how the `Transaction` class only has to implement the `IEntity` interface and not inherit from the `EntityBase` class. This works out well because although a Transaction is an Entity, it does not need all of the functionality that the `EntityBase` class has, and therefore I can keep it lightweight.

Designing the Synchronization

Figure 10.3 is a drawing showing the different pieces involved in the SmartCA synchronization strategy.

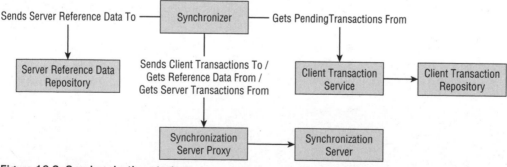

Figure 10.3: Synchronization strategy.

The diagram shows the pieces involved in getting transactions that happen on the client up to the server, as well as getting reference data and transactions from the server down to the client. There is a lot going on in this diagram, and many new classes will need to be added to support the new synchronization functionality.

Writing the Unit Tests

In this section, I am going to show the tests for the IClientTransactionRepository interface, mainly because it is this interface that is going to be called the most on the client whenever an IUnitOfWork instance is going to commit a transaction.

Very similarly to how I tested the other Repository interfaces, I have written a suite of unit tests that will test an instance of the IClientTransactionRepository interface that is returned from the ClientTransactionRepositoryFactory (which I have not shown yet, but I will later in this chapter).

The IClientTransactionRepositoryAddTest Method

This method tests the process of adding a new ClientTransaction to the IClientTransactionRepository instance.

```
/// <summary>
///A test for adding a Transaction
///</summary>
[DeploymentItem("SmartCA.sdf"), TestMethod()]
public void IClientTransactionRepositoryAddTest()
{
    IClientTransactionRepository target =
        ClientTransactionRepositoryFactory.GetTransactionRepository();
    TransactionType type = TransactionType.Insert;
    Company entity = new Company();
    entity.Name = "Test 123";
    object unitOfWorkKey = Guid.NewGuid();
    target.Add(new ClientTransaction(unitOfWorkKey, type, entity));
}
```

The method starts out by first getting an instance of the IClientTransactionRepository interface, and it then builds up a ClientTransaction instance filled with a new Company (which is an IEntity) instance, and then calls the Add method of the IClientTransactionRepository interface.

The FindPendingTransactionsTest Method

The purpose of this method is to test how the system finds all of the pending transactions on the client:

```
/// <summary>
/// A test for finding all of the pending transactions
/// </summary>
[DeploymentItem("SmartCA.sdf"), TestMethod()]
public void FindPendingTransactionsTest()
{
    // Make sure there is at least one pending transaction
    this.IClientTransactionRepositoryAddTest();

    // Get the pending transactions
    IClientTransactionRepository target =
        ClientTransactionRepositoryFactory.GetTransactionRepository();
    IList<ClientTransaction> transactions = target.FindPending();
    Assert.IsTrue(transactions.Count > 0);
}
```

This test starts out by first calling the IClientTransactionRepositoryAddTest method in order to make sure that there is at least one Transaction that needs to be synchronized on the client. Next, it makes the usual call to the factory to get the instance of the IClientTransactionRepository, and then it calls the FindPending method to get the list of all pending transactions on the client. Finally, it asserts that there is more than one pending transaction on the client.

The SetLastSynchronizationTest Method

This method is really simple; it tests how the system sets the last time that synchronization has occurred on the client:

```
/// <summary>
///A test for SetLastSynchronization
///</summary>
[DeploymentItem("SmartCA.sdf"), TestMethod()]
public void SetLastSynchronizationTest()
{
    IClientTransactionRepository target =
        ClientTransactionRepositoryFactory.GetTransactionRepository();
    target.SetLastSynchronization(DateTime.Now);
}
```

The first line is the familiar call of getting the instance of the IClientTransactionRepository. The next line simply calls the SetLastSynchronization method and passes in the current DateTime as the argument.

The GetLastSynchronizationTest Method

This test method exercises and tests the GetLastSynchronization method of the IClientTransactionRepository interface:

```
/// <summary>
///A test for GetLastSynchronization
///</summary>
[DeploymentItem("SmartCA.sdf"), TestMethod()]
public void GetLastSynchronizationTest()
{
    IClientTransactionRepository target =
        ClientTransactionRepositoryFactory.GetTransactionRepository();
    target.SetLastSynchronization(DateTime.Now);
    DateTime? lastSynchronization = target.GetLastSynchronization();
    Assert.IsTrue(lastSynchronization.HasValue);
    Assert.IsTrue(DateTime.Now > lastSynchronization.Value);
}
```

It starts out with the familiar, by getting an instance of the IClientTransactionRepository instance. It then calls the SetLastSynchronization method and passes in the current DateTime value to the method. Next, it calls the GetLastSynchronization method to get the DateTime value of the last time that the synchronization occurred, and then it makes sure that the synchronization DateTime value is in the past.

The Solution

There really are two main parts to the synchronization solution. The first part is all of the changes required to the Unit of Work implementation in order to support the saving of client transactions as messages. The second part is everything that is involved in getting the client transactions up to the server, and getting the server transactions and reference data from the server and into the client application.

I am splitting up the work in this fashion because the first part happens synchronously while a Unit of Work is committing the changes to Entities, and the second part does not need to happen right away; it can, and should, be an asynchronous operation. I say that it should be an asynchronous operation because I do not want the synchronization to freeze the application while it is running; again, think Microsoft Outlook here. This is why I chose to use a local database such as SQL Server CE in the first place. It allows me to work happily in my client domain and not have to worry about the server, since I can concern myself with the server during the synchronization process. Since the synchronization will be happening without blocking the main thread, the user experience is not impacted nearly as much as it would be if this synchronization were synchronous. The users can keep doing work with the application and not have their screen freeze up. This is exactly how Microsoft Outlook 2003 and above behaves when it synchronizes with a Microsoft Exchange mail server.

Unit of Work Refactoring

For the synchronization, I need to know what has changed on the client, without having to resort to doing a lot of low-level database queries and comparisons. As I was thinking about how to do this, I realized that I already have code that knows all about what changes are being persisted on the client, and that is my Unit of Work implementation.

The Commit Method

The code that knows about changes being persisted on the client is the Commit method. In that method, I already iterate through everything that has been changed, added, and deleted in the current Unit of Work transaction.

```
public void Commit()
{
    using (TransactionScope scope = new TransactionScope())
    {
        foreach (EntityBase entity in this.deletedEntities.Keys)
        {
            this.deletedEntities[entity].PersistDeletedItem(entity);
        }

        foreach (EntityBase entity in this.addedEntities.Keys)
        {
            this.addedEntities[entity].PersistDeletedItem(entity);
        }

        foreach (EntityBase entity in this.changedEntities.Keys)
        {
            this.changedEntities[entity].PersistDeletedItem(entity);
```

(continued)

(continued)

```
                }

                scope.Complete();
        }

        this.deletedEntities.Clear();
        this.addedEntities.Clear();
        this.changedEntities.Clear();
    }
```

I can simply add more code to this method to save these transactions as messages that need to be sent to the server for processing:

```
    public void Commit()
    {
        using (TransactionScope scope = new TransactionScope())
        {
            foreach (EntityBase entity in this.deletedEntities.Keys)
            {
                this.deletedEntities[entity].PersistDeletedItem(entity);

                this.clientTransactionRepository.Add(
                    new ClientTransaction(this.key,
                    TransactionType.Delete, entity));
            }

            foreach (EntityBase entity in this.addedEntities.Keys)
            {
                this.addedEntities[entity].PersistNewItem(entity);

                this.clientTransactionRepository.Add(
                    new ClientTransaction(this.key,
                    TransactionType.Insert, entity));
            }

            foreach (EntityBase entity in this.changedEntities.Keys)
            {
                this.changedEntities[entity].PersistUpdatedItem(entity);

                this.clientTransactionRepository.Add(
                    new ClientTransaction(this.key,
                    TransactionType.Update, entity));
            }

            scope.Complete();
        }

        this.deletedEntities.Clear();
        this.addedEntities.Clear();
        this.changedEntities.Clear();

        this.key = Guid.NewGuid();
    }
```

In the new code, you should notice a new Repository reference, the clientTransactionRepository class-level variable, and a new class-level variable, the key variable.

The UnitOfWork Key

The `key` variable is the primary identifier for the transaction, and it lets me know what operations in the transaction are tied together. The key variable is a `System.Guid` data type. Notice how when the transaction is committed and all of the dictionaries are emptied, I assign the `key` variable a new value. This signals that the `UnitOfWork` is cleared and ready to start up a new transaction.

New Properties and Changes to the Constructor

Here are the private variables in the `UnitOfWork` class:

```
private Guid key;
private IClientTransactionRepository clientTransactionRepository;
private Dictionary<EntityBase, IUnitOfWorkRepository> addedEntities;
private Dictionary<EntityBase, IUnitOfWorkRepository> changedEntities;
private Dictionary<EntityBase, IUnitOfWorkRepository> deletedEntities;
```

Here are the new properties exposing the new private fields as read-only:

```
public object Key
{
    get { return this.key; }
}

public IClientTransactionRepository ClientTransactionRepository
{
    get { return this.clientTransactionRepository; }
}
```

If you remember from the design earlier in the chapter, these properties were already added to the `IUnitOfWork` interface, and they are just being implemented here.

The Transaction Class Implementations

In this section, I will take a look at the implementations for the `Transaction`, `ClientTransaction`, and `ServerTransaction` classes.

The Transaction Class

Both the `ClientTransaction` and `ServerTransaction` classes inherit from the `Transaction` abstract class, which itself only holds two properties, `Type` and `Key`. The `Type` property represents the three different types of transaction operations, Insert, Update, and Delete, and the `Key` property represents the unique identifier for the Transaction.

```
using System;
using SmartCA.Infrastructure.DomainBase;

namespace SmartCA.Infrastructure.Transactions
{
    public abstract class Transaction : IEntity
    {
        private object key;
        private TransactionType type;
```

(continued)

(continued)

```csharp
        protected Transaction(object key, TransactionType type)
        {
            this.key = key;
            if (this.key == null)
            {
                this.key = Guid.NewGuid();
            }
            this.type = type;
        }

        public TransactionType Type
        {
            get { return this.type; }
        }

        #region IEntity Members

        public object Key
        {
            get { return this.key; }
        }

        #endregion

        #region Equality Tests

        /// <summary>
        /// Determines whether the specified transaction is equal to the
        /// current instance.
        /// </summary>
        /// <param name="entity">An <see cref="System.Object"/> that
        /// will be compared to the current instance.</param>
        /// <returns>True if the passed in entity is equal to the
        /// current instance.</returns>
        public override bool Equals(object transaction)
        {
            return transaction != null
                && transaction is Transaction
                && this == (Transaction)transaction;
        }

        /// <summary>
        /// Operator overload for determining equality.
        /// </summary>
        /// <param name="base1">The first instance of an
        /// <see cref="Transaction"/>.</param>
        /// <param name="base2">The second instance of an
        /// <see cref="Transaction"/>.</param>
        /// <returns>True if equal.</returns>
        public static bool operator ==(Transaction base1,
            Transaction base2)
        {
            // check for both null (cast to object or recursive loop)
```

```csharp
            if ((object)base1 == null && (object)base2 == null)
            {
                return true;
            }

            // check for either of them == to null
            if ((object)base1 == null || (object)base2 == null)
            {
                return false;
            }

            if (base1.Key != base2.Key)
            {
                return false;
            }

            return true;
        }

        /// <summary>
        /// Operator overload for determining inequality.
        /// </summary>
        /// <param name="base1">The first instance of an
        /// <see cref="Transaction"/>.</param>
        /// <param name="base2">The second instance of an
        /// <see cref="Transaction"/>.</param>
        /// <returns>True if not equal.</returns>
        public static bool operator !=(Transaction base1,
            Transaction base2)
        {
            return (!(base1 == base2));
        }

        /// <summary>
        /// Serves as a hash function for this type.
        /// </summary>
        /// <returns>A hash code for the current Key
        /// property.</returns>
        public override int GetHashCode()
        {
            return this.key.GetHashCode();
        }

        #endregion
    }
}
```

As mentioned in the design section, the `Transaction` class implements the `IEntity` interface, and, therefore, it has to expose a `Key` property. The rest of the class is equality logic tests and probably could be refactored out into some type of Generic class at a later time.

Chapter 10: Synchronizing With the Server

The ClientTransaction Class

As you might have expected by the name, the `ClientTransaction` class inherits from the `Transaction` class. It contains an instance of the `IEntity` that the current Transaction is acting upon.

```
using System;
using SmartCA.Infrastructure.DomainBase;

namespace SmartCA.Infrastructure.Transactions
{
    public class ClientTransaction : Transaction
    {
        private IEntity entity;

        public ClientTransaction(object key, TransactionType type,
            IEntity entity)
            : base(key, type)
        {
            this.entity = entity;
        }

        public IEntity Entity
        {
            get { return this.entity; }
        }
    }
}
```

The ServerTransaction Class

The `ServerTransaction` class is almost the same as the `ClientTransaction` class except that it holds an instance of a `ContractBase` class instead of an `IEntity` instance:

```
using System;
using SmartCA.Infrastructure.DomainBase;
using SmartCA.DataContracts;

namespace SmartCA.Infrastructure.Transactions
{
    public class ServerTransaction : Transaction
    {
        private ContractBase contract;

        public ServerTransaction(object key, TransactionType type,
            ContractBase contract)
            : base(key, type)
        {
            this.contract = contract;
        }

        public ContractBase Contract
```

```
            {
                get { return this.contract; }
            }
        }
    }
```

Data Contracts

The `ContractBase` class is the Data Contract equivalent of the `EntityBase` class:

```
using System;

namespace SmartCA.DataContracts
{
    [Serializable]
    public abstract class ContractBase
    {
        private object key;

        /// <summary>
        /// An <see cref="System.Object"/> that represents the
        /// primary identifier value for the class.
        /// </summary>
        public object Key
        {
            get { return this.key; }
            set { this.key = value; }
        }
    }
}
```

So, the question you probably are asking now is what in the world is a Data Contract? It is basically a Data Transfer Object (DTO) used to get data back and forth from the client to the server. All of the Data Contract classes are nothing but data, that is, they contain just a bunch of property setters and getters. Their main purpose in life is to be serialized and sent across the wire and then deserialized on the receiving end of the wire. I will go into more detail on these classes in the section of this chapter that deals with the server.

The only Data Contract classes that inherit from the `ContractBase` class are those that represent the Entity Root classes in the domain model. An example would be a `CompanyContract` class, whose main purpose is to represent the data of the Company Domain Model class in a way that is easily serializable.

The Client Transaction Repository Implementation

Since I am going to be storing the client transactions as messages that will be sent later, I need a way to save them, and what better way than to use the existing Repository pattern already being used everywhere else in the domain model.

The ClientTransactionRepositoryFactory Class

In order to program against this interface, just like I have with the other Repository interfaces in this application, I need a Factory to give the correct instance of the interface. This is a little bit different from the Repository Framework that I developed earlier for the other Entity Repositories, so I have created a new Factory for this implementation, and I am calling it the `ClientTransactionRepositoryFactory` class. Here is what it looks like:

```csharp
using System;
using SmartCA.Infrastructure.Transactions;
using SmartCA.Infrastructure.RepositoryFramework.Configuration;
using System.Configuration;

namespace SmartCA.Infrastructure.RepositoryFramework
{
    public static class ClientTransactionRepositoryFactory
    {
        private static IClientTransactionRepository transactionRepository;

        public static IClientTransactionRepository GetTransactionRepository()
        {
            // See if the ITransactionRepository instance was already created
            if (ClientTransactionRepositoryFactory.transactionRepository == null)
            {
                // It was not created, so build it now
                RepositorySettings settings =
                    (RepositorySettings)ConfigurationManager.GetSection(
RepositoryMappingConstants.RepositoryMappingsConfigurationSectionName);

                // Get the type to be created
                Type repositoryType =
                    Type.GetType(
settings.RepositoryMappings["IClientTransactionRepository"].RepositoryFullTypeName);

                // Create the repository, and cast it to the
                // ITransactionRepository interface
                ClientTransactionRepositoryFactory.transactionRepository =
                    Activator.CreateInstance(repositoryType)
                    as IClientTransactionRepository;
            }

            return ClientTransactionRepositoryFactory.transactionRepository;
        }
    }
}
```

I was not able to use the existing `RepositoryFactory` class because it has the `IRepository` constraint, and the `IClientTransactionRepository` interface does not extend that interface, nor does it make sense for it to extend it.

The ClientTransactionRepository Class

The `ClientTransactionRepository` class is an abstract class that is intended to abstract away the implementation of the `Add` method of the `IClientTransactionRepository` interface.

```
using System;
using SmartCA.Infrastructure.DomainBase;
using SmartCA.Infrastructure.Transactions;
using SmartCA.DataContracts.Helpers;
using System.Collections.Generic;

namespace SmartCA.Infrastructure.Repositories
{
    public abstract class ClientTransactionRepository :
        IClientTransactionRepository
    {
        #region IClientTransactionRepository Members

        public abstract DateTime? GetLastSynchronization();
        public abstract void SetLastSynchronization(DateTime? lastSynchronization);

        public void Add(ClientTransaction transaction)
        {
            // Convert the entity to one of the data contract types
            object contract = Converter.ToContract(transaction.Entity);

            // Serialize the data contract into an array of bytes
            byte[] serializedContractData = Serializer.Serialize(contract);

            // Persist the transaction (delegate to the derived class)
            this.PersistNewTransaction(transaction.Type,
                serializedContractData, transaction.Key);
        }

        public abstract IList<ClientTransaction> FindPending();

        #endregion

        protected abstract void PersistNewTransaction(TransactionType type,
            byte[] serializedContractData, object transactionKey);
    }
}
```

As you can see, it implements the `IClientTransactionRepository` interface methods by exposing all of them as abstract methods or properties, except for the `Add` method. In the `Add` method, it takes care of converting the `ClientTransaction`'s `IEntity` instance into a Data Contract, and then serializes the Data Contract to an array of bytes so that it can be persisted. By taking advantage of the Template Method pattern, it leaves the persistence of the data up to the derived class, via the `PersistNewTransaction` abstract method that it calls in its `Add` method.

The SqlCeClientTransactionRepository Class

As you might expect, this class inherits from the `ClientTransactionRepository` class. Its purpose is to persist `ClientTransaction` objects to and from the local SQL CE database.

Constructor

The constructor is similar to the `SqlCeRepositoryBase<T>` constructor, as it grabs an instance of the Enterprise Library's Database class for use in some of its methods:

```
using System.Data.Common;
using System.Data;
using System.Collections.Generic;
using SmartCA.Infrastructure.EntityFactoryFramework;
using System.Text;

namespace SmartCA.Infrastructure.Repositories
{
    public class SqlCeClientTransactionRepository : ClientTransactionRepository
    {
        private Database database;

        public SqlCeClientTransactionRepository()
        {
            this.database = DatabaseFactory.CreateDatabase();
        }
```

The PersistNewTransaction Method

This is the override of the abstract method on the base class, `ClientTransactionRepository`:

```
protected override void PersistNewTransaction(TransactionType type,
    byte[] serializedContractData, object transactionKey)
{
    // See if the parent transaction already exists

    // Perform a query to see if it exists
    StringBuilder builder = new StringBuilder(100);
    builder.Append("SELECT 1 FROM ClientTransaction ");
    builder.Append(string.Format("WHERE ClientTransactionID='{0}';",
        transactionKey));
    object result = this.database.ExecuteScalar(
        this.database.GetSqlStringCommand(builder.ToString()));

    // Test the result of the query to see if it exists
    if (result == null)
    {
        // It does not exist, so create a new parent transaction
        builder = new StringBuilder(100);
        builder.Append("INSERT INTO ClientTransaction ");
        builder.Append("(ClientTransactionID) ");
        builder.Append(string.Format("VALUES ('{0}');", transactionKey));
        this.database.ExecuteNonQuery(
            this.database.GetSqlStringCommand(builder.ToString()));
    }

    // Insert the details of the transaction,
    // including the serialized object's byte array
```

```
            builder = new StringBuilder(100);
            builder.Append("INSERT INTO ClientTransactionDetail ");
            builder.Append("(ClientTransactionID,TransactionType,ObjectData) ");
            builder.Append(string.Format("VALUES ('{0}',{1},@data);",
                transactionKey, (int)type));
            using (DbCommand command =
                this.database.GetSqlStringCommand(builder.ToString()))
            {
                this.database.AddInParameter(command, "@data",
                    DbType.Binary, serializedContractData);
                this.database.ExecuteNonQuery(command);
            }
        }
```

This code first has to detect whether a parent transaction has already been started, based upon the value of the `transactionKey` (which is the new Key property I added to the IUnitOfWork interface). It does this by executing a query and seeing whether the query returned null. If the parent transaction does not exist, then the code creates it by executing a SQL insert statement. The last step is to insert the details of the transaction, which contains the main piece of data for the transaction, the serialized Data Contract's byte array.

The FindPending Method

The job of this method is to find all pending transactions in the repository:

```
        public override IList<ClientTransaction> FindPending()
        {
            List<ClientTransaction> transactions = new List<ClientTransaction>();
            StringBuilder builder = new StringBuilder(100);
            builder.Append("SELECT ctd.ClientTransactionID,");
            builder.Append("ctd.TransactionType,ctd.ObjectData ");
            builder.Append("FROM ClientTransaction ct ");
            builder.Append("INNER JOIN ClientTransactionDetail ctd ");
            builder.Append("ON ct.ClientTransactionID = ctd.ClientTransactionID ");
            builder.Append("WHERE ct.ReconciliationResult = 1;");
            using (DbCommand command =
this.database.GetSqlStringCommand(builder.ToString()))
            {
                using (IDataReader reader = this.database.ExecuteReader(command))
                {
                    IEntityFactory<ClientTransaction> entityFactory =
                        EntityFactoryBuilder.BuildFactory<ClientTransaction>();
                    while (reader.Read())
                    {
                        transactions.Add(entityFactory.BuildEntity(reader));
                    }
                }
            }
            return transactions;
        }
```

This method builds a query to pull all of the pending transaction data from the data store and then uses the `ClientTransactionFactory` to transform the results into `ClientTransaction` instances:

```csharp
using System;
using SmartCA.Infrastructure.EntityFactoryFramework;
using SmartCA.Infrastructure.Transactions;
using System.Data;
using SmartCA.Infrastructure.DomainBase;
using SmartCA.DataContracts;
using SmartCA.DataContracts.Helpers;

namespace SmartCA.Infrastructure.Repositories
{
    public class ClientTransactionFactory : IEntityFactory<ClientTransaction>
    {

        internal static class FieldNames
        {
            public const string ClientTransactionId = "ClientTransactionID";
            public const string ReconciliationResult = "ReconciliationResult";
            public const string ReconciliationErrorMessage =
                "ReconciliationErrorMessage";
            public const string TransactionType = "TransactionType";
            public const string ObjectData = "ObjectData";
        }
        #region IEntityFactory<ClientTransaction> Members

        public ClientTransaction BuildEntity(IDataReader reader)
        {
            byte[] objectData =
                DataHelper.GetByteArrayValue(reader[FieldNames.ObjectData]);
            ContractBase contract =
                Serializer.Deserialize(objectData) as ContractBase;
            EntityBase entity = Converter.ToEntity(contract);
            return new ClientTransaction(reader[FieldNames.ClientTransactionId],

(TransactionType)DataHelper.GetInteger(reader[FieldNames.TransactionType]),
                    entity);
        }

        #endregion
    }
}
```

Most of the code in this method is the standard implementation of the Entity Factory Framework that I have been using in all of the chapters. There is an interesting aspect in the implementation, particularly where the byte array is retrieved from the `IDataReader` instance and deserialized into its proper

ContractBase instance via the Serializer class. As you might expect, the Serializer class contains two methods, Serialize and Deserialize. The job of the Serialize method is to take a ContractBase instance and turn it into an array of bytes using binary formatting:

```
public static byte[] Serialize(object graph)
{
    byte[] serializedData = null;
    using (MemoryStream stream = new MemoryStream())
    {
        BinaryFormatter formatter = new BinaryFormatter();
        formatter.Serialize(stream, graph);
        serializedData = stream.ToArray();
    }
    return serializedData;
}
```

This method takes an object instance and uses the BinaryFormatter class to serialize the object graph into an array of bytes.

The Deserialize method does just the opposite. It takes an array of bytes and deserializes it into an object.

```
public static object Deserialize(byte[] serializedData)
{
    object graph = null;
    if (serializedData != null)
    {
        using (MemoryStream stream = new MemoryStream())
        {
            for (int i = 0; i < serializedData.Length; i++)
            {
                stream.WriteByte(serializedData[i]);
            }
            stream.Position = 0;
            BinaryFormatter formatter = new BinaryFormatter();
            graph = formatter.Deserialize(stream);
        }
    }
    return graph;
}
```

It is nice to encapsulate this functionality because it guarantees that each time I serialize or deserialize an object I know that it will be done the same way in the same format.

The next interesting part of the BuildEntity method in the ClientTransactionFactory class is where it takes the array of bytes returned from the Serializer class and then uses a Converter helper class to convert the ContractBase instance into an IEntity instance. This magic is done in the Converter class using reflection.

Here is the code for the `Converter` class's `ToEntity` method:

```
public static IEntity ToEntity(ContractBase contract)
{
    // Do reflection to call the right method here
    string methodName = string.Format("To{0}",
        contract.GetType().Name.Replace("Contract", ""));
    MethodInfo method = typeof(Converter).GetMethod(methodName);
    return method.Invoke(null, new object[] { contract }) as IEntity;
}
```

I know this code may look a little funky, but it gets rid of a giant switch statement of method names to do this conversion. For every class in the domain model, there is an equivalent Data Contract class, and, for each set of classes, there is a To *[Entity Name]* method and a To *[Entity Name]*Contract method. For example, the Company Domain Model class has a `ToCompanyContract` method (from a Company Entity) and a `ToCompany` method (from a Company Data Contract).

To further illustrate the concept, here is the `ToCompanyContract` method:

```
public static CompanyContract ToCompanyContract(Company company)
{
    CompanyContract contract = new CompanyContract();
    contract.Key = company.Key;
    contract.Abbreviation = company.Abbreviation;
    foreach (Address address in company.Addresses)
    {
        contract.Addresses.Add(Converter.ToAddressContract(address));
    }
    contract.FaxNumber = company.FaxNumber;
    contract.HeadquartersAddress =
        Converter.ToAddressContract(company.HeadquartersAddress);
    contract.Name = company.Name;
    contract.PhoneNumber = company.PhoneNumber;
    contract.Remarks = company.Remarks;
    contract.Url = company.Url;
    return contract;
}
```

Here is the `ToCompany` method:

```
public static Company ToCompany(CompanyContract contract)
{
    Company company = new Company(contract.Key);
    company.Abbreviation = contract.Abbreviation;
    foreach (AddressContract address in contract.Addresses)
    {
        company.Addresses.Add(Converter.ToAddress(address));
    }
    company.FaxNumber = contract.FaxNumber;
    company.HeadquartersAddress =
        Converter.ToAddress(contract.HeadquartersAddress);
    company.Name = contract.Name;
```

```
        company.PhoneNumber = contract.PhoneNumber;
        company.Remarks = contract.Remarks;
        company.Url = contract.Url;
        return company;
    }
```

As you can see, these two methods are pretty straightforward and are just the inverse of each other.

The ToEntity method assumes that the naming is consistent in the Converter class, and uses reflection to call the right method to convert a ContractBase instance to an IEntity instance. I know that this is a lot of plumbing, but that's why it lives in the Infrastructure namespace; the domain model is still free from this clutter!

The GetLastSynchronization Method

This method is used to retrieve the last DateTime value a Synchronization with the server occurred:

```
public override DateTime? GetLastSynchronization()
{
    string query = "SELECT LastSynchronization FROM Synchronization";
    using (DbCommand command =
        this.database.GetSqlStringCommand(query))
    {
        return DataHelper.GetNullableDateTime(
            this.database.ExecuteScalar(command));
    }
}
```

This code is pretty simple; it performs a query on the Synchronization table (which is always a one-row table) in order get the Nullable DateTime value.

The SetLastSynchronization Method

This method is just the opposite of the GetLastSynchronization method; it updates the date that the last synchronization with the server took place:

```
public override void SetLastSynchronization(DateTime? lastSynchronization)
{
    if (lastSynchronization.HasValue)
    {
        string query = "SELECT COUNT(*) FROM Synchronization";
        bool synchronizationRecordExists = false;
        using (DbCommand command =
            this.database.GetSqlStringCommand(query))
        {
            synchronizationRecordExists =
                ((int)this.database.ExecuteScalar(command) > 0);
        }

        StringBuilder builder = new StringBuilder(50);

        if (synchronizationRecordExists)
```

(continued)

(continued)

```
            {
                builder.Append("UPDATE Synchronization ");
                builder.Append(
                    string.Format("SET LastSynchronization = '{0}'",
                    lastSynchronization.Value));
            }
            else
            {
                builder.Append("INSERT INTO Synchronization ");
                builder.Append("(LastSynchronization) ");
                builder.Append(string.Format("VALUES ('{0}')",
                    lastSynchronization));
            }
            using (DbCommand command =
                this.database.GetSqlStringCommand(builder.ToString()))
            {
                this.database.ExecuteNonQuery(command);
            }
        }
    }
```

The ClientTransactionService Class

This class is similar to a lot of the other service classes in that it is acting as a façade to a Repository interface instance, in this case the IClientTransactionRepository interface:

```
using System;
using System.Collections.Generic;
using SmartCA.Infrastructure.RepositoryFramework;

namespace SmartCA.Infrastructure.Transactions
{
    public static class ClientTransactionService
    {
        private static IClientTransactionRepository repository =
            ClientTransactionRepositoryFactory.GetTransactionRepository();

        public static IList<ClientTransaction> GetPendingTransactions()
        {
            return ClientTransactionService.repository.FindPending();
        }

        public static DateTime? GetLastSynchronization()
        {
            return ClientTransactionService.repository.GetLastSynchronization();
        }

        public static void SetLastSynchronization(DateTime? lastSynchronization)
        {

ClientTransactionService.repository.SetLastSynchronization(lastSynchronization);
        }
    }
}
```

As you can see, it is delegating to the `IClientTransactionRepository` methods and then exposing them via its static methods. I do not necessarily have to have this class, but it does make it easy to call static methods.

Synchronizing with the Synchronizer Class

Now that I have covered persisting transactions on the client, it is time to cover how to send the transactions to the server, and also how to get the transactions and reference data from the server.

If you remember from the diagram at the beginning of the chapter, the `Synchronizer` class was the class that was controlling everything in the synchronization process. The `Synchronizer` class is a static `Service` class whose job is to orchestrate the process of getting the transaction messages processed back and forth from the server.

Constructor

This `static` class does have a static constructor, and it is used to initialize the last time that the client synchronized with the server.

```
using System;
using SmartCA.Infrastructure.Transactions;
using System.Collections.Generic;
using SmartCA.Infrastructure.DomainBase;
using SmartCA.DataContracts.Helpers;
using SmartCA.Infrastructure.RepositoryFramework;
using System.Reflection;
using SmartCA.Infrastructure.ReferenceData;

namespace SmartCA.Infrastructure.Synchronization
{
    public static class Synchronizer
    {
        private static DateTime? lastSynchronized;

        static Synchronizer()
        {
            Synchronizer.GetLastSynchronized();
        }
```

The last synchronized value is used later in the class when communicating with the server.

The GetLastSynchronized Method

This method uses the `ClientTransactionService` to get the last time the client has synchronized with the server:

```
        private static void GetLastSynchronized()
        {
            Synchronizer.lastSynchronized =
                ClientTransactionService.GetLastSynchronization();
        }
```

This code is really just a pass-through to the Service method, but it is still useful for it to be wrapped in this method, as it makes the code more readable. This method is only called from the constructor.

The SetLastSynchronized Method

This method is the inverse of the GetLastSynchronization method:

```
private static void SetLastSynchronized()
{
    // Persist the last synchronized datetime
    Synchronizer.lastSynchronized = DateTime.Now;
    ClientTransactionService.SetLastSynchronization(
        Synchronizer.lastSynchronized);
}
```

This method is always called at the end of the synchronization process. Besides the obvious job of setting the last synchronized value, this method also persists the value via the ClientTransactionService. Where it is persisted is up to the IClientTransactionRepository instance that the ClientTransactionService refers to at run time.

The ProcessReferenceData Method

The ProcessReferenceData method takes in a composite DataContract that contains all of the collections of reference data items from the server, and then proceeds to send this data to the ReferenceDataRepository for persistence on the client:

```
private static void ProcessReferenceData(
    ReferenceDataContract referenceData)
{
    if (referenceData != null)
    {
        IReferenceDataRepository repository =
            ReferenceDataRepositoryFactory.GetReferenceDataRepository();

        if (referenceData.Disciplines != null)
        {
            repository.Add(referenceData.Disciplines);
        }
        if (referenceData.ItemStatuses != null)
        {
            repository.Add(referenceData.ItemStatuses);
        }
        if (referenceData.Sectors != null)
        {
            repository.Add(referenceData.Sectors);
        }
        if (referenceData.Segments != null)
        {
            repository.Add(referenceData.Segments);
        }
        if (referenceData.SpecSections != null)
```

```
            {
                repository.Add(referenceData.SpecSections);
            }
        }
    }
```

This code first gets a reference to the IReferenceDataRepository interface instance via the
ReferenceDataRepositoryFactory and then calls the appropriate Add method overloads to persist
each type of reference DataContract type.

The IReferenceDataRepository Interface

The IReferenceDataRepository interface is a very simple interface with one method, the Add
method, but with an overload of the Add method consisting of an IList type for each type of reference
DataContract:

```
using System;
using System.Collections.Generic;
using SmartCA.DataContracts;

namespace SmartCA.Infrastructure.ReferenceData
{
    public interface IReferenceDataRepository
    {
        void Add(IList<DisciplineContract> disciplines);
        void Add(IList<ItemStatusContract> itemStatuses);
        void Add(IList<MarketSectorContract> sectors);
        void Add(IList<MarketSegmentContract> segments);
        void Add(IList<SpecificationSectionContract> specSections);
    }
}
```

The ReferenceDataRepositoryFactory Class

Following the same pattern that I have used all along when programming to an interface, I created
an instance of the IReferenceDataRepository interface via a Factory. In this case, the Factory, the
ReferenceDataRepositoryFactory, is just like the ClientTransactionRepositoryFactory. Again,
I was not able to reuse the Repository Factory Framework I used for all of the other Repository interfaces
in the domain model. I probably should refactor the ClientTransactionRepositoryFactory and the
ReferenceDataRepositoryFactory into one class, but I have not done that yet.

```
using System;
using SmartCA.Infrastructure.RepositoryFramework.Configuration;
using System.Configuration;
using SmartCA.Infrastructure.ReferenceData;

namespace SmartCA.Infrastructure.RepositoryFramework
{
    public static class ReferenceDataRepositoryFactory
    {
        private static IReferenceDataRepository referenceDataRepository;

        public static IReferenceDataRepository GetReferenceDataRepository()
```

(continued)

(continued)

```
    {
        // See if the IReferenceDataRepository instance was already created
        if (ReferenceDataRepositoryFactory.referenceDataRepository == null)
        {
            // It was not created, so build it now
            RepositorySettings settings =
                (RepositorySettings)ConfigurationManager.GetSection(

RepositoryMappingConstants.RepositoryMappingsConfigurationSectionName);

            // Get the type to be created
            Type repositoryType =
                Type.GetType(

settings.RepositoryMappings["IReferenceDataRepository"].RepositoryFullTypeName);

            // Create the repository, and cast it to the
            // IReferenceDataRepository interface
            ReferenceDataRepositoryFactory.referenceDataRepository =
                Activator.CreateInstance(repositoryType) as
IReferenceDataRepository;

        }

        return ReferenceDataRepositoryFactory.referenceDataRepository;
    }
    }
}
```

As you can see, the only real difference between the two repositories is that the interface type instance is returned. The nice thing is that I have created unit tests for these factories, so I can refactor them as much as I like and just re-run my tests until they pass.

The IReferenceDataRepository Implementation – The SqlCeReferenceDataRepository Class

This class is very similar to the `SqlCeClientTransactionRepository` implementation. As you can probably guess from its name, its job is to persist reference data to the local SQL CE database. As you can see from the `IReferenceDataRepository` interface, it does not perform any searching operations; it is strictly adding and updating reference data on the client.

Its private field and constructor are pretty much identical to the `SqlCeClientTransactionRepository` constructor as well:

```
using System;
using System.Collections.Generic;
using SmartCA.Infrastructure.ReferenceData;
using Microsoft.Practices.EnterpriseLibrary.Data;
using SmartCA.DataContracts;
using System.Text;

namespace SmartCA.Infrastructure.Repositories
```

```
{
    public class SqlCeReferenceDataRepository : IReferenceDataRepository
    {
        private Database database;

        public SqlCeReferenceDataRepository()
        {
            this.database = DatabaseFactory.CreateDatabase();
        }
```

All of the interface methods that it implements delegate out to private helper methods, as shown here:

```
#region IReferenceDataRepository Members

public void Add(IList<DisciplineContract> disciplines)
{
    foreach (DisciplineContract discipline in disciplines)
    {
        this.AddDiscipline(discipline);
    }
}

public void Add(IList<ItemStatusContract> itemStatuses)
{
    foreach (ItemStatusContract itemStatus in itemStatuses)
    {
        this.AddItemStatus(itemStatus);
    }
}

public void Add(IList<MarketSectorContract> sectors)
{
    foreach (MarketSectorContract sector in sectors)
    {
        this.AddMarketSector(sector);
    }
}

public void Add(IList<MarketSegmentContract> segments)
{
    foreach (MarketSegmentContract segment in segments)
    {
        this.AddMarketSegment(segment);
    }
}

public void Add(IList<SpecificationSectionContract> specSections)
{
    foreach (SpecificationSectionContract specSection in specSections)
    {
        this.AddSpecificationSection(specSection);
    }
}

#endregion
```

The private helper methods just execute basic insert SQL statements on the local database. I am not going to show all of them here, but this is what the first one looks like:

```
private void AddDiscipline(DisciplineContract discipline)
{
    StringBuilder builder = new StringBuilder(100);
    builder.Append("INSERT INTO Discipline ");
    builder.Append("(DisciplineID,DisciplineName,Description) ");
    builder.Append(string.Format("VALUES ({0},'{1}','{2}');",
        discipline.Key, discipline.Name, discipline.Description));
    this.database.ExecuteNonQuery(
            this.database.GetSqlStringCommand(builder.ToString()));
}
```

As you can see, this method takes in the `DataContract` for a Discipline and uses it to build an insert SQL statement, and then executes the SQL statement.

The ProcessServerTransactions Method

Now that I have covered `Synchronizer` class's `ProcessReferenceData` method, it is time to move on to the last method in the `Synchronizer` class, which is the `ProcessServerTransactions` method:

```
private static void ProcessServerTransactions(
    IList<ServerTransaction> serverTransactions)
{
    IEntity entity = null;
    Type serviceType = null;
    string saveMethodName = string.Empty;
    MethodInfo method = null;

    foreach (ServerTransaction transaction in serverTransactions)
    {
        // Convert the DataContract into an EntityBase
        // and use the right service class to save it

        // 1. Get the EntityBase from the DataContract
        entity = Converter.ToEntity(transaction.Contract);

        // 2. Get the right service class type for the entity
        serviceType = Type.GetType(string.Format("{0}Service",
            entity.GetType().Name));

        // 3. Use reflection to get the correct Save method
        saveMethodName = string.Format("Save{0}", entity.GetType().Name);
        method = serviceType.GetMethod("Save");

        // 4. Call the Save method
        method.Invoke(null, new object[] { entity });
    }
}
```

This method takes a collection of server transactions, iterates through them, converts each server transaction that is represented by the `DataContract` back into an Entity, and then uses the Entity's associated Repository to persist it. Remember, the `ServerTransaction` class was covered in the beginning of the chapter, but this is the first time that I am using it. It really is about the same as the `ClientTransaction` class, except that it holds a reference to a `DataContract` instance instead of an `IEntity` instance.

Iterating through the server transactions and persisting them sounds pretty simple, but the way this method has to do it is a little bit tricky. The first thing the method has to do is to convert the `DataContract` instance of the `ServerTransaction` into an `IEntity` instance. This is done via the `ToEntity` method of the `Converter` class, which we looked at earlier in the chapter. The next step is to figure out the type name of the Entity, that is, Company, and then use that type name to figure out the associated Service for that Entity's Repository. For the Company example, it knows to get the `System.Type` of the type name of `CompanyService`. Then, once it has the `System.Type` reference, it reflects on the type to get an instance of the `Save[Entity Name]` method; in the case of the `CompanyService`, it would be `SaveCompany`. When it has the reference to the reflected method, it invokes the method, which in turn saves the Company instance to its proper Repository.

The Main Method – the Synchronize Method

You may have noticed that all of the methods I have shown so far in the `Synchronizer` class are all private methods. I wanted to show them to you so you could understand how the class works. The main entry point to the class, however, is one public static method, and that is the `Synchronize` method. This method is a Controller method, that is, it coordinates calls to other methods in the class that enable it to perform the overall synchronization with the server.

```
public static void Synchronize()
{
    // Send pending transactions to the server
    SynchronizationServerProxy.SendTransactions(
        ClientTransactionService.GetPendingTransactions());

    // Get reference data from the server
    ReferenceDataContract referenceData =
        SynchronizationServerProxy.GetReferenceData(lastSynchronized);

    // Process the reference data
    Synchronizer.ProcessReferenceData(referenceData);

    // Get transactions from the server
    IList<ServerTransaction> serverTransactions =
        SynchronizationServerProxy.GetTransactions(lastSynchronized);

    // Process the server transactions
    Synchronizer.ProcessServerTransactions(serverTransactions);

    // If the synchronization was successful,
    // then record the timestamp
    Synchronizer.SetLastSynchronized();
}
```

As you can see, it coordinates all of the calls to the private methods that I have just shown, but it calls them in the proper order required for Synchronization. There are two calls in this controller method that are not calls to private methods, and those are the calls to the server to get the reference data and the server transactions. These calls are done with a class called `SynchronizationServerProxy`. This class is mocked up for now, but this is the class that will actually make the calls to the server. It is the application's proxy to the server. Here is what the class looks like now:

```
using System;
using System.Collections.Generic;
using SmartCA.Infrastructure.Transactions;

namespace SmartCA.Infrastructure.Synchronization
{
    public static class SynchronizationServerProxy
    {
        public static void SendTransactions(
            IList<ClientTransaction> transactions)
        {
        }

        public static IList<ServerTransaction> GetTransactions(
            DateTime? lastSynchronized)
        {
            return new List<ServerTransaction>();
        }

        public static ReferenceDataContract GetReferenceData(
            DateTime? lastSynchronized)
        {
            return null;
        }
    }
}
```

I probably will refactor this class into an interface and create a Factory to give me different instances of the interface. This will allow me to use a mocked up `SynchronizationServerProxy` class that does pretty much what this one is doing, which will make my unit tests fast. When it comes time for actual integration with the server, I will create the real implementation of the interface and have the application configured to use that one for the actual synchronizations with the server.

Summary

In this chapter, I tackled the concept of how to synchronize the client's offline data with the server. I came to the conclusion that it was better to make my synchronization process more business-driven than data-driven, and therefore I chose not to use database replication or to use the new ADO.NET Synchronization Services. Instead, I went with a message-based approach and ended up refactoring my Unit of Work implementation to store transaction messages on the client. I then came up with a strategy and implementation for synchronizing those messages stored on the client with the messages on the server. Overall, the solution feels fairly elegant to me, and how it works makes sense. What I did not do is figure out how to reconcile synchronization conflicts, but that can be done in a later iteration of the application. The important point is that the synchronization process has been brought back and tied into the domain model, so any logic that needs to be performed to reconcile synchronization conflicts can be easily refactored into the domain model, which is where it belongs.

The Client Membership System

In the last chapter, I talked about synchronizing data with the server and how important it was to be able to work offline. In this chapter, I am going to discuss how to implement membership features, such as authentication, in an offline scenario.

The Problem

Now that the application has a nice, service-based way of working offline and synchronizing all of its data with the server, there needs to be a way to enable authentication and authorization while offline as well.

Users should be able to authenticate (i.e., log in to the application) and be able to perform work based on their assigned role(s) in the system. This is easy to do in an online ASP.NET application using the ASP.NET Membership System, but it is a lot trickier in a smart client application. One way of implementing these features is to call web services on the server that will authenticate the user and provide authorization information. The web services could actually wrap methods on the ASP.NET Membership System. The problem with that approach in the SmartCA application is that it requires that the user has a network or Internet connection, and if you remember from Chapter 1, the users sometimes are out in the middle of nowhere with no access to any type of network connection.

The Design

Since I already have a nice data synchronization strategy in place, why not use that to help solve the problem of performing membership tasks offline? After thinking about it for a while, I thought, why not put the membership data that is normally on the server down on the client? This would allow the users to authenticate themselves locally and do things like change their passwords locally. If any changes were then made on the server, or if the user changed any of his or her membership data on the client, the changes could be synchronized using the existing framework from the last chapter.

Password Security

One of the key factors about trying something like that is how to secure stored passwords on the client. The ASP.NET Membership Service specifies three formats for storing a password — in clear text, encrypted, or hashed, as defined in the `PasswordFormat` enumeration.

Password Format Setting	Description	Password Retrieval
PasswordFormat.Clear	The password is stored in clear text.	Yes
PasswordFormat.Hashed	A one-way hash of the password is stored.	No
PasswordFormat.Encrypted	The password is stored in encrypted format.	Yes

It should be obvious, but for security reasons, the option of storing passwords in clear text is definitely out. That would essentially allow any user who could figure out how to open and read the SQL CE database file to see all of the other users' passwords!

Encryption is definitely a better option than clear text. In order to perform password comparisons when passwords are stored in the encrypted format, the stored password must be decrypted first. To me, this still presents a problem, because that means someone could possibly figure out the algorithm to decrypt the passwords.

The best option is hashing. To compare passwords when they are stored in the hashed format, a hash using the same key is calculated on the supplied password and then compared against the stored hash. This is one-way encryption, that is, the password can never be decrypted. This means that once the password is created, it can never be decrypted back into plain text again. Nobody can ever retrieve their password with this option. If a user forgets his or her password, a new one must be created.

Designing the Client Membership System

I have decided for this application that I will implement a Membership System very similar to the ASP .NET Membership System, but with a "Client Membership" type of API. What this means is that I want users to be able to authenticate locally when using the application offline. The users will not only be able to authenticate themselves, but it will also be able to change and reset their passwords and password questions and answers.

All other functions, such as creating and managing users will be handled by the server. The client will communicate its Membership changes via the Synchronization Framework from the last chapter. In addition to sending the server membership data, the client will also receive updates to its membership data from the server as well.

In order to make it easier to synchronize data, I have decided to make the Client Membership System behave as close as possible to the ASP.NET Membership System. What I mean by that is that I am going with a provider-based model for accessing the Client Membership data. I know, you might be thinking, why not a repository like the ones I have been using all along? Well, the reason why is because the user data that I am holding on the client does not really fit that pattern. I am not really going to need to access it like an in-memory collection. All I really need to be able to do is retrieve and update the current User from the Client Membership System.

One of the main differences between my Membership implementation on the client and Microsoft's ASP .NET Membership implementation is that I am keeping my membership-related logic in the domain model, whereas with the ASP.NET Membership there is logic scattered across several classes and even in stored procedures in the out of the box `SqlMembershipProvider` implementation that comes with the ASP.NET Provider Toolkit.

The diagram in Figure 11.1 shows how the Client Membership system interacts with the user data.

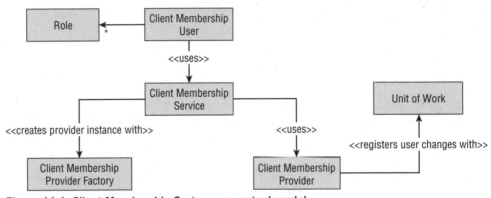

Figure 11.1: Client Membership System conceptual model.

In the diagram, you can see how this looks relatively similar to what I have been doing all along, except, instead of a repository behind the Service class, now there is a Provider behind it. The Provider is still kept abstract via an interface, and I still use a Factory to create an instance of the interface, thus allowing me to keep a dependency to only the interface of the Provider in my domain model.

An important item to note in the diagram is that the Client Membership provider is using a Unit of Work to register any changes to User instances, such as changed passwords, account lockouts, and so on. Since the Unit of Work implementation is tied into the synchronization strategy from the last chapter, this means that all of the User instance change transactions will be propagated to the server when the Synchronizer runs. Also, any relevant Membership transactions and refer to data from the server side will also be brought down to the client with the Synchronizer. I will go into more detail into how that works later in the chapter.

The Solution

The solution for the Client Membership System is mainly divided into two areas, the domain model and the Provider Framework.

The Client Membership System Domain Model Classes

Instead of just having one `User` class, I decided to try to split out some of the security-related data and behavior from the User class into a separate ClientMembershipUser class. Consumers of the Client Membership System should only ever have to work with the User class; the `ClientMembershipUser` class shields them from having to know all of the security-related details, such as keeping track of bad login attempts, locking users out, and so on. When I show the interface for the Client Membership Provider later in the chapter, you will see how this encapsulation is enforced by the interface.

The diagram in Figure 11.2 shows how the Client Membership System classes interrelate to each other.

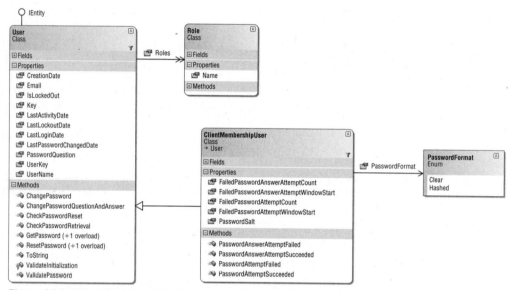

Figure 11.2: Client Membership System domain model classes.

The User Class

Since the `User` class is the main class that developers will be using to interact with the Client Membership System, I will cover it first.

Class Signature and Private Fields

Note that the `User` class implements the `IEntity` interface, which will prove to be very important later on when I need this class to participate in the Synchronization Framework:

```
using System;
using System.Collections.Generic;
using System.Text.RegularExpressions;
using SmartCA.Infrastructure;
using SmartCA.Infrastructure.DomainBase;

namespace SmartCA.Model.Membership
```

```
{
    public class User : IEntity
    {
        #region Private Fields

        private Guid userKey;
        private DateTime creationDate;
        private string email;
        private bool isLockedOut;
        private DateTime lastActivityDate;
        private DateTime lastLockoutDate;
        private DateTime lastLoginDate;
        private DateTime lastPasswordChangedDate;
        private string passwordQuestion;
        private string userName;
        private List<Role> roles;

        #endregion
```

As you can see, this class is not holding any security-sensitive information, such as the User's password or password answer. This data fields in this class are very similar to the ASP.NET `MembershipUser` class, but as you will see, there is much more logic in this class.

The Constructor

The constructor for this class essentially makes it mandatory for all of the data to be passed into the class in order to use it. This is similar to Value class functionality, but the `User` class is definitely an Entity.

```
        #region Constructors

        public User(Guid userKey, string name, string email,
            string passwordQuestion, bool isLockedOut,
            DateTime creationDate, DateTime lastLoginDate,
            DateTime lastActivityDate, DateTime lastPasswordChangedDate,
            DateTime lastLockoutDate)
        {
            this.userKey = userKey;
            if (name != null)
            {
                name = name.Trim();
            }
            if (email != null)
            {
                email = email.Trim();
            }
            if (passwordQuestion != null)
            {
                passwordQuestion = passwordQuestion.Trim();
            }
            this.userName = name;
            this.email = email;
            this.passwordQuestion = passwordQuestion;
            this.isLockedOut = isLockedOut;
```

(continued)

(continued)

```
            this.creationDate = creationDate.ToUniversalTime();
            this.lastLoginDate = lastLoginDate.ToUniversalTime();
            this.lastActivityDate = lastActivityDate.ToUniversalTime();
            this.lastPasswordChangedDate
                = lastPasswordChangedDate.ToUniversalTime();
            this.lastLockoutDate = lastLockoutDate.ToUniversalTime();
            this.roles = new List<Role>();
            this.ValidateInitialization();
        }


    #endregion
```

The constructor starts out by cleaning up the name, email, and passwordQuestion arguments before assigning them to their respective class fields. The next interesting bit of logic is the conversion of all of the DateTime argument values to Universal Time. Doing this allows the Client Membership system to standardize on one time zone for users who may be working around the country or the world.

The last task for the constructor is to validate the data passed in, and this is done via the ValidateInitialization method:

```
        protected virtual void ValidateInitialization()
        {
            SecurityHelper.CheckParameter(this.userName, true, true, true,
                ClientMembershipService.Application.MaxUsernameSize, "username");
            SecurityHelper.CheckParameter(this.email, true, true, true,
                0, "email");
            SecurityHelper.CheckParameter(this.passwordQuestion, true, true, true,
                ClientMembershipService.Application.MaxPasswordQuestionSize,
                "passwordQuestion");
        }
```

This method validates the username, email, and passwordQuestion fields that were passed in from the constructor. To do this validation, the SecurityHelper class's CheckParameter method is used:

```
        public static void CheckParameter(string param, bool checkForNull,
            bool checkIfEmpty, bool checkForCommas, int maxSize, string paramName)
        {
            if (param == null)
            {
                if (checkForNull)
                {
                    throw new ArgumentNullException(paramName);
                }
            }
            else
            {
                param = param.Trim();
                if (checkIfEmpty && (param.Length < 1))
                {
                    throw new ArgumentException("Parameter cannot be empty",
                        paramName);
                }
                if ((maxSize > 0) && (param.Length > maxSize))
```

```
        {
            throw new ArgumentException("Parameter too long",
                paramName);
        }
        if (checkForCommas && param.Contains(","))
        {
            throw new ArgumentException("Parameter cannot contain commas",
                paramName);
        }
    }
}
```

This method is very flexible; it lets the caller specify, via its Boolean arguments, what types of checks should be made. The first check that is made, without giving the caller a choice, is whether the parameter is null. If it is null, then an ArgumentNullException is thrown.

The next check is for an empty parameter. If the call specified that it wanted this checked, then it is checked. If it turns out that the parameter is empty, then an ArgumentException is thrown. The checks for parameter length and commas perform the exact same pattern; that is, the method is only checking if instructed to do so, and then throwing exceptions if the check does not pass.

You can see in the ValidateInitialization method that everything is being checked for the username, email, and passwordQuestion fields.

The Properties

There really is not that much interesting about the properties of this class from a code and logic point of view; however, there is some nice encapsulation done with the private fields. Almost all of the properties are read-only, except for the LastActivityDate, Email, and LastLoginDate properties. For all of the DateTime properties, all of their getters return the DateTime value in the LocalTime format:

```
public DateTime CreationDate
{
    get { return this.creationDate.ToLocalTime(); }
}
```

Some of the properties do have setters, but they are protected setters, meaning they needed to be opened up for changing to any classes that derive from the User class. This will make more sense when I show you the ClientMembershipUser class a little later. Here is an example of one of the properties with a protected setter:

```
public bool IsLockedOut
{
    get { return this.isLockedOut; }
    protected set { this.isLockedOut = value; }
}
```

This is useful because it means that I could put some logic in a derived class that may need to change depending on whether the User is in a locked out state.

The Methods

Unlike some of the other classes in the SmartCA domain model, this class has a lot of behavior in it.

The ChangePassword Method

This is the first of several methods that will be delegating any heavy lifting to the `ClientMembershipService` class, which I will look at later in the chapter.

```
public void ChangePassword(string oldPassword, string newPassword)
{
    SecurityHelper.CheckPasswordParameter(oldPassword, 0, "oldPassword");
    SecurityHelper.CheckPasswordParameter(newPassword, 0, "newPassword");
    User.ValidatePassword(newPassword);
    ClientMembershipService.ChangePassword(this.UserName,
        oldPassword, newPassword);
}
```

This method starts out by first validating its arguments, and then calls the static `ValidateUser` method.

```
public static void ValidatePassword(string password)
{
    SecurityHelper.CheckParameter(password, true, false, false,
        0, "password");

    Application application = ClientMembershipService.Application;

    if (password.Length < application.MinRequiredPasswordLength)
    {
        throw new ArgumentException("Password too short",
                    "password");
    }

    int count = 0;

    for (int i = 0; i < password.Length; i++)
    {
        if (!char.IsLetterOrDigit(password, i))
        {
            count++;
        }
    }

    if (count < application.MinRequiredNonAlphanumericCharacters)
    {
        throw new ArgumentException
            ("Password needs more non alphanumeric chars",
            "password");
    }

    if (application.PasswordStrengthRegularExpression.Length > 0)
    {
        if (!Regex.IsMatch(password,
            application.PasswordStrengthRegularExpression))
        {
            throw new ArgumentException
                ("Password does not match regular expression",
                "password");
        }
```

```
        }

        if (password.Length > application.MaxPasswordSize)
        {
            throw new ArgumentException("Password too long",
                "password");
        }
    }
```

I made this method static so I would be able to centralize this logic in the domain, in order for it to be reused from a Client Membership Provider. This method does a very exhaustive job of validating the password.

It ends up conducting five different tests on the password parameter:

1. It first checks to see whether the parameter is null via the CheckParameter method shown previously.

2. The next check is to make sure that the password meets the minimum length requirements of the Client Membership System. If it does not, then you guessed it, an ArgumentException is thrown.

3. The next check is a little bit more complicated. It iterates through all of the characters of the password and makes sure that it has the minimum number of non-alphanumeric characters in it.

4. The last test is to see whether the password meets the regular expression criteria of the Client Membership System. If that test passes, then the last test is to make sure that the password is not too long.

Now, let's go back to the ChangePassword method that I was originally showing. After performing all of the necessary checks, the last thing the ChangePassword method needs to do is to change the User's password! This is done by using the ChangePassword method of the ClientMembershipService class, and passing in the User's UserName property value, their old password, and their new password.

The ChangePasswordQuestionAndAnswer Method

This method is for changing the User's password question and password answer. It requires the password to be passed in, in order for the provider to authenticate the user before changing the User's password question and answer values.

```
public void ChangePasswordQuestionAndAnswer(string password,
    string newPasswordQuestion, string newPasswordAnswer)
{
    SecurityHelper.CheckPasswordParameter(password, 0, "password");
    SecurityHelper.CheckParameter(newPasswordQuestion, false, true,
        false, 0, "newPasswordQuestion");
    SecurityHelper.CheckParameter(newPasswordAnswer, false, true,
        false, 0, "newPasswordAnswer");
    ClientMembershipService.ChangePasswordQuestionAndAnswer(this.UserName,
        password, newPasswordQuestion, newPasswordAnswer);
    this.passwordQuestion = newPasswordQuestion;
}
```

It starts out by validating all of the arguments with the `SecurityHelper` class. It then goes on to delegate to the `ClientMembershipService` class the changing of the User's password question and answer. The last thing it does is to update the `passwordQuestion` field of the User class to the value of the `newPasswordQuestion` argument passed in.

The ResetPassword Method

The `ResetPassword` method has two overloads; the first one takes no parameters:

```
public string ResetPassword()
{
    User.CheckPasswordReset(null);
    return ClientMembershipService.ResetPassword(this.UserName);
}
```

This method first calls the `CheckPasswordReset` static method to verify that the Client Membership System is configured to allow password resets:

```
public static void CheckPasswordReset(string passwordAnswer)
{
    Application application = ClientMembershipService.Application;

    if (!application.EnablePasswordReset)
    {
        throw new NotSupportedException
            ("Not configured to support password resets");
    }

    if (string.IsNullOrEmpty(passwordAnswer))
    {
        if (application.RequiresQuestionAndAnswer)
        {
            throw new NotSupportedException
                ("Must reset password with a password answer");
        }
    }
}
```

This method first checks to see whether the Client Membership System allows password resets. If no password answer was passed in, it checks to see whether the Client Membership System requires a password answer to be supplied before it resets the password. If any of those tests does not pass, it throws a `NotSupportedException` exception.

The `ResetPassword` method finishes by calling the `ResetPassword` method of the `ClientMembershipService` class.

The second overload of the `ResetPassword` method takes in a `passwordAnswer` argument, and passes the argument, along with the `UserName` property value to the `ResetPassword` method of the `ClientMembershipService` class.

```
public string ResetPassword(string passwordAnswer)
{
    User.CheckPasswordReset(passwordAnswer);
    return ClientMembershipService.ResetPassword(
        this.UserName, passwordAnswer);
}
```

The ClientMembershipUser Class

The ClientMembershipUser class contains the logic and data for auditing and managing User authentication.

Class Signature and Private Fields

As previously mentioned, the ClientMembershipUser class derives from the User class, and its behavior affects some of the data in the User class:

```
using System;
using SmartCA.Model.Membership;

namespace SmartCA.Model.Membership
{
    public class ClientMembershipUser : User
    {
        #region Private Fields

        private string passwordSalt;
        private PasswordFormat passwordFormat;
        private int failedPasswordAttemptCount;
        private DateTime failedPasswordAttemptWindowStart;
        private int failedPasswordAnswerAttemptCount;
        private DateTime failedPasswordAnswerAttemptWindowStart;

        #endregion
```

This class holds password and password answer authentication auditing information. This class also has a lot of behavior in it that helps it manage its auditing information.

The Constructor

The Constructor for the ClientMembershipUser class is very similar to that of the User class; all of the data for its fields must be passed in:

```
#region Constructor

public ClientMembershipUser(User user, string passwordSalt,
    PasswordFormat passwordFormat, int failedPasswordAttemptCount,
    DateTime failedPasswordAttemptWindowStart,
    int failedPasswordAnswerAttemptCount,
    DateTime failedPasswordAnswerAttemptWindowStart)
    : base(user.UserKey,
    user.UserName, user.Email, user.PasswordQuestion,
    user.IsLockedOut, user.CreationDate, user.LastLoginDate,
```

(continued)

(continued)

```
                  user.LastActivityDate, user.LastPasswordChangedDate,
                  user.LastLockoutDate)
      {
          if (passwordSalt != null)
          {
              passwordSalt = passwordSalt.Trim();
          }
          this.passwordSalt = passwordSalt;
          this.passwordFormat = passwordFormat;
          this.failedPasswordAttemptCount = failedPasswordAttemptCount;
          this.failedPasswordAttemptWindowStart
              = failedPasswordAttemptWindowStart;
          this.failedPasswordAnswerAttemptCount
              = failedPasswordAnswerAttemptCount;
          this.failedPasswordAnswerAttemptWindowStart
              = failedPasswordAnswerAttemptWindowStart;
      }

      #endregion
```

Almost all of the arguments being passed in are `Integer` and `DateTime` data types, except for the `passwordSalt` argument, which is a string. Just like before, the string argument is trimmed before being assigned.

The Properties

I am not going to show any of the code for the properties here, since there is nothing special code-wise about them. All of the properties are read-only representations of the field data for the class.

The Methods

The only way the internal data in the class can be changed is through its methods. The methods contain all of the logic for successful logins, bad logins, successful password answer authentications, and failed password answer authentications.

The PasswordAttemptFailed Method

This method changes the state of the class appropriately whenever a failed password verification attempt occurs:

```
      public void PasswordAnswerAttemptFailed()
      {
          DateTime currentDateTime = DateTime.Now.ToUniversalTime();

          if (currentDateTime >
              this.failedPasswordAnswerAttemptWindowStart.AddMinutes(
              ClientMembershipService.Application.PasswordAttemptWindow))
          {
              this.failedPasswordAnswerAttemptWindowStart = currentDateTime;
              this.failedPasswordAnswerAttemptCount = 1;
          }
```

```
            else
            {
                this.failedPasswordAnswerAttemptCount++;
            }

            if (this.failedPasswordAnswerAttemptCount >
                ClientMembershipService.Application.MaxInvalidPasswordAttempts)
            {
                this.IsLockedOut = true;
                this.LastLockoutDate = currentDateTime;
            }

            this.LastActivityDate = currentDateTime;
        }
```

The logic in this method first captures the current timestamp in Universal Time (UTC) format. Next, a check is made to see if the timestamp is greater than the failed password attempt window plus the number of minutes configured for the window in the Client Membership System. The time window represents the `DateTime` from the last failed password. When this occurs, the failed password attempt time window starts ticking. If the current timestamp is greater than that time window plus the minutes from configuration, then the method knows that it is time to start the time window over again. This concept is probably best illustrated with an example. Take the case where a User has a bad login two days ago. Today he has another bad login. In this case, a new time window starts, and the failed password attempt count is set to 1 because it has been too long since the last bad login. This behavior is intended to prevent people from guessing passwords through some type of dictionary attack.

If it turns out that the bad password attempt did occur within the time window, then the failed password attempt counter is incremented by one. After that logic has completed, the next step is to see whether the User should be locked out. If the number of bad password attempts is greater than that allowed in the Client Membership System configuration, then the User is locked out of the account.

Notice how the method is setting the `IsLockedOut`, `LastLockedOut`, and `LastActivityDate` base class property values. This is made possible because they are marked with the protected keyword, which means that only classes that derive from the User class can set those values. Here is the `IsLockedOut` property of the `User` class again:

```
public bool IsLockedOut
{
    get { return this.isLockedOut; }
    protected set { this.isLockedOut = value; }
}
```

This is a nice little trick because the property is encapsulated from outside users of the class, but I am still able to change its values from the derived class.

The PasswordAttemptSucceeded Method

As you can probably infer by the name, this method is almost exactly the opposite of the previous method.

```
public void PasswordAttemptSucceeded()
{
    DateTime currentDateTime = DateTime.Now.ToUniversalTime();
    this.failedPasswordAttemptWindowStart = DateTime.MinValue;
    this.failedPasswordAttemptCount = 0;
    this.IsLockedOut = false;
    this.LastLockoutDate = DateTime.MinValue;
    this.LastActivityDate = currentDateTime;
}
```

This method starts out the same as the one before it, also by capturing the current timestamp. Since it represents a successful login, it resets the failed password attempt window to the lowest DateTime possible, and it resets the failed password attempt count to zero. Just to make sure, it sets the IsLockedOut property value of the User class to false, as well as setting the LastLockoutDate property value to the lowest DateTime value possible. Finally, it sets the LastActivityDate property for auditing purposes.

The PasswordAnswerAttemptFailed Method

This method is almost exactly the same as the PasswordAttemptFailed method, only instead of tracking bad password attempts, it is tracking bad password answer attempts.

```
public void PasswordAnswerAttemptFailed()
{
    DateTime currentDateTime = DateTime.Now.ToUniversalTime();

    if (currentDateTime >
        this.failedPasswordAnswerAttemptWindowStart.AddMinutes(
        ClientMembershipService.Application.PasswordAttemptWindow))
    {
        this.failedPasswordAnswerAttemptWindowStart = currentDateTime;
        this.failedPasswordAnswerAttemptCount = 1;
    }
    else
    {
        this.failedPasswordAnswerAttemptCount++;
    }

    if (this.failedPasswordAnswerAttemptCount >
        ClientMembershipService.Application.MaxInvalidPasswordAttempts)
    {
        this.IsLockedOut = true;
        this.LastLockoutDate = currentDateTime;
    }

    this.LastActivityDate = currentDateTime;
}
```

There really is not much different here from the PasswordAttemptFailed method—the logic is identical. The only difference is that I am tracking failed password answer attempts, but I still use the same logic as before for the time window and locking the User's account out if necessary.

The PasswordAnswerAttemptSucceeded Method

Again, the name of this method should give you a hint that it is very similar to the `PasswordAttemptSucceeded` method.

```
public void PasswordAnswerAttemptSucceeded()
{
    DateTime currentDateTime = DateTime.Now.ToUniversalTime();
    this.failedPasswordAnswerAttemptWindowStart = DateTime.MinValue;
    this.failedPasswordAnswerAttemptCount = 0;
    this.IsLockedOut = false;
    this.LastLockoutDate = DateTime.MinValue;
    this.LastActivityDate = currentDateTime;
}
```

The only thing different about this method is that it resets the values for the failed password answer attempt fields instead of the failed password attempt fields.

The Application Class

I have already shown parts of the `Application` class being used in the methods of the `User` and `ClientMembershipUser` classes. The `Application` class is a `Value` class that is only meant to store the configuration values of the Client Membership System. Here is the signature and data fields for the `Application` class:

```
using System;

namespace SmartCA.Model.Membership
{
    public class Application
    {
        #region Private Fields

        private string name;
        private bool enablePasswordReset;
        private bool enablePasswordRetrieval;
        private int maxInvalidPasswordAttempts;
        private int minRequiredNonAlphanumericCharacters;
        private int minRequiredPasswordLength;
        private int passwordAttemptWindow;
        private PasswordFormat passwordFormat;
        private string passwordStrengthRegularExpression;
        private bool requiresQuestionAndAnswer;
        private bool requiresUniqueEmail;
        private bool isDecryptionKeyAutogenerated;
        private bool isHashAlgorithmFromMembershipConfig;
        private string hashAlgorithmType;
        private int maxPasswordSize;
        private int maxPasswordAnswerSize;
        private int maxUsernameSize;
        private int maxPasswordQuestionSize;

        #endregion
```

I am not going to show the constructor and properties of the Application class here. Since it is a standard Value class, all of its properties are read-only and the constructor requires all of the field data to be passed in as arguments.

Its job is to represent the configuration from the Client Membership System, thus allowing me to not have to hard-code any values in the domain model or Providers.

The Client Membership System Provider Framework and Implementation

The Client Membership System Provider is very much like that of a repository, only it does not necessarily represent an in-memory collection of Aggregate Root Entities. In this case, the Client Membership provider's job is to provide the necessary data and persistence behavior for storing and retrieving Client Membership System data.

The IClientMembershipProvider Interface

Following the same pattern as with repositories, I am keeping the interface for the Client Membership System Provider in the domain model, along with its associated Service class. This way I can use it from my Domain Model classes but only be tied to the interface and not to the implementation.

The IClientMembershipProvider interface provides all of the functionality that my domain model needs in a nice, clean, well-encapsulated interface:

```
namespace SmartCA.Model.Membership
{
    public interface IClientMembershipProvider
    {
        #region Methods

        User GetUser(object userKey);
        User GetUser(string username);
        string GetPassword(string username);
        string GetPassword(string username, string answer);
        bool ChangePassword(string username, string oldPassword,
            string newPassword);
        bool ChangePasswordQuestionAndAnswer(string username, string password,
            string newPasswordQuestion, string newPasswordAnswer);
        string ResetPassword(string username);
        string ResetPassword(string username, string answer);
        void UpdateUser(User user);
        bool ValidateUser(string username, string password);

        #endregion

        #region Properties

        Application Application { get; }

        #endregion
    }
}
```

There are few things to notice on this interface; the first is that it has a property on it as well as methods. That property is the Application property, which represents an instance of the Application class that I just demonstrated.

The next important item to note is that it offers methods to change the User's password and password answer values, as well as for password retrieval. Since I have decided to use hashed passwords for the Client Membership System, these password retrieval methods probably should not be there, but I left them there in case, later, someone wanted to change to an encryption algorithm that would support retrieving passwords.

The last important piece of functionality this interface offers is the ability to get a User instance from a data store and also update that instance and have the changes persisted to a data store.

The ProviderFactory Class

Just like the RepositoryFactory class from the Repository Framework, the ProviderFactory class is used to create instances of the IClientMembershipProvider interface implementation class:

```csharp
using System;
using System.Configuration;
using SmartCA.Infrastructure.RepositoryFramework.Configuration;

namespace SmartCA.Infrastructure.Membership
{
    public static class ProviderFactory
    {
        private static object provider;

        public static T GetProvider<T>() where T : class
        {
            // See if the provider instance was already created
            if (ProviderFactory.provider == null)
            {
                // It was not created, so build it now
                RepositorySettings settings =
                    (RepositorySettings)ConfigurationManager.GetSection(
RepositoryMappingConstants.RepositoryMappingsConfigurationSectionName);

                // Get the type to be created
                string interfaceTypeName = typeof(T).Name;
                Type repositoryType =
                    Type.GetType(
settings.RepositoryMappings[interfaceTypeName].RepositoryFullTypeName);

                // Create the provider
                ProviderFactory.provider =
                    Activator.CreateInstance(repositoryType);
            }

            return ProviderFactory.provider as T;
        }
    }
}
```

This code is very similar to the RepositoryFactory code from Chapter 2, but it is a little bit more scaled down. In order to make things easier, it actually uses the same configuration code as the RepositoryFactory class.

Again, just like with the Repository interfaces and the RepositoryFactory, by using the combination of interface and Factory, it allows me to implement the Separated Interface Pattern (Fowler). In other words, I can keep the interface separate from the implementation and yet still create instances of the interface and use those instances without even knowing what they are.

The ClientMembershipProvider Class

This is probably the most complicated class in the Client Membership System, or at least it was the hardest one for me to create. I wanted to make sure that I did not hide any domain logic in this class; I really wanted the domain logic to stay in the domain model where it is supposed to be.

This class kind of resembles the MembershipProvider class of the ASP.NET Membership system, but the main difference is that it implements the IClientMembershipProvider interface.

Class Signature and Private Fields

The first thing to notice about this class is that it is abstract and implements two different interfaces:

```
using System;
using System.Globalization;
using System.Security.Cryptography;
using System.Text;
using SmartCA.Infrastructure.DomainBase;
using SmartCA.Infrastructure.RepositoryFramework;
using SmartCA.Model.Membership;

namespace SmartCA.Infrastructure.Membership.Providers
{
    public abstract class ClientMembershipProvider
        : IClientMembershipProvider, IUnitOfWorkRepository
    {
        #region Constants

        private static class Constants
        {
            public const int SaltSizeInBytes = 0x10;
            public const string NoEncryptedPasswordsWithAutoGenKeys =
                "Cannot use encrypted passwords with autogenerated keys";
            public const string CannotDecodeHashedPassword =
                "Provider cannot decode hashed password";
            public const string NoPasswordRetrieval =
                "Password retrieval is not supported";
            public const int PasswordSize = 14;
        }

        #endregion

        #region Private Fields
```

```
        private IUnitOfWork unitOfWork;

    #endregion
```

The first interface that this class implements is the `IClientMembershipProvider` interface. This should not be a surprise, and makes total sense from what I have shown so far. The second one, the `IUnitOfWorkRepository` interface, is a little bit more intriguing. By implementing this interface, this allows me to let the Client Membership System take part in the Synchronization Framework introduced in the last chapter. This is very important, because this allows the Client Membership System to stay synchronized with the membership data on the server.

The next important thing about this class is that it is an abstract class. By being abstract, it can absorb and encapsulate any type of Client Membership Provider logic and make it easier to write the Client Membership Provider implementations. As you will later see, this class uses the Template Method pattern all over the place to make implementing a Client Membership provider as simple as storing and retrieving data from a data store.

The Constructor

The constructor for the class does not do much, except instantiate a `UnitOfWork` class and delegate for the Provider to initialize itself:

```
    #region Constructors

    protected ClientMembershipProvider()
    {
        this.unitOfWork = new UnitOfWork();
        this.Initialize();
    }

    #endregion
```

Note that it is protected, and that the `Initialize` method that it is calling is also abstract. This is the first occurrence of the Template Method pattern in the class.

Here is the `Initialize` method signature:

```
    protected abstract void Initialize();
```

The method is protected, which helps encapsulate the provider implementation by not allowing other callers to initialize it except the `ClientMembershipProvider` class.

The Methods

Probably the easiest way to look at the methods in the `ClientMembershipProvider` class is to look at them from the perspective of the `IClientMembershipProvider` interface. The first two methods of the `IClientMembershipProvider` interface are implemented as pass-through methods to the derived Provider:

```
        public abstract User GetUser(object userKey);
        public abstract User GetUser(string username);
```

They are both marked as abstract, so it is up to the derived Provider to retrieve the User instances from the data store properly.

The next two methods of the interface implementation are the GetPassword overloaded methods. I will only show the code for one of the overloads here:

```
public virtual string GetPassword(string username, string answer)
{
    ClientMembershipUser user = this.GetClientMembershipUser(username);
    return this.GetPassword(user, answer);
}
```

Notice how this method is marked virtual. I made it virtual in case someone else writing a Client Membership Provider wanted to override the logic in this method. You will see this pattern repeated on all of the methods implemented for the IClientMembershipProvider interface in this class.

This method first gets a ClientMembershipUser instance from the username argument. This is something you will see a lot in this class, because the ClientMembershipUser class has all of the security-related data and behavior that the Provider needs. This happens with the GetlClientMembershipUser method:

```
private ClientMembershipUser GetClientMembershipUser(string username)
{
    return this.GetUser(this.GetUser(username));
}
```

This method is calling two methods in a nested fashion. Here is the outer method:

```
protected abstract ClientMembershipUser GetUser(User user);
```

This method is implemented in the derived Client Membership provider and is protected, which is good encapsulation. The purpose of the method is to take a User instance and decorate it with the necessary data to be a ClientMembershipUser instance. The inner GetUser method looks like this:

```
public abstract User GetUser(string username);
```

This method should look familiar, as I showed it earlier in this section. Finally, the GetPassword method finishes by calling the class's protected virtual GetPassword method:

```
protected virtual string GetPassword(ClientMembershipUser user,
    string passwordAnswer)
{
    // Make sure password retrievals are allowed
    User.CheckPasswordRetrieval();

    // Validate the user's password answer
    this.ValidateUserWithPasswordAnswer(user, passwordAnswer, true);

    // Get the user's password from persistence
    return this.GetPasswordFromPersistence(user);
}
```

This method first checks to see whether password retrievals are even allowed in the Client Membership System. Next, it authenticates the user with the User's supplied password answer via the `ValidateUserWithPasswordAnswer` method:

```
private void ValidateUserWithPasswordAnswer(ClientMembershipUser user,
    string passwordAnswer, bool throwIfFails)
{
    if (passwordAnswer != null)
    {
        passwordAnswer = passwordAnswer.Trim();
    }

    SecurityHelper.CheckParameter(passwordAnswer,
        this.Application.RequiresQuestionAndAnswer,
        this.Application.RequiresQuestionAndAnswer,
        false, this.Application.MaxPasswordAnswerSize,
        "passwordAnswer");

    string passwordAnswerFromPersistence =
        this.GetPasswordAnswerFromPersistence(user);

    try
    {
        if (!this.CheckPasswordAnswer(passwordAnswer,
            passwordAnswerFromPersistence,
            user.PasswordFormat, user.PasswordSalt))
        {
            user.PasswordAnswerAttemptFailed();
            if (throwIfFails)
            {
                throw new SecurityException
                    ("The password answer supplied was not correct");
            }
        }
        else
        {
            user.PasswordAnswerAttemptSucceeded();
        }
    }
    finally
    {
        this.PersistUser(user);
    }
}
```

This method first starts out by validating all of the arguments passed in. The next step it needs to perform is to get the User's password answer from the data store so that it can compare it to the password answer that the User supplied. It gets the User's password answer from the data store via the `GetPasswordAnswerFromPersistence` method, which is another protected, abstract method:

```
protected abstract string GetPasswordAnswerFromPersistence(
        ClientMembershipUser user);
```

Once the password answer is obtained, the next step is to check to see if the password answer supplied equals the password answer from the data store. This is where the `CheckPasswordAnswer` method comes in:

```
private bool CheckPasswordAnswer(string passwordAnswer,
    string passwordAnswerFromPersistence,
    PasswordFormat passwordFormat, string salt)
{
    return this.CheckPassword(
        passwordAnswer.ToLower(CultureInfo.InvariantCulture),
        passwordAnswerFromPersistence, passwordFormat, salt);
}
```

This method does a pass-through to the `CheckPassword` method. I did this, instead of just having one method, to make the code more readable. Here is the `CheckPassword` method:

```
private bool CheckPassword(string password, string passwordFromPersistence,
    PasswordFormat passwordFormat, string salt)
{
    string encodedPassword = this.EncodePassword(password,
        passwordFormat, salt);
    return passwordFromPersistence.Equals(encodedPassword);
}
```

The important thing to take away from this code is that the password answer from the data store is already hashed. I have to hash the password answer that is being passed in, so I can compare apples to apples. The way I hash the value is to call the `EncodePassword` method:

```
private string EncodePassword(string password,
    PasswordFormat passwordFormat, string salt)
{
    if (passwordFormat == PasswordFormat.Clear)
    {
        return password;
    }
    byte[] bytes = Encoding.Unicode.GetBytes(password);
    byte[] source = Convert.FromBase64String(salt);
    byte[] destination = new byte[source.Length + bytes.Length];
    byte[] passwordBytes = null;
    Buffer.BlockCopy(source, 0, destination, 0, source.Length);
    Buffer.BlockCopy(bytes, 0, destination, source.Length, bytes.Length);
    if (passwordFormat == PasswordFormat.Hashed)
    {
        HashAlgorithm algorithm = HashAlgorithm.Create(
            this.Application.HashAlgorithmType);
        if ((algorithm == null) &&
            this.Application.IsHashAlgorithmFromMembershipConfig)
        {
            this.ThrowHashAlgorithmException();
        }
        passwordBytes = algorithm.ComputeHash(destination);
    }
    return Convert.ToBase64String(passwordBytes);
}
```

This code essentially takes a password string and a password salt, and then encodes the password using the salt in the manner specified in the `passwordFormat` argument. In the case of the current configuration of the Client Membership System, it will be using a `PasswordFormat` enumeration value of `Hashed`.

The next `IClientMembershipProvider` interface method implementation is the `ChangePassword` method:

```
public virtual bool ChangePassword(string username, string oldPassword,
    string newPassword)
{
    ClientMembershipUser user = this.GetClientMembershipUser(username);
    this.ChangePassword(user, oldPassword, newPassword);
    return true;
}
```

This method is also marked virtual for flexibility reasons and starts out just like the `GetPassword` method by calling the `GetClientMembershipUser` method to get a `ClientMembershipUser` instance. It then passes that instance on to the protected `ChangePassword` method:

```
protected virtual void ChangePassword(ClientMembershipUser user,
    string oldPassword, string newPassword)
{
    SecurityHelper.CheckParameter(oldPassword, true, true, false,
        this.Application.MaxPasswordSize, "oldPassword");
    SecurityHelper.CheckParameter(newPassword, true, true, false,
        this.Application.MaxPasswordSize, "newPassword");

    // Validate the user before making any changes
    this.ValidateUserWithPassword(user, oldPassword, true);

    // Make sure the new password is ok
    User.ValidatePassword(newPassword);

    // encode the new password
    string encodedPassword = this.EncodePassword(newPassword,
        user.PasswordFormat, user.PasswordSalt);

    if (encodedPassword.Length > this.Application.MaxPasswordSize)
    {
        throw new ArgumentException("Membership password too long",
            "newPassword");
    }

    // Save the new password
    this.PersistChangedPassword(user, encodedPassword);
}
```

I marked this method as protected in order to encapsulate it and made it virtual, so the derived provider would have some flexibility in using it. This code starts out with very familiar methods for validating the password values passed in. It then authenticates the user with the `oldPassword` argument value that was passed in via the `ValidateUserWithPassword` method:

```
private void ValidateUserWithPassword(ClientMembershipUser user,
    string password, bool throwIfFails)
{
    if (password != null)
    {
        password = password.Trim();
    }

    SecurityHelper.CheckParameter(password,
        true, true, true,
        this.Application.MaxPasswordAnswerSize,
        "password");

    string passwordFromPersistence =
        this.GetPasswordFromPersistence(user);

    try
    {
        if (!this.CheckPassword(password,
            passwordFromPersistence,
            user.PasswordFormat, user.PasswordSalt))
        {
            user.PasswordAttemptFailed();
            if (throwIfFails)
            {
                throw new SecurityException
                    ("The password supplied was not correct");
            }
        }
        else
        {
            user.PasswordAttemptSucceeded();
        }
    }
    finally
    {
        this.PersistUser(user);
    }
}
```

Very similar to the `ValidateUserWithPasswordAnswer` method previously shown, this method's job is to authenticate a user based on their user password value. Its logic is almost identical to the `ValidateUserWithPasswordAnswer` method, except that it validates the user using their password instead of their password answer.

Okay, going back to the `ChangePassword` method, the next step after authenticating the user is to encode the new password via the previously shown `EncodePassword` method. Once the new password is encoded, it is then checked to make sure it is not too long.

```
if (password.Length > this.Application.MaxPasswordSize)
{
    throw new ArgumentException("Membership password too long",
        "newPassword");
}

this.PersistChangedPassword(user, password);
```

Once the check of the newly encoded password is done, then the User's new password is saved to the data store via the PersistChangedPassword method:

```
protected abstract void PersistChangedPassword(ClientMembershipUser user,
        string newPassword);
```

The PersistChangedPassword method is another protected abstract method that the derived Client Membership Provider must override. Its job is to save the User's data, including their new password, to the data store.

The next IClientMembershipProvider interface method implementation is the ChangePasswordQuestionAndAnswer method:

```
public virtual bool ChangePasswordQuestionAndAnswer(string username,
    string password, string newPasswordQuestion,
    string newPasswordAnswer)
{
    ClientMembershipUser user = this.GetClientMembershipUser(username);
    this.ChangePasswordQuestionAndAnswer(user, password,
        newPasswordQuestion, newPasswordAnswer);
    return true;
}
```

This method first obtains a ClientMembershipUser instance, and then passes that instance to the protected virtual ChangePasswordQuestionAndAnswer method:

```
protected virtual void ChangePasswordQuestionAndAnswer(
    ClientMembershipUser user, string password,
    string newPasswordQuestion, string newPasswordAnswer)
{
    SecurityHelper.CheckParameter(newPasswordQuestion,
        this.Application.RequiresQuestionAndAnswer,
        this.Application.RequiresQuestionAndAnswer, false,
        this.Application.MaxPasswordQuestionSize, "newPasswordQuestion");

    if (newPasswordAnswer != null)
    {
        newPasswordAnswer = newPasswordAnswer.Trim();
    }

    SecurityHelper.CheckParameter(newPasswordAnswer,
        this.Application.RequiresQuestionAndAnswer,
        this.Application.RequiresQuestionAndAnswer, false,
```

(continued)

381

(continued)

```
                        this.Application.MaxPasswordAnswerSize, "newPasswordAnswer");

            // Validate the user before making any changes
            this.ValidateUserWithPassword(user, password, true);

            string encodedPasswordAnswer;

            if (!string.IsNullOrEmpty(newPasswordAnswer))
            {
                encodedPasswordAnswer = this.EncodePassword(
                    newPasswordAnswer.ToLower(CultureInfo.InvariantCulture),
                    user.PasswordFormat, user.PasswordSalt);
            }
            else
            {
                encodedPasswordAnswer = newPasswordAnswer;
            }

            SecurityHelper.CheckParameter(encodedPasswordAnswer,
                this.Application.RequiresQuestionAndAnswer,
                this.Application.RequiresQuestionAndAnswer, false,
                this.Application.MaxPasswordAnswerSize, "newPasswordAnswer");

            this.PersistChangedPasswordQuestionAndAnswer(user, password,
                newPasswordAnswer);
        }
```

This method starts out by validating all of the parameters passed into it, as well as authenticating the User based on the password argument passed in. Once all of those tests pass, it encodes the new password answer string using the familiar `EncodePassword` method. Once the password answer has been encoded, it must be validated again in order to make sure that it does not exceed the maximum password size limits of the Client Membership System. Once the encoded password answer has passed all of these tests, the password question and answer are then persisted to the data store via the `PersistChangedPasswordQuestionAndAnswer` method:

```
protected abstract void PersistChangedPasswordQuestionAndAnswer(
        ClientMembershipUser user, string password,
        string newPasswordAnswer);
```

Since this method is abstract, it is implemented in the derived Client Membership Provider.

The next method in the `IClientMembershipProvider` interface is the `ResetPassword` method, which has one overload. I will just show the code for the `ResetPassword` method that requires a password answer to be passed in:

```
        public virtual string ResetPassword(string username, string answer)
        {
            ClientMembershipUser user = this.GetClientMembershipUser(username);
            return this.ResetPassword(user, answer);
        }
```

This method gets the `ClientMembershipUser` instance and then passes it to the protected virtual `ResetPassword` method:

```
protected virtual string ResetPassword(ClientMembershipUser user,
    string passwordAnswer)
{
    // Are password resets allowed?
    User.CheckPasswordReset(passwordAnswer);

    // Validate the user's password answer
    this.ValidateUserWithPasswordAnswer(user, passwordAnswer, true);

    int maxPasswordSize =
        (this.Application.MinRequiredPasswordLength <
            Constants.PasswordSize)
                ? Constants.PasswordSize :
                this.Application.MinRequiredPasswordLength;

    // Create the new password
    string newPassword = System.Web.Security.Membership.GeneratePassword(
        maxPasswordSize,
        this.Application.MinRequiredNonAlphanumericCharacters);

    // Encode the password
    string newEncodedPassword = this.EncodePassword(newPassword,
        user.PasswordFormat, user.PasswordSalt);

    // Save the user's new password
    this.PersistResetPassword(user, newEncodedPassword);

    // return the new password (not the encoded one!)
    return newPassword;
}
```

This method first checks to see whether password resets have been configured to be allowed in the Client Membership System. If that test passes, then the User is authenticated with his or her password answer. If that test passes, then the `Membership` class of the .NET Framework's `System.Web.Security` namespace is used to generate a new password via its `GeneratePassword` method. After getting the newly generated password, it is encoded via the `EncodePassword` method and then saved to the data store. Finally the new password value is returned in clear text to the caller.

The next `IClientMembershipProvider` interface method implementation is the `UpdateUser` method:

```
public virtual void UpdateUser(User user)
{
    ClientMembershipUser clientMembershipUser = this.GetUser(user);
    this.unitOfWork.RegisterChanged(clientMembershipUser, this);
    this.unitOfWork.Commit();
}
```

This method is interesting to me because instead of just delegating to the protected abstract method `PersistUser`, it instead calls the `RegisterChanged` method of the `IUnitOfWork` instance. Then it calls the `Commit` method on the `IUnitOfWork` instance. This is very significant because this is how the Provider is hooking in to the Synchronization Framework from the last chapter. When the `IUnitOfWork` instance's `Commit` method is called, it calls back into the `IUnitOfWorkRepository` interface passed in with the `RegisterChanged` method. This is better known as a double dispatch.

If you recall from earlier in the chapter, the `ClientMembershipProvider` class implements the `IUnitOfWorkRepository` interface, whose methods are called in the `IUnitOfWork`'s `Commit` implementation. Here is the `IUnitOfWorkRepository` interface implementation:

```
#region IUnitOfWorkRepository Members

public void PersistNewItem(IEntity item)
{
    throw new NotImplementedException();
}

public void PersistUpdatedItem(IEntity item)
{
    ClientMembershipUser user = (ClientMembershipUser)item;
    this.PersistUser(user);
}

public void PersistDeletedItem(IEntity item)
{
    throw new NotImplementedException();
}

#endregion
```

As you can see, the only method implemented on the interface is the `PersistUpdatedItem` method. This is because all I am doing in the `ClientMembershipProvider` with the User instances is updating them, I am not adding new users or deleting users—those types of activities are all done on the server.

The `PersistUpdatedItem` method is very simple; it casts the `IEntity` instance passed into it to a `ClientMembershipUser` instance, and then passes that to the protected abstract `PersistUser` method previously shown.

The SqlCeClientMembershipProvider Class

The `SqlCeClientMembershipProvider` class inherits from the `ClientMembershipProvider` abstract class. Its main purpose is to persist User data to and from the local SQL CE database.

Class Signature and Private Fields

The signature is similar to the `SqlCeRepositoryBase<T>` signature, as it contains a private field for the Enterprise Library's `Database` class for use in some of its methods:

```
using System.Data;
using System.Data.Common;
using System.Text;
using Microsoft.Practices.EnterpriseLibrary.Data;
using SmartCA.Infrastructure.EntityFactoryFramework;
using SmartCA.Infrastructure.Helpers;
using SmartCA.Model.Membership;

namespace SmartCA.Infrastructure.Membership.Providers
{
    public class SqlCeClientMembershipProvider : ClientMembershipProvider
    {
        private Database database;
        private Application application;
```

The Initialize Method Override

This is the method override that the constructor of the `ClientMembershipProvider` base class calls:

```
protected override void Initialize()
{
    this.database = DatabaseFactory.CreateDatabase();
    string sql = "SELECT * FROM Application;";
    using (DbCommand command = this.database.GetSqlStringCommand(sql))
    {
        using (IDataReader reader = this.database.ExecuteReader(command))
        {
            if (reader.Read())
            {
                this.application =
                    ApplicationFactory.BuildApplication(reader);
            }
        }
    }
}
```

The main tasks that this method performs are to initialize the database field value and to populate the application field value with the Client Membership System configuration information from the database.

The GetUser Method Overrides

There are three method overrides for `GetUser`. Here are the first two:

```
public override User GetUser(object userKey)
{
    return this.GetUserFromSql(string.Format
        ("SELECT * FROM [User] WHERE UserId = '{0}'", userKey));
}
```

(continued)

385

(continued)

```
public override User GetUser(string username)
{
    return this.GetUserFromSql(string.Format
        ("SELECT * FROM [User] WHERE UserName = '{0}'", username));
}
```

As you can see, they both only differ by their SQL statements and both of them use the `GetUserFromSql` helper method:

```
private User GetUserFromSql(string sql)
{
    User user = null;
    using (DbCommand command = this.database.GetSqlStringCommand(sql))
    {
        using (IDataReader reader = this.database.ExecuteReader(command))
        {
            IEntityFactory<User> entityFactory =
                EntityFactoryBuilder.BuildFactory<User>();
            if (reader.Read())
            {
                user = entityFactory.BuildEntity(reader);
            }
        }
    }
    return user;
}
```

This code in this method should look pretty familiar by now; it is following the standard pattern laid out for converting data from the database into `IEntity` instances.

The third method override for `GetUser` is a little bit different; it takes an existing `User` instance and adds the necessary data to it in order to make it a `ClientMembershipUser` instance:

```
protected override ClientMembershipUser GetUser(User user)
{
    ClientMembershipUser membershipUser = null;
    string sql = string.Format(
        "SELECT * FROM [User] WHERE UserId = '{0}'",
        user.UserKey.ToString());
    using (DbCommand command = this.database.GetSqlStringCommand(sql))
    {
        using (IDataReader reader = this.database.ExecuteReader(command))
        {
            if (reader.Read())
            {
                membershipUser =
                    ClientMembershipUserFactory.BuildClientMembershipUser(
                        user, reader);
            }
        }
    }
    return membershipUser;
}
```

This code follows almost the same pattern as the GetUserFromSql method, except that it does not use the IEntityFactory<T> class to build the ClientMembershipUser instance.

The Other Method Overrides of the SqlCeClientMembershipProvider Class

All of the other methods in this class are just performing simple read and update operations in the SQL CE database, so I do not think there is any point in boring you with that code here. The important thing to note about this class is that almost all of its methods are either protected or private, which is really good from an encapsulation standpoint. Almost all of the retrieval logic is stored in the ClientMembershipProvider base class. The only two public methods on this class are two of the GetUser methods, which simply take a parameter and return a User instance.

The ClientMembershipService Class

This class is very similar to the other service classes in that it acts as a façade to an interface, in this case the IClientMembershipService interface. Here is what its signature and constructor look like:

```
using SmartCA.Infrastructure.Membership;

namespace SmartCA.Model.Membership
{
    public static class ClientMembershipService
    {
        private static IClientMembershipProvider provider;

        static ClientMembershipService()
        {
            ClientMembershipService.provider =
                ProviderFactory.GetProvider<IClientMembershipProvider>()
                as IClientMembershipProvider;
        }
```

This should look pretty familiar by now; the constructor is using the ProviderFactroy to instantiate an instance of the IClientMembershipProvider interface for the class to use.

I am not going to show all of the methods from the Service class, since they are all simply wrapping the interface and passing the argument data through. Here is a sample so that you can see what I am talking about:

```
        public static User GetUser(object userKey)
        {
            return ClientMembershipService.provider.GetUser(userKey);
        }

        public static User GetUser(string username)
        {
            return ClientMembershipService.provider.GetUser(username);
        }
```

Both of these GetUser methods pass their call through to the interface instance held by the Service.

Client Membership System Unit Tests

Instead of showing UI code exercising the Client Membership System, I thought it might be better if I show some of the unit tests used to develop the Client Membership System. This way you can see the data going in and out and get a better feel for how to use the system. All of the following tests will be going against the ClientMembershipService class.

The Login Test

This test verifies the behavior of the ValidateUser method:

```
/// <summary>
///A test for logging in
///</summary>
[TestMethod()]
public void ValidateUserTest()
{
    string username = "timm";
    string password = "Password!23";
    bool expected = true;
    bool actual = ClientMembershipService.ValidateUser(username, password);
    Assert.AreEqual(expected, actual);
}
```

As you can see, all of the complexity of the back-end system is masked by the façade, and the call to authenticate a User is very easy to make. As long as the Assertion returns true, then the unit test will pass.

The Change Password Test

This test is for changing a User's password:

```
/// <summary>
///A test for ChangePassword
///</summary>
[TestMethod()]
public void ChangePasswordTest()
{
    string username = "timm";
    string oldPassword = "Password!23";
    string newPassword = "Password!24";
    bool expected = true;
    bool actual = ClientMembershipService.ChangePassword(username,
        oldPassword, newPassword);
    Assert.AreEqual(expected, actual);

    // Change it back so the other tests don't fail
    ClientMembershipService.ChangePassword(username,
        newPassword, oldPassword);
}
```

Notice how, at the end, I have to change the password again to what it was originally. This is so the rest of the Client Membership System unit tests will pass because they are expecting the data to be in the same state as it was at the beginning of this method.

The Change Password Question and Answer Test

This test is for changing a User's password question and answer:

```
/// <summary>
///A test for ChangePasswordQuestionAndAnswer
///</summary>
[TestMethod()]
public void ChangePasswordQuestionAndAnswerTest()
{
    string username = "timm";
    string password = "Password!23";
    string newPasswordQuestion = "What color is the sky?";
    string newPasswordAnswer = "Grey";
    bool expected = true;
    bool actual = ClientMembershipService.ChangePasswordQuestionAndAnswer(
        username, password, newPasswordQuestion, newPasswordAnswer);
    Assert.AreEqual(expected, actual);

    // Change it back so the other tests don't fail
    ClientMembershipService.ChangePasswordQuestionAndAnswer(
        username, password, newPasswordQuestion, "Blue");
}
```

Summary

In order to satisfy the requirement of allowing users to be able to perform Membership-related tasks in an offline scenario, I created the Client Membership System in this chapter. This involved a very rich domain model for representing the Users and their membership data, as well as a new concept of using a Provider instead of a repository for interacting with the data store. It also was able to piggyback on the Synchronization Framework from the last chapter, which meant that all local Membership transactions would be replayed on the server as well as all server Membership transactions being played back on the client.

This chapter was by the far the most difficult code to implement, but that is also why it was so much fun! Probably the one thing that made this chapter's code easier to correct and implement were my unit tests. I was able to do a lot of refactoring with the comfort of knowing that as long as my unit tests passed I was all right.

I sure have come a long way since the first chapter! If you remember, I started out with nothing more than a problem statement and some design ideas to build a smart client application. During the course of the book, I took you on a journey of building a pretty robust Repository Framework (that was refactored several times), introduced WPF and the Model-View-ViewModel pattern, implemented lot of business logic for the various functional areas of the application, built a Synchronization Framework, and finally concluded with a Client Membership System. If nothing else, I hope you at least got some great reusable code from all of these exercises that I took you on throughout the book! Finally, I want to thank you for being patient enough to read through this book, I appreciate the fact that you are reading it right now!

Index

A

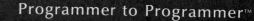